POLITICS
IN RUSSIA

The Longman Series in Comparative Politics

Almond/Powell   *Comparative Politics Today: A World View,* Sixth Edition
Almond/Powell   *Comparative Politics Politics: System, Process and Policy,*
Second Edition

Country Studies

Aborisade/Mundt   *Politics in Nigeria*
Bill/Springborg   *Politics in the Middle East,* Fourth Edition
Ehrmann/Schain   *Politics in France,* Fifth Edition
Dalton   *Politics in Germany,* Second Edition
Remington   *Politics in Russia*
Rose   *Politics in England,* Fifth Edition
Wiarda   *Politics in Iberia*

Analytic Studies

Monroe   *The Economic Approach to Politics*

Regional Studies

Almond/Dalton/Powell   *European Politics Today*

POLITICS IN RUSSIA

Thomas F. Remington
Emory University

 LONGMAN

An imprint of Addison Wesley Longman, Inc.

New York • Reading, Massachusetts • Menlo Park, California • Harlow, England
Don Mills, Ontario • Sydney • Mexico City • Madrid • Amsterdam

Marketing Manager: Megan Galvin
Project Manager: Bob Ginsberg
Design Manager: Rubina Yeh
Text Designer: Carole Desnoes
Cover Designer Rubina Yeh
Art Studio: Mapping Specialists Limited
Prepress Services Supervisor: Valerie A. Vargas
Electronic Production Manager: Heather Peres
Senior Print Buyer: Hugh Crawford
Electronic Page Makeup: Ruttle, Shaw & Wetherill, Inc.
Printer and Binder: The Maple-Vail Book Manufacturing Group
Cover Printer: Coral Graphic Services, Inc.

Library of Congress Cataloging-in-Publication Data

Remington, Thomas F., (date)
    Politics in Russia / Thomas F. Remington.
        p.   cm. — (Longman series in comparative politics)
    Includes index.
    ISBN 0-321-00493-0
    1. Russia (Federation)—Politics and government—1991-
2. Constitutional history—Russia (Federation) 3. Soviet Union-
-Politics and government.   I. Title.   II. Series.
JN6695.R46 1998
320.947'09'049—dc21
                                                    98-4968
                                                      CIP

Please visit our website at http://longman.awl.com

ISBN 0-321-00493-0
  2345678910—MA—010099

Contents

Preface

This book is a successor to Frederick C. Barghoorn's book *Politics in the USSR*, the third edition of which appeared in 1986, but it is an entirely new work. Since *Politics in the USSR* last came out, the Union of Soviet Socialist Republics (USSR) has dissolved into its constituent national republics, posing challenges for students, teachers, policymakers—and above all for the citizens of what was once a vast, powerful, multinational communist state. In this volume, I have chosen to discuss the political system of only one of those constituent republics of the union, Russia. Since the USSR was in many ways a phase in the history of the Russian state, it is reasonable to see Russia as the principal successor state of the USSR. But it is not the only one, and the other newly independent states that were former Soviet republics have followed a very diverse range of paths in their postcommunist development. For the sake of clarity and consistency, I have focused in this book on *Russia's* political development.

The emphasis here is on Russia's political institutions and processes in the post-1991 period, when it became formally independent. Still, there is a good deal of material covering the old regime, since an understanding of how its political system worked is essential to an understanding of the current Russian system. Students need to bear in mind that the communist system developed in Russia in the early decades of this century became the model for communist regimes throughout much of Europe and Asia, and set in motion the dynamics that divided much of the international system between the two great political blocs.

Those reading this text will certainly appreciate that Russia's political life is subject to rapid and often unexpected change. The book covers events roughly through the middle of 1997. It proceeds from the premise that the elements of a system are becoming visible and I have tried to identify some of the forces influencing its development, particularly those stemming from the transformation of its economy from a centrally planned state-socialist system to one with private property and market relations. These changes have been extremely controversial, inviting fierce policy disputes over whether and how reform might have been handled differently, as well as deep theoretical disagreements over how we should understand what has happened. Some of the analytical issues that arise as we compare Russia with other political systems are made explicit and readers are invited to work through the evidence and arguments themselves and come to their own conclusions about how and why Russia has changed.

Acknowledgments

In writing this book I have incurred many intellectual debts, which it is a pleasure to acknowledge. First, my mentor, the late Frederick C. Barghoorn, a pioneer in integrating the study of Russian politics into the field of comparative political analysis, set a great example as a scholar who brought sympathy and objectivity to the study of Russia. Gabriel A. Almond, whose seminal contributions to the comparative study of politics continue to shape the discipline, offered steady encouragement and support throughout the writing of the book. It is a great privilege to be associated with him in this comparative politics series.

Colleagues and students have made Emory a stimulating and enjoyable environment in which to work, and have provided valuable feedback on earlier versions of various chapters. The following readers made a number of excellent criticisms and suggestions for which I am grateful, even when I did not entirely follow their advice: Johnathan Adelman, University of Denver; Harold J. Berman, Emory University; Terry D. Clark, Creighton University; Linda J. Cook, Brown University; Jane Dawson, University of Oregon; and Darrell P. Hammer, Indiana University.

It is to my Russian friends to whom I owe the most. They have shared their knowledge and insights with patient generosity over these past years. They have shown great forbearance in allowing an outsider to try to understand their country. I hope that they will find the result worthy of their faith.

I wish also to express my appreciation to IREX and the National Council for Eurasian and East European Research, whose support made it possible for me to make a number of visits to Russia over the past several years to study Russia's emerging political institutions. Both organizations should be absolved of responsibility for any shortcomings of this book and for the opinions expressed in it.

I am particularly grateful for the opportunity to have worked with Vladimir Podoprigora and many other of Russia's political leaders in a series of workshops under the auspices of the East-West Parliamentary Practice Project. Their love and devotion for their country inspire faith in her future.

Finally, I wish to dedicate this book to my son, Alexander Frederick Remington. Born on the sixty-sixth anniversary of the October Revolution, Alexander is old enough to remember the experience of living in the USSR for several of its final months, and young enough to have lived most of his life in the post-Cold War world.

THOMAS F. REMINGTON

Regions of the Russian Federation, 1993

Northern region
1 Karelia Republic
  Komi Republic
2 Nenets AOkr
  Other Arkhangel'sk Oblast
3 Nenets AOkr
  Arkhangel'sk Oblast
4 Vologda Oblast
  Murmansk Oblast

Northwestern region
5 Leningrad
  St. Petersburg city
  Leningrad Oblast
6 Novgorod Oblast
7 Pskov Oblast

Central region
8 Bryansk Oblast
9 Vladimir Oblast
10 Ivanovo Oblast
11 Kaluga Oblast
12 Kostroma Oblast
13 Moscow
  Moscow city
  Moscow Oblast
14 Orel Oblast
15 Ryazan' Oblast
16 Smolensk Oblast
17 Tver' Oblast
18 Tula Oblast
19 Yaroslavl' Oblast

Volgo-Vyatsk region
20 Mariy El Republic
21 Mordova Republic
22 Chuvash Republic
23 Kirov Oblast
24 Nizhnii Novgorod Oblast

AO—Autonomous Oblast
AOkr—Autonomous Okrug

Central Black Earth region
25 Belgorod Oblast
26 Voronezh Oblast
27 Kursk Oblast
28 Lipetsk Oblast
29 Tambov Oblast

Volga region
30 Kalmykia Republic
31 Tatarstan Republic
32 Astrakhan' Oblast
33 Volgograd Oblast
34 Penza Oblast
35 Samara Oblast
36 Saratov Oblast
37 Ul'yanovsk Oblast

Volga region
38 Adygei Republic
39 Dagestan Republic
40 Kabardino-Balkar Republic
41 Karachay-Cherkess Republic
42 North Osetian Republic
43 Chechen and Ingush Republics
44 Krasnodar Krai
45 Stavropol' Krai
46 Rostov Oblast

Urals region
47 Bashkortostan Republic
48 Udmurt Republic
49 Kurgan Oblast
50 Orenburg Oblast
51 Perm' Oblast
52 Komi-Permyat AOkr
  Other Perm' Oblast
53 Sverdlovsk Oblast
54 Chelyabinsk Oblast

West Siberian region
55 Altai Republic
  Altai Krai
56 Kemerovo Oblast
57 Novosibirsk Oblast
58 Omsk Oblast
  Tomsk Oblast
59 Tiumen' Oblast
  Khanty-Mansiisk AOkr
60 Yamalo-Nenetsk AOkr
  Other Tiumen' Oblast

East Siberian region
61 Buryatia Republic
62 Tuva Republic
63 Khakassia Republic
  Krasnoyarsk Krai
  Taymyr AOkr
  Evenki AOkr
  Other Krasnoyarsk Krai
64 Ust'-Ordyn Buryat AOkr
  Other Irkutsk Oblast
  Chita Oblast
65 Agin AOkr
  Other Chita Oblast

Far Eastern region
  Sakha Republic
  Primorsk Krai
  Khabarovsk Krai
66 Jewish AO
  Other Khabarovsk
  Amur Oblast
67 Kamchatka Oblast
68 Koryak AOkr
  Other Kamchatka Oblast
  Magadan Oblast
  Chukotka AOkr
  Other Magadan Oblast
  Sakhalin Oblast
69 Kaliningrad Oblast

Location of Republics, Krais, Oblasts, Autonomous Oblasts, and Autonomous Okrugs in Russia

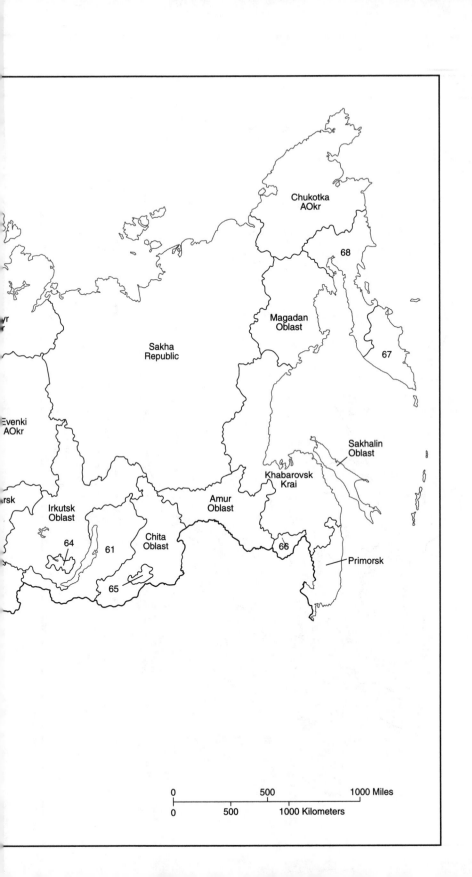

Location of the Regions of Western Russia

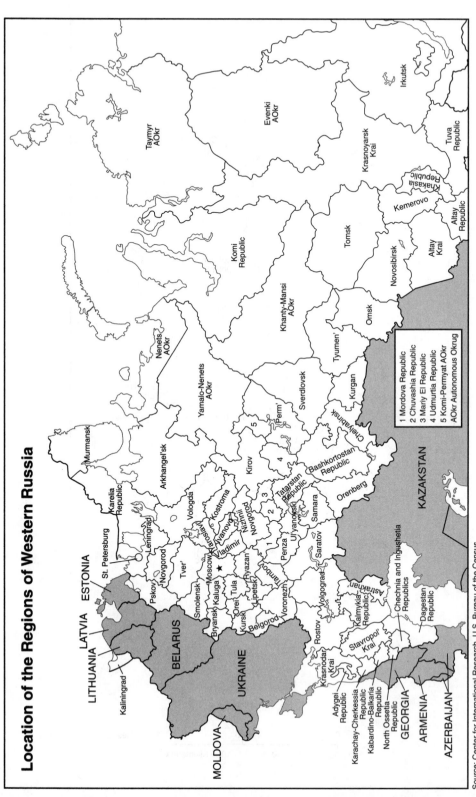

Source: Center for International Research, U.S. Bureau of the Census

Economic Regions of Russia, 1993

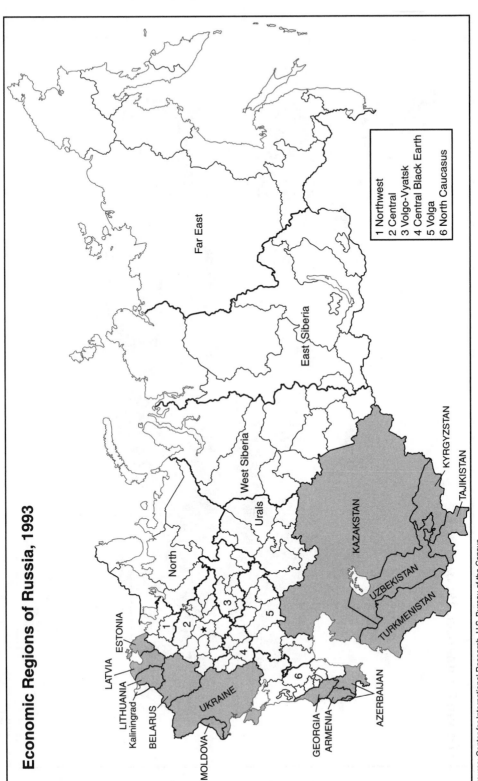

1 Northwest
2 Central
3 Volgo-Vyatsk
4 Central Black Earth
5 Volga
6 North Caucasus

Source: Center for International Research, U.S. Bureau of the Census

Urban Population, 1993

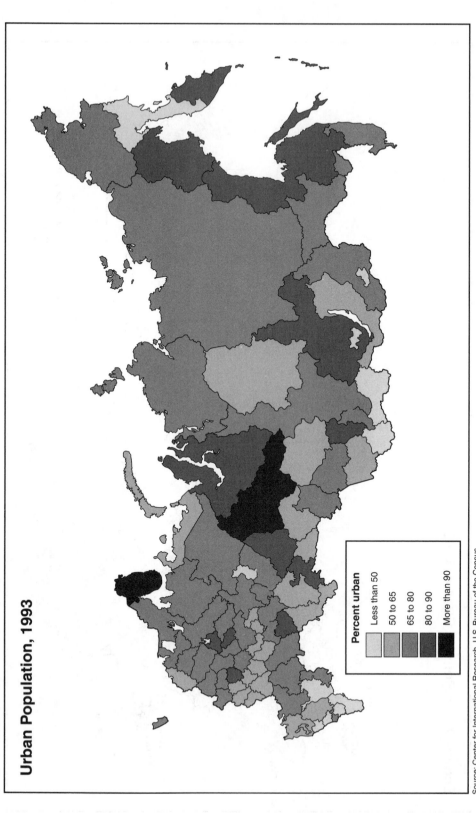

Percent urban

Less than 50
50 to 65
65 to 80
80 to 90
More than 90

Source: Center for International Research, U.S. Bureau of the Census

POLITICS
IN RUSSIA

Chapter 1

Russia and the End of Soviet Communism

Russia's political system today reflects the influence of a thousand-year history of statehood. For most of the twentieth century, Russia was ruled as a communist state and formed part of a larger state called the Union of Soviet Socialist Republics (USSR, also often called the Soviet Union). Since 1991, however, Russia has been an independent country, officially called today the Russian Federation *(Rossiiskaia Federatsiia)*. Although the communist regime fell along with the Soviet state, many of the institutions and processes of that system are still intact in Russia.

In other respects, however, Russia is a new country. Legally speaking, it became sovereign upon the dissolution of the Soviet Union, when it took on its present political identity. Many of its political institutions are also new since they were not part of the Russian political system either under Soviet rule or under the tsars. Among these are the presidency, the Constitutional Court, and federalism. This book will concentrate on the structure and functioning of Russia's contemporary political system. In doing so, we will often need to refer to the previous political system, that of the Soviet Union, in order to understand present-day Russia in light of Soviet and pre-Soviet history.

In this chapter we will review the changes that have taken place over the last decade that have brought about the collapse of the Soviet Union and the formation of an independent new Russian Federation. These changes have been extraordinarily tumultuous and are often confusing—no less for Russians than for outside observers. The chapter will discuss three sets of these changes:

- The breakup of the union into its 15 constituent parts, the union republics, of which Russia was the largest;
- The end of the communist political regime, known as *communist* because the Communist Party of the Soviet Union held a monopoly on the exercise of political power; and

1

- The end of the centrally planned economy in which the country's political leadership decided what the economy was to produce, and in which the state owned all productive property.

Because these changes have occurred simultaneously, they have been much more wrenching and difficult than regime transitions in other societies that have witnessed the fall of an authoritarian regime and the establishment of democratic institutions. These changes have created enormous uncertainty for Russia's citizens, which has undermined their faith in the future. Few people can be confident that the coming decade will bring about a more stable democratic and market-based social order. Society's lack of confidence in the future tends to undermine the forms of social behavior and relations that would reinforce stable democratic institutions.

The premise of the book, therefore, is that Russia's political system combines *democratic* and *authoritarian* elements. It is no longer a communist, post-totalitarian system, but it also is not a full democracy. By *democracy* I mean a political system in which the entire adult population has the freedom to take part in the choice of leaders and policies, exercising this freedom through elections under rights of association, conscience, speech, and participation. By *authoritarianism* I refer to a political system in which these rights are denied to a part of the citizenry or are restricted to a limited set of political issues. Those who make decisions about policy are not held accountable to the citizenry in any meaningful way. The Soviet regime (1917–91) represented a particular form of authoritarian rule known as *communism,* in which the state owned all productive property and political power was monopolized by the Communist Party. Communist regimes—sometimes also called *totalitarian,* because, like the Nazi regime under Adolf Hitler in Germany in 1933–45 and the fascist regime in Italy under Benito Mussolini in 1922–43, they aspired to give the rulers of the state total control over society—concentrated far more power in the party and government leaders than is found in other types of authoritarian regimes because the rulers controlled both economic and political processes. For this reason, then, the transition from communist rule to democratic rule in Russia represents a greater discontinuity than the recent transitions from authoritarianism in Latin America or Southern Europe.[1]

The transition in Russia from communist rule to a freer, more open political system presents us with an extraordinary opportunity to understand regime change. In this book we will study the way social change over the past several decades resulted in a more demanding and articulate society in the Soviet Union. In turn we will examine how society responded with explosive energy to the new freedoms to voice concerns and to organize for collective action that were introduced by the reformist leadership under Mikhail Gorbachev in the late 1980s. A large part of the transition was fueled by pressure "from below" as society organized to voice grievances and demands for change. The mobilization of discontent, however, is only part of the story. We must also consider the choices made by political actors as they created new arenas of political action and new structures of government and devised stratagems for gaining and building power. Often, due to leaders' miscalculations and unex-

---

[1]Juan J. Linz and Alfred Stepan, *Problems of Democratic Transition and Consolidation: Southern Europe, South America, and Post-Communist Europe* (Baltimore and London: Johns Hopkins University Press, 1996).

pected moves by other political actors, these had entirely unforeseen consequences. For instance, it is clear now that the central party leadership in the late 1980s seriously underestimated the strength of ethnic-national attachments in the union republics, so that when they granted greater political liberty to Soviet citizens, much of the new ferment that followed swelled into nationalist movements demanding independence for the union republics.

Another critical issue in understanding regime change is the relationship between economic and political liberalization. Scholars actively debate how closely linked are the development of liberal democracy and the development of market capitalism. In the long run, most observers agree, the two are interdependent. But in the short run, the relationship is less clear, and there is disagreement about how market reform may reinforce or undermine democratic reform. There is a school of thought which believes that it may be necessary to restrict democratic freedoms for a period of time when painful market-oriented reforms are begun. Those who think this way argue that such reforms create widespread hardship for society in the short run, and therefore are susceptible to being reversed unless they are protected by strong executive power. The specific tasks of such reforms, which are aimed at laying the foundations of a capitalist economy, include ending inflation, restoring growth, encouraging investment, and liberalizing capital markets. These favorable economic conditions, according to the theory, then facilitate the expansion of political rights in a later phase, once a strong, secure, and self-confident middle class has arisen that supports the rule of law and democratic government. Advocates of this point of view frequently point to the newly industrialized states of East Asia, such as Taiwan, South Korea, and Singapore, to justify their view that society as a whole is better off if democracy is postponed for a time while it establishes a firm footing of economic prosperity.

Against this is the view that the adjustment of an economy to liberal capitalism creates so much discontent in a society that it can only be contained by granting citizens democratic rights, particularly if the society already has a number of internal divisions. Transition to a more open, market-oriented capitalist system generates numerous hardships: inequality often grows in the early stages of economic development before it declines again in later stages; the demands of workers can readily consume resources needed for investment unless held in check; prices of industrial and commercial goods may outpace prices for agricultural goods, leading to urban–rural tension; and cutting off tariff protection and state economic subsidies to inefficient firms can result in widespread unemployment and economic insecurity. Many workers, farmers, pensioners, and other social groups are likely to suffer a decline in living standards as wages lag behind prices, at least in the short run, before the economy begins responding to the market-oriented stimuli and production and consumption can begin rising again. For this reason, the second school argues, an inclusive and democratic order is required that allows diverse social interests political voice so as to get through the worst of the early period of economic adjustment. Thus there is a great debate over the optimal sequence of reform: first, economic reform, then political reform versus simultaneous economic and political reform.

This issue is not only of academic interest. Russia's experience is seen as a case from which other countries can draw lessons. Russia and China are often compared in this connection.[2] In 1978 China began a series of economic reforms that emphasized liberalization of the economy. Farmers and small-scale entrepreneurs were given freedom to produce food and other goods for the market and to accumulate wealth. At the same time, however, the Chinese Communist Party made it clear that no challenge to its political dominance would be tolerated. The bloody events of June 1989, when military units massacred students demonstrating for democracy on Tiananmen Square in Beijing, confirmed the Chinese leadership's resolve in this policy. Gorbachev, in contrast, introduced deep political reforms in the Soviet Union when his early economic reforms failed to produce results. Therefore the Soviet Union and China are often cited as contrasting models of reform strategy. For example, leaders in China and elsewhere often point to the Soviet Union as an object lesson in the harmful consequences that come from opening a system up politically before a strong market economy is in place. They say that the Soviet leaders failed to foresee that political liberalization would have extremely destructive consequences, among them the collapse of the union state, the breakdown of political order, and the resulting insecurity and uncertainty which sabotaged both economic and political reform. Soviet leaders respond that Soviet Union had no choice, because the only way to overcome the old communist system was to launch radical political and economic reform simultaneously in order to break permanently the power of the old bureaucratic ruling class and set in motion liberalizing, competitive forces.

Another reason for studying the transition in Russia is its position in the international system. As the heir of the Soviet Union, Russia inherited an enormous military arsenal and vital geo-strategic location. For most of the post–World War II period—from the late 1940s until the late 1980s—the United States and other Western democracies were engaged in a fundamental competition with the Soviet Union for influence over Europe and other regions of the world. This was largely a result of the fact that communism began as a revolutionary movement aimed at overthrowing international capitalism and "bourgeois" (liberal democratic) governments around the world. From the time that the communists took power in Russia in 1917, their regime adopted a posture of fundamental hostility to the West. For most of the period of communist rule (1917–91), Soviet rulers alternated between an aggressive, expansionist policy toward the Western world and an accommodative and pragmatic one. They pursued "peaceful coexistence" but competed for influence by supporting radical socialist movements and fought the spread of the basic democratic and capitalist values of the West. Observers have long noted that in its external relations, the Soviet Union proceeded along two tracks simultaneously.[3] On one track, the regime sought stable economic and diplomatic relations with the powerful

---

[2] A useful comparison of the Soviet and Chinese reform strategies and their consequences is Minxin Pei, *From Reform to Revolution: The Demise of Communism in China and the Soviet Union* (Cambridge: Harvard University Press, 1994).

[3] Studies of Soviet foreign policy include Peter Zwick, *Soviet Foreign Relations: Process and Policy* (Englewood Cliffs, NJ: Prentice Hall, 1990); Joseph L. Nogee and Robert H. Donaldson, *Soviet Foreign Policy since World War II*, 4th ed. (New York: Macmillan, 1992); Alvin Z. Rubinstein, *Soviet Foreign Policy since World War II: Imperial and Global*, 4th ed. (New York: HarperCollins, 1992). A magisterial study of Soviet foreign policy in Adam Ulam, *Expansion and Coexistence: Soviet Foreign Policy, 1917–1973*, 2nd ed. (New York: Praeger, 1974).

countries of the capitalist world. On the other, it constructed a network of political and military alliances with socialist and revolutionary regimes and groups with the goal of increasing its global influence at the expense of that of the West. The antagonism and rivalry between the democratic and market-oriented states of the West and the socialist bloc led by the Soviet Union created a bipolar distribution of power in world politics which lasted from shortly after World War II until the momentous reforms of Mikhail Gorbachev.[4]

The strategic rivalry between the two superpowers, the United States and Soviet Union, shaped both political and military relations. Both countries devoted enormous efforts to preparing for possible war. Each side came to accept that a general nuclear war between them would be so devastating to each side, no matter which began it, that it could never be fought; each accepted that the terrible threat of such a war served to deter the other from taking excessive or provocative risks. Both, moreover, continually upgraded their nuclear arsenals during this period, emphasizing qualities such as destructive power, accuracy, invulnerability, and mobility. The Soviet Union and United States each built around 10,000 long-range nuclear weapons capable of striking each other's military, industrial, political, and communications centers. They also accumulated tens of thousands more shorter-range nuclear weapons that were part of the land, naval, and air forces stationed in Europe and Asia.[5] Some of these weapons have been dismantled as a result of arms reduction agreements signed between the two sides, but most remain in the American and Russian arsenals. If the START II (Strategic Arms Reduction Talks, round II) agreement is ratified and put into force, the two sides will each reduce their nuclear arsenals by about two-thirds, leaving each with around 3,500 strategic warheads.[6] The political balance in Russia will determine whether this major step toward reducing the threat of nuclear arms competition is taken or whether the two sides return to a posture of mutual hostility and confrontation.

The Soviet Union and United States were also rivals in ideology. Soviet doctrine claimed that the socialist system was intrinsically superior to capitalism because it

---

[4]World War II ended in 1945, and the postwar era of antagonism between the United States and its allies and the Soviet Union and its allies began in 1947–48. Mikhail Gorbachev, the last leader of the Soviet Union, assumed power as General Secretary of the Communist Party of the Soviet Union in March 1985. In 1990 he created and assumed the position of President of the Soviet Union. He resigned formally from this position in December 1991. The Union of Soviet Socialist Republics formally dissolved as a legal entity on December 31, 1991. The Soviet leaders and the dates of their rule since the Bolshevik Revolution in 1917, when the Soviet regime was established, are as follows:

1. Vladimir Lenin (1917–24)

2. Iosif Stalin (1924–53)

3. Nikita Khrushchev (1953–64)

4. Leonid Brezhnev (1964–82)

5. Yuri Andropov (1982–84)

6. Konstantin Chernenko (1984–85)

7. Mikhail Gorbachev (1985–91)

[5]Coit D. Blacker, *Reluctant Warriors: The United States, the Soviet Union, and Arms Control* (New York: W. H. Freeman & Co., 1987), p. 25.

[6]As of January 1998, both sides had signed the treaty, and the U.S. Senate had ratified it; but the Russian parliament had not yet acted on it.

did away with the exploitation of labor by capitalists, and because it concentrated control over productive resources in the hands of leaders who could build up the country's productive potential. The doctrine held that, unlike capitalism, socialism had a determinate goal and would one day advance to the "communist" stage of development, when all property and power would be held in common and all people would be equal. In earlier periods, many Soviet citizens as well as sympathetic foreign observers believed that the Soviet system did indeed offer an alternative model of economic development and social justice to that represented by capitalism. Over time, however, the socialist model lost its attractiveness both at home and abroad. Soviet leaders became unable to persuade their population or the outside world that the bright future of communism would ever arrive. When it collapsed, the communist system collapsed quickly and comprehensively, indicating how little popular support communist rule in fact possessed. But it has proven far easier to dismantle the former structures of communist rule than to replace them with new structures. For many people in the former Soviet Union, the hopes that the construction of a democratic and prosperous new order would be relatively smooth have been frustrated and instead replaced with bitterness or anger at the authorities. The transition period has left many living in the former Soviet Union materially worse off, at least for the present. Many, indeed, feel that they have lost their very national identity.

A successful outcome of the transition in Russia would mean, therefore, that the strategic confrontation between the Western powers and Russia could finally give way to a relationship of cooperation, even partnership. An economically healthy and democratic Russia would be a stabilizing factor in the multiple regions on which Russia borders: Eastern Europe, the Middle East, and Northeast and Northwest Asia. On the other hand, the renewal of authoritarianism in Russia would very likely herald a return to a climate of international tension, a new division of Europe, and a new arms race between East and West.

Three Domains of Change

Let us review the changes that have occurred in the last several years in three basic areas: national identity, political institutions, and the economy.

THE QUESTION OF IDENTITY: IMPERIAL RUSSIA—USSR— RUSSIAN FEDERATION

As of January 1, 1992, the Union of Soviet Socialist Republics no longer existed. The white-blue-red tricolor of the Russian state now flew over Moscow's Kremlin—the physical and symbolic seat of Russian state power for 400 years—in place of the Soviet Union's red flag with its hammer and sickle. Soviet communism had come to an end, and a newly sovereign Russia took control of that portion of the USSR's territory—comprising some three quarters of the physical area and half the population—which had formed the Russian Soviet Federative Socialist Republic. (Today the RSFSR has been renamed the Russian Federation or simply Russia.) The 15 republics which had made up the Soviet Union were now independent states.

The relationship between the Soviet Union and postcommunist Russia can be confusing, both for outside observers and for the people who suddenly found themselves citizens of a new state. Many people thought of Russia and the Soviet Union as interchangeable names for the same country, which was an understandable mental shortcut given Russia's dominance of the union politically and culturally. Formally, however, Russia was only one of 15 nominally equal federal republics making up the union. Each republic had an ethnic-national identity but the union itself had no ethnic or national affiliation—only an ideological one.

The union collapsed when the governments of Russia and other member republics refused to accept the authority of the central government any longer. Mikhail Gorbachev, the reform-minded leader of the Soviet Union, struggled to find some new framework to preserve the unity of the union, but he was outmaneuvered by Boris Yeltsin, head of the Russian republic, and frustrated by the powerful aspirations for self-rule on the part of peoples in many of the republics. On June 12, 1990, the Russian Congress of People's Deputies—the newly elected legislative assembly of the RSFSR—approved a sweeping endorsement of Russian sovereignty within the USSR: Russia would only observe those USSR laws that it consented to acknowledge. A year later, on June 12, 1991, Boris Yeltsin was elected president of Russia in the first direct popular presidential elections that Russia had ever had. Probably few Russians foresaw that the union itself would eventually collapse as an outgrowth of these developments. Other events were equally momentous. The Communist Party ceased to rule the country. The familiar contours of the state-owned, state-planned economy were giving way to contradictory tendencies: production in the state enterprises fell, while energetic, if frequently corrupt, private entrepreneurship spread. Inequality and poverty increased sharply. Everyone agreed that the old Soviet system had broken down, while a new system had not yet fully formed.

The August 1991 Coup Before the final breakup of the USSR as a going concern, one last dramatic confrontation between the old and new worlds occurred. For certain elite groups—particularly in the military, KGB (Committee for State Security, also known as the secret police), economic bureaucracy, and Communist Party—the declining power of the union and the assertion of sovereignty by its constituent republics were a mortal threat. But large groups of the population, both in other union republics and, significantly, in Russia itself, saw the union government as an oppressive, exploitative, and alien power. They demanded sovereignty for the constituent republics of the union as the only way to achieve economic progress, democracy, and freedom. Even some bureaucratic elites in the republics themselves, while cool to the idea of democracy and a market economy, supported loosening the stranglehold of the union government as a way of increasing their own power over their republics. Public opinion data from 1990 showed overwhelming support in Russia and other republics for increasing the autonomy of the republics in the union and opposition to the authority of the union's center.[7]

---

[7]Vicki L. Hesli and Joel D. Barkan, "The Center-Periphery Debate: Pressures for Devolution Within the Republics," in Arthur H. Miller, William M. Reisinger, and Vicki L. Hesli, eds., *Public Opinion and Regime Change: The New Politics of Post-Soviet Societies* (Boulder: Westview Press, 1993), pp. 131–133, 149.

In August 1991 these contradictory pressures reached a climax. Gorbachev was preparing to enact a treaty between himself, as president of the USSR, and the heads of the republics making up the union, which would have laid a new foundation for the country as a looser federation. The treaty would have granted the republics substantial powers to control the economic resources of their own territories. Most of the leaders of the constituent republics were prepared to accept this agreement, but we will never know whether it might have served as a viable basis for a new, post-Soviet union. One day before the scheduled signing of the treaty, a self-appointed "State Committee for the State of Emergency," consisting of a group of senior officials from the central government, police, KGB, military, and Communist Party, seized power. They placed Gorbachev under house arrest and declared a state of emergency in an attempt to reimpose the power and integrity of the USSR which they believed Gorbachev was about to destroy for good. Immediately, masses of citizens in Moscow and Leningrad rallied in protest. Thousands of citizens stood up to the tanks sent out by the "State Committee" to defend the principle of Russian sovereignty and democratic liberty. Instead of restoring the old order, the coup's organizers gave up after three days when key military units refused to obey their orders in the face of widespread popular protest. At that moment—August 19–21, 1991— many citizens of Russia considered Russian national sovereignty, political democracy, and the end of state socialism to be bundled together in the same cause.[8] Having defeated the combined forces of the old, oppressive, bureaucratic Soviet order, they thought a sovereign Russia would speedily move on to a prosperous new order.

The Commonwealth of Independent States (CIS) The coup attempt accelerated the pace of the union's disintegration. One by one the union republics issued declarations of independence. The power structures of the union soon were unable to exercise authority. The Finance Ministry could not collect taxes, the military could not conscript soldiers. Trade ties were breaking down across regions and republics. As revenues fell, the Central Bank pumped more and more money into circulation that was not backed up by real values. The economy was sinking into chaos. Union bureaucracies operating on Russian territory were taken over by the Russian government; those in other republics were similarly nationalized by those republics.

---

[8]On the coup, see "Anatomy of a Failed Coup," in Ch. 5, John B. Dunlop, *The Rise of Russia and the Fall of the Soviet Empire* (Princeton: Princeton University Press, 1993), pp. 186–255. One of many mysteries about the coup is the degree of foreknowledge that Gorbachev may have had about it. There is a good deal of speculation that Gorbachev allowed the coup's organizers to seize power in the hopes that they would call him back to power after they had crushed Yeltsin and other republican political forces seeking independence. Gorbachev himself, however, has strongly denied all such accounts.

There is an extensive memoir literature now by some of the principals. Gorbachev's account is Mikhail Gorbachev, *The August Coup: The Truth and the Lessons* (New York: HarperCollins, 1991). Boris Yeltsin's fascinating recollections are in his book, *The Struggle for Russia*, trans. Catherine A. Fitzpatrick (New York: Random House, 1994). One of the principals, the chairman of the Russian parliament, discusses the coup and his own rather ambiguous role in it in A. Luk´ianov, *Perevorot: Mnimyi i nastoiashchii* [The coup: apparent and real] (Voronezh: Voronezhskaia oblastnaia organizatsiia Soiuza zhurnalistov Rossii, 1993).

In October Yeltsin announced that Russia would proceed with radical market-oriented reform along the lines of Poland's "big bang."[9] On December 1, 1991, a referendum was held in the Ukrainian republic on national independence. When the proposal to declare Ukrainian independence passed with 90 percent of the vote, politicians throughout the Soviet Union recognized that the breakup of the union was irreversible, and they looked for ways to preserve at least some of the formal ties among the republics. The leaders of the three Slavic core states—Russia, Ukraine, and Belorussia—met near Minsk, capital of Belorussia, on December 8, and on their own authority declared the USSR dissolved. In its place they agreed to form a new entity, a framework for coordinating their economic and strategic relations, called the Commonwealth of Independent States (CIS). Thirteen days later the CIS was expanded to include all the former republics except for Georgia and the three Baltic states of Lithuania, Latvia, and Estonia. In 1993, Georgia also joined.

Although less than a government, the CIS is more than a purely symbolic organization. It has gained some coordinating powers in the realms of trade, finance, lawmaking, and security. The great obstacle to the growth of integration and hence of coordinating power for the CIS is the unwillingness of other member states to turn over much power to the huge Russian state. This issue illustrates the point that the Soviet Union functioned as a sovereign state only by weakening Russia's own status as a member state, and turning power over instead to a nominally federal, Communist Party-controlled central government. For this reason, it is probably the case that Russia had no chance of becoming a democratic state unless in fact it jettisoned the union. But without Russia, of course, there could be no union.

On Christmas Day, 1991, Gorbachev announced his resignation as president and turned state powers over to Yeltsin. The group who plotted to take over the state to restore the Soviet state's power had accomplished precisely the opposite outcome. Russia could now chart its own destiny without reference to the larger union state.

Three years later, however, opinion polls were registering a wave of public resentment and disillusionment over the failure of popular hopes for rapid improvement of their lives. By a large majority, Russian citizens in late 1993 condemned the breakup of the Soviet Union as harmful.[10] Two-thirds of Russians blamed the breakup of the Soviet Union for their current economic woes. A majority of citizens said that they did not consider themselves Europeans and a majority

---

[9]Poland's "big bang" refers to a comprehensive package of policy reforms that Poland's democratically elected government introduced on January 1, 1990. These reforms drastically cut state spending, let prices float upward until demand met supply, and opened the borders to free trade. These reforms resulted in a sharp, one-time upward surge in prices for most goods. Shortages quickly disappeared, but many people's living standards initially fell. However, Poland's currency quickly stabilized and positive economic growth followed soon afterward. Poland thus represents a successful application of the market-oriented, anti-inflationary stabilization measures prescribed by the International Monetary Fund and other world financial institutions for economies struggling to overcome crises of chronic high inflation and low growth. In Chapter Six below we will discuss the rationale for and results of a similar program of economic reform that Russia enacted in 1992.

[10]Jerry F. Hough, "The Russian Election of 1993: Public Attitudes Toward Economic Reform and Democratization," *Post-Soviet Affairs* 10:1 (January–March 1994), p. 13.

gave a positive rating to the old, communist regime (although only a quarter would support its restoration).[11] A majority was even willing to agree with the proposition that the West was trying to weaken Russia with its economic advice.[12]

It is hardly surprising that Russians were struggling to grasp the significance of the breakup of the union and tended to blame it for the hardships they were experiencing. Yet in the perspective of history, we should see the Soviet Union as one phase in Russia's political evolution, and a relatively brief one at that. Soviet communism in Russia lasted only 74 years, from October 1917 until December 1991, whereas the Russian state dates its origins to the city-state of Rus that arose around Kiev, in present-day Ukraine, at the end of the ninth century. The Soviet period is thus a brief though momentous episode in the thousand-year history of the political entity we call Russia. And, as historians such as Roman Szporluk have pointed out, Russia's political evolution differed from the typical path taken by Western countries.[13] In Western Europe, nations formed as social communities in territories defined through contests and treaties among state rulers. In Russia, by contrast, the state created a territorial empire spanning a huge landmass and populated by a diverse array of European and Asian peoples, who differed profoundly among themselves in religion, way of life, and relationship to Russian authority. Russian national consciousness was based less on ethnicity, therefore, than on identification with a powerful imperial state. Russia's history lacks a model of a nation-state to serve as a precedent for the postcommunist period.

Of course the collapse of the multinational Soviet state did not restore the prerevolutionary status quo: instead, the fifteen union republics that constituted the nominal federation of equal republics each acquired formal independence. Thus, although the Soviet state was the heir of the Russian imperial state, contemporary Russia is only one of fifteen successor states of the Soviet Union. Some had possessed national statehood before being annexed into the Soviet Union, but others gained the institutional infrastructure of nationhood in the course of Soviet rule. The Soviet regime's policies affected different nationalities in the union differently: some small peoples assimilated into larger groups; in many cases the national culture of a people was severely restricted; in yet others, the formal features of national existence that the federal model of the Soviet state provided tended to stimulate the rise of a national consciousness. The breakup of the Soviet Union has not simply restored the status quo ante.[14]

Although in this book we will focus on Russia's political system, we should note that the dissolution of the centrally run union state has resulted in enormous variety among the successor states with respect to their domestic political and economic orders, their mutual relations, and their relationships with Russia.

---

[11]Richard Rose, "After Communism: What?" *Daedalus* 123:3 (Summer 1994), pp. 46, 56.

[12]Hough, "The Russian Election," p. 6.

[13]Roman Szporluk, "The Imperial Legacy and the Soviet Nationalities," in Lubomyr Hajda and Mark Beissinger, eds., *The Nationalities Factor in Soviet Politics and Society* (Boulder: Westview Press, 1990), pp. 1–23; and idem, "Dilemmas of Russian Nationalism," in Rachel Denber, ed., *The Soviet Nationality Reader: The Disintegration in Context* (Boulder: Westview Press, 1992), pp. 509–543.

[14]Ronald Grigor Suny, *The Revenge of the Past: Nationalism, Revolution, and the Collapse of the Soviet Union* (Stanford: Stanford University Press, 1993).

The three Baltic states, Lithuania, Latvia, and Estonia, have established stable democracies and market-dominated economies which are increasingly being integrated into the larger European economy. These states do not belong to the Commonwealth of Independent States and their relations with Russia range from correct to frosty. It is worth noting, in passing, that, of the former Soviet states, only the Baltic states have parliamentary political systems and only they are securely democratic. The other twelve successor states all have presidential systems, and only a few adhere consistently to basic democratic principles.

For instance, most of the Central Asian states—Tajikistan, Kyrgyzstan, Turkmenistan, and Uzbekistan, and their huge neighbor Kazakstan—have become less democratic since the union's breakup. Their presidents have claimed sweeping powers and restricted citizens' rights although they all also seek foreign capital investment in their economies. Most have sought close relations with Russia as well. Indeed, Tajikistan, which has suffered from a violent civil war between Islamic fundamentalists and government forces, has accepted a status akin to that of a protectorate of Russia.

Russia has also gained a dominant strategic position with respect to the security and energy interests of other former Soviet republics, including the three Transcaucasian states of Armenia, Azerbaijan, and Georgia. These states differ in the degree to which democracy and the rule of law are honored, but each has had to accept a degree of Russian domination as the price for political peace and stability.

Belarus, under its authoritarian president Alexander Lukashenka, has in fact made union with Russia a principal goal. Despite the formal agreements on union that have been signed, however, neither Belarus nor Russia has been prepared to relinquish any of its sovereignty to a superior union government. The union has consequently remained a dead letter.

Ukraine's political stance will be critical to determining whether the future will bring about any restoration of a new union of former Soviet states. Its leadership has been united in the aim of maintaining independence from Russia politically and economically. Ukraine's political and economic development has lagged behind Russia's both in the consolidation of democratic institutions and in the spread of market-oriented relations: to a considerably greater extent than in Russia, the old Soviet-style, state-centric social order remains intact in Ukraine, propped up in large measure by the appeal to anti-Russian Ukrainian nationalism. Russia and Ukraine have nonetheless succeeded in keeping their relations on a reasonably harmonious track despite recurrent tensions over issues such as the disposition of the old Soviet Black Sea fleet and the status of the naval port Sevastopol.

The diversity of political and economic interests of the successor states has so far limited the capacity of the institutional framework created by the Commonwealth of Independent States to exercise any real authority. Such capacity as the CIS has is the product of Russia's military, economic, and political clout, which it has exercised on occasion with all the bluntness of a nineteenth-century imperial hegemon. Yet at the same time, democratic and market reforms have proceeded further in Russia than in nearly any other CIS state.

Although it was the product of a movement which sought to ignite an international revolution, the Soviet communist state established its rule in Russia in 1917, defended its power against domestic and foreign enemies, and proceeded to reannex many of the same territories which the tsarist state had conquered. Denying that this multinational, communist state was in any way a Russian empire—the very name was meant to show that the state was neither Russian by national identity nor an empire politically—the communist regime imposed a common socialist model of economic ownership and administration on the entire territory of the state. Although Soviet ideology held that in the long run, national differences would be subsumed in a common Soviet national identity, during the late 1980s, leaders in the 15 republics pursued demands for greater autonomy for their republics, and in many republics, mass movements for national independence grew powerful. With the breakup of the USSR, the Russian state regained a national identity, but at the price of giving up the larger union.

Each year since 1990, Russia has observed a holiday on June 12 called "Independence Day." On June 12, 1990 the newly elected Russian legislature adopted its "Declaration of Sovereignty," and exactly one year later, Boris Yeltsin was elected president. Since then, Yeltsin's government has sought to recapture the optimistic mood and democratic aspirations of 1990 and 1991 by celebrating June 12 as a commemoration of Russia's hopes for a bright future as a sovereign nation. Yet the attitude of many Russians toward the holiday is one of irritation and indifference: independence has brought few perceptible benefits. "What is there to celebrate?" one Moscow resident commented in puzzlement. "I don't understand. What are we independent of?"[15]

TRANSITION TO PLURALIST DEMOCRACY

At the same time that Russian leaders and citizens have struggled to redefine Russia's national identity, they have been partners in the revolutionary enterprise of remaking the country's political institutions. This process began with the deep political reforms launched by Mikhail Gorbachev, who came to power as General Secretary of the Communist Party of the Soviet Union (CPSU) in 1985. Although Gorbachev did not intend for his reform policies to bring about the dissolution of the Soviet Union, he did push for a far-reaching and radical set of changes in the economic and political institutions of the regime. These changes, in turn, stimulated demands for still more autonomy by regional and republican leaders and led to the mobilization of protest against the existing regime by large segments of the population in many republics. In Russia, Boris Yeltsin and other political leaders successfully challenged Gorbachev and the union government for power by championing the cause of liberal democracy, the market economy, and national sovereignty for Russia. With the breakup of the Soviet Union, President Yeltsin and his government have continued to press for radical economic reform. In doing so they have, at times, used undemocratic methods. Yet there can be no question that Russia enjoys significantly more political freedom today than it did for nearly the whole Soviet period or, for that matter, at almost any time in its history. Two-thirds of Russian respondents in a nationwide survey in summer 1993 said that they had more freedom of religion, speech, and association now than under the old regime.[16]

---

[15]In 1997, the government finally gave up trying to treat the holiday as a celebration of independence, and simply renamed June 12 "the day of Russia."

[16]Richard Rose, "Postcommunism and the Problem of Trust," *Journal of Democracy* 5:3 (July 1994), p. 24; idem, "After Communism, What?" p. 52.

Democratization in Russia, although neither complete nor secure, has brought about fundamental changes of at least three kinds.

Individual Rights First, the barriers to individual political liberties which the communist regime imposed have largely been lifted: the intrusive Communist Party mechanism for enforcing ideological discipline in public discourse is gone and with it, political censorship; persecution of religious practice has ended and the state has instead embraced religion, particularly the Russian Orthodox Church, as an ally in strengthening public morality; citizens are now free to organize independent political parties and associations; and, gradually, the courts have been gaining independence in the enforcement of individuals' legal rights. A large body of research suggests that commitment to democratic principles of individual rights is widely shared although not uniformly practiced.[17] Citizens' ability to defend these rights against encroachment by central or local authorities remains tenuous, however.

Organizational Pluralism A second type of change that advances democracy is the emergence of autonomous social and civic organizations. Under the old regime, public organizations were monitored and sometimes directly controlled by the Communist Party. In the Stalin era (1928–53), the major public organizations, such as trade unions and youth leagues, were considered to be "transmission belts" linking society to the political authorities. These "transmission belt" organizations provided regime-sponsored outlets for organized collective action and ensured that they would serve the regime's political goals. In the Gorbachev period, a large number of new, autonomous social organizations sprang up under the influence of the regime's political reforms, some with avowedly political purposes, others for cultural or philosophical pursuits.[18] After the demise of the communist regime, many of these organizations vanished. With time, however, a more stable set of interest groups began to develop. Among these are organizations defending the interests of regions, collective and state farms, state industrial firms, new entrepreneurs, private farmers, and industrial workers, not to mention a shifting array of political parties, groups, movements, and blocs competing for attention and influence.

Contested Elections The third change in the democratic process is that elections have become competitive and regular. Between the first contested elections of

---

[17]James L. Gibson, Raymond M. Duch, and Kent L. Tedin, "Democratic Values and the Transformation of the Soviet Union," *Journal of Politics* 54:2 (May 1992), pp. 329–371; James L. Gibson, "A Mile Wide But an Inch Deep (?): The Structure of Democratic Commitments in the Former USSR," Paper delivered at the 1994 meeting of the American Political Science Association, New York, September 1994; William Zimmerman, "Markets, Democracy and Russian Foreign Policy," *Post-Soviet Affairs* 10:2 (April–June 1994), pp. 103–126; Stephen Whitefield and Geoffrey Evans, "The Russian Election of 1993: Public Opinion and the Transition Experience," *Post-Soviet Affairs* 10:1 (January–March 1994), pp. 38–60.

[18]Jim Butterfield and Marcia Weigle, "Unofficial Social Groups and Regime Response in the Soviet Union," in Judith B. Sedaitis and Jim Butterfield, eds., *Perestroika from Below: Social Movements in the Soviet Union* (Boulder: Westview Press, 1992), pp. 175–195; Marcia A. Weigle and Jim Butterfield, "Civil Society in Reforming Communist Regimes: The Logic of Emergence," *Comparative Politics* 25:1 (October 1992), pp. 1–23; Thomas Remington, "A Socialist Pluralism of Opinions: *Glasnost'* and Policy-Making under Gorbachev," *Russian Review* 48:3 (July 1989), pp. 271–304.

USSR deputies in 1989 and the presidential election of June 1996, Russian voters went to the polls eight times in nationwide elections:

- 1989: election of USSR deputies
- 1990: election of RSFSR and local deputies
- 1991: March: referenda on preserving union and creating Russian presidency
- 1991: June: election of RSFSR president
- 1993: April: referendum on approval of Yeltsin and government
- 1993: December: election of deputies to new parliament and referendum on draft constitution
- 1995: December: election of deputies to parliament
- 1996: June/July: election of president

1999: Dec: election of deputies to parl

These elections varied in the degree to which they were honest, open, and fair. But the principle of democratic elections as a means of conferring legitimate power on political leaders is now well established, both in political practice and public opinion.

In other respects the political system remains authoritarian, however. One result of the democratic movement of 1989–91 was the creation of a powerful state presidency invested with enormous power to overcome resistance to reform. The new constitution ratified in the nationwide referendum in December 1993 embodies President Yeltsin's conception of the presidency: the president has wide powers to issue decrees with the force of law and faces few constraints on the exercise of his powers. In practice the president directly oversees foreign policy and national security. President Yeltsin has interpreted this power, reinforced by the constitutional provision that the president is the supreme commander-in-chief of the armed forces, as authorization to send the armed forces into action to preserve order. President Yeltsin ordered the military to shell the parliament building in October 1993 to destroy the last remnants of the groups that had attempted an armed uprising to seize power. In December 1994 he again ordered the army and security troops to conquer the forces fighting for the independence of the separatist Chechen Republic. This action resulted in massive destruction of Grozny, the capital city, and of many other cities and towns in the republic. Tens of thousands of people were killed, close to half a million people fled the republic, and hundreds of thousands more were left homeless by the fighting, which continued until a cease-fire was reached in late 1996. Federal government spokesmen denied that federal armed forces had engaged in massive bombardment of civilian targets, but, significantly, the central authorities did not go so far as to suppress all independent news reporting about the war. This allowed independent national television and newspaper correspondents to expose the government's statements as fabrications.

The concentration of political power in the president and the executive agencies he oversees, and the weakness of checks on his use of his wide powers, are reinforced by the rampant lawlessness and corruption in the country. Organized crime has flagrantly defied the law, and law enforcement officials have appeared to be helpless in the face of widespread criminality. Highly publicized killings of prominent citizens—for example, three members of parliament were murdered in 1994 alone—have strengthened the central authorities' demand for sweeping powers of surveillance and investigation. Often, ironically, it has been some of President

Yeltsin's communist opponents who have attempted to block the aggrandizement of power by the security police.

The tendencies toward a new concentration of authoritarian power in the executive are echoed in many regions of the country where powerful local bosses rule. Often individuals who have successfully survived the upheavals of the past several years, these regional chief executives have established strong political machines that make them relatively independent of both federal power and accountability to the local citizens. In a few cases, local officials have suppressed political opposition and arrested their opponents. Both at the federal and regional levels, then, the outcome of the struggle for the rule of law remains in doubt.

ECONOMIC TRANSFORMATION

In addition to the wrenching change in national identity and the uneven movement toward liberal democracy, a third and equally momentous change has been underway in Russia. This is the transformation from the state-owned, centrally administered economy to one approximating a market system. In a market economy, the right of private ownership of productive resources enjoys legal guarantees; decisions on production and consumption are made by producers and consumers; and the coordination of the myriad activities of individuals and organizations is accomplished primarily through their interaction in a competitive environment. Russia remains far from having reached this point—in fact, no economy in the real world completely matches this description. But in Russia the state has gone very far to dismantle the former socialist system in favor of a rudimentary market framework. Russia's method of enacting economic reform—rapid, radical price liberalization, combined with sharp decreases in state spending and increases in taxation—has been called "shock therapy." Russia's version of shock therapy was a very crude policy instrument and it was often quietly sabotaged in the course of implementation. It may have been the only means available to policymakers for making rapid and irreversible changes in the behavior of economic actors, but it created many unwanted side effects and did not succeed in setting Russia onto a path where market incentives would stimulate economic growth.

Among the several painful side effects of the reforms, which included the decontrol of most prices, was a huge jump in prices in 1992 and uneven but slowly declining inflation thereafter. Another consequence has been a profound and lasting economic depression: industrial output fell by half in the first five years of the reform, and a severe liquidity crisis is reflected in a massive problem of arrears in wages, interfirm payments, and government tax revenues and budget spending. On the other hand, the reform did succeed in making some crucial changes in the economy. One was to give money real value as a medium of exchange, as opposed to the communist period when it was an accounting unit but because of the planning system could not be used for most kinds of transactions. Another was to end most shortages of goods and services in major cities: queues largely disappeared, basic consumer needs could be satisfied, and imported food and other goods became widely available throughout the country.

The most striking consequence of the economic reform has been the sharp rise in rates of poverty and inequality. Figures on these politically sensitive subjects are not always reliable, but one estimate shows that the ratio of the average per capita income of the richest 10 percent of the population to that of the poorest 10 percent has risen from 5.4 in 1991 to almost 11 at the end of 1993, and, according to some reports, to 15 by the end of 1994. The richest 10 percent of the population were said to be receiving 30 percent of total income, and the poorest only 1.9 percent.[19] As of summer 1994, the number of people living below the poverty line reached 24 million, or 16.4 percent of the population.[20] Through 1995 and 1996, some sectors of the economy remained relatively healthy, particularly those that lived off the export of Russia's extraordinary natural mineral wealth. But many others remained plunged in deep depression without signs of recovery amidst a mounting financial crisis.

Besides the attempt to bring about a macroeconomic balance between state revenues and state expenditures, a second major feature of economic transformation has been the shift to private ownership of productive resources. This has come about in two ways. First has been the program of privatization of state assets through their transfer to citizens.[21] By the middle of 1994, when the first phase of mass privatization by vouchers ended, 70 percent of large and medium-sized industrial firms had been privatized, as had 80 percent of small firms. And second, private entrepreneurship has grown as well: as of the middle of 1994, some 10 percent of the population were self-employed, and their numbers had risen by 25 percent since the beginning of the year.[22] Around one million small and medium-sized private businesses were in existence as of mid-1994, and they employed around 12 million people.[23] The results of these policies have been mixed. Market forces now play a far greater role than in the past. But control over real economic assets of factories and farms often remains in the hands of the same managers and officials who held them in the past, only with the difference that now they have acquired legal title. The separation between political and economic sources of power is still far from complete.[24]

---

[19]OMRI Daily Digest, January 6, 1995, citing figures in the Russian newspaper *Vecherniaia Moskva*. (OMRI, or Open Media Research Institute, is the successor organization to Radio Free Europe/Radio Liberty, a radio and research service covering affairs in Eastern Europe and the former Soviet Union previously funded by the U.S. government.)

[20]Russian Ministry of Labor statistics cited in RAU-Corporation, *Obozrevatel'-Observer (Special Issue): Natsional'naia doktrina Rossii (problemy i prioritety)* [National Doctrine of Russia: Problems and Priorities] (Moscow: Agenstvo "Obozrevatel'," no. 5–8, 1994), p. 173; RFE/RL Daily Report for August 1, 1994. The poverty line as of the beginning of 1994 was considered to be around 90,000 rubles, or 45 U.S. dollars per month. A good overview of the economy's performance as of fall 1994 is "Russian Capitalism," *The Economist*, October 8, 1994, pp. 21–23.

[21]On privatization, see Lynn D. Nelson and Irina Y. Kuzes, *Property to the People: The Struggle for Radical Economic Reform in Russia* (Armonk, NY: M. E. Sharpe, 1994); Pekka Sutela, "Insider Privatization in Russia: Speculations on Systemic Changes," *Europe-Asia Studies* 46:3 (1994), pp. 417–435; Peter Rutland, "Privatisation in Russia: One Step Forward: Two Steps Back?" *Europe-Asia Studies* 46:4 (1994), pp. 1109–1131.

[22]Russian Statistical Committee figures cited in the newspaper *Segodnia*, August 9, 1994.

[23]*Segodnia*, September 1, 1994.

[24]Peter Rutland, "The Economy: The Rocky Road from Plan to Market," in Stephen White, Alex Pravda, and Zvi Gitelman, eds., *Developments in Russian and Post-Soviet Politics* (London: Macmillan, 1994), p. 161; Rutland, "Privatisation in Russia," p. 1125.

Choices and Changes in Russian Politics

These have been huge changes in Russia—the dismantling of the communist political system, the change in national identity of the state, and the shift toward market capitalism. Have they resulted in a new democratic order? How much have they changed the distribution of *real* power in the country?

The degree of political change has been much less than many Russians hoped for, but it has been significant. Observing the extraordinary upheavals of the last decade, we might estimate that the end of the old socialist economic structures, union state framework, and communist party rule and their replacement by new institutions amount to a break with the past comparable in depth with, say, the formation of the Soviet regime in 1917. The temptation to overstate change can lead us to take pronouncements by political leaders as statements about the actual state of affairs or to mistake a policy's goals for its effects. As we know, the formal rules laid out in the constitution or a law do not always describe the way political actors in fact behave. The equivalent error in the past was to take Soviet propaganda at face value, thus interpreting the USSR's political processes through the prism of the regime's ideologically defined categories. This is analogous to a Type I error in scientific research (a "false positive"), where the observer erroneously detects an effect that is not there in fact.

Still, we must also avoid the equivalent reciprocal error of overlooking important changes. That is, keen to expose the realities hidden behind surface appearances, we may dismiss all the innovations in law, policy, doctrine, and pronouncements as mere subterfuge and façade. It is easy enough to point out the resurrection of older forms of governance, such as the dual executive of autocrat and government, the impotence of legal institutions, the pervasiveness of corruption, the proliferation of centralized state agencies together with the inability to accomplish stated policy purposes, the practically unlimited power of the security police, and the survival of the former regime's ruling elite in positions of power. Looking at these phenomena, we might jump to the conclusion that nothing essential has changed, except that social disorder and distress have grown. People are even more likely to say this when they have personally been caught up in hopes and expectations that were subsequently betrayed. Many Russians today say that the apparent democratic revolution in Russia was a fraud and illusion which simply allowed a new group of greedy, power-hungry elites to win a share of control of the country's property and power.

However, it would be as wrong to exaggerate the degree of continuity with the past as it would be to overlook the ways in which the transition from communist authoritarianism to a democratic system is incomplete. The dismantling of the old communist party mechanisms for exercising and maintaining its monopolistic power means that political and economic processes are somewhat more open and competitive. The diversity of political interests has now moved from the arena of behind-the-scenes bureaucratic politics to a more open competition of interest groups and parties for influence over policy. Individual rights are far stronger than in the past. The movement of people, ideas, and resources between Russia and the outside world has expanded enormously. Many more economic actors are influenced by the pressures of the marketplace. Overall, these changes in national identity, political institutions, and economic system amount to a revolution. When we remember the level of violence required to carry out the communist revolution and establish the Soviet system in Russia, the peaceful nature of the transition from the old regime is astonishing.

In the following chapters, I shall argue that the reason that change has been largely peaceful is twofold. First, the Soviet regime's modernizing policies had the effect of creating a much more conducive environment for pluralistic democracy than existed before the October Revolution. Second, many of the powerful elite groups and political structures which persisted from the Soviet period into the post-Soviet system successfully adapted to the new political and social conditions. In doing so, however, they modified the operating rules and principles of the new system to their benefit, resulting in a political system that is not fully democratic. The mutual adaptation of elites and institutions may have been the price paid for averting more serious social conflict during the transition.

At a more basic level, the Russian case offers us a powerful test of the effects of institutional engineering. To what extent is democracy a product of long-term social and economic processes that produce conducive economic and cultural conditions? Moreover, to what extent can democracy be created by the adoption of democratic institutions? This issue has been the subject of intense research by political scientists in recent years.[25] Some political scientists believe that certain social conditions are prerequisites or facilitating factors in the establishment and consolidation of democracy. These include a political culture dominated by democratic values, a flourishing network of civic associations, and a reasonable level of economic prosperity and equality.[26] Other scholars argue that there is a very wide range of different social conditions in which democracy may be created and that there is no clear causal relationship between a particular set of social conditions and a particular type of political system. They believe, instead, that a democratic system can result from the willingness of rival sets of political leaders to abide by a common set of rules and procedures to govern their competition for power.[27]

Russia will not conclusively prove one side or the other right in this debate. Whatever the final outcome of Russia's transition, people will disagree over its causes. If democracy fails, some will say that Russia's postcommunist constitution was poorly designed (for instance, that it granted too much power to the president and too little to other institutions), while others will say that the political culture or the economy were still too powerfully influenced by the communist system to permit a democratic experiment to succeed. If it succeeds, some will say that democracy was

---

[25]See, for instance, Adam Przeworski, *Democracy and the Market: Political and Economic Reforms in Eastern Europe and Latin America* (Cambridge: Cambridge University Press, 1991); Giuseppe DiPalma, *To Craft Democracies: An Essay on Democratic Transitions* (Berkeley: University of California Press, 1990); Guillermo O'Donnell, Philippe C. Schmitter, and Laurence Whitehead, eds., *Transitions from Authoritarian Rule: Prospects for Democracy* (Baltimore: Johns Hopkins University Press, 1986); Samuel P. Huntington, *The Third Wave: Democratization in the Late Twentieth Century* (Norman and London: University of Oklahoma Press, 1991).

[26]Seymour Martin Lipset, "Some Social Requisites of Democracy: Economic Development and Political Legitimacy," *American Political Science Review* 53 (1959), pp. 69–105; Larry Diamond, "Economic Development and Democracy Reconsidered," *American Behavioral Scientist* 35 (1992), pp. 450–499.

[27]The seminal statement of this view is Dankwart Rustow, "Transitions to Democracy: Toward a Dynamic Model," *Comparative Politics* 2:3 (April 1970), pp. 337–364.

the product of long-term changes in the domestic and international environment that created a more demanding, individualistic populace that could no longer be ruled by autocratic methods. Others will say that radical reforms made it possible for Russia to escape its state-centered, authoritarian past, and to create a new path of political development for itself. In the study of politics, unlike the study of the natural world, we do not have laboratory conditions for isolating and testing the effects of causal agents. We draw our analytical judgements from observations of a sometimes murky, confusing reality, so our generalizations are inevitably tentative. We can show, however, that the choices political actors made at certain important turning points had major consequences. Much of Russia's contemporary political system is the product of the behavior of its citizens rather than simply the force of circumstance.

PLAN OF THE BOOK

In this chapter we have reviewed the ways in which Russia's political system has undergone deep changes in its identity as a national community, in its political institutions, and in its economic environment. We have seen that there exist sharply different perspectives on how to understand these changes. Some observers see them as primarily the product of social forces in Russia and the outside world, and others as the consequences of political decisions made by Russian citizens and leaders. Some consider Russia a model of how *not* to reform, an object lesson in the folly of trying to pursue both radical liberalization and market adjustment at the same time, while others believe that political and economic power were so tightly connected under the old regime that only simultaneous political and economic reform would have defeated the old bureaucratic elite. Finally, some people minimize the degree of change that has taken place, and rather emphasize how similar the new order is to the old, while others believe that fundamental changes have occurred in the political and economic realms. The premise of this book is that Russia's future is still open. There is no assumption here that having departed the station of "communist authoritarianism," the train will reach the station of "liberal democracy." Many stops and detours in between are possible, and the train can reverse direction numerous times. Our task, therefore, is to see whether there is some overall direction to the development of Russia's political system.

The rest of the book will explore the institutions and processes of Russia's political system in greater detail. Chapter Two provides a brief overview of the political history of the last decade, when the old Soviet regime collapsed, and a new political order in Russia took shape. The chapter details the main changes in the structures and processes of rule since the late Soviet period, describing the Communist Party–dominated regime of the Soviet period and showing how power was organized and used. The Gorbachev reforms are discussed along with their objectives and the succession of schemes Gorbachev advanced to reorganize the political system. The chapter shows that the reforms had unanticipated effects that resulted in Gorbachev's loss of control over political developments. When the Soviet regime collapsed in 1991, it was succeeded by newly independent successor regimes in the former republics. Already, however, the Russian republic had initiated its own major reforms which culminated in a political crisis in 1993 and the adoption of a new constitution which is in force today. We will discuss the 1993 constitution, pointing out continuities and changes between it and the old Soviet regime in institutional structures and processes.

Chapter Three assesses the findings of public opinion surveys about the values and beliefs of Russians. It observes that although the median Russian voter seems to be "social-democratic" in outlook, the political system remains polarized between communists and their opponents. It shows that although large shares of Russian citizens continue to express support for political democracy, their disillusionment with the way political and economic reforms have worked out in practice is reflected in very low levels of confidence in state institutions, and a reaction against the institutions of market capitalism. But there is also a strong reluctance to return to the old communist order.

In Chapter Four we look at how the public participates in the political system. The nature of popular participation in politics has changed greatly since the Soviet era. Today it is far less widespread but also far less ceremonial, regimented, and controlled. Many of the "informal organizations" that sprang up during the late Soviet period have become the basis for political parties and interest groups in the present period, and we inquire into the forms and nature of their activity. We also look at the place of elections in the system of participation.

The second part of the chapter takes up the subject of elite recruitment. In every political system, popular participation in politics is closely related to the process of elite recruitment: through elections, organizational activism, and the exercise of influence over policymakers, some individuals grow particularly active and interested in politics; of them, some become full-time political professionals. Of considerable interest in this connection is the question of the relation between the old political elite in Russia (sometimes called "the nomenklatura") and the contemporary political elite. Is it true, as some charge, that the same crowd is still running things? Or is there new blood? And what has happened to the old communist elite?

In Chapter Five we ask how Russians voice their political demands and interests. We discuss the relevance of three basic models of interest articulation (statism, corporatism, and pluralism) to interest group activity in present-day Russia. We review several categories of actors—enterprise managers, organized labor, regional governors, and particular sectors such as the gas and oil industries, defense industry, and agro-industrial complex—to see how the social changes of the last five years have altered the balance of power and interests among old and new groups.

In the second part of the chapter we ask how political parties are developing. How do they tie different groups of the population to the national political arena? What are the main partisan tendencies of the population, and how strong are they? Are parties forming "from below" or "from above" and what differences does this make for the political system's ability to accommodate the severe tensions of the transition period?

Chapter Six is a case study in policy-making focusing on the radical economic reform called "shock therapy." The chapter discusses the aims of the reformers and the tools at their disposal to carry out their policy. It shows that the programs of macroeconomic stabilization were modified, and in fact distorted, to satisfy the demands of the most powerful constituencies in society. In the end, the reformers' inability to enforce the policy rigorously against the demands by powerful economic interest groups for concessionary credits and subsidies left the program only partly implemented. Producers' economic behavior did not take the desired forms that would have contributed to noninflationary growth, and the simultaneous application of deflationary monetary policy and restrictive fiscal policy led to a deep depression, widespread evasion of the controls, rising protectionism, and a general outcry for a more relaxed fiscal and monetary regime.

Chapter Seven assesses the legal system, asking whether Russia is moving toward the rule of law. The chapter discusses the problem of law and legal institutions at two levels: the task of putting the activity of state officials and private citizens securely under the rule of law, and the effectiveness of legal institutions in enforcing constitutional and legal rules. The chapter reviews the major institutions of the judicial and law enforcement systems and the reforms that are being made in these systems. Of particular interest is the emergence of a mechanism for judicial review of the acts of other government institutions. We discuss the obstacles toward the rule of law, including the power of organized crime, pervasive corruption, and the failure of accountability on the part of government officials for their use of financial and other resources.

The last chapter offers an overview of Russian politics, returning to the problem of Russia's development. We ask about the prospects for the establishment of democracy in the future. The chapter argues that Russia faces a choice between an imperial and a democratic path of development, and that it is the simultaneous interaction of millions of individual actions which will ultimately determine how Russia develops. The relations of people in society can reinforce a virtuous cycle which builds democracy and pluralism, or can make antidemocratic pessimism a self-fulfilling prophecy. Russia has a heavy burden of historical precedent but it is not an insurmountable one. Democracy remains one of several possible outcomes of Russia's transition.

Chapter 2

Toward a New Constitutional Order: Leadership and Political Institutions

The Old Regime

The Russian communists took power in October 1917. Their aim was to create a socialist society in Russia and, eventually, to spread revolutionary socialism throughout the world. Socialism, as the communists—also called the Bolsheviks—understood it, meant a society without private ownership of the means of production, where the state owned and controlled all important economic assets, and where political power was exercised in the interests of the working people. *Vladimir Ilyich Lenin* (1870–1924) was the leader of the Russian Communist Party and the first head of the Soviet Russian government.[1] In keeping with Lenin's model of the Com-

---

[1]Vladimir Ilyich Lenin (1870–1924) was the leader of the wing of the Russian Marxist movement which insisted that socialism in Russia would only be possible if the revolutionaries seized state power and used it to construct a modern, industrial, and socialist economic base in Russia, as well as to launch similar revolutions elsewhere. This wing, which later became a separate party, was called the Bolsheviks. Still later it was renamed the Russian Communist Party, and finally the Communist Party of the Soviet Union. Lenin and his fellow Bolsheviks carried out their plan after seizing power in October 1917 in the name of the workers and peasants, and establishing a government formed around state socialist principles. As de facto leader of the Bolshevik (later Communist) party, and chairman of the new Soviet Russian government, Lenin established the basic governing institutions of the new Soviet regime. Throughout Soviet history, Soviet citizens were taught to revere Lenin as the infallible source of guidance about ideological doctrine, and his teachings were codified, systematized, and joined to official versions of Marxist theory. Together, these bodies of official teachings were given the name "Marxism–Leninism." In the Soviet Union and throughout the communist world, Marxism–Leninism had the status of dogma.

munist Party as a "vanguard party," the Soviet regime divided power between the *soviets,* which were the representative organs through which workers and peasants could voice their desires, and the Communist Party, which would direct the soviets. Soviets originated in the revolutionary period as grass roots councils to represent industrial workers, peasants, soldiers, and sailors. The Bolsheviks considered soviets to be well-suited to form the backbone of the new, socialist state they intended to construct: they were vehicles of mass democracy which could also be dominated and manipulated by the more tightly organized and disciplined Communist Party. The party would guide and direct the soviets and their executive organs, but it would remain organizationally separate from them.[2]

This model proved highly effective in several respects. It ensured that the party could penetrate and control government without itself becoming government. It created opportunities for mass participation and the recruitment of leaders, and gave experience in government to ordinary working people. It presented a democratic façade to the Soviet population and the outside world. It could be adapted to the formally federal makeup of the state, while ensuring that there was a hierarchical chain of command through the executive branch. When the Soviet Union formed as a federal state made up of nominally equal, sovereign national republics, each republic had its own representative and executive organs, but these were strictly subordinated to the will of the center.

The Soviet system differed from liberal democracy in a number of ways, including the fact of the party's monopoly on political power and the state's ownership of productive resources. The system's institutional features were so tightly woven together that they formed an integrated whole that lasted until the system's sudden collapse in 1991. Four characteristics can be singled out as defining elements of the Soviet system:

1. Formal organization of state power in the soviets;
2. Ethnically based federalism;
3. State ownership of the means of production; and
4. Dominance of the Communist Party in elite recruitment, ideological control of communications, and policy-making.

Let us examine each of these in turn before asking why it was that Gorbachev's attempts to reform the system led unexpectedly to its total collapse.

ORGANIZATION OF STATE POWER IN SOVIETS

Soviets are councils: the word soviet in Russian means council (as well as counsel). On paper, the system of soviets resembled a pyramid of democratic representative assemblies. Soviets were organized as elective bodies of self-government that represented voters and set basic policy. In theory, the soviets embodied all state power in the Soviet Union: the principle of separation of powers was not recognized. The voters of every village and town, province and republic, elected representatives, called

---

[2]Two useful recent historical surveys of the Soviet regime are Mary McAuley, *Soviet Politics: 1917–1991* (New York: Oxford University Press, 1992); Ronald Grigor Suny, *The Soviet Experiment: Russia, the USSR, and the Successor States* (New York: Oxford University Press, 1998).

deputies, to the soviet to serve as the body of representative power for that territory. Deputies served on a part-time, voluntary basis, and were expected to look out for the local needs of their constituents although it was generally understood that the soviets had no real policy-making power. Generally speaking, soviets were quite large compared to city councils or state legislatures in the United States. Some were as large as the parliaments of an entire country: the city of Moscow, with a population of nine million in 1989, had a soviet with 500 deputies. The USSR Supreme Soviet had 1,500 deputies.

In fact the large size of many soviets was an indication of the powerlessness and ceremonial character of these structures. The USSR Supreme Soviet, for instance, met only twice a year, and then for a few days each time, to hear official reports and approve motions proposed by the leadership. At lower levels, there were more debates and behind-the-scenes politicking, but generally, everyone accepted that the soviets served the function of creating a formal appearance of representative democracy, while in fact the party and the executive organs of government made all the major decisions. The only sense in which the soviets "represented" the public was descriptive, in that the candidates were selected by the party to ensure the presence of fixed shares of deputies from each major demographic category by occupation, sex, age, ethnic group, and party status. This allowed the regime to boast that large proportions of particular groups of the population were serving as elected representatives. However, since generally only one candidate ran for a given seat, the elections offered voters only the opportunity to vote for or against the candidate proffered. Elections were not an institution for making officials accountable to voters for their actions.

Formally, the executive arm of each soviet was accountable to the soviet for its actions. Thus a soviet "elected" a set of executive officials to manage government in its jurisdiction. In reality, the soviet simply ratified a choice which had been made by the communist party authorities. Nonetheless, the power of executive officials was real. The executive branch at lower levels of the pyramid of soviets was called the "executive committee" (*ispolnitel'nyi komitet,* or *ispolkom,* in Russian). It consisted of a chairman, the deputy chairs, and the heads of government departments, such as the departments for transportation, finance, public catering, and education. These officials were formally accountable to the soviets, but in fact they answered to two sets of superior authorities: higher level government executive officials, and communist party officials. Thus the old communist regime of the Soviet Union devised overlapping mechanisms of supervision to ensure that government officials carried out policy: an executive branch chain of command which stretched all the way from the lowest level of government up to Moscow, and a Communist Party organization which supervised and directed—but was not supposed to usurp—the work of government executives.

At the highest levels, such as those at the level of union republics and the all-union central government, this model of soviet and executive committee took on a more elaborate form. Instead of a soviet, there was a Supreme Soviet, which had the power to enact laws. Instead of an executive committee, there was a Council of Ministers. The USSR Council of Ministers was thus formally equivalent to the cabinet of a parliamentary government in a Western democracy and its chairman was the functional equivalent of a prime minister. As the person in charge of the executive branch for the entire Soviet Union, the chairman of the Council of Ministers was in fact a very powerful figure—but never as powerful as the head of the Communist Party of the Soviet Union.

ETHNIC FEDERALISM

Federalism in the Soviet state originated with the Bolsheviks' aim to grant symbolic rights to ethnic minorities, especially those located on the outer perimeter of Russia's territory that had traditions of national autonomy or statehood. So, unlike federalism in the United States or Germany, the constitutional form that federalism took in the Soviet Union was linked to the goal of giving ethnic-national populations a means to maintain their national cultures but to do so without challenging the center's power.

In Soviet federalism, 15 nominally sovereign republics were considered to be the constituent units of a federal union. Each republic gave a particular ethnic nationality a certain formal opportunity for representation. Most structures of power at the central level were replicated in the 15 union republics; of course, the control of the military and the money supply were exclusively central functions. The model was not quite symmetrical in that certain structures were not replicated in the Russian Republic itself. The reason is that the existence of a full-fledged branch of the Communist Party, a branch of the KGB (Committee for State Security—the secret police), a trade union council, an Academy of Sciences, and the like at the Russian republic level would have threatened the power of the union-level structures. Union-level party and state organs thus doubled as Russian ones.

Power was so highly centralized in the Soviet regime that the federal structure of the state was largely a formality. Yet federalism did allow national self-awareness to spread in the republics, while the centralization of political and economic power in Moscow prevented the national leaders of the federal republics from making any serious claims on the union government for greater autonomy. As time passed, members of the indigenous nationalities in the republics came to take certain rights for granted. Among these were the principles that the leader of the communist party organization in that republic would be a member of the indigenous nationality, and that national cultural traditions could be honored and developed to the extent that these did not directly contradict Soviet ideological doctrine. The stability of these informal rules and understandings about how far each nationality could go in preserving its national identity fostered a tendency for the leaders and peoples in the republics to think of the territory and institutions of the republic as "theirs," a kind of collective national patrimony. Coupled with the steady rise in the population's educational levels over the decades of Soviet rule, this tacit but powerful assumption contributed to the growth of ethnic self-consciousness in each republic among the indigenous nationality.

Soviet federalism tended to foster the formation of a national intelligentsia and a national political elite in each republic. At the same time, by isolating and segmenting national republics, the regime limited their ability to influence federal policy. The titular nationality of each republic might have had some opportunity to preserve its national culture but had little influence over cultural or other policies affecting the entire union. Russian as well as union domination of the republics was facilitated by the penetration of union-wide control structures such as the party, KGB, army, and economic bureaucracy into each republic. The center, not the republican governments, controlled the way resources were exploited and developed in each republic. Yet the republics possessed a certain limited autonomy, which allowed the national languages and heritages of the titular nationalities to be disseminated—often at the expense of indigenous ethnic-national minorities residing within their borders. It is important to recognize that the Soviet model of federalism affected different groups differently. For some groups, it tended to create a new sense of nationhood, while other groups—particularly those which had possessed independent statehood before the imposition of Soviet rule—harbored grievances over the memory of lost national sovereignty.[3]

In keeping with the formally federal structure of state power, the Soviet legislature, the Supreme Soviet of the USSR, was bicameral. Its upper chamber, the Soviet of Nationalities, provided equal numbers of seats to each of the union republics, large and small, and equal but lesser numbers of seats to the lower-status ethnic territories that existed within several of the republics. This corresponded formally to the bicameralism used in some other federal legislatures (such as the United States Congress), in which the upper chamber represents regional units of the federation while the lower chamber is composed on the basis of districts of equal size. Bicameralism became much more important in the late 1980s, when the Soviet system began to open up. After the breakup of the Soviet Union, a federal, bicameral legislature was embodied in the 1993 constitution that Yeltsin sponsored in Russia as a way of guaranteeing federal rights for Russia's regions.

The Soviet state was unitary in fact, federal in form. In federalism, the constituent regions possess a constitutionally protected domain of power in which they are autonomous and can make policy so long as they do not violate constitutional rules. In the Soviet Union, the central government—the Communist Party leadership and central executive authorities—had ultimate control over the political, economic, and cultural life of the republics, choosing how much autonomy the republics could exercise at any given time. Each jurisdictional unit was treated as subordinate to the higher-level unit within which it was located, in keeping with the chain of command principle. The union center controlled major productive resources throughout the country, including land, natural resources, industry, and human capital, while the constituent republics were given the right to manage lesser assets on their territories. Strategic decisions about economic development in the republics were determined by the center. This pattern resembled colonial imperialism in that a dominant metropolitan state developed the economies of peripheral territorial possessions for its own benefit.

Yet reality and perception diverged. In the USSR, the balance of trade among republics was not always favorable to Russia, even though Russia dominated the union politically. Because of the deliberately low prices set for energy and other industrial inputs supplied by Russia, in many respects, Russia ended up subsidizing the development of other republics. By 1991, Russia was providing the equivalent of one-tenth of its gross domestic product to other republics in the form of implicit

[3]Ronald Grigor Suny, *The Revenge of the Past: Nationalism, Revolution, and the Collapse of the Soviet Union* (Stanford: Stanford University Press, 1993).

trade subsidies.[4] Centralized planning and controlled prices made it impossible to judge who was exploiting whom, and within each republic people became convinced that the union was exploiting their republic.[5] Meanwhile, ethnic federalism enabled republican party and state leaders to build up political machines and expand their own political control. Many republican political and cultural leaders were keen to gain greater control over state resources, not necessarily to put them to better or more productive use, but to acquire greater control over the flow of benefits they yielded. Political economists term this "rent-seeking," when the possessor of a productive asset restricts market competition, so as to be able to monopolize a stream of private benefits from it. When the political leaders in the union republics demanded the *decentralization* of economic administration, often what they wanted was to capture control over state resources for their own political benefit rather than to make more productive use of them—to transfer the *union's* bureaucratic control over the economy to control by the *republican* bureaucracy. Decentralization in this sense was neither democratic nor market-oriented.

This point is a clue to the struggle for power between the union and Russian republican levels of the Soviet system, so often interpreted simply as a struggle between old-style hard-liners and insurgent democrats (or, still more simply, as a fight between Gorbachev and Yeltsin). The demand for decentralization was one on which both democratic forces and bureaucratic officials in the republics could agree: the democrats wanted to break the hold of the communist party and the central government over citizens' political rights, while the republic-level officials were eager to claim a share of control over Soviet state assets located in their republics. They found common cause in the desire to weaken the central government. Thus, to a large extent, the struggles over sovereignty in 1989–91 resulting in the breakup of the Soviet Union were a contest for control over state resources between elites whose institutional position was at the union level and the political forces gathered at the next hierarchical level down who sought to gain autonomy within their territorial jurisdictions. As far as the Russian Republic was concerned, this strategy meant that the Russian leaders gained autonomous control over the Russian territory at the expense of influence over other republics.

STATE OWNERSHIP OF THE MEANS OF PRODUCTION

Political and economic power were closely intertwined in the Soviet system. The relationship between these two domains is the key to understanding the difference between the Soviet system and liberal democracies, even those where the state has a large ownership stake in the economy. Even the most strongly social democratic polity in Europe differs sharply from the state socialism of the Soviet-type system.

---

[4]Anders Åslund, *How Russia Became a Market Economy* (Washington, D.C.: Brookings Institution, 1995), p. 108.

[5]Stephen White, Graeme Gill, and Darrell Slider, *The Politics of Transition: Shaping a Post-Soviet Future* (Cambridge: Cambridge University Press, 1993), p. 85.

The famous theory of the "new class" developed by the dissident Yugoslav communist Milovan Djilas helps to explain why.[6] In contrast to societies where there is private ownership of productive property, in the Soviet system an individual's power, prestige, and wealth depended on his or her position in the political hierarchy. Productive wealth could not be passed on through inheritance to others.[7] State ownership of productive resources meant that political and social status derived from the same source; even the most powerful leaders depended on the favor of party officials because all lines of advancement and opportunity converged in the Communist Party. The "new class"—those who rose to power and privilege in the system—sought to use the Communist Party to protect their interests, but the absence of firm political rights or popular legitimacy created insecurity which they compensated for by the use of propaganda and repression that fended off political challenges to their positions. Djilas and later scholars who investigated the relations between the party elite and other managerial and specialist elites saw that their mutual dependence contained elements of tension and competition.

In turn, the size and scale of the great manufacturing enterprises (of which there were only around 50,000 in the country) lent their managers enormous clout. The heads of enterprises were under intense pressure to fulfill their plan targets, and generally the authorities gave them substantial autonomy in choosing how to meet their output goals. Managers could usually get away with cutting corners, for instance, by reducing quality, so long as they met the basic target for raw output set by the planners. Managers had little incentive to innovate or modernize since the risk that a new technology might fail outweighed the potential benefits of increased productivity or efficiency. In short, the incentives faced by enterprise managers tended to militate against flexibility, adaptiveness, entrepreneurship, and innovation. As a result, with time, the economy became stagnant and unable to compete in the global market.

Stalin's strategy of industrializing Russia rapidly in the late 1920s and 1930s led to another important feature of the state socialist model—the reliance on the enterprise as a source of noneconomic benefits to the populace. Goods such as housing, child care, subsidized meals, and groceries and scarce durable goods such as cars and subsidized vacations have long been allocated through enterprises alongside the ordinary retail distribution system. In the late 1970s, when the economy's performance began slipping seriously and food rationing had to be introduced in many cities, enterprise "social funds" assumed a greater political importance. To the extent that the retail markets in housing, food, and ordinary services fell further behind the demand, enterprise managers exercised still more leverage over the state. Workers and managers were tightly bound to one another in mutual need. Managers needed a large and cheap labor force to enable them to fulfill their plan targets, and workers needed a secure position in a state enterprise in order to obtain a range of social benefits that were unavailable except through the enterprise. This created a sort of collusive relationship between workers and managers, rather than

---

[6]Milovan Djilas, *The New Class: An Analysis of the Communist System* (New York: Praeger, 1957).

[7]A person could leave "personal" property to his or her heirs, including money, but not property which was used to create other forms of wealth or income.

———————————————————TABLE 2.1———————————————————

Average Annual Growth of the Soviet Economy, 1961–85, Net Material Product

	1961–65	1966–70	1971–75	1976–80	1981–85
Official	6.5	7.8	5.7	4.3	3.6
Selyunin and Khanin	4.4	4.1	3.2	1.0	0.6

Source: Anders Åslund, *How Russia Became a Market Economy* (Washington D.C.: Brookings Institution, 1995), p. 43. Reprinted by permission.

an adversarial relationship. It tended to weaken trade unions (which, in the Soviet model, were organized around entire economic branches, so that the managers of a firm were members of the same trade union as the engineers, the bench workers, and the cafeteria staff). It gave both managers and workers an incentive to pressure the state to maintain a steady stream of orders and financing regardless of whether the enterprise was profitable or productive. Just as the economy created little incentive for entrepreneurship or innovation, it also discouraged the restructuring or closing of loss-making firms.

Moreover, the weakness of financial constraints on enterprises' appetites for resources created a chronic syndrome of excess demand, shortages, and repressed inflation.[8] Low efficiency and failure to innovate on the part of enterprises did not incur economic penalties. To some extent enterprises were able to conceal the facts of their performance, and to some extent the center simply lacked the clout to improve productivity through administrative pressure. The center itself was constantly pressured to satisfy the needs of powerful industrial and regional interests. As a result, the system settled into inertia and decay: each year the plan represented a modest incremental change over the previous year. Any serious attempts at reform were defeated by the combination of weakness at the center and inertial resistance by those who were called upon to carry out the reform. A very powerful latent coalition of interests—ministries, regional officials, enterprise directors, and workers—shared an interest in the preservation of the status quo since any serious change threatened them. Yet continuation of the status quo allowed the economy to reach the point where it had essentially stopped growing. Table 2.1 indicates the trend.[9]

The table provides two alternative series on economic output over time. One is the official Soviet statistical report, and the other is a reconstruction of Soviet economic performance by two Soviet economists using an alternative, unofficial methodology which attempts to find measures not subject to the distortions of inflation and over-reporting. As is evident, the alternative series yields far lower estimates

---

[8]Janos Kornai, *The Socialist System: The Political Economy of Communism* (Princeton: Princeton University Press, 1992).

[9]This table is taken from Anders Åslund, *How Russia Became a Market Economy* (Washington, D.C.: Brookings Institution, 1995), p. 43.

of the size and growth rate of Soviet output. If the second set of figures is accurate, by the time Gorbachev came to power, defense expenditures were running at about a quarter of gross domestic product, and the share was still increasing.[10] The heavy and rising burden of military expenditures on a stagnant economy was one of the major reasons Gorbachev undertook his program of radical reform.

In the post-Stalin period, a set of tacit mutual expectations began to arise in the relations between the regime and the working class. Often this is called the "social contract." Some observers see the "social contract" as an explicit strategy on the part of the political elite which was matched by a complementary response in mass behavior. The regime committed itself to providing job security, social benefits, and relative income equality, in exchange for quiescence and compliance from workers. The theory implies that the regime was prepared to go to great lengths to maintain its end of the tacit bargain, but when it could not do so, workers withdrew their support of the regime.[11]

The deteriorating performance of the economy in the 1960s, 1970s, and 1980s placed a greater burden on the regime's ability to meet social expectations. Fewer and fewer people were able to rise above the class into which they were born. In turn, the slowing of upward social mobility seems to have brought about a subtle shift in the terms of the tacit understanding between regime and society. Gradually workers seem to have come to believe that no matter how low productivity fell, they were secure in their jobs and other social benefits.

In addition, the slowing of economic growth meant that fewer jobs were opening up in managerial and professional positions. Yet the stream of graduates with specialist degrees kept growing. More and more people occupied jobs below their educational qualifications. This affected both manual and specialist social strata. Many groups considered themselves underpaid and undervalued. Many of the grievances voiced in the early years of *glasnost´* centered around the low professional autonomy and esteem of managerial and professional groups, including the administrative staff of the Communist Party itself. These strains were in part the consequence of the Brezhnev leadership's policy of "levelling" (reducing income differentials across occupational groups) by raising the wage levels and educational qualifications at the lower end of the social hierarchy without achieving a corresponding transformation of the structure of labor. As a result, a sizable part of the workforce occupied jobs for which they were significantly overqualified.

The Soviet trade unions were not an effective instrument for renegotiating the terms of the social contract. Trade unions were organized in keeping with Stalin's vision of a society where the rulers controlled the population through great "transmission belt organizations" that would penetrate and channel participation.[12] The trade unions in Soviet society were used by the regime to supplement the administra-

---

[10]Ibid.

[11]Linda Cook, *The Soviet Social Contract and Why It Failed: Welfare Policy and Workers' Politics from Brezhnev to Yeltsin* (Cambridge: Harvard University Press, 1993).

[12]The "administered mass organization" has been an instrument of mass control in many totalitarian and authoritarian modern societies. See Gregory J. Kasza, *The Conscription Society: Administered Mass Organizations* (New Haven, CT: Yale University Press, 1995).

tion of social benefits and the political and economic control of the work force. When mass unrest began developing, the trade unions took a conservative posture, provoking some labor groups to break away and form their own independent unions.

Economic stagnation exacerbated popular resentment of the privileges of the political elite. Crucial to understanding the explosive quality of social protest in the late 1980s was the growing popular alienation, which readily took nationalist forms, but which also arose from other issues, such as environmental degradation, the perception that the ruling *nomenklatura* was indifferent and parasitic, anger over shortages in the economy, and the conviction on the part of nearly every region and republic that it was being economically exploited by a distant, bureaucratized center. Under Brezhnev, the regime generally observed the "social contract," although the cost was high. After Brezhnev, faced with the unacceptably high cost to the economy's efficiency of maintaining the compact, Gorbachev struggled to alter its terms but shrank from renouncing it completely. Yet the reforms he introduced in the economic and political realms had consequences that made it impossible for his regime to fulfill its end of the bargain. Large-scale labor unrest in 1989 and 1991 was one result.

POLITICAL DOMINANCE OF THE COMMUNIST PARTY

The final crucial element of the Soviet system was the monopoly of political power by the Communist Party. Lenin's model of rule ensured that the organizational structure of the Communist Party maximized central control over all levels of government. The party itself was kept rather small, emphasizing that membership was a privilege and an obligation, and taking pains to admit only individuals whose political loyalties and social backgrounds passed stringent review. At its peak, the Communist Party had around 20 million members, around 9 percent of the adult population.[13] In many professions the membership rate was higher, and generally membership was higher among the more highly educated strata of the population. Among individuals in positions of high political and administrative responsibility— including those with offices in government, law enforcement, culture and communications, diplomacy, science, education, the military, and economic management—party membership was well nigh obligatory. Indeed, for most individuals with high career ambitions, party membership was, at the very least, useful, and often it was indispensable.

The party's own organization paralleled that of the government, which it supervised and directed. In every territorial jurisdiction—district, town, province, and so on—the party maintained its own small but powerful full-time organization. This was divided into functional departments that were overseen by senior party officials called secretaries. Every party member belonged to a "Primary Party

---

[13]On the Communist Party, see Ronald J. Hill and Peter Frank, *The Soviet Communist Party*, 3rd ed. (Boston: Allen & Unwin, 1986); Graeme J. Gill, *The Collapse of a Single Party System: The Disintegration of the CPSU* (Cambridge: Cambridge University Press, 1994).

Organization" or PPO at his or her place of work. Larger PPOs had their own paid, full-time secretaries as well as a group of volunteer activists who carried out party work in the enterprise, organizing meetings and ceremonies, checking on personnel, overseeing the admission of new members. Smaller PPOs relied solely on volunteer party activists to carry out these tasks. Every place of work in the country had its own PPO.

At higher levels the party was organized along territorial lines. Every territorial subdivision of the state contained a party organization. We will use a city as an example, but the same pattern applied symmetrically in every territorial jurisdiction. Each city had a city CPSU organization with its own governing committee, a more powerful inner body called a "bureau," functional departments, and full-time party secretaries. The first secretary of the party organization of the city was always the city's most powerful official. The top party official was not the chief executive of the city: that was, as we have seen, the chairman of the local executive committee of the city soviet. Nominally, the chairman of the city executive committee was answerable to the elected city soviet, but in actuality, he or she was accountable first and foremost to the party officials of the city. The first secretary of the party organization worked closely with the chairman of the executive committee of the city, but the party official was superior in status. Directives and advice from the party secretary were binding on executive branch officials, but, by the same token, when the city government needed special help from Moscow, the party offered a direct channel of access to the highest levels of power in the country.

At each level of the territorial pyramid the pattern was repeated. A set of full-time Communist Party organs paralleled and supervised the governmental system for the given territorial unit. At the top, final power to decide policy rested in the CPSU Politburo. The Politburo was a small committee made up of the country's most powerful leaders: the General Secretary of the CPSU, the Chairman of the Council of Ministers, a few other senior secretaries of the CPSU Central Committee, one or two of the First Secretaries of the communist party organizations in union republics, the Minister of Defense, the Chairman of the KGB, and the Foreign Minister. Although no fixed number of members was set, generally there were around twelve full, voting members, and another six candidate, or nonvoting, members. The Politburo made decisions in all important areas of policy at its weekly meetings.

Supporting the Politburo, helping to develop its agenda, structuring the options for each decision, and seeing to it that its decisions were carried out, was the powerful Secretariat of the Central Committee of the Communist Party. The Secretariat ran the party's central headquarters which was linked to all lower party organizations. Here the party monitored the political and economic situation throughout the country and around the world, and determined which problems needed to be addressed, developing policy options for the Politburo. Here the party managed the political careers of thousands of top political officials. Here it determined the ideological line that was to be echoed and reinforced throughout the country through the channels of party propaganda and the mass media. And here it supervised the vast government bureaucracy, the army, the police, the law enforcement system, the KGB, and the governments of the republics and regions.

THREE DOMAINS OF POWER

The Communist Party's political role was described in the 1977 Soviet Constitution as being "the leading and guiding force of Soviet society, the nucleus of its political system and of [all] state and public organizations."[14] More concretely, the party exercised its power over three major domains of the political system.

First was its decisive voice in policy-making. At the top, the party set general guidelines for national policy, both domestic and foreign. This included setting overall targets for economic growth and the particular priorities—heavy or light industry, agriculture, defense, regional development, and so forth—which were embodied in the national five-year production plans. Meeting weekly, the CPSU Politburo heard reports and recommendations forwarded to it from its Secretariat, which structured the decision options that the Politburo discussed. The General Secretary performed something of the same role that a prime minister might play in a British Cabinet meeting: chairing the session, determining whether and when to put an issue to a vote, and, very importantly, summing up or "calling" the results of the deliberation. Like the prime minister in a parliamentary system, the General Secretary might be relatively powerful or relatively weak, or something in between, at any given point in his relationship with the other members of the Politburo. A General Secretary who was just selected, and one whose physical and mental powers were severely waning, might have little independent influence over the other members of the group. But one who had consolidated power and proven his clout could manipulate the Politburo decision-making process and bend it to his will. Since the General Secretary also supervised the work of the full-time Secretariat, he could control how the policy choices presented to the Politburo were structured and timed. Thus the party institutionally, the party leaders collectively, and the General Secretary individually, structured the policy agenda and had the final say in setting policy directions.

The party exercised the same policy-making powers at each level of the territorial hierarchy. The head of each republic's party organization, its First Secretary, similarly oversaw the party's machinery and its decision-making processes for that republic. The party ensured that government and social organizations operated in a way faithful to the party's overall policy directions. The same was true at the level of the province and city. At every level, disputes over priorities were referred to and settled by the party officials, and the party's internal decision-making structures set the general course for the behavior of its own members, as well as state and social institutions.[15]

The second domain of power was elite recruitment. The party held a monopoly on the power to fill positions of power and authority in the party itself, in government, and in all organized areas of social life. The system of maintaining lists of jobs

---

[14]From Article Six of the USSR constitution as given in Robert Sharlet, *The New Soviet Constitution of 1977: Analysis and Text* (Brunswick, OH: King's Court Communications, 1978), p. 78.

[15]The classic study of the duties of a regional party first secretary in the economic sphere is Jerry F. Hough, *The Soviet Prefects: The Local Party Organs in Industrial Decision-Making* (Cambridge, MA: Harvard University Press, 1969).

which could only be filled on the party's recommendation or approval, and records on the personnel filling those positions, was called the *nomenklatura*. Through the nomenklatura system, the top leader and subordinate party officials monitored and selected candidates for appointment to leading positions throughout the government, society, and the party itself, even appointing people to positions which were formally elective. The nomenklatura system was hierarchical and encompassing: at each level of the pyramid was a set of posts deemed by the party to be critical to the maintenance of the regime, and so these fell under the nomenklatura. These included, of course, the party's own full-time officials, but they also included the top positions in many other government and social organizations.[16] A person chosen to occupy a nomenklatura position had to have been approved by the appropriate party committee's personnel department. But once a person had succeeded in entering the nomenklatura, he or she had a certain degree of job security and social status. People tended to move up the ladder to higher-level nomenklatura positions, or, at worst, laterally to other positions at the same level. Such people came to be regarded as members of a privileged social–political elite, where access to power defined their social standing and material perquisites. In everyday language, they were collectively called the nomenklatura and thought of as a ruling class.[17] In Chapter Four, we shall return to this group and see how they have fared since the breakdown of the communist system.

The final class of powers exercised by the party concerned the ideological sphere. As if persuaded of the truth of Lenin's oft-quoted maxim that "any weakening of socialist ideology must inevitably result in the strengthening of bourgeois ideology," the party strove to ensure that all channels of culture and communications bore messages that reinforced party doctrine. The party's doctrine was itself a mixture of Marxist philosophical and economic principles and current party policy statements; it was itself broad, vague, heterogeneous and often self-contradictory, but it effectively established a boundary line between precepts that supported the Soviet system and those that were "anti-Soviet." For making anti-Soviet utterances—whether poems, theoretical tracts, political opinions, or other forms of communication—the criminal code specified that a person could be legally punished. The party supervised the mass media, the arts, libraries, schools, the censorship agency, and any other organized form of communications and culture and dictated that certain ideas be emphasized and others buried. It monitored the flow of information and ideas, allowing a somewhat richer stream to reach political and professional elites, and a more standardized, ideologically homogeneous environment to surround the general public. To be sure, the party generally did not penetrate certain private social spheres with its control over ideology; family and friendship were extremely important channels for forming and exchanging alternative values and ideas. But the sphere of public discourse fell under the party's intended span of ideological control, making dissenting opinions easier to spot and isolate, and defeating efforts at

---

[16]Bohdan Harasymiw, *Political Elite Recruitment in the Soviet Union* (New York: St. Martin's Press, 1984).

[17]Michael Voslensky, *Nomenklatura: The Soviet Ruling Class. An Insider's Report,* trans. Eric Mosbacher (Garden City, NY: Doubleday, 1984).

organizing counter-ideological political movements. In the next chapter we shall consider the nature of the party's political socialization effort in more detail.

As sweeping as the party's powers were, they were undermined by bureaucratic immobilism. This problem grew more severe in the 1970s and 1980s for many reasons, among them the growing complexity of the political system, the loss of social cohesion, and the declining capacity of the aging leaders to manage the system coherently. The role that fear of arrest had played in reinforcing central power in the Stalin era gradually diminished, and gave way to the certainty on the part of many officials that they could behave incompetently or even criminally with impunity. Certainly a universal observation of hierarchical organizations is that over-centralization brings its own pathologies of control, through distortions of information flow, tacit resistance to the center's orders by officials at lower levels who have their own agenda, and the force of inertia.[18] By the time Mikhail Gorbachev was elected General Secretary of the CPSU in 1985, the political system of the USSR had grown top-heavy, unresponsive, and muscle-bound.[19]

POWER AND POLICY IN THE OLD REGIME

The Soviet regime placed a heavy emphasis on adherence to set rules and procedures of decision-making, which were followed almost ritualistically. Formal political processes were designed as displays of unity and solidarity. However, more than in political systems where law and custom generally govern the way power is exercised by those holding office, Soviet politicians had to struggle for power constantly, even when they occupied important positions. Merely holding an office did not guarantee its incumbent the ability to exercise the power that was nominally associated with that office. Below the calm surface of consensus, therefore, politicians competed fiercely to acquire and maintain power. Naturally, Soviet leaders did not advertise their moves in this game. Nonetheless, by close examination of the public record, it is possible to identify the political alliances and commitments formed by top political leaders of the CPSU. Contenders for power consolidated power by showing that they could solve policy problems: successes in policy tended to strengthen their hand in attracting supporters and eliminating opponents, while failures weakened the incentives that other officials had for supporting them.[20] The contest was not carried out in the electoral realm since there was no electoral link between the desires of the public and the policy choices considered by the regime. Nonetheless, the contest was real, and played for high stakes. It resembled games of bureaucratic politics played out in other complex hierarchical organizations but with lower agreement over the rules and with a high risk factor: failure in the political arena could lead, at best, to forced retirement and disgrace, and, at worst, to arrest and imprisonment—in Stalin's time, to the concentration camps.

---

[18]Anthony Downs, *Inside Bureaucracy* (Boston: Little-Brown, 1967).

[19]Philip G. Roeder, *Red Sunset: The Failure of Soviet Politics* (Princeton: Princeton University Press, 1993).

[20]George W. Breslauer, *Khrushchev and Brezhnev as Leaders: Building Authority in Soviet Politics* (Boston: Allen & Unwin, 1982).

A serious weakness of the old regime was its inability to transfer power in a regular and peaceful fashion from one leader to another. The struggle for power became even more intense when succession drew near. Still, the enormous potential powers of the country's top leader—the General Secretary of the CPSU—enabled him to stay in power as long as he could count on the backing of the Politburo and Secretariat. By appointing his supporters to leading party posts in the Secretariat and the regions (and removing in time those who might oppose him), the General Secretary could expect to stay in office until the end of his life. Most in fact did so. The result was a gradual aging of the entire ruling elite of the USSR, illustrated by the long and increasingly undistinguished tenure of Leonid Ilyich Brezhnev.

Born in 1906, Brezhnev reached the summit of power when he was appointed First Secretary of the CPSU in 1964 following a conspiracy among top party leaders to remove Nikita Khrushchev. Soon consolidating his own power, Brezhnev renamed the position "General Secretary" and built a power base that allowed him to remain in that office, despite obviously worsening health, until his death in November 1982.

Brezhnev was succeeded by Yuri Andropov, who had served as chairman of the KGB and as a secretary of the CPSU Central Committee. Although Andropov initially launched a policy program to reverse the decline in national economic performance, it soon turned out that he was gravely ill and could only rule from his hospital bed. When he, in turn, died in February 1984, he was succeeded by another aging, ailing member of the Brezhnev generation, Konstantin Chernenko. Chernenko had been a loyal member of Brezhnev's personal circle and tried to hold on to power by allying himself with the remnants of the old Brezhnev political machine. This meant halting the limited reform programs launched under Andropov and returning to the conservatism and drift of the Brezhnev era. But Chernenko, too, was fatally ill, and died in March 1985.

At this point, the senior leadership was evidently concerned by the impression of debility and weakness created by this rapid succession of deaths, and agreed to turn to a much younger, more dynamic, and open-minded figure as the new General Secretary. Mikhail Sergeevich Gorbachev was the youngest member of the Politburo at the time he was named its leader; born in 1931, he was only 54 when he took over. Gorbachev quickly grasped the levers of power that the system granted the General Secretary, and moved both to strengthen his own political base, and to carry out a program of economic reform.

Two great mysteries about Gorbachev will long be discussed. First, how did so radical a figure manage to become the leader of the Communist Party and to launch his earth-shaking reforms? Second, why did he fail so profoundly to achieve his goals? We can shed some light on these questions by referring to the close link between the contest for power and the policy process.

In Soviet politics, as in democratic pluralism, political leaders who aspired to move up in the power hierarchy endeavored to broaden their base of support. In this way they tended to assemble loose networks of interest groups and power centers, such as regions, industrial branches, and occupational and professional groups. In effect, this is a crude form of interest aggregation—the process by which demands and interests of particular groups are enlarged and generalized into options for policy. In Soviet politics, the game tended to work as follows. One contender might reach out for tacit support in elements of the army, the heavy industrial ministries, and certain powerful cities and regions, and the backing of the segments of the party apparatus which oversaw them. Another figure might be more sympathetic to the intelligentsia, light industries, and modernizers within the party and government. Thus, behind the rivalries of senior party officials one can discern the general outlines of certain recurrent types of policy conflict.

Broadly speaking, we can identify three tendencies in the policy outlooks of party leaders: conservative, nationalist, and liberal. At any given time, one or another of these tendencies predominated. Khrushchev and Gorbachev built a coalition of more reform-oriented groups, while Brezhnev (and later, his protégé Chernenko) relied on a conservative, standpat-oriented coalition. Certain phases in the Brezhnev, and later, Andropov, periods hinted at the existence of a network of intellectuals and officials in the security police and army who were attracted to an old-fashioned, imperialist Russian nationalism. They may have believed that the Soviet regime would be more popular if it appealed to a traditionalist mixture of Russian nationalism, imperialism, and Orthodox Church support. But, if so, this strategy was never explicitly pursued. Up to the very end, the regime professed a commitment to the universalist, internationalist precepts of Marxism–Leninism.

GORBACHEV COMES TO POWER

Reformist and nationalist tendencies in policy were not necessarily incompatible so long as they could agree on attacking the corruption and indiscipline that beset the system. There was a wing of conservatives who believed that Soviet socialism needed a strong dose of bitter medicine—strict discipline, accountability, and adherence to the socialist doctrine. These conservatives could accept a certain amount of administrative reform in the interests of strengthening socialism. Some of them had been pushed out of the top leadership under Brezhnev, and were willing to support someone from outside Brezhnev's political machine. They, and pro-reform elements in the party apparatus and intelligentsia, were therefore a natural base of support for an ambitious and ingenious political leader such as Mikhail Gorbachev.

Gorbachev's initial base of support, therefore, was a coalition of disciplinarians and reformers. This alliance began to form well before Brezhnev's death, and was reflected in Gorbachev's remarkable rise beginning in the late 1970s. In 1978 he was named Secretary of the Central Committee; in 1979 he became candidate member, and in 1980 full member of the Politburo. When long-time ideological arbiter Mikhail Suslov died in January 1982, Yuri Andropov replaced him as Central Committee Secretary. Gorbachev's position grew stronger when Andropov succeeded Brezhnev as general secretary in November 1982 and launched a discipline drive which entailed, among other things, a small press campaign for franker exposure of problems. Once both Andropov and his successor Chernenko had died and been succeeded by Gorbachev himself in 1985, the Soviet leadership consisted of a mixture of Brezhnevites and disciplinarians. Gorbachev needed to build a broader base of support in the Politburo for a policy of reform and used his credentials as Andropov's ally and de facto head of the party secretariat to carry out an anticorruption drive. This gave him the opportunity to build his coalition of supporters against the Brezhnevites. To help persuade his colleagues to embark on real reform, Gorbachev needed to generate an elite perception of impending crisis in order to overcome their cautious reluctance to accept the risks of major reform.

Emphasizing the need for greater openness—*glasnost'*—in relations between political leaders and the populace, Gorbachev stressed that the ultimate test of the party's effectiveness lay in improving the economic well-being of the country and its people. By highlighting such themes as the need for market relations, pragmatism in economic policy, and less secretiveness in government, he identified himself as a champion of reform.[21] The party amplified his modestly unorthodox message through its propaganda machine, disseminating to officials and citizens everywhere the new leader's appeals for *glasnost'*, modernization, and intensification of economic development.

Gorbachev moved rapidly to consolidate his own power using the general secretary's power over the recruitment of ranking elites. Acting cautiously at first, and then with increasing decisiveness, Gorbachev removed opponents and promoted supporters. By the middle of 1986, he had replaced one-third of the powerful regional first secretaries and two-thirds of the party's senior staff officials in Moscow (Central Committee secretaries and department heads). By June 1987 he had replaced two-thirds of all USSR ministers and state committee chiefs and over half of the regional party first secretaries.[22] In April 1989 he engineered a mass resignation of 110 members from the party's Central Committee. Perhaps most significant was the fact that Gorbachev's closest advisors and the government's senior ministers—including the prime minister—were left off the new Politburo of the CPSU when it was formed at the end of the 28th Party Congress in July 1990. Gorbachev not only stripped power away from the Brezhnev-era old guard, but he began transferring power away from the Communist Party altogether.

Similarly, Gorbachev made use of the party's control of national policy to set new directions in domestic and foreign policy. In the economic sphere, he demanded acceleration of technological progress and economic growth through an infusion of capital, including stepped-up foreign investment. He promised a loosening of the suffocating bureaucratic controls that discouraged innovation and risk on the part of enterprise managers. He called for breathing new life into the desiccated democratic forms of Soviet political life by making elections and public debate real and meaningful. In the sphere of foreign policy he pursued a new, active diplomacy in Europe and Asia, served up a series of disarmament proposals, and promised greater flexibility and understanding in relations with the West.

These early policy initiatives resembled those of Nikita Khrushchev, who succeeded Stalin as party leader in 1953 and liberalized somewhat the harsh and bleak Soviet regime. Like Gorbachev, Khrushchev assumed the leadership at a time of economic stagnation and widespread political apathy. Similarly, he tried to break the impasse of mutual hostility in East–West relations by a series of gestures, some for show, some substantive, aimed at defusing some of the confrontational atmosphere of the Cold War.[23] Khrushchev, however, remained faithful to the Marxist–Leninist

[21]Archie Brown, *The Gorbachev Factor* (New York: Oxford University Press, 1996).

[22]Thane Gustafson and Dawn Mann, "Gorbachev's Next Gamble," *Problems of Communism* 36:4 (July–August 1987), pp. 1–20.

[23]Martin McCauley, ed., *Khrushchev and Khrushchevism* (Bloomington: Indiana University Press), 1987; William J. Tompson, *Khrushchev: A Political Life* (New York: St. Martin's Press, 1995).

heritage of the regime and was in turn its victim when he was deposed by a conspiracy of senior party leaders in 1964.

Western and Soviet observers alike, therefore, were startled by the radical turn Gorbachev took beginning around 1987. He not only called for political democratization, but he pushed through a reform bringing about the first contested elections for local soviets in many decades.[24] He sponsored a law on state enterprise that was intended to break the stranglehold that industrial ministries held over enterprises through their powers of plan-setting and resource allocation. He legalized private, market-oriented enterprise for individual and cooperative businesses and encouraged them to fill the many gaps in the economy left by the inefficiency of the state sector. He called for a "law-governed state" (*pravovoe gosudarstvo*) in which state power—including the power of the Communist Party—would be subordinate to law. He welcomed the explosion of informal social and political associations that formed. He made major concessions to the United States in the sphere of arms control, resulting in a treaty which, for the first time in history, stipulated the destruction of entire classes of nuclear missiles.

In 1988, he proposed still more far-reaching changes at an extraordinary gathering of party members from around the country, where in a nationally televised address he outlined a vision of a democratic, but still socialist, political system. In it, legislative bodies made up of deputies elected in open, contested races would exercise the main policy-making power in the country. The Supreme Soviet would become a genuine parliament, debating policy, overseeing government officials, and adopting or defeating bills. Moreover, the judiciary would be separated from party control, and at the top of the system there would be a body called upon to adjudicate the constitutionality of legislative acts. The party conference itself was televised, and treated the Soviet public to an unprecedented display of open debate among the country's top leaders. Using the general secretary's full authoritarian powers, Gorbachev quickly railroaded his proposals for democratization through the Supreme Soviet, and in 1989 and 1990 the vision Gorbachev had laid out before that party conference was realized as elections were held, deputies elected, and new soviets formed at the center and in every region and locality. When nearly half a million coal miners went out on strike in the summer of 1989, Gorbachev declared himself sympathetic to their demands.

Gorbachev's radicalism received its most dramatic confirmation through the astonishing developments of 1989 in Eastern Europe. All the regimes making up the socialist bloc collapsed and gave way to multiparty parliamentary regimes in virtually bloodless popular revolutions—Romania was the only country where the ouster of the ruling communist elite was accompanied by widespread bloodshed—and the Soviet Union stood by and supported the revolutions![25] The overnight dismantling of communism in Eastern Europe meant that the elaborate structure of

---

[24]Stephen White, "Reforming the Electoral System," *Journal of Communist Studies* 4:4 (1988), pp. 1–17.

[25]The eyewitness reports by Timothy Garton Ash, *The Magic Lantern* (New York: Random House, 1990), are exceptionally valuable firsthand accounts as well as brilliant political analysis of the revolutions of 1989 in Eastern Europe. A thorough history of this period is Gale Stokes, *The Walls Came Tumbling Down: The Collapse of Communism in Eastern Europe* (New York: Oxford University Press, 1993).

party ties, police cooperation, economic trade, and military alliances that had developed since Stalin imposed communism on Eastern Europe after World War II now vanished. Divided Germany was allowed to reunite, and, after initial reluctance, the Soviet leaders even gave their sanction to the admission of the reunited Germany to the North Atlantic Treaty Organization (NATO). In the Soviet Union itself, meanwhile, the Communist Party was facing massive popular hostility and a critical loss of authority. Gorbachev forced it to renounce the principle of the "party's leading role" and to accept the legitimacy of private property and free markets. Real power in the state was being transferred to the elective and executive bodies of government—marked, above all, by the powerful new office of state president that Gorbachev created for himself in March 1990.[26] The newly elected governments of the national republics making up the Soviet state were one by one declaring their sovereignty within the union; and the three Baltic republics had declared their intention to secede altogether from the union. Everywhere, within and without the Soviet Union, communist party rule was breaking down.

Political Institutions of the Transition Period: Demise of the USSR

Gorbachev's inability to overcome the party and state bureaucracy's resistance to his economic programs undoubtedly prompted the radicalization of his reforms. He was careful not to go too far, however. His design for the democratization of the soviets had clear roots in the Leninist past, and, not incidentally, also served to reinforce his own power at the top. In introducing his political reforms in 1988, Gorbachev made it amply clear that he was not endorsing a move to a multiparty system. Parliamentarism was all very well and good as a further extension of *glasnost´*, Gorbachev seemed to think, but it must be kept firmly in its place. The power to make major decisions on domestic and national policy was to remain with the Communist Party leadership. Gorbachev sought to play the new parliamentary structures off against the party bureaucracy, bringing pressure to bear on party officials to carry out his reform policies, while ensuring that the newly elected deputies would not overstep the boundaries of their power. In the language of game theory, Gorbachev's political reforms had a strategic purpose. Gorbachev intended them to mobilize new allies by creating new political arenas in which supporters of liberal reform could gain influence. But by creating these new arenas of participation—*glasnost´*, elections, democratized soviets—Gorbachev made it possible for radical democrats, hard-line communist conservatives, and nationalist movements to seize the initiative and oppose his policies.

In retrospect it is clear that Gorbachev underestimated the centrifugal force of demands for national sovereignty and independence in a number of the union republics. As the liberalization of political life enabled new autonomous political movements to press for changes going far beyond what he was then prepared to tolerate, he concluded that the two posts he held—general secretary of the CPSU and

---

[26]On Gorbachev's autocratic methods in forcing through the constitutional amendments needed to create a powerful presidency, see David Shipler, "Between Dictatorship and Anarchy," *The New Yorker,* 25 June 1990.

chairman of the Supreme Soviet of the USSR—did not give him the power he desired. Although he had initially opposed the idea of creating a state presidency, he decided early in 1990 that only as president would he able to control the executive branch. Accordingly, in March 1990, he railroaded constitutional amendments creating a presidency through the Congress of People's Deputies. He coupled this with a change in the constitution which had the effect of legalizing multiparty competition. Both of these reforms, needless to say, seriously threatened the Communist Party's power. Now Gorbachev would be initiating policy and controlling the bureaucracy in his capacity as president, not as general secretary; even worse from the Communist Party's standpoint was the fact that the party would be forced to compete for popular support in competitive elections against legal rivals.

Again, Gorbachev's reforms had consequences he clearly did not intend. Although he was readily elected president of the Soviet Union, he was elected by the Congress of People's Deputies, not in a direct popular election (which he might have lost). Elimination of the long-standing provision that assigned the Communist Party the "leading role" in government and society authorized opposition movements to contest the party's mandate to rule. Therefore, the 1990 elections of deputies to the Supreme Soviets in all 15 republics, and to soviets in regions and towns all across the country, stimulated competition among political movements and parties. In Russia, a coalition of democratic reformers ran under the banner of a movement called "Democratic Russia" which sought to form caucuses in each soviet to which its candidates were elected. In the March 1990 elections the Democratic Russia movement succeeded in winning a majority of seats in both the Moscow and Leningrad (later the city took back its old name of St. Petersburg) soviets. And in the races for the Russian Congress of People's Deputies, the Democratic Russia contingent claimed as many as 40 percent of the newly elected deputies as adherents. (Of course, as events later showed, many of these deputies had only a very weak, opportunistic commitment to the radical democratic tenets of its program.) A roughly equal number of the new Russian deputies identified themselves with the conservative, antireform, pro-socialist ideology of the communists of Russia. Under the influence of the democratic aspirations and national self-awareness that the electoral campaign stimulated, the Congress narrowly elected Boris Yeltsin as chairman of the Russian Supreme Soviet in June 1990. As chief of state in the Russian Republic, Yeltsin was now well positioned to challenge Gorbachev for preeminence in the country.[27]

A course of developments then followed in the Russian Republic which paralleled those occurring at the level of the USSR federation during the previous year.

---

[27]On the 1989 and 1990 elections and the new representative bodies they formed, see Yitzhak M. Brudny, "The Dynamics of 'Democratic Russia,' 1990–1993," *Post-Soviet Affairs* 9:2 (1993), pp. 141–170; Giulietto Chiesa, with Douglas Taylor Northrop, *Transition to Democracy: Political Change in the Soviet Union, 1987–1991* (Hanover and London: Dartmouth College, University Press of New England, 1993); Robert T. Huber and Donald R. Kelley, eds., *Perestroika-Era Politics: The New Soviet Legislature and Gorbachev's Political Reforms* (Armonk: M.E. Sharpe, 1991); Brendan Kiernan, *The End of Soviet Politics: Elections, Legislatures and the Demise of the Communist Party* (Boulder: Westview Press, 1993); Michael E. Urban, *More Power to the Soviets: The Democratic Revolution in the USSR* (Aldershot, England and Brookfield, Vermont: Edward Elgar, 1990); Thomas F. Remington, ed., *Parliaments in Transition: The New Legislative Politics in Eastern Europe and the Former USSR* (Boulder: Westview Press, 1994). For more bibliographic information on Boris Yeltsin, see "Yeltsin and Electoral Politics" in Chapter Four.

Like Gorbachev a year earlier, Yeltsin, too, decided in early 1991 to create a state presidency in Russia. Unlike Gorbachev, Yeltsin put the matter to a national referendum. But he did so in such a way as to counter Gorbachev further. When Gorbachev held a USSR-wide referendum in March 1991 on whether the populace desired to preserve the Soviet Union in some new, vaguely defined form, Yeltsin added a question to the ballot distributed in the Russian Republic. This asked whether voters approved the idea of instituting a national presidency for the Russian Republic. Both measures passed by wide margins—71 percent of Russian voters supported preservation of the union, 70 percent a Russian presidency—but the popularity of the principle of a Russian presidency effectively undercut Gorbachev's desire to win a national mandate for his efforts to defend central power.

Moreover, Yeltsin linked his power and the cause of Russian national freedom with a program of radical market-oriented economic reform. In the spring of 1990, Yeltsin had endorsed a program of rapid, uncompromising economic transformation intended to dismantle the old system of state ownership and planning, and set loose the forces of private enterprise. The strategy discussed by Yeltsin's economic advisors had much in common with the programs of stabilization being adopted in Poland and Czechoslovakia. First, the central government would relinquish many of its administrative controls over the economy, allowing prices to rise to meet demand and freeing producers to determine their own production goals. Second, the government would launch a massive effort to privatize state assets and create a broad base of property owners who would help ensure that communism would never return. In Russia, the "500 Days" program embodying these ideas had the added feature of allowing the republics to claim sovereign control over the assets on their territories. This provision helped make the program acceptable to republic leaders and publics, but would have eliminated most remaining controls that the union center still had to regulate the economy. Little wonder that Gorbachev, pressured by conservative elements in the Politburo, military, government, and KGB, rejected the plan after having initially considered it; and little wonder that Yeltsin embraced it in his struggle with Gorbachev.

The winter of 1990–91 saw an intense political struggle between Gorbachev and Yeltsin. Gorbachev fought to hold onto his own power in the central leadership while maneuvering to defeat Yeltsin. By April 1991, Yeltsin had succeeded in defeating the conservative forces in the Russian parliament and Gorbachev had failed to bring Yeltsin down. Gorbachev was forced to accept Yeltsin's power, and that of Russia's sovereign status within the federal union. Gorbachev thereupon sought to find terms for a new federal or confederal union that would be acceptable to Yeltsin and the Russian leadership, as well as to the leaders of the other republics. He began a set of negotiations with the republic leaders aimed at drafting a new constitutional framework for the Soviet Union. In pursuing these talks, though, he was negotiating from a position of weakness: he lacked the support of the conservative, bureaucratic elements of the union government, and democratic forces were shifting their support to Yeltsin and the cause of a sovereign Russia.

Nonetheless, in April 1991 Gorbachev succeeded in reaching agreement on the outlines of a new treaty of union with 9 of the 15 republics, including Russia. Called the "9 + 1" agreement, it would have established a new balance of power between the federal union government and the constituent republics. The union government would have preserved its responsibility to set policy for defense and security, energy and transportation, money and finance, and to exercise other coordinating functions. The member republics would have gained the power to make economic policy and control productive assets within their territories. Most of the power of the union bureaucracy would have been transferred to the republics.

Gorbachev once again underestimated the strength of his opposition, based in the great bureaucracies of the union government. On August 19, 1991, his own vice-president, prime minister, defense minister, KGB chief, and other senior officials acted to prevent the signing ceremony of the treaty by forming the "State Committee on the State of Emergency" and seizing power in the coup attempt that was described in the first chapter. When the coup attempt failed, they were arrested and Gorbachev returned again as president. But his power was now fatally weakened. Neither union nor Russian power structures heeded his commands. Through the fall of 1991, the Russian government absorbed the union government ministry by ministry. In November 1991, President Yeltsin issued a decree formally outlawing the Communist Party of the Soviet Union. By December, Gorbachev was a president without a country. On December 25, 1991, he resigned as president of the USSR and turned the powers of his office over to Boris Yeltsin.

Institutions of the Transition Period: Russia

The Russian Republic followed the example of the USSR and adopted its own constitutional amendments creating a Congress of People's Deputies and Supreme Soviet. With the breakup of the Soviet Union, these representative bodies became the supreme organs of legislative power in a sovereign state, rather than simply the legislatures of the fifteen republics. As we have seen, the Russian Republic also followed the union government's lead in establishing a state presidency. Boris Yeltsin was elected president of the Russian Federation in June 1991 in a contested, direct election. After the election, he left his position as chairman of the Supreme Soviet, and, in October 1991, his deputy chairman, Ruslan Khasbulatov, was elected to the vacant post. Over the next two years, Khasbulatov and the legislature moved from a posture of enthusiastic support for Yeltsin and his policies to one of adamant opposition. The conflict reached a bloody climax in September and October 1993 when Yeltsin dissolved parliament by decree, and the opposition forces launched an armed uprising against him, which he suppressed. The two years between the crises of August 1991 and October 1993 show that the transition to a settled constitutional order was almost as difficult for Russia as it had been for the USSR.

1990–93: DEEPENING CONSTITUTIONAL CONFLICT

Like Gorbachev before him, Yeltsin demanded and received extraordinary powers from parliament to cope with the country's economic problems. In October 1991, following the August coup attempt, he sought and was given the power to carry out his radical economic program by decree from the Russian Congress of People's Deputies. The congress also consented to his demand that he be authorized to appoint the heads of government in each region of the country, rather than hold local elections for heads of the executive branch. Yeltsin then named himself acting prime minister and proceeded to form a government led by a group of young, Western-oriented leaders determined to carry out a decisive economic transformation. Charged with planning and carrying out the program was his deputy prime minister, Egor Gaidar.

Under the program—widely called "shock therapy"—the government took several radical measures simultaneously which were intended to stabilize the economy by bringing government spending and revenues into balance, and by letting market demand determine the prices and supply of goods. Under the reforms, the government let most prices float, raised taxes, and cut back sharply on spending in industry and construction. These policies caused widespread hardship as many state enterprises found themselves without orders or financing. The rationale of the program was to squeeze the built-in inflationary pressure out of the economy so that producers would begin making sensible decisions about production, pricing, and investment instead of chronically overusing resources. By letting the market rather than central planners determine prices, product mixes, output levels, and the like, the reformers intended to create an incentive structure in the economy where efficiency and risk would be rewarded and waste and carelessness would be punished. Removing the causes of chronic inflation, the reform program's architects argued, was a precondition for all other reforms: hyperinflation would wreck both democracy and economic progress; only by stabilizing the state budget could the government proceed to restructure the economy. A similar reform program had been adopted in Poland in January 1990, with generally favorable results.

However, in every country where it is applied, radical economic stabilization affects many interests and causes acute hardship, at least in the short run. Groups that lose out make their voice heard through the political process. In Russia's case, the program led to an intense confrontation between the president and the parliament. Each claimed to represent Russia's true interests.

The reform program took effect on January 2, 1992. The first results were immediately felt as prices skyrocketed, government spending was slashed, and heavy new taxes went into effect. Quickly a number of politicians began to distance themselves from the program: even Yeltsin's vice-president, Alexander Rutskoi, denounced the program as "economic genocide."[28] The chairman of the Russian Supreme Soviet, Ruslan Khasbulatov, also came out in opposition to the reforms, despite still claiming to support President Yeltsin's overall goals. Through 1992, opposition to the reform policies of Yeltsin and Gaidar grew stronger and more intransigent. Increasingly, the political confrontation became centered in the two branches of government. President Yeltsin expanded the powers of the presidency beyond constitutional limits in carrying out the reform program. In the Russian Congress of People's Deputies and the Supreme Soviet, the deputies refused to adopt a new constitution which would enshrine presidential power into law. They refused to allow Yeltsin to continue to serve as his own prime minister, and rejected his attempt to nominate Gaidar. They demanded modifications of the economic program and directed the Central Bank, which was under parliament's control, to continue issuing credits to enterprises to keep them from shutting down. The Cen-

---

[28]Celestine Bohlen, "Yeltsin Deputy Calls Reforms 'Economic Genocide,'" *New York Times*, February 9, 1992.

tral Bank's liberality wrecked the regime of fiscal discipline that the government was attempting to pursue: the money supply tripled in the third quarter of 1992 and for the year, prices rose over 2300 percent.[29] Through 1992, Yeltsin wrestled with the parliament for control over government and policy.

In March 1993, Yeltsin threatened to declare a regime of special emergency rule in the country and to suspend parliament, but then backed down. The Congress of People's Deputies immediately met and voted on a motion to impeach Yeltsin. The motion failed by a narrow margin. Yeltsin countered by convening a large conference of political leaders from a wide range of government institutions, regions, public organizations, and political parties, to hammer out a constitution that would give him the presidential powers he demanded. On September 21, shortly before the deputies were to meet to adopt a law that would have lowered the threshold for majorities in the congress and thus would have made it easier for them to impeach the president, Yeltsin declared the parliament dissolved, and called for elections to a new parliament to be held in December. Yeltsin's enemies then barricaded themselves inside the White House, as the building where the parliament was situated was popularly known. Refusing to submit to Yeltsin's decrees, they held a rump congress which declared Alexander Rutskoi president. After 10 days, during which Yeltsin shut off electric power to the building, they joined with some loosely organized paramilitary units outside the building and assaulted the building next door where the Moscow mayor's offices were located. Then they tried to take over Ostankino, the television tower where Russia's main national television broadcast facilities are housed, driving trucks through the entrance, smashing offices, and exchanging gunfire with police. Rutskoi and Khasbulatov evidently hoped their action would set off a national revolt against Yeltsin or win the army over to their side. Finally, the army decided to back Yeltsin and suppress the uprising. Khasbulatov, Rutskoi, and the other leaders of the rebellion were arrested. The army even lobbed artillery shells against the White House, killing several dozen people inside.

In subsequent decrees soon afterward, Yeltsin dissolved local (city, district, and village) soviets and called for the formation of new kinds of local representative bodies. He also called upon regional soviets to disband and hold new elections to new assemblies under guidelines that he also issued. Yeltsin was in fact ending the system of soviet power. He had made his views on this issue amply clear the previous June when, at the constitutional assembly that he convened, he declared that the system of soviet power was intrinsically undemocratic because it failed to separate legislative from executive power. In place of soviets he decreed that there be small, deliberative bodies at the local and regional levels, and a national parliament called the Federal Assembly representing Russia as a whole.

Yeltsin's plan for the parliament was embodied in the draft constitution that he put before the country in December 1993. According to the draft constitution, the Federal Assembly would have two chambers. The upper house, the Council of the Federation, would give equal representation to each of Russia's 89 regions and republics (called "subjects of the federation"). As in other European parliaments, it would be weaker than the lower, or popular, chamber. The latter, called the State Duma, would be formed in a manner entirely new to Russia. It was to have 450 seats.

---

[29]See Table 6.3 in Chapter Six.

Half were to be filled in proportion to the share of votes that parties received for their party lists.[30] The other 225 seats were to be filled in traditional single-member district races. Each voter in December 1993 therefore cast four votes for the Federal Assembly: two for the seats from his or her region in the Council of the Federation, and two for the deputies of the State Duma. One of these was for a candidate running for the local district seat, and one was for a party list.[31]

In the national referendum on December 12, 1993, Yeltsin's constitution was approved. According to the official figures, turnout was 54.8 percent, and of those who voted, 58.4 percent voted in favor of the constitution.[32] The constitution therefore came into force.

THE 1993 CONSTITUTION AND THE PRESIDENCY

The new constitution was designed to establish a dominant presidency: Yeltsin referred to the model as a "presidential republic." Using a typology proposed by political scientists Matthew Shugart and John Carey, we can call the Russian system "presidential-parliamentary." In such a system the president appoints the cabinet ministers, but the cabinet must also have the confidence of parliament to govern.[33] In Russia, the president does have the power to make law by decree, and to dissolve parliament, although he is subject to several specific constitutional constraints. His decrees may not violate existing law and can be superseded by laws passed by parliament. The president appoints the prime minister (who is formally termed the chairman of the government), subject to the approval of parliament. The Duma can refuse to confirm the president's choice, but if after three attempts the president still fails to win the Duma's approval of his choice, he dissolves the Duma and calls for new elections. Likewise the Duma may hold a vote of no confidence in the government. The first time a motion of no confidence carries, the president and government may ignore it, but if it passes a second time, the president must either dissolve parliament or dismiss the government. The president's power to dissolve

---

[30]To receive any seats, however, a party or electoral association had to have been legally registered and to have won at least 5 percent of the party list votes. For the 225 proportional representation seats, the entire Russian federation was considered a single district. Votes for each party's list were added, and the sum was divided by the total number of votes cast to determine the share of proportional representation seats that each party would receive. Certain parties further divided their lists into regional sublists to determine which of their candidates would win parliamentary mandates.

[31]On the new parliament and the manner of its formation, see Thomas F. Remington and Steven S. Smith, "The Early Legislative Process in the Russian Federal Assembly," *Journal of Legislative Studies* 2:1 (Spring 1996), pp. 161–192.

[32]Serious charges of fraud in the vote counting were made by a team of Russian analysts. Combining individual reports of irregularities from a number of regions with statistical modeling techniques, they estimate that actual turnout may have been as low as 46 percent and that, as a result, the constitution did not pass. They also claimed that the results of the vote for parliamentary candidates were extensively falsified as well. Although these accusations created a stir, all sections of the political elite tacitly agreed not to challenge the validity of the referendum or the elections.

[33]Ch. 2, "Defining Regimes with Elected Presidents," in Matthew S. Shugart and John M. Carey, *Presidents and Assemblies: Constitutional Design and Electoral Dynamics* (New York: Cambridge University Press, 1992), pp. 18–27. An alternative type of system is "premier-presidential" where the president lacks the power to appoint and dismiss cabinet ministers unilaterally.

parliament and call for new elections is also limited by the constitution. He may not dissolve parliament within one year of its election, or once it has filed impeachment charges against the president, or once the president has declared a state of emergency throughout Russia, or within six months of the expiration of the president's term.[34] Thus although the constitution gives the president the upper hand in relations with parliament, it is not an entirely free hand.

The constitution calls the president "head of state" and "guarantor of the constitution." He "ensures the coordinated functioning and collaboration of bodies of state power" (Article 80, paragraphs 1 and 2). He is not made chief executive. Although the president's nominee for prime minister must be confirmed by parliament, the president can appoint and remove deputy prime ministers and other ministers without parliamentary consent. These decisions are, nonetheless, to be made "on the proposal" of the prime minister (Article 83, para. e). On this point the president's power is the same as that of the French president, and the language of the relevant provisions of the two constitutions is the same.[35] As in France, the Russian constitution seems to allow a good deal of room for variation in the possible relationship between a president and a prime minister, depending on the personalities and political tendencies of each. And, as in France, it may be that the dual executive system works more harmoniously in practice if the two avoid competing for direct executive control over the same spheres of policy. In Russia, a certain division of labor seems to have evolved tacitly between the president and the prime minister. The prime minister is directly responsible for economic management, while the president oversees foreign and security policy, provides strategic direction, and enforces the loyalty of regional governments to central government.

To be sure, the two offices differ considerably in scope and power. President Yeltsin's reach extends over a wide range of political institutions at the center and in the regions. The president exercises his power through a staff structure called the "presidential administration." To some extent, the presidential administration duplicates the ministries of government. Some units of it work to ensure that governments in the regions carry out federal policy. The "power ministries"—the Foreign Ministry, Federal Security Service (formerly the Committee for State Security, or KGB), Defense Ministry, and Interior Ministry—now answer directly to the president. Indeed, they have been called "presidential ministries." There are, in addition, a large range of official and quasi-official commissions and administrations that are funded and directed by the president which carry out a variety of supervisory and advisory functions. The president also directly oversees the Security Council, which consists of a full-time secretary, the heads of the power ministries and other security-related agencies, the prime minister, and, more recently, the finance minister and chairs of the two chambers of parliament. Its powers are broad but

---

[34]The restriction on dissolving the Duma within one year of its election applies to the no confidence procedure but not to the requirement of parliament confirmation of the president's nominee for prime minister. Thus while the president may not dissolve the Duma twice within one year of its last election in the case where it votes no confidence in the government twice within three months or defeats a motion of confidence in the government, he is not so limited if the Duma rejects the candidates he nominates for prime minister three times in a row.

[35]The French Constitution, Article 8, says that "On the proposal of the Prime Minister, he [the president] shall appoint and dismiss the other members of the Government."

shadowy. Most observers believe that this body made the principal decisions on the invasion of Chechnia in December 1994 and the subsequent military operations there. But little is known about the degree of its authority or the way in which it makes decisions.[36]

When President Yeltsin wanted to reinforce his chances of victory in the runoff round of the presidential election in the summer of 1996, he invited General Alexander Lebed´—who as a candidate in the first round of the presidential election had won 15 percent of the vote and enjoyed a reputation as a straight-shooting, tough-minded independent—to join the presidential administration as secretary of the Security Council and national security advisor. To persuade Lebed´ to accept, Yeltsin promised him an extremely broad mandate to fight crime and corruption in the country. Yeltsin even charged him with the mission of finding an honorable solution to the war in Chechnia. The move was politically shrewd, but potentially dangerous, since the Security Council lacks any executive authority of its own, and still lacks a legal definition of its rights and authority. Lebed´ did succeed in signing an agreement on the cessation of hostilities with the Chechen leadership, which he claimed as a personal policy triumph. This success reinforced his ambitious conception of his mandate as head of the Security Council. Lebed´ then proceeded to lock horns with nearly every other official in the presidential administration and the government—many of whom, jealous of his personal stature, undercut him in bitter turf battles. Finally Yeltsin unceremoniously tossed him out in October 1996, three months after his appointment.

The Lebed´ case illustrates an important point. Many state structures in the young postcommunist state are closely tied to the personalities of their chief executives: the leader's personal priorities often define the rights and responsibilities of the office. Rules remain undeveloped and fluid. There is still no regular civil service in Russia protected from political pressure.[37] The consolidation of a more law-governed political process will take some time. Contributing to the stabilization of institutions is the fact that for the first time in Russian or Soviet history, there is a Constitutional Court adjudicating jurisdictional disputes among branches of government and levels of state authority. Generally the struggle for political power takes more open forms than it did during the communist or autocratic era, when there was no open party competition or legal constraints on the state's sovereignty.

On the other hand, as many observers point out, the new Russian political system bears many similarities to the tsarist and communist regimes which preceded it. The weakness of institutions, the drive for concentrated, centralized power at the top, and the hierarchical organization of political life all have left a strong mark on the present regime. First of all, the Russian presidency has come to resemble the central communist party organs of the Soviet era. The president is a kind of gener-

---

[36]On the Security Council and the December 1993 reorganization of security agencies in Russia, see Victor Yasmann, "Security Services Reorganized: All Power to the Russian President?" *RFE/RL Research Report* 3:6 (February 11, 1994), pp. 7–14.

[37]Eugene Huskey, "Democracy and Institutional Design in Russia," *Demokratizatsiya: The Journal of Post-Soviet Democratization*, no. 4 (1996), p. 459.

al secretary, his administration something like the machinery of the Central Committee.[38] Both in structure and function, the comparison is apt. The reason that a similar pattern of organization has emerged in the post-Soviet period, as Eugene Huskey argues, is the same dilemma that the communist authorities faced. In the absence of a rational-legal foundation for bureaucratic authority, and of a professionally oriented civil service, direct political supervision from above seems to be the only means Russian rulers know for controlling the sprawling state bureaucracy. It is unlikely that Yeltsin or his successors will soon voluntarily relinquish the vast powers that the presidency gives them.

THE GOVERNMENT

Successful performance under a mixed, dual executive system requires a constructive working relationship between president and prime minister and a mutually acceptable demarcation between their respective spheres of authority. In Russia, Prime Minister Viktor Chernomyrdin and President Yeltsin enjoyed a fairly harmonious relationship until Yeltsin abruptly dismissed Chernomyrdin and the whole government in March 1998. First appointed prime minister in December 1992, Chernomyrdin had a surprisingly long tenure in office.

The Chairman of the Government is head of the executive branch, which consists of over 60 ministries and state agencies. Each administers a different branch of government, such as the Ministry of Finance, the Ministry of Fuel and Energy, the State Tax Service, and so on. (However, as noted above, the ministries immediately concerned with national security are under the president's direct control.) The prime minister directs the government through an intermediate layer of deputy prime ministers. In August 1996, these included three first deputy chairmen and eight regular deputy chairmen of government, each of whom oversaw a particular bloc of ministries and agencies. As has been true in Russia for centuries, the fine distinctions in administrative rank matter acutely for the individuals concerned, because they determine how material and political privileges are allocated. When Sergei Kirienko was confirmed as prime minister in spring 1998, he promised to cut the number of deputy prime ministers and to streamline government structure.

Unlike most parliamentary systems, in Russia the government does not directly reflect the balance of party forces in parliament. The relationship between the distribution of seats in parliament and the makeup of government is extremely loose. So far, most members of the government have been career administrators rather than party politicians. Some, however, have direct ties to parties. In 1995, Yeltsin appointed a member of the Communist Party as Minister of Justice; outraged, his party immediately expelled him. Likewise Yeltsin appointed a leading member of the Agrarian Party as deputy chairman of government in charge of agricultural policy. He, too, was kicked out of his party. Yeltsin has consistently rejected

[38]Eugene Huskey, "Yel´tsin as State Builder," *Soviet and Post-Soviet Review* 21:1 (1994), pp. 61–62.

demands by Zhirinovsky to appoint members of the extremist Liberal-Democratic Party of Russia as members of government, but he has appointed two leading members of the Yabloko parliamentary faction (which favors market reform but is sharply critical of Yeltsin's policies) to serve as Minister of Finance and Minister of Labor.

To some degree, the makeup and policy direction of the government must reflect the political composition of the parliament because the Duma has the power to deny the government its confidence. Yet because the Duma's members have been highly reluctant to give the president a reason to dissolve parliament, Yeltsin has been able to appoint and dismiss members of his government more or less at will and force parliament to accept his choices. After his reelection in summer 1996, Yeltsin reappointed Chernomyrdin to head the government. The constitution requires that the Duma approve the nomination. Despite the opposition majority in the Duma, the nomination passed (in a secret ballot) by a surprisingly wide margin—314 to 85 votes, with 3 abstentions. Evidently the opposition parties decided it was preferable to allow Chernomyrdin to continue in office than to give Yelstin a reason to dissolve parliament and call new elections.

A similar test of executive-legislative power occurred again in March-April 1998 after Yeltsin unexpectedly dismissed the entire government, provoking a month of high-stakes brinkmanship with the Duma. Yeltsin nominated a young, relatively inexperienced figure, Sergei Kirienko, to replace Chernomyrdin as head of government. The State Duma refused to confirm Kirienko on the first two votes (which were by shows of hands), but on the third vote, held by secret ballot, the nomination was approved with a 25-vote margin. Once again, the deputies showed themselves to be unwilling to let President Yeltsin dissolve the Duma and force new elections. Kirienko was regarded by most observers as a competent administrator, close to the reformist camp. On the other hand, Kirienko lacked an independent base of political support, and so could not be considered a threat or rival to President Yeltsin. This lent support to the supposition that Yeltsin had fired Chernomyrdin out of a fear of Chernomyrdin's political ambitions.

THE PARLIAMENT

The parliament, or Federal Assembly, has proven to be a relatively authoritative and effective body despite the turmoil that surrounded its creation. Several features distinguish it from its predecessor institutions. One is the important role played by party factions in organizing its proceedings. Another is its bicameral nature; in contrast to the past, its two chambers differ markedly in their makeup and operations. The lower house, or State Duma, is given the constitutional right to originate legislation except for certain categories of policy which are under the jurisdiction of the upper house, the Council of the Federation. Upon passage in the State Duma, a bill goes to the Council of the Federation. If the upper house rejects it, the bill goes back to the Duma, where a commission comprising members of both houses may seek to iron out differences. If the Duma rejects the upper house's changes, it may override the Council of the Federation by a two-thirds vote.

When the bill has cleared parliament, it goes to the president for signature. If the president refuses to sign the bill, it returns to the Duma. The Duma may pass it with the president's proposed amendments by a simple absolute majority, or override the president's veto, for which a two-thirds vote is required. The Council of the Federation must then also approve the bill, by a simple majority if the president's amendments are accepted, or a two-thirds vote if it chooses to override the president. The Duma has overridden the president's veto on rare occasions, and it has overridden Council of the Federation rejections several times. In other cases, the Duma has passed bills rejected by the president after accepting the president's amendments. For the most part, the parliament and president have consciously avoided provoking a conflict that could trigger a major constitutional crisis.

The upper house is designed as an instrument of federalism in that, like the U.S. Senate, every constituent unit of the federation is represented by two deputies. Thus the populations of small ethnic-national territories are greatly overrepresented compared with more populous regions. Members of the Federation Council were elected by direct popular vote in December 1993, but since the constitution was silent on how they were to be chosen in the future, a law was adopted in 1995 governing the formation of the chamber. Under the law, the heads of the executive and legislative branches of each constituent unit of the federation automatically hold seats in the Council of the Federation. Not intended as a full-time chamber, the Council of the Federation does have certain important prerogatives in addition to its role as a check on the actions of the lower house. It approves presidential nominees for high courts such as the Supreme Court and the Constitutional Court. It approves presidential decrees declaring martial law or a state of emergency, and any actions altering the boundaries of territorial units in Russia. It must consider any legislation dealing with taxes, budget, financial policy, treaties, customs, and declarations of war. The Council of the Federation defied the president's will on a number of issues, rejecting some of his nominees for the Constitutional Court, as well as his candidate for Procurator-General.[39]

The State Duma has emerged as an assertive and active body. Opponents of President Yeltsin and his policies are stronger in the Duma than are his allies, but no one party or coalition has a majority. Unlike the Federation Council, the Duma is organized by party faction. Representatives of its factions—one from each registered group or party faction regardless of size—comprise its steering body, the Council of the Duma.[40] The Council of the Duma makes the principal decisions in

---

[39]The Procurator-General oversees the procuracy, a branch of the legal system equivalent to government prosecutors in the American system. For more details, see Chapter Eight.

[40]Any party which has won at least 5 percent of the party list vote and thus obtained seats through the proportional representation vote is entitled to form its own political faction in the Duma which is given full rights to maintain a staff and participate in the legislative process. Groups of deputies from outside parties may also organize. If a group has 35 members, it may register as a recognized parliamentary group and enjoy the same rights and privileges as party factions. Each faction and registered group is entitled to have one representative—generally its leader—on the Council of the Duma, which steers the chamber. It is important to note that the Russian Duma therefore does not favor the majoritarian structure, used by the U.S. House and Senate and the British House of Commons. Every party and group has an equal voice in setting the agenda and managing the proceedings.

the Duma with respect to legislative agenda and proceedings, and acts on occasion to broker compromise agreements that overcome deadlocks among the deeply opposing political groups represented in the Duma. The Duma also created 23 standing committees—expanded to 27 in the second Duma—whose leadership and membership positions are distributed in rough proportion to factional strength in the chamber. Some, such as the budget committee, have become influential in shaping national economic policy. One reason the Duma has been able to modify government policy without provoking a destructive collision with President Yeltsin is that its first chairman, Ivan Rybkin, showed himself to be a flexible and capable builder of consensus. Observers were impressed at his skill and moderation in the chairman's post since he had been a leader of the communist faction in the previous parliament and had run for the Duma as a candidate of the pro-communist Agrarian Party. In the Duma which convened in 1996 following the 1995 parliamentary elections, the communists were much stronger, and succeeded in winning the election of one of their leading members, Gennadii Seleznev, as chairman of the Duma. Like Rybkin, he has generally sought to avoid head-on clashes with President Yeltsin and instead to promote compromise and conciliation.

THE CONSTITUTIONAL COURT

The Yeltsin constitution also provided for a means of judicial review through a Constitutional Court. The Court is empowered to consider the constitutionality of actions of the president, the parliament, and lower level governments. Through 1996, the court had not issued any decisions restricting President Yeltsin's powers in any significant way but it had decided several thorny constitutional issues, including the relations between the two chambers of parliament and the delineation of powers between the central and regional governments. Moreover, the present court has two important predecessor bodies, whose success in limiting presidential power may serve as precedent in the future.

The first was the "Committee for Constitutional Oversight" proposed by Gorbachev as part of his great political reform package of 1988. In one of its first decisions, in September 1990, it found unconstitutional a decree Gorbachev had issued unilaterally claiming for himself as president the power to approve or prohibit demonstrations within the city of Moscow. Gorbachev chose not to challenge the ruling, thus tacitly acknowledging its validity.

While this USSR-level body was not itself a court, the Russian Republic established a Constitutional Court by constitutional amendment in July 1991. One of its first rulings in early 1992 also found a presidential action unconstitutional. The court struck down President Yeltsin's decree merging two ministries into one. He too complied with the ruling, again accepting the principle that the court had jurisdiction to adjudicate constitutional disputes to which he was a party. To be sure, since then, Yeltsin has taken several baldly unconstitutional steps, among them the dissolution of parliament and suspension of the Constitutional Court itself in September 1993. As we shall see in Chapter Seven, however, the Constitutional Court finally resumed its work in early 1995, and has issued a number of rulings that resolved disputes arising among branches and levels of government. So far, though, it has refrained from attempting to restrain the president's freedom of action in any significant way.

EXECUTIVE–LEGISLATIVE RELATIONS

The president's powers vis-à-vis parliament are great but should not be exaggerated. Certainly the constitution makes it extremely difficult for the parliament to remove the president. As in the United States, the legislature's sole device for forcing out the president is the drastic means of impeachment. The word impeachment is used in the constitution to refer to the actual removal from office, rather than, as in the United States, to the "indictment" enacted by the House of Representatives preparatory to Senate action. The Russian procedure is even more cumbersome than the American.[41] Parliament's power to check the president has little to do with the threat of impeachment, however. Rather it stems from two more immediate considerations: the need for the parliament's approval of any piece of legislation, and the constitutional requirement of parliamentary confidence in the government. A president who ruled by decree could not be certain that the government would comply with his directives; this consideration appears to have moved Yeltsin to use his decree power rather sparingly, to invite parliament to pass its own legislation on some matters, and even in certain cases to amend decrees to satisfy parliamentary objections.[42] Of course there are large swaths of executive power—particularly those relating to foreign policy and national security policy—where the parliament's influence is diminished because they are directly overseen by the president.

The Russian president's ability to make policy against parliament's will faces certain limits even in foreign and defense policy domains. This is because parliament, by rejecting a candidate for prime minister three times or denying a government its confidence twice within three months, can force the president to choose whether to dissolve the government or dissolve the parliament and call new elections. The president must therefore calculate whether by dissolving parliament and holding new elections he will wind up with a friendlier or more hostile parliament. Over 1994–97 President Yeltsin evinced little desire to invoke this procedure. Moreover, as we have seen, he is constitutionally prohibited from doing so within one year of a parliament's election, within six months of a new presidential election, or if the Duma

---

[41]The constitution provides that the president can only be removed in case of serious crime or high treason and specifies the sequence of procedures required: one-third of the members of the Duma must initiate the process; the decision must be considered by a special commission of the Duma; the Duma must approve the action by a two-thirds vote; the Supreme Court must issue a ruling finding that the president's actions constituted a grave crime or act of treason; the Constitutional Court must find that the parliament acted properly; and the Federation Council must finally approve removal by a two-thirds vote.

[42]Over 1994–95, the Duma passed 461 laws, and of them 282 were signed by the president. Around 100 of the latter were major regulatory or distributive policy acts in areas such as budget appropriations, social welfare, reform of state political institutions, and reform of law-enforcement and the judicial system (*Segodnia*, December 23, 1995). Over the same period, the president issued approximately 4,000 decrees (*ukazy*), most of them of minor significance—such as appointing individuals to state positions or awarding honors for merit. A few, however, were highly important because they attempted to shape major national policy. These included the terms of privatization of shares of the state television and radio company, the powers that law enforcement bodies would have to prosecute organized crime, and decisions on which enterprises were subject to privatization in the current cash phase of the privatization program. In the case of the cash privatization program, the president's decree was modified to accommodate some of parliament's concerns, and in the case of the decree on fighting organized crime, the president invited parliament to pass its own more sweeping crime-fighting legislation.

has, by the required two-thirds vote, approved a motion calling for the removal of the president through impeachment. Thus the balance of power, while asymmetrical, is by no means as one-sidedly tilted in favor of the president as is often thought. Figure 2.1 provides a schematic picture of the present constitutional arrangements.

One question for Russia's development as a democracy will be whether an effective working relationship develops between the presidency and the parliament. This problem is all the greater given the requirement that the government must enjoy parliament's confidence, but also must answer to the president. As political scientists have pointed out, a system in which the government is subordinate to the president, while it must simultaneously be able to command a majority in parliament, often produces severe confrontations between president and parliament.[43] It may be that in Russia, periods of stability in relations between president and parliament come about when there is no stable opposition majority that can provoke a crisis by forcing the government's fall through a vote of no confidence. Alternatively, with time, the presidency may be occupied by less activist figures, and the government and parliament will play a more prominent part in determining policy. In this instance, again, France may provide a model of stable development under a mixed parliamentary/presidential system.

The circumstances under which the constitutional referendum and elections to the new parliament were held were hardly auspicious. For one thing, Yeltsin decreed that national elections were to be held for a legislature that did not, constitutionally, yet exist. Moreover, the government imposed severe limitations on party competition during the electoral campaign, outlawing some parties, and disqualifying others from running candidates. Senior officials tried to impose press censorship (which was quickly lifted) and to prohibit public criticism of the constitution by candidates.[44] Observers inside and outside Russia were further alarmed at the electoral success of antidemocratic forces.

Yet despite the inauspicious circumstances attending its birth, the new constitutional order achieved some successes in its first years. It relieved some of the tensions and conflicts of the previous period. Despite their deep political differences, the parties in the parliament were able to reach agreement on a number of difficult issues, such as the choice of a chairman, the leadership of the committees, and the nature of the rules of procedure. Parliament and government succeeded in reaching agreement over some major pieces of legislation, such as the budgets for 1994, 1995, 1996, and 1997. Parliament passed and the president signed a major overhaul of the criminal justice system and a new Civil Law Code enshrining property rights. Five laws on electoral procedures have been passed: regarding parliamentary elections, presidential elections, voters' rights throughout the federation, referenda, and the formation of the upper house of parliament. On these and a number of

---

[43]On this point, see Juan J. Linz, "Presidential or Parliamentary Democracy: Does It Make a Difference?" in Juan J. Linz and Artura Valenzuela, *The Failure of Presidential Democracy: Comparative Perspectives* (Baltimore and London: Johns Hopkins University Press, 1994), pp. 3–90; also Scott Mainwaring, "Presidentialism, Multipartism, and Democracy," *Comparative Political Studies* 26 (1993), pp. 198–228; Alfred Stepan and Cindy Skach, "Constitutional Frameworks and Democratic Consolidation: Parliamentarism versus Presidentialism," *World Politics* 46 (1993), pp. 1–22.

[44]A good account of these events is Michael Urban, "December 1993 as a Replication of Late-Soviet Electoral Practices," *Post-Soviet Affairs* 10:2 (1994), pp. 127–158, esp. pp. 129–139.

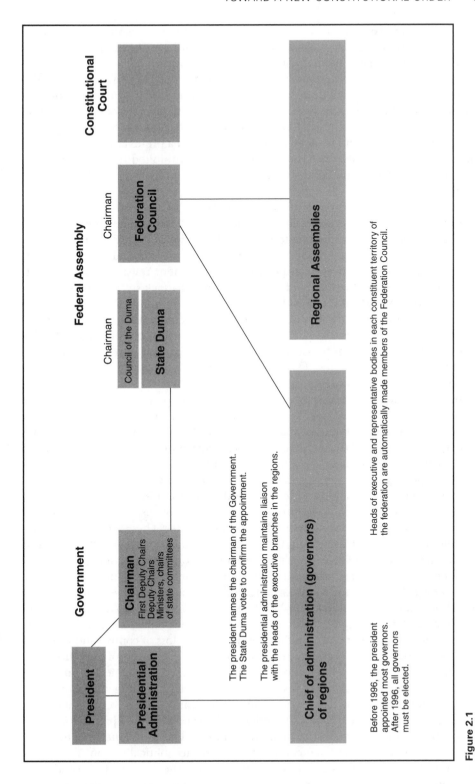

Figure 2.1
The 1993 Russian Constitution

other issues, the president and government showed themselves willing to bargain and compromise in their dealings with parliament. For its part, parliament has usually adopted a pragmatic line in dealing with the executive.

Certainly members of parliament are aware that if they seriously challenge the president, he might respond by dissolving parliament and holding new elections. To do this, he could instruct the government to demand that a vote of confidence be held: it would almost certainly fail. Since the deputies do not relish the prospect of facing the voters, they tend to avoid giving the president a pretext for dissolving parliament. But by the same token, the president also is inhibited from invoking this procedure, since he cannot be sure that a newly elected parliament will be any more sympathetic to his policies.

To be sure, serious threats to the consolidation of the constitutional order remained. Spells of passivity and ill health on the part of President Yeltsin created fears that the president was unable to exercise the duties of his office with any consistency or impose a common policy line on the huge presidential administration. Indeed, for nearly the entire second half of 1996 President Yeltsin devoted very little time to performing the duties of his office. A heart attack suffered between the first and second rounds of the presidential election in the summer required that he undergo a heart bypass, which was performed in November 1996. Preparation for the surgery and recuperation from it, followed by severe pneumonia, left him unable to make all but the most pressing decisions for well over half a year. He resumed a more normal schedule only in spring 1997.

Controlling the vast, burgeoning presidential administration would tax the physical powers of even the healthiest president. A great deal of power is therefore vested in the president's chief of staff, the "head of the presidential administration." Following his reelection, Yeltsin appointed Anatolii Chubais—formerly the head of the State Property Committee and the architect of mass privatization (see Chapter Six)—as his chief of staff. He gave Chubais wide power to reorganize the presidential administration and impose greater order and rationality on it. But Chubais faced powerful political enemies both inside and outside the presidential administration, and it was not clear that he would be able to control it. Aggressive nationalist elements within the state bureaucracy pressed for more hard-line statist policies. These are most likely the elements responsible for instigating the costly and brutal war against the separatist Chechen Republic. Some of Yeltsin's most ardent supporters from among the reform movement, such as former prime minister Egor Gaidar, bitterly denounced the war and broke with Yeltsin over it. Most alarming, as the operation unfolded, were the signs that Yeltsin himself was not in control of the situation. Yeltsin complained, for example, that his orders for a halt in the bombing were ignored. Still more dangerous than the high concentration of power in the presidency is the loss of control and responsibility that can occur if the president does not command the powers of the office.

After the December 1995 elections, where the communists made a strong showing, Yeltsin shifted the makeup of his entourage to the left, pushing out many of the remaining reformers from the presidential administration and government. Then, following his dramatic victory in the presidential election in June–July 1996, Yeltsin brought back some reformers into his administration. This is evidence that the president does play the role of balancer and arbiter in the political system. Yeltsin has refused to form a political party, but he has exercised the powers of his office in a highly political way, seeking to make Russia's turn from communism irrevocable. It may be that history will judge that he should have built a lasting political organization that united a following throughout the country and gave reform-minded politicians a common cause. On the other hand, a party affiliation might have made it more difficult for Yeltsin to maneuver politically in order to preserve his power and win support for his policies.

The constitutional order remains subject to change. Stimulated by President Yeltsin's sweeping use of his decree power, a number of politicians have called for constitutional amendments restricting the president's powers, and some seek to change the way the president is elected. Some political forces reject the constitutional order that Yeltsin had introduced and demand some form of dictatorial rule. Yet most political tendencies active in politics are represented in parliament and thus have a stake in preserving representative institutions.

Russia bears some similarities to other political systems where the presidency is invested with enormous power and legal checks on its exercise are weak.[45] In such a country, the presidency is the greatest prize in politics, and the struggle to win it provokes intense political struggle. In 1996, Yeltsin ran for reelection as president and won in the second round with a convincing victory against his opponent, communist party leader Gennadii Ziuganov. Because the incumbent president was reelected, Russia still has not undergone a test of its political institutions' ability to manage the transfer of power from one leader to a democratically elected winner. Therefore deep uncertainty hangs over the future of democracy in Russia. The stakes are so high that those determined to keep or win control of the Kremlin are strongly tempted to resort to undemocratic means. In 1996, for example, some of Yeltsin's closest advisors, fearful that he would lose the race for reelection, reportedly urged him to find a pretext for cancelling the elections.[46] A peaceful transfer of power from an incumbent to a challenger following a free and fair election would be the single greatest impetus to democracy that could be made at present. Equally important is the observance of constitutional principles by the winner of the election. Violation of them before, during, or after the election by the incumbent or a challenger would compromise democracy gravely.

The Center and the Regions

Notwithstanding the Chechen war, Russia's path of development during the transition period has not culminated in the state's dissolution along national-territorial lines like that which ended the Soviet Union's existence. As was true of the USSR under Gorbachev, Yeltsin's government has confronted the twin crises of maintaining relations between the central government and the constituent members of the federation, and of carrying out deep economic reform in the face of powerful opposition. The breakdown of the Soviet order eroded both the central government's power to enforce its authority in the regions and reduced the benefits it could offer

---

[45]The political scientist Guillermo O'Donnell has termed such systems "delegative democracies." Guillermo O'Donnell, "Delegative Democracy," *Journal of Democracy* 5 (1994), pp. 55–69.

[46]Stephen White, Richard Rose, and Ian McAllister, *How Russia Votes* (Chatham, NJ: Chatham House, 1996), pp. 253–254.

regional governments to induce their compliance with federal law. Since both Gorbachev and Yeltsin had made liberal offers of autonomy to the subnational governments of Russia as part of their rivalry in 1990–91, Russia found it particularly difficult to reestablish the primacy of its own central authority. Conflicts between the subnational governments and the Russian federal authorities over the appropriate spheres of rights and powers are substantial. This is particularly true for several of the ethnic-national territories which enjoy a privileged constitutional status in Russia and are unwilling to relinquish it. By far the most intractable case is that of the Chechen Republic, whose leaders declared independence in 1991. In December 1994 Russia launched a large-scale military assault to restore central rule, employing heavy and often indiscriminate force. Fighting between Russian federal troops and the forces fighting for Chechen independence continued until October 1996, punctuated by mass hostage-taking raids by Chechens on Russia soil, and unsuccessful cease-fire declarations. Nevertheless, the Chechen war proved to be the sole case where the federal government had to resort to force to preserve the unity of the state. Unlike the union government, the Russian state preserved itself despite centrifugal pressures from the regions. Several factors distinguishing Russia's situation from that of the USSR help to explain the different outcomes.

One is the demographic factor. The Soviet population was more ethnically fragmented than that of the Russian republic. Whereas half of the Soviet population was ethnically Russian, and the other half was a diverse array of smaller national groups, Russia's population is 80 percent Russian. As Table 2.2 indicates, its ethnic minorities thus form a very small proportion of the total. The Soviet population, moreover, was never an ethnic nationality, whereas Russia's national culture provided a historic identity which encouraged (and sometimes required) other national groups to assimilate to it. Finally, the national republics of the Soviet Union were all located on the perimeter of the country, and thus bordered other countries. The national territories of Russia are mainly internal to the Russian republic, and thus have had less direct interaction with the outside world.[47]

A second factor has to do with Russia's internal administrative structure. In Russia, only around 17 percent of the population lives in territories designated as ethnic homelands.[48] In the Soviet state, by contrast, all territory was included in one or another of the ethnic-national republics. The republic of Russia took up three quarters of Soviet territory and half its population. In the Soviet state, most of the national groups giving their names to the republics had lived in the territory of their republics for centuries, and had some reason to consider them "national homelands." In most cases, these peoples had a national history and had been subjugated by the Soviet Russian state. Like the USSR, the Russian Republic was also formally considered a federation and had internal ethnic-national subdivisions. But in contrast to the larger union, only some of its constituent members are ethnic-national

---

[47]Ian Bremmer and Ray Taras, eds., *New States, New Politics: Building the Post-Soviet Nations* (Cambridge: Cambridge University Press, 1997).

[48]Note that some of these territorial units are huge in physical terms: Sakha (formerly Yakutia) alone constitutes 17 percent of the territory of Russia. Altogether around half of Russian territory belongs to ethnic republics and regions.

TABLE 2.2

Population of Major Nationalities of the Russian Federation (in thousands)

	1970	1979	1989
TOTAL	130079	137410	147022
Russians	107748	113522	119866
Tatars	4755	5006	5522
Crimean Tatars*	2.9	5.2	21
Ukrainians	3346	3658	4363
Chuvash	1637	1690	1774
Bashkirs	1181	1291	1345
Belorussians	964	1052	1206
Mordva	1177	1111	1073
Chechens	572	712	899
Germans	762	791	842
Udmurts	678	686	715
Mari	581	600	644
Kazak	478	518	636
Avar	362	438	544
Jews	792	692	537
Peoples of the north	168	170	199

*Crimean Tatars are enumerated as a separate ethnic group from Volga Tatars.

territories. Most are pure administrative subdivisions, populated mainly by Russians. In the past, Russia's internal ethnic-national territories were classified by size and status into autonomous republics, autonomous provinces, and national districts; today all the autonomous republics are simply termed republics. In many, the indigenous ethnic group comprises a minority of the population. Since 1991, the names and status of some of the constituent units in Russia have changed. As of 1996, Russia comprises 89 constituent territorial units; in Russian constitutional language, these are called the "subjects of the federation." Of these, 21 are republics, 6 are krais (territories), 10 are autonomous districts (all but one of them located within other units), 1 is an autonomous oblast, 2 are cities (Moscow and St. Petersburg), and 49 are oblasts. (See Table 2.3.) Republics, autonomous okrugs (districts) and the one autonomous oblast are units created specifically to give certain political rights to populations living in territories with significant ethnic minorities. Autonomous okrugs are located within larger territorial entities, although they also are treated as "subjects of the federation." Republics, on the other hand, are treated constitutionally as though they had a share of sovereignty. They have the right to adopt their own constitution so long as it does not contradict the federal constitution. They have the right to enact their own laws. In contrast, oblasts and krais are simply administrative subdivisions with no special constitutional status. Not surprisingly, there is constant rivalry between the oblasts and krais, on the one hand, and the republics on the other. Leaders of oblasts and krais complain of the special privileges that republics are given which enable them to circumvent federal law but receive benefits such as federal subsidies. Unable to even out the constitutional status of the two kinds of entities by lowering the constitutional status of republics, they have occasionally

—————————————————TABLE 2.3—————————————————
Constituent Members of the Russian Federation, January 1, 1993

Name of unit	Territory (in thousands sq. km.)	Population (in thousands)
Russian Federation	17075.4	148673
Northern Region		
Republic of Karelia	172.4	800
Komi Republic	415.9	1246
Arkhangel'sk oblast includes:	587.4	1562
Nenetsk autonomous okrug	176.7	52
Vologda oblast	145.7	1362
Murmansk oblast	144.9	1117
Northwestern Region		
St. Petersburg (city) ⎱	85.9	4952
Leningrad oblast ⎰		1674
Novgorod oblast	55.3	752
Pskov oblast	55.3	840
Kaliningrad oblast*	15.1	906
Central Region		
Bryansk oblast	34.9	1468
Vladimir oblast	29.0	1654
Kaluga oblast	29.9	1086
Kostroma oblast	60.1	812
Moscow (city) ⎱	47.0	8881
Moscow oblast ⎰		6682
Orel oblast	24.7	909
Ryazan' oblast	39.6	1342
Smolensk oblast	49.8	1165
Tver' oblast	84.1	1663
Tula oblast	25.7	1840
Yaroslavl' oblast	36.4	1467
Volga-Viatka Region		
Mariy-El Republic	23.2	764
Mordova SSR	26.2	964
Chuvash Republic	18.3	1359
Kirov oblast	120.8	1701
Nizhnii Novgorod oblast	74.8	3697
Central–Black Earth Region		
Belgorod oblast	27.1	1423
Voronezh oblast	52.4	2488
Kursk oblast	29.8	1341

*Kaliningrad oblast is physically separate from Russia. Before World War II it was part of Eastern Prussia. It is situated on the Baltic Sea and borders on Lithuania and Poland.

Name of unit	Territory (in thousands sq. km.)	Population (in thousands)
Central–Black Earth Region (Continued)		
Lipetsk oblast	24.1	1241
Tambov oblast	34.3	1314
Volga Region		
Republic of Kalmykia (Khalmg Tangch)	76.1	322
Republic of Tatarstan	68.0	3723
Astrakhan´ oblast	44.1	1013
Volgograd oblast	113.9	2660
Penza oblast	43.2	1522
Samara oblast	53.6	3312
Saratov oblast	100.2	2722
Ul´yanovsk oblast	37.3	1462
North Caucasus Region		
Adygei Republic	7.6	447
Dagestan Republic	50.3	1925
Kabardino-Balkar Republic	12.5	786
Karachaev-Cherkess Republic	14.1	434
North Osetian SSR	8.0	651
Chechen and Ingush Republics**	19.3	1307
Krasnodar krai	76.0	4879
Stavropol´ krai	66.5	2580
Rostov oblast	100.8	4383
Urals Region		
Republic of Bashkortostan	143.6	4042
Udmurt Republic	42.1	1643
Kurgan oblast	71.0	1118
Orenburg oblast	124.0	2219
Perm´ oblast includes:	160.6	3106
Komi-Permyak autonomous okrug	32.9	161
Sverdlovsk oblast	194.8	4698
Chelyabinsk oblast	87.9	3634
Western Siberian Region		
Altai Republic	92.6	197
Altai krai	169.1	2682
Kemerovo oblast	95.5	3177
Novosibirsk oblast	178.2	2803

**Figures for the Chechen and Ingush Republics are reported as if they were still a single republic. Since 1992 they have been separated into two republics.

Table 2.3 (Continued)

Table 2.3 *(continued)*
Constituent Members of the Russian Federation, January 1, 1993

Name of unit	Territory (in thousands sq. km.)	Population (in thousands)
Western Siberian Region *(continued)*		
Omsk oblast	139.7	2176
Tomsk oblast	316.9	1008
Tiumen´ oblast includes:	1435.2	3120
Khanty-Mansiisk autonomous okrug	523.1	1301
Yamalo-Nenetsk autonomous okrug	750.3	465
Eastern Siberian Region		
Republic of Buryatia	351.3	1057
Republic of Tuva	170.5	306
Republic of Khakassia	61.9	583
Krasnoyarsk krai includes:	2339.7	3048
Taimyr (Dolgano-Nenetsk autonomous okrug)	862.1	51
Evenki autonomous okrug	767.6	24
Irkutsk oblast includes:	767.9	2872
Ust´-Ordyn Buryat autonomous okrug	22.4	142
Chita oblast includes:	431.5	1376
Agin-Buryat autonomous okrug	19.0	79
Far Eastern Region		
Republic of Sakha-Yakutia	3103.2	1074
Jewish autonomous oblast	36.0	219
Chukotka autonomous okrug	737.7	124
Primorsk krai	165.9	2302
Khabarovsk krai	788.6	1621
Amur oblast	363.7	1063
Kamchatka oblast includes:	472.3	456
Koryak autonomous okrug	301.5	38
Magadan oblast	461.4	327
Sakhalin oblast	87.1	714

Source: State Committee on Statistics of the Russian Federation, *Rossiiskaia Federatsiia v 1992: Statisticheskii ezhegodnik* (The Russian Federation in 1992: Statistical Annual) (Moscow: 1993).

attempted to raise their own status to that of republic. In 1993, the soviet of Sverdlovsk oblast, in the Urals, decided to change the region's constitutional status to that of a republic, and declared itself the "Urals Republic." Immediately President Yeltsin overturned the decision, and sacked the chairman of the soviet. He made it clear that the contagion of separatism would not be allowed to spread.

Republics, in turn, jealously guard their special status. Over 1990–92, all the republics adopted declarations of sovereignty and two made attempts to declare full or partial independence from Russia. In the mountainous region of the North Caucasus, between the Black and Caspian Seas, lies a belt of ethnic republics that includes the Chechen Republic (Chechnia) and several other predominantly Muslim republics. (Note that Dagestan is a kind of "dormitory" republic providing a common homeland to several small mountain peoples.) The other republic that sought to separate itself from Russia was the Tatar Republic, situated on the Volga, in an oil-rich and heavily industrialized region. Eventually Russia and Tatarstan worked out a special treaty arrangement satisfactory to both sides, and the separatist movement in Tatarstan gradually subsided.

Under the old regime, federalism in Russia, as in the Soviet Union, was largely formal. In recent years, Russia's constitutional order has evolved toward a more meaningful form of federalism, where constituent units of the federation possess a certain sphere of autonomy. The new constitution adopted in December 1993 did not settle the problem of federalism entirely, and largely preserved the status quo. But the new bicameral structure of the parliament went some way to making federalism real by ensuring that each of the 89 federal subjects had an equal number of representatives in the Council of the Federation. The Council of the Federation was given certain specific rights over matters of direct concern to regions, including budget and taxation policy. The Council of the Federation has strongly defended the prerogatives of the regions, which has helped to mitigate some of the intensity of the problem. With time, some of the nationalist passions that helped to drive the movements for separatism in the republics have subsided as populations have concluded that their economies are not likely to benefit from independence.

The relations between the central government and the governments of regions and republics vary considerably. Some subcentral governments have worked out special arrangements under which they are exempt from certain taxes, or permitted to retain a higher share of earnings from the exploitation of regional resources. In 1994, when the new Russian constitutional order was particularly fragile and fears of regional separatism were acute, the central government signed bilateral treaties with the Tatar Republic and Bashkir Republic (also known as Bashkortostan) under which the center conceded special privileges to the republics in return for their acknowledgment of the sovereignty of the federal state. Since then, the use of individually negotiated bilateral treaties has spread. By March 1997 the central government had concluded such treaties with 27 republics and regions. There was an especially intense phase of treaty-making when President Yeltsin was out on the hustings during his 1996 presidential election campaign. Typically, as part of a visit to a region, he would ceremoniously sign a treaty on power-sharing with the governor or head of state, clearly using the occasion of a treaty between the federal government and a region as a means of appealing to the regional authorities for their electoral support.[49] After the election the pace of treaty-making slowed down.

At the local level, Russia's constitutional order remains unsettled. The respective powers of regional and local governments still must be worked out in law and practice. After protracted battles, parliament passed a law granting local governments an autonomous sphere of power. However, the law remains largely an empty shell because there are still no clear legal guidelines specifying the taxing and

---

[49]OMRI Russian Regional Report, Vol. 2, No. 9, March 6, 1997.

spending powers of local governments. The problem arises from the fact that *regional* governments resist allowing local governments to exercise any significant powers of their own, and regional governments have a great deal of clout through their representation in the Federation Council. Moscow and St. Petersburg are exceptional cases because they have the status of regions. Therefore they are treated as "subjects of the federation" along with the other republics and regions, with their chief executives and the chairs of their legislative assemblies serving as members of the Federation Council. (The mayor of Moscow, Yuri Luzhkov, in fact wields a great deal of political power at the level of the federal government and is often mentioned as a possible contender for the presidency.) Other cities lack the power and autonomy of Moscow and St. Petersburg, and must bargain with their superior regional governments for shares of power.

At present, executive power in Russia's regions is a good deal more powerful than the legislative bodies in each region. Since Yeltsin decreed the dissolution of local soviets and the election of new representative bodies, nearly all regions and towns have elected new organs of representative power, called "dumas" and "assemblies." These are far smaller than the old soviets, and generally very weak. Regional and local executives dominate government; very often, staff officials of the executive branch form the largest contingent of representatives to the local assemblies. There is little separation of powers at the regional and local level.[50] A recent report by the Central Electoral Commission found that of the deputies elected to representative bodies in the regions in 1996, 20 percent were employees of commercial firms and banks, 25 percent were employed in municipal enterprises, and 25 percent were government employees and others on government payrolls, such as teachers.[51] Surveys have also found that the public has little confidence in the legislative branch of regional government but considerably more in the executive branch.[52]

Until 1996, President Yeltsin exercised direct administrative control over the oblasts and krais by appointing their chiefs of administration, often called "gubernatory" or governors.[53] The governor and his administration replace the former structure of regional power under the soviet system but, as in the past, are expected to be directly subordinate to the will of the center. Under a law passed by the Russian parliament in 1991, the heads of administration were to be elected by the voters in each region but Yeltsin persuaded the parliament to allow elections to be postponed for a year so that he could carry out his economic reforms. Finally, following the presidential elections in 1996, elections were held for the position of chief executive in most of the regions. In a majority of cases, the incumbent won. Elections of regional legislatures were also held in most regions, but these elections have seen a

---

[50]L. Smirnyagin, "Razdeleniia vlastei na mestakh bol´she ne sushchestvuet [Separation of Powers in the Localities No Longer Exists]," *Segodnia*, August 2, 1994. Leonid Smirnyagin is a distinguished Russian geographer and a former member of the presidential advisory council.

[51]*Segodnia*, February 22, 1997.

[52]Ibid.

[53]A valuable discussion of the evolution of regional governments' relations with the center in the post-Soviet period is Darrell Slider, "Federalism, Discord, and Accommodation: Intergovernmental Relations in Post-Soviet Russia," in Theodore H. Friedgut and Jeffrey W. Hahn, eds., *Local Power and Post-Soviet Politics* (Armonk, NY: M. E. Sharpe, 1994), pp. 239–269. The book contains several case studies as well.

near-total turnover in office. The results generally indicate that incumbent chief executives were able to persuade voters that despite the current economic hardships, keeping them in power was preferable to electing a new team which might be even worse.

In addition to the appointed chiefs of administration, in most regions Yeltsin also maintains a "presidential representative" who serves as his political eyes and ears, and helps keep tabs on local government and politics. Under a 1993 decree, the presidential representatives are also expected to coordinate the activity of federal organs on their territories, thus setting up a certain rivalry between the presidential representatives and the chiefs of administration. This rivalry is often intensified by the fact that for the most part, the presidential representatives belong to the democratic movement that entered politics in 1990 and 1991, while the heads of administrative tend to be conservative, pragmatic creatures of the old regime with strong roots in the local establishment. In July 1997, following the round of gubernatorial elections which gave most governors greater political independence, President Yeltsin issued a decree strengthening the institution of presidential representatives. Aiming to employ them as a counterweight to the newly elected governors, Yeltsin decreed that the representatives were to supervise the heads of regional branches of federal agencies, coordinate their work, and oversee the spending of federal funds. This was an effort to take back control over the appointment of the chiefs of the federal government's executive agencies in the regions, which had been effectively relegated to the governors. Thus Yeltsin was attempting to reassert the prerogatives of the federal executive in the face of the new electoral independence of the regional governments.[54]

The 21 republics have the constitutional power to determine their own form of state power so long as their decisions do not contradict federal law. The chief executive is either an elected president or the chairman of the republican parliament, usually still called, as in the past, the Supreme Soviet. In most, presidencies have been instituted. The republic leaderships are often adept at building their own powerbases around appeals to ethnic solidarity and demands to preserve the cultural autonomy of the indigenous nationality. In many cases, however, republic leaders have turned the inherited institutions of the Soviet system into personal political resources, and are very slow to expand political and economic rights. The center's power to enforce law is somewhat weaker in the republics than in ordinary regions, and hence tends to rely more on a combination of fiscal sticks and carrots.

Relations between the federal government and the governments of regions and republics reveal a considerable degree of conflict. Many regions have passed laws which, at least according to federal-level authorities, violate the Russian constitution. However, most of these disputes are coming before the Constitutional Court rather than being resolved by force. The Court has shown itself to be politically shrewd in defending the prerogatives of the federal government, trying to reconcile the interests of the center and the regions while reinforcing its own legitimate authority as an arbiter in intergovernmental disputes. It has struck down several laws adopted in republics and in ordinary territorial subjects that it found to conflict with the federal constitution, but it has also upheld several appeals from the regions

[54]*Segodnia*, March 31, 1997; RFE/RL Newsline, Vol. 1, No. 73, Part I, 15 July 1997.

against the unconstitutional intrusion of the federal government into the sphere of their legal power. Increasingly, much as in other federal states, the politics of federalism in Russia revolves around a continuous renegotiation of the relative powers of the center and the constituent members of the federation.

The fears that Russia would split apart much as the Soviet Union did proved to be exaggerated despite the tragic case of Chechnia. Although Russia also underwent a wave of ethnic-national mobilization within its national republics, separatism never reached the point where Russia itself as a national state was at the point of dissolution. The different demographic and administrative makeup of Russia, and Moscow's willingness to negotiate special arrangements with some of the national republics, have preserved Russia's integrity and begun the process of establishing a meaningful form of federalism. On the other hand, the central government's power over regional governments is very weak, and in many areas, local authorities wield arbitrary power much as they did before communism fell. Now that the chief executives of the regions and republics hold their office as a result of popular elections, their role as members of the Federation Council gives them even more influence and independence in national politics. Increasingly, Russian politics is becoming defined by the problems of federalism rather than by the struggle for democratic and market reform.

In this chapter we have surveyed the development of Russia's political institutions from the Soviet period to the present. We examined the four principal structural elements of the old Soviet system—the hierarchy of soviets, ethnic federalism, state socialism, and communist party dominance—and pointed out reasons why Gorbachev's attempts to reform the system from within produced radical unanticipated effects that finally brought the system down. Gorbachev successfully built a coalition of political leaders supportive of reform, and created new arenas and bases of power. By doing so they increased opportunities for other political forces to oppose democratic change. Some of the new movements aspired to replace the Soviet system with a liberal democratic one, others demanded independence for the national republics. Still others insisted on the restoration of the old communist system. Ultimately no compromise was possible among these incompatible forces.

Yeltsin succeeded in building a broad base of support in Russia by uniting radical democratic reformers with bureaucratic nationalists. With the help of this odd coalition of forces, he challenged Gorbachev for preeminence within Russia. He used his institutional prerogatives as president of the Russian republic to initiate a program of deep market-oriented reform and ultimately to disband the parliament when it came to be dominated by his opposition. Although he used force to end the institutional framework of the 1990–93 period, the new constitution that came into force in December 1993 provided a basis for democratic stability. Over 1994–97 the political system operated without major system-threatening crises and confrontations. But the great power that Yeltsin assigned to the presidency in the new constitution tempted both reformers and their opposition to circumvent constitutional principles in their drive to win control of it. In each period—during Gorbachev's reforms, the interim period in Russia, and the post-1993 period—leaders chose new structures for the exercise of power which affected their opponents' calculations. Future behavior of the still deeply divided political forces will determine whether the new political institutions in Russia can withstand the stresses of their competition for power.

Chapter 3

The Dynamics of Political Culture

One benefit of the democratic revolution in Russia is the opportunity it presents to Russians and outside observers to study objectively the way people evaluate the tremendous changes their society has undergone. We now have a great deal of information gathered from survey research. To be sure, the findings are often contradictory. Perhaps it is not surprising to find that popular attitudes about political and economic reform are inconsistent or subject to change, in view of the rapid pace of social change. In this century, Russia has undergone two great revolutionary upheavals, one in the second decade, when the tsarist autocracy fell and gave way to a new, revolutionary communist regime, and one at the beginning of the 1990s, when the communist regime in turn fell and gave way to a regime espousing liberal democratic and market principles. These experiences have left their imprint on contemporary Russian political culture, as has the equally profound shift from a rural, uneducated society to one that is overwhelmingly urban and highly educated.

Before we look at Russia's political culture more closely, however, let us take a short theoretical excursus to inquire what we mean by political culture, how we study it, and what bearing it has on a country's politics.

Political Culture Theory

Political scientists define political culture as the distribution of generalized orientations toward politics found in a given society. These orientations include values, i.e. the normative dimension (evaluative, or "ought" statements); beliefs, the cognitive dimension (what one believes to be true); and affective (emotional) dispositions, that is, those matters about which people experience pride, shame, desire, anger, or other feelings.[1]

---

[1]Gabriel A. Almond and Sidney Verba, *The Civic Culture: Political Attitudes and Democracy in Five Nations* (Boston: Little-Brown, 1965).

The subject of political culture has been the source of lively controversy in political science, not least in the field of Soviet and communist studies.[2] A major point of contention is how political culture is related to the structures and institutions of a political system. Political culture is never changeless, but tends to change gradually and incrementally, whereas political regimes sometimes undergo drastic and discontinuous changes. Therefore if political culture *directly* determined how a national political system operated, we could not explain some of the startling transformations in regimes that we have observed in our time. Some countries formerly considered to have deeply conservative, authoritarian political cultures have succeeded in sustaining viable and successful democratic polities after a major constitutional transition. Other countries considered to have pro-democratic political cultures have docilely accepted spells of authoritarian rule. Clearly there can be no simple causal arrow pointing from the distribution of values and beliefs in a society to its form of government at any given point in time. But is the obverse true, that the political and social institutions of a country determine the nature of its political culture? If so, we could not explain why so many regimes which have poured resources into shaping their populace's hearts and minds have had so little to show for their effort. Political culture may be malleable, but only up to a point.

Another related question is whether we should define political culture to include behavior or not.[3] If so, how would we separate out the influence of values and beliefs from other factors shaping people's political activity? But if it is treated separately, what reliable gauge do we have as to the real underlying structures of opinion which exist in the society? Survey research may not give us an accurate reading of a society's political culture since our own cultural biases affect the very measures we use. Ideally we would like to know what goals motivate people even if they are unable to act on them in the present. But it may be difficult to gain access to the real passions and motives of people, particularly where political oppression makes it impossible for them to express their views freely.

Over time, differences across countries in the composition of political cultures are stable but certainly not static. "Culture," political scientist Ronald Inglehart writes, "is not a constant. It is a system through which a society adapts to its environment: Given a changing environment, in the long run it is likely to change."[4] He provides evidence that national political cultures exert a major influence on their countries' political and economic performance, although, of course, their performance has in turn a feedback effect on the political culture. A successful democracy tends to reinforce the public's conviction that democratic institutions work better than the alternatives. But political cultures can evolve, sometimes taking significant turns, and Inglehart shows that one major way in which conditions may affect the values and beliefs of the members of a society is through generational suc-

---

[2]Gabriel A. Almond and Sidney Verba, eds. *The Civic Culture Revisited* (Boston: Little-Brown, 1980); Archie Brown, ed. *Political Culture and Communist Studies* (Armonk, NY: M. E. Sharpe, 1985); Ronald Inglehart, *Culture Shift in Advanced Industrial Society* (Princeton: Princeton University Press, 1990); Stephen White, *Political Culture and Soviet Politics* (London: Macmillan, 1979).

[3]Frederick J. Fleron, Jr., "Post-Soviet Political Culture in Russia: An Assessment of Recent Empirical Investigations," *Europe-Asia Studies* 48 (1996), pp. 225–260.

[4]Inglehart, *Culture Shift*, p. 55.

cession. People in their late teens and early twenties are especially susceptible to formative influences in their political and economic environment. At that age people often come to adhere to orientations which shape their outlook on politics and society for the rest of their lives. We shall see evidence of this phenomenon in Russia.

But if there is a feedback loop created by the constant interaction between political institutions and political culture, how can we determine how the political culture of a country is affecting the development of its political system? The effect is likely to differ between democratic and nondemocratic regimes.

To clarify these issues, let us suppose that there is a hypothetical country, country A. For any important political value, there is a distribution of opinion across the citizens—some citizens share the value strongly, some oppose it, some are ambivalent. One value we might be interested in is support for political liberty: how widely distributed is the view that political liberty is desirable? This is an empirical question, so we can conduct a survey of the attitudes of the population. Suppose that we administer a questionnaire to a random sample of respondents in country A, structured in such a way as to be representative of the adult population of the country. We might ask the following question: "Do you agree with the view that in the interests of protecting social order, the state should restrict individual liberties?" Suppose that at the moment we take our survey, which we shall call time t_0, we find the following distribution of opinion:

Country A, Time t_0: Support for Order Over Liberty (in Percentages)

Agree fully	10
Agree more than disagree	25
Sometimes yes, sometimes no	30
Disagree more than agree	25
Disagree fully	10

Some prefer order to liberty, others prefer liberty to order, and the largest percentage consider them to be roughly equal in importance.

Suppose further that we repeat our survey 40 years later and find that liberty is now more highly valued. Perhaps in the intervening period, educational levels have grown higher and people become more demanding and individualistic. Perhaps the society suffered under a dictatorship and people came to value liberty highly. In any case, we now find (at time t_1) the following distribution of responses:

Country A, Time t_1: Support for Order Over Liberty (in Percentages)

Agree fully	5
Agree more than disagree	10
Sometimes yes, sometimes no	20
Disagree more than agree	30
Disagree fully	35

The distribution has shifted considerably in the direction of support for liberty over order.

How would we expect the government to be affected by the change in the distribution of political values in the society? If the political system is a democracy, then we would imagine that newer generations of politicians would rise to power by promising to widen the sphere of individual liberty in order to appeal to voters. They might pass new laws limiting government's rights to conduct wiretaps and infiltrate radical organizations.

But what if the political system is not a democracy? In a case where the regime's policies grow increasingly unpopular, but there is no way in which the citizens can affect them, we would expect that the citizens would become increasingly dissatisfied with the entire system. Since it is not a democracy, the citizens cannot change the direction of policy through elections and public opinion. If there is public protest, the regime will probably repress it by force. But how long can the regime draw down the reserves of support it possesses without replenishing them through policy successes? Often such systems drift to a frontier where catastrophe strikes: lacking the ability to gauge reliably the point at which the society will simply balk at going along with the regime's demands any longer, the authorities rule with a mixture of carrots and sticks. They punish those who dissent from the system, and reward those who make notable contributions to it. But they operate in fear and insecurity about when and whether they will reach a point of crisis, where they will face a massive general strike or popular uprising.

The early Bolshevik regime faced a situation somewhat like this in early 1921, when the sailors at the key naval garrison of Kronstadt, located in the mouth of the Gulf of Finland, outside Petrograd,[5] mutinied against Bolshevik rule, calling for "soviets without Bolsheviks." Just before this, widespread strikes among urban workers broke out in Petrograd and Moscow. And in the countryside, there was a large-scale peasant rebellion that the Red Army was trying to suppress. All at once, and on multiple fronts, the fledgling Bolshevik regime faced the possibility of breakdown, almost without warning, after having weathered the terrible storm of the civil war against the anticommunist White armies.[6] Why exactly did breakdown occur at that moment? For that matter, why did the tsarist regime break down suddenly in February 1917, or the Soviet and other East European communist regimes unravel so suddenly in the 1989–91 period? One reason is that the authorities, lacking a mechanism to recognize and respond to grave popular discontent, only saw the crisis after it had burst into the open. As the system draws closer to the frontier beyond which people will not tolerate it any longer, the calculus of risks and benefits for the regime's officials and for ordinary citizens to support the regime shifts at an increasing pace. Going along with the system brings ever fewer rewards while turning against it seems less dangerous. People begin to see the once mighty regime as weak. Finally, once the balance of incentives turns enough so that refusing to go

---

[5]Petrograd was the city's name from 1914–24. When Lenin died the city was given the name Leningrad in his honor. After the end of the Soviet regime it took back its original name of St. Petersburg.

[6]The regime replied with both force and concessions. Suppressing the Kronstadt uprising by bloody force, they simultaneously announced the relaxation of the draconian restrictions on private production and trade that had been enforced during the civil war period. Thus, under duress, they introduced the New Economic Policy (1921–29) which allowed a mixed economy comprising both state ownership of heavy industry and private peasant production for the market.

along is less risky than joining the opposition, no one wants to be the last to leave the losing side and the withdrawal of support resembles a stampede. When collapse in an authoritarian system comes, it can come with extraordinary rapidity and force.[7]

It oversimplifies the concept of political culture to suppose that a society has one dominant central tendency in its political culture. There are, of course, many important issues over which citizens hold opinions, values, and feelings. But regardless of how many major dimensions a particular political culture possesses, one crucial question is how consensual or how divided the society is.

Let us take another hypothetical example. Suppose we find in a survey of a second country, country B, that instead of one predominant value orientation in the society, there are two. Our survey yields the following results, suggesting that society is polarized between two very different subcultures that are roughly equal in strength:

Country B, Time t_1: Support for Order Over Liberty (in Percentages)

Agree fully	30
Agree more than disagree	15
Sometimes yes, sometimes no	10
Disagree more than agree	15
Disagree fully	30

Polarization of this degree might come about if a society comprises two or more culturally distinct communities, such as ethnic or religious groups. Their political cultures may be closely tied to their group identities. Change over time or dissent within the group can threaten the group's cohesiveness or even survival. But over time change may come as one group grows in population size more than the other, or grows more urbanized or prosperous. If the political culture is differentiated by cleavages stemming from ethnic and religious identity, a shift in the relative size and weight of the different groups might result in the unraveling of the very political regime—unless there is some way to accommodate the demands of the assertive group that does not deprive another group of rights and privileges it has formerly enjoyed. In a more homogeneous political culture, a single national identity may be dominant, and then the national culture may define itself and claim its rights through a relationship with a neighboring nation. Cultural differences within or between societies may reinforce differing identities and conflicting claims to territory, resources, and political rights.[8]

In each case, whether the political system is democratic and responds to changes in the distribution of political attitudes and values in society through the electoral process, or is authoritarian and faces the risk of crisis and breakdown through the unseen effects of change, or whether culture is tied up in a bundle with

[7]Mancur Olson, "The Logic of Collective Action in Soviet-type Societies," *Journal of Soviet Nationalities* I:2 (Summer 1990), pp. 8–27.

[8]Donald Horowitz, *Ethnic Groups in Conflict* (Berkeley: University of California Press, 1985).

group identities and demands, political culture affects the way political elites interact with the populace of a country. It does not do so by itself, of course: it does so
through the medium of political action by interested individuals, such as party leaders, interest group activists, government officials, and elected representatives. In a
democracy elites compete for power through appeals for popular support: they seek
to respond to, or even to sharpen, differences in orientations on the part of different segments of the citizenry, or they may establish broad coalitions of support by
aggregating the demands of many different groups. Changes and diversity in political culture provide politicians in democratic societies with challenges and opportunities. They seek politically usable openings to intensify differences or soften them,
and in doing so, they typically shape and direct the course of policy and the structure of institutions.

In the case of authoritarian systems, elites resort to a variety of means to mold
political culture to their purposes, and suppress any expression of dissenting views.
They attempt to inspire popular identification with symbols of national power and
purpose, but they always worry whether some catastrophic failure of national unity
awaits them around the next bend.

For societies where the political culture is tightly bound up with national identity, politicians may outbid rival politicians for power and support by exacerbating
the conflict between one national community and another, within or across state
boundaries. Others, however, may link their political fate to the pursuit of national
greatness through other forms of collective purpose, such as hard work, high savings, and low consumption. The old is redefined and made to serve the new. Or
politicians may arise in a region where a particular group predominates and call
into question the legitimacy of the state, demanding sovereignty or even secession.
Conflicting claims to sovereign control over the homeland may be irreconcilable
within a particular constitutional framework.

In short, one way in which political culture affects the development of political
systems is through the strategies of political elites. Through their political parties
and interest groups, their electoral campaigns and stump speeches, political elites
convert the broad sets of political values, beliefs, and emotions that pervade society
into programs, ideologies, and policies. For this reason, we now turn from the examination of the ways that Russia's political leadership formed, reformed, and
responded to the institutions of government, and survey the composition and development of Russian political culture.

Russian Political Culture in the Post-Soviet Period

How are values and attitudes about political freedom and order and other key issues
distributed in Russian society? On some points, the findings of a large number of
recent opinion studies converge. Survey researchers have found a sturdy core of
commitment to democratic values in Russian society together with very high dissatisfaction with the current regime and very low levels of confidence in existing political institutions. Support for some features of a market economy is high but low for

others, and dissatisfaction with the performance of the current economic system is even higher than that with the political regime. A number of studies have also found that a majority of the population supports the idea that the state should own heavy industry.[9] Generally speaking, surveys show that there is a high level of support for principles associated with liberal democracy: political tolerance; political liberty; individual rights; rights of opposition and dissent; independence of the communications media; and competitive elections.[10] James Gibson and Raymond Duch sum up their findings on these questions by observing that there is widespread support for the values and institutions of liberal democracy but that support for political rights for oneself is higher than acceptance of the rights of one's political opponents, and that a conception of democracy as majority rule is widely embraced, but respect for the rights of minorities is less firm.[11]

Dissatisfaction with the current political arrangements is very high: by a majority, Russians rate the present system negatively and by an even wider majority, they rate the pre-Gorbachev communist system favorably. However, Russians also rate very favorably the greater political freedoms that they possess now, and very few would wish to restore the old communist system. Surveys from the New Russia Barometer conducted by Richard Rose and his associates based on a sample representing the adult Russian population confirm the contradictory nature of these currents of public opinion.[12] See Table 3.1 and Table 3.2.

The rather high levels of support found for basic democratic principles such as religious liberty, freedom of speech, competitive elections, and other rights challenge an impression that was widely held in the West, that Russian political culture was conservative, traditional, and influenced by decades of Soviet communist practice and indoctrination. In some respects, indeed, Soviet propaganda reinforced older official values, such as the enormous emphasis placed on state power, the expectation that the state would provide for the material well-being of its citizens, the hierarchical way of conceptualizing formal authority, and the priority of collective over individual needs. Consequently, it is not surprising to find a rather high

---

[9]Stephen Whitefield and Geofrey Evans, "The Russian Election of 1993: Public Opinion and the Transition Experience," *Post-Soviet Affairs* 10 (1994), pp. 46–49; William Zimmerman, "Markets, Democracy and Russian Foreign Policy," *Post-Soviet Affairs* 10 (1994), pp. 103–126; Donna Bahry, "Society Transformed? Rethinking the Social Roots of Perestroika," *Slavic Review* 52:3 (Fall 1993), pp. 511–554.

[10]James L. Gibson and Raymond M. Duch, "Emerging Democratic Values in Soviet Political Culture," in Arthur H. Miller, William M. Reisinger, and Vicki L. Hesli, eds., *Public Opinion and Regime Change* (Boulder: Westview Press, 1993), pp. 69–94; William M. Reisinger, Arthur H. Miller, and Vicki L. Hesli, "Political Values in Russia, Ukraine and Lithuania: Sources and Implications for Democracy," *British Journal of Political Science* 24 (1994), pp. 183–223; and Jeffrey W. Hahn, "Continuity and Change in Russian Political Culture," *British Journal of Political Science* 21(4) (1991), pp. 393–421.

[11]James L. Gibson, "A Mile Wide But an Inch Deep (?): The Structure of Democratic Commitments in the Former USSR," *American Journal of Political Science* 40 (1994), pp. 396–420; James L. Gibson and Raymond M. Duch, "Emerging Democratic Values in Soviet Political Culture."

[12]Table 3.1 from: Richard Rose and Evgeny Tikhomirov, "Trends in the New Russia Barometer, 1992–1995," paper no. 256, Studies in Public Policy (Glasgow, UK: University of Strathclyde, 1995), p. 21; Table 3.2 from: Stephen White, Richard Rose, and Ian McAllister, *How Russia Votes* (Chatham, NJ: Chatham House, 1996), p. 46.

──────────────────────────TABLE 3.1──────────────────────────

Distribution of responses to the question: Compared to our system of government before perestroika, would you say that our current system is better, much the same, or not so good as the old system in allowing people to:

	1993 (Percentage)	1994 (Percentage)	Change (Percentage)
Everybody has freedom of choice in religious matters			
Better	71	83	12
Much the same	29	15	−14
Worse	6	2	−4
Everybody has a right to say what they think			
Better	65	73	8
Much the same	27	18	−8
Worse	8	8	0
One can join any organization one likes			
Better	63	77	14
Much the same	28	18	−10
Worse	9	5	−4
Everyone can decide individually whether or not to take an interest in politics			
Better	57	62	5
Much the same	39	33	−6
Worse	4	5	1

Source: Richard Rose and Evgeny Tikhomirov, "Trends in the New Russian Barometer 1992–1995," paper no. 25, Studies in Public Policy (Glasgow, UK: University of Strathclyde, 1995), p. 21. Reprinted by permission.

──────────────────────────TABLE 3.2──────────────────────────

Distribution of responses to the question: Our current political system is not the only possible one. Some people say that another would be better for us. What do you think? Here are some statements; please tell me to what extent you agree with each of them.

Strongly Agree	Agree	Disagree	Strongly Disagree	Don't Know
Experts, not parliament and government, should make the most important economic decisions.				
26 %	28 %	12 %	6 %	28 %
We do not need parliament or elections, but instead a strong leader who can make decisions and put them into effect fast.				
21	22	20	20	16
It would be better to restore the former communist system.				
9	14	28	34	15
The army should rule.				
3	7	23	55	12
The tsar should be restored.				
4	5	18	52	21

Source: Stephen White, Richard Rose, and Ian McAllister, *How Russia Votes* (Chatham, NJ: Chatham House, 1996), p. 46. Reprinted by permission.

degree of continuity in the level of support for values concerning the state's respon-sibility for ensuring society's prosperity and for providing individuals with material security.[13]

A set of surveys of the general public and of political elites conducted by William Zimmerman in 1993 tapped attitudes about political and economic values. To measure whether people generally preferred market or socialist institutions, Zimmerman asked a battery of questions about acceptance of economic competi-tion, entrepreneurial risk, inequality of earnings, and state ownership of heavy industry. The responses to these items were combined into a single index to mea-sure whether respondents favored a socialist or a market system. Only about 27 per-cent of the general public fell more on the pro-market side of the spectrum. But among respondents who had had at least some higher education, 54 percent were supporters of the market. And among the 200 individuals who were sampled from Russia's governmental, media, military, foreign policy, and economic elites, 80 per-cent favored the market.[14] Other surveys also find that a majority of Russians favor extensive state economic controls and protections even while they are willing to express support for some principles of market competition.[15] It may be that higher levels of education tend to bring about higher levels of ideological consistency in people's outlooks on basic political and economic choices. But it is scarcely surpris-ing that the central tendency in Russians' economic values should favor a mixed economy with an interventionist state.

What is more surprising is the high level of support for democratic values that developed during the period of Soviet rule despite official antagonism to liberal democracy. Before looking more closely at the structure of political values and beliefs in contemporary Russian society, let us examine the old regime's program to shape the values and beliefs of Soviet citizens. Then we may be able to understand better the level and nature of support for democratic values.

Soviet Political Socialization

Throughout the regime's history, Soviet rulers placed a high priority on inculcating knowledge of and commitment to regime doctrine among the population. The sys-tem of formal political socialization embraced virtually every setting of education and communication in society—from schools and youth activity, to the mass media, to the arts and popular culture, and to collective activity in the workplace, place of residence, and avocational groups. As much as possible, influences that contradict-ed Marxist–Leninist doctrine were suppressed, while the rhetoric of public life con-stantly reaffirmed the doctrine of the leading role of the Communist Party, the supe-riority of socialism, devotion to the Soviet fatherland, and the correctness of the

---

[13]James R. Millar and Sharon L. Wolchik, "Introduction: The Social Legacies and the Aftermath of Com-munism," in James R. Millar and Sharon L. Wolchik, eds., *The Social Legacy of Communism* (Washington, D.C. and Cambridge: Woodrow Wilson Press and Cambridge University Press, 1994), p. 16.

[14]William Zimmerman, "Markets, Democracy and Russian Foreign Policy," *Post-Soviet Affairs* 10 (1994), pp. 103–126; William Zimmerman, "Synoptic Thinking and Political Culture in Post-Soviet Russia," *Slav-ic Review* 54 (1995), pp. 630–641.

[15]Whitefield and Evans, "The Russian Election of 1993."

party's general policies at home and abroad. Because of the importance the regime assigned to the means of mass communications as agencies of political socialization and of mass mobilization, it saturated Soviet society with multiple channels of print and broadcast communications.[16]

The doctrine of Marxism–Leninism which guided political socialization was based on the ideas of Karl Marx and Friedrich Engels as interpreted and applied by Vladimir Lenin and the Soviet communist party's leaders. Each new leadership that came to power reinterpreted Marxist–Leninist ideas to serve its policy interests, often discarding concepts promulgated by the preceding leaders. The doctrine was highly flexible and was interpreted to justify the preferences and decisions of the party leadership. Ideological doctrine and political authority were always closely linked because power and ideology legitimated one another. This pattern was a source of strength so long as there was no serious challenge to the leaders' power or policy. But it also gave rise to a dogmatic intolerance of any criticism of the tenets of the doctrine itself, or of the leaders' interpretation of it. Dogmatism in the Brezhnev period, as under Stalin, stifled innovation and serious discussion of the trends affecting society.

The party's demand for full loyalty to the party and its doctrines prohibited any alternative doctrines from being aired in public life. In foreign policy, the doctrine of "peaceful coexistence" with the capitalist world referred to the possibility that conflicting social systems, socialism and capitalism, might have correct and even cooperative relations at the level of diplomacy, trade, and cultural and scientific contacts, but that at the fundamental level of ideas, the two ideologies were ultimately incompatible and in the end socialism would triumph over capitalism because of its intrinsic superiority. Soviet leaders, especially the more conservative of them, were always suspicious of any notion that the struggle between the world system of capitalism and the world system of socialism should be put aside in favor of a convergence of ideologies. They often quoted Lenin to the effect that any weakening of socialist ideology would inevitably lead to a strengthening of bourgeois ideology. The state's propaganda system thus had a twofold purpose: to persuade Soviet people of the correctness of party doctrine, and to prevent hostile ideologies from winning adherents.

The elaborate machinery for propagating and defending ideology included the following features:

1. *Family.* Efforts were made to persuade parents to make the family an instrument for raising children steeped in communist morality, firm faith in the party and its leadership, a positive attitude toward labor, confidence in the socialist future, and intolerance toward hostile world views, such as religion. But, because the family was the least amenable to control by the party authorities, and because it tended to protect value systems at odds with the official ideology, the family has

---

[16]On the impact of television in Soviet society, see Ellen Mickiewicz, *Split Signals: Television and Politics in the Soviet Union* (New York and Oxford: Oxford University Press, 1988); on propaganda and mass communications more generally, see Stephen White, *Political Culture and Soviet Politics* (London: Macmillan, 1979), and Thomas F. Remington, *The Truth of Authority: Ideology and Communication in the Soviet Union* (Pittsburgh: University of Pittsburgh Press, 1988).

long been the most important agency of transmission of liberal democratic values, national awareness, and religious faith.

2. *School.* Schooling contributed to political socialization both through the curriculum, where lessons in history, social studies, literature, and other subjects were used to reinforce political doctrines, and through a system of youth groups which organized school-time and after-school activities.

3. *Youth groups.* The regime maintained a set of organized youth leagues for different age categories that combined political indoctrination with organized activities such as field trips, hobby clubs, service activities, summer camps, and study circles. The three groups—Octobrists, for 7- to 9-year-olds; Pioneers, for 9- to 14-year-olds; and Komsomol (the acronym for the Communist Youth League), for 14- to 28-year-olds—each combined play, recreation, and basic socialization with political indoctrination appropriate to the age level. Many youths who remained active in Komsomol into their 20s were admitted directly to the Communist Party from Komsomol on the strength of their good records as Komsomol members.

4. *The mass media.* Officially the broadcast and print media were to serve as instruments of political socialization, in addition to their roles as conduits of needed information, exhorters to work hard and well, critics of social problems, and providers of feedback from the public. They were thus called upon to mold the consciousness of the population while at the same time combatting the system's inefficiencies. All mass media organizations were under the ideological authority of the party through its department of propaganda and similar departments charged with ideological oversight in every lower party committee.

5. *Adult political education.* The party oversaw a system of workplace talks and political study groups for various categories of the population—workers, managers, political executives, and so on. Party-run schools gave local party staff members up-to-date instruction on current party doctrine and policy; some even conferred graduate degrees in such topics as the theory of scientific communism.

Despite the enormous effort devoted to political indoctrination, studies showed that the impact of this effort was extremely low and was even counter-productive. Why then did the party persist in keeping it going? Various reasons have been proposed. One is inertia. The section of the party concerned with ideological propaganda and control justified its existence by ever greater displays of quantitative success, increasing the number of people reached and activists recruited. Another is fear. The leadership behaved as though it genuinely believed its claim that any weakening of socialist ideology must necessarily lead to a rise of hostile counter-ideologies. However ineffective the party's ideological effort may have been, it helped to combat the spread of ideas and values opposed to Marxism–Leninism. Ultimately, the reason ideological control over society was so important to the party was that it prevented the formation of opposition movements espousing alternative ideologies. In any event, no Soviet leader until Gorbachev was willing to relinquish the party's monopoly upon ideology, and even Gorbachev, when he first came to office, used the traditional powers of the general secretary to reprogram and redirect party propaganda, rather than to dismantle the system itself.

Gorbachev very quickly set his own stamp upon the propaganda system, declaring that society was in need of an "acceleration" of the tempo of socioeconomic progress. This was to be achieved by a campaign to upgrade the technological level of Soviet industry, especially by introducing computers and information technology widely into the economy. Another one of Gorbachev's early policy themes, around which an old-fashioned ideological campaign was mounted, was his assault on alcohol abuse. Within two months of his coming to power, officials were forbidden to drink in public, many liquor stores were closed, hours for purchases of liquor were limited, and a number of plants producing wines and spirits were closed or turned to other purposes.[17] Still another one of the new policy themes was encouragement for more honest and open criticism of problems in society—a policy identified by the term *glasnost´*.

At first, the reformist line of the new leadership in the mid-1980s hardly affected either the forms or content of "communist upbringing." In day-care facilities and in schools, teachers continued to teach children to revere Lenin as one who loved mankind and embodied its highest ideals. As in the past, basic moral education was identified with communist philosophy. Even in secondary school and higher educational institutions, the curriculum was little affected by the ideological ferment occurring in society until around 1989. Students continued to be required to pass courses on Lenin's and the party's teachings. A scandal occurred in the spring of 1988 when, all across the Soviet Union, history exams in secondary schools had to be cancelled because the old textbooks were considered inaccurate (they glossed over the magnitude of Stalin's terror) and new textbooks were not available. Yet, on the whole, the old structures of ideological indoctrination and control continued to soldier on in a traditional spirit until 1989–90, when the radical changes in the leadership's thinking and behavior finally provoked a crisis at all levels of the propaganda and socialization system.

The mass media also reflected the inertia and slowness with which the ideological changes made at the top rippled out across the hierarchy of media organizations. Before Gorbachev the mass media had been under pervasive political control. The supply of newsprint was controlled by a state monopoly. All printing equipment had to be licensed by the government. The Communist Party selected all senior editors. The content of everything published or aired was subject to prior review by the party's ideological sector. Although unofficial, independent publications existed (called *samizdat,* or "self-publishing"), these were illegal and their publishers and distributors could be arrested and charged with spreading anti-Soviet propaganda.

But after a slow start, the *glasnost´* campaign gained momentum: ultimately it had far-reaching consequences.[18] Eventually it produced significant feedback on the party's socialization program by discrediting socialism both in theory and practice. By late 1990, public opinion polls revealed that no more than 10–20 percent of the population professed support for the socialist principles on which the state was

---

[17]Stephen White, *Russia Goes Dry: Alcohol, State and Society* (Cambridge: Cambridge University Press, 1996). This study uses the anti-alcohol campaign of the early Gorbachev period as an illustration of the weakness of policy implementation in the late Soviet period.

[18]Thomas Remington, "A Socialist Pluralism of Opinions: Glasnost´ and Policy-Making under Gorbachev," *Russian Review* 48 (1989), pp. 271–304.

founded.[19] A poll of nearly 2,700 people throughout the Soviet Union in December 1989 found that 48 percent considered themselves religious believers, but only 6 percent thought that Marxism–Leninism had the answers to the country's problems.[20] Another nationwide survey in 1989 found that 61 percent of the respondents supported the principle of legalizing private property and only 11 percent opposed it.[21] Over 1989 and 1990 there were many other indications of the power and speed of popular rejection of communist ideology. Close to two million members—one-tenth of the membership—quit the Communist Party before Yeltsin banned it in September 1991. A radical reform wing of the Communist Party itself threatened to break away and form an alternative party.

At the same time, the policy positions taken by Gorbachev and the party leadership grew progressively more unorthodox, until by 1990 almost nothing of the old Marxist–Leninist doctrine remained. The theory of the international class struggle between capitalism and socialism was gone; the party's leading role had been abandoned in favor of support for multiparty competition and parliamentary politics; and Gorbachev called his domestic program a transition to a "social market economy." In the document adopted as a basis for economic policy for 1991 and 1992, Gorbachev endorsed the following statement, which acknowledged the failure of the system of central planning imposed under Stalin:

> There is no alternative to switching to a market. All world experience has shown the viability and effectiveness of the market economy. The switch to such an economy in our society is dictated solely by people's interests and aims to create a socially oriented economy, gear all production to consumer needs, overcome the shortages and disgraceful queues, ensure citizens' de facto economic freedom, and establish conditions for encouraging hard work, initiative, and high productivity.
>
> The transition to the market does not contradict our people's socialist choice. Only the market, combined with the humanist orientation of all society, is capable of ensuring the satisfaction of people's needs, the fair distribution of wealth, social rights and guarantees for citizens, and the strengthening of freedom and democracy.[22]

By the end of 1990, Marxism–Leninism was essentially defunct. The doctrine had been abandoned in all essential points by the Communist Party, and the party itself

---

[19]Bill Keller, "At Mrs. Gorbachev's School, Hardly a Commuinist in Sight," *New York Times*, November 4, 1990.

[20]Yu. Levada et al., "Homo Sovieticus: A Rough Sketch," *Moscow News*, no. 11 (1990), p. 11.

[21]Tatiana Zaslavskaia, "Vesti dialog s liud´mi," *Narodnyi deputat*, no. 2 (1990), pp. 25–27. Zaslavskaia is a distinguished sociologist who was one of the most important theorists of reform in the pre-Gorbachev and early Gorbachev periods. A member of the Academy of Sciences and a deputy to the Congress of People's Deputies, she founded a new institute to conduct public opinion surveys throughout the Soviet Union.

[22]"Main Directions for the Stabilization of the National Economy and the Transition to a Market Economy," as published in the British Broadcasting System Summary of World Broadcasts (BBC SWB), SU/0900, 20 October 1990, p. C/1. This policy statement was adopted as the basis of national economic policy by the USSR Supreme Soviet on October 19, 1990. It is important mainly as a statement of goals and principles rather than as a working program of action.

had lost its power to rule the country's ideological life. Both among the leadership and among the populace, only a small minority remained willing to defend communist ideology. Indeed, there is evidence that political elites are more supportive of liberal democratic values than is the general public—more inclined, for instance, to disagree with the idea that only one philosophy in the world is correct.[23]

As Marxism–Leninism declined, what political values gained strength? The many surveys that have been conducted give us some convergent evidence on this point.

Support for Democratic Values

In early 1990 a political scientist named James Gibson and a team of American and Soviet researchers conducted a survey of 504 residents of the Moscow *oblast*—the region around the city of Moscow—to determine support for important values associated with liberal democracy. They found surprisingly high levels of support for liberal values. On such issues as whether freedom of speech should always be respected, they found the Soviet respondents to hold roughly the same views as citizens of West European countries (77 percent in agreement for the Moscow province population, 78 percent for the West Europeans). On a series of items, measured by the percent agreeing that a particular right ought always to be respected, Soviet citizens were extraordinarily similar to West Europeans. Table 3.3 reports their findings.[24]

Note that the only area in which the Moscow population appears to differ from Western citizens is in unequivocal support for the right to associate. This difference lends some credence to the possibility that these responses are not simply instances of the often-noted tendency of Soviet citizens to agree with the conventional wisdom of the time.

In addition, Gibson et al. found that education was positively associated with rights consciousness, much as age and being female were negatively correlated with it; these were the only significantly associated variables they established from analysis of demographic factors. The impact of education was particularly strong: on average, the higher a person's educational level, the more likely he or she was to endorse the principle of individual political rights. By the same token, the older a person was, all else being equal, the weaker the support for individual rights. Women were on the whole slightly less supportive of individual rights than were men, even after controlling for the effects of education and age.

Gibson's group extended the survey to the entire western portion of the USSR in May 1990 and found remarkably similar responses—that is, extremely high levels of support for liberal values with the single exception of the freedom of association, where fewer than half of the respondents agreed that the right must be respected

---

[23]Of an elite sample studied by William Zimmerman 93 percent disagreed with this statement, as did about 60 percent of the respondents in a mass sample. Zimmerman, "Markets, Democracy and Russian Foreign Policy."

[24]James L. Gibson, Raymond M. Duch, and Kent L. Tedin, "Democratic Values and the Transformation of the Soviet Union," *Journal of Politics* 54 (1992), p. 346.

--------------------TABLE 3.3--------------------
Rights Consciousness, European Community and Moscow Oblast

	All EC	Moscow Oblast
Freedom of speech	78.4	77.0
Personal safety	88.8	92.9
Freedom of association	64.9	50.0
Cultural autonomy	82.0	93.3
Freedom of conscience	85.9	91.7
Equality before the law	90.0	95.6
Right of asylum	55.1	–
Right to work	91.9	93.7
Right to property	82.0	90.7
Right to education	95.5	95.0
Freedom of information	85.1	83.3
Right to privacy	94.1	80.6
Right to travel abroad	–	71.0
Percentage demanding *all* rights	25.7	36.3

Source: James L. Gibson, Raymond M. Duch, and Kent L. Tedin, "Democratic Values and the Transformation of the Soviet Union," *Journal of Politics* 54 (1992), p. 346. Reprinted by permission.

always, and around 40 percent believed that it depends on circumstances.[25] Once again, education and age were significantly correlated with rights consciousness: education positively, age negatively.

Given Russia's authoritarian history, it is reasonable to wonder whether findings such as these tap into deep and lasting convictions of the public, or capture the shibboleths and hopes of a particularly optimistic moment in time. Let us address two separate aspects of this question. First is the matter of whether these values are real and meaningful for Russian citizens or whether instead they represent glittering abstractions with no bearing on the actual day-to-day choices that citizens face in their interactions with the political system. One way to test this possibility is to examine how different kinds of democratic values are interrelated. Do democratic values cluster together in a logically coherent way, such that a person who supports the idea of competitive elections also values personal liberty, a free press, and the right of dissent? Employing factor analysis, a statistical technique which reveals underlying patterns of association among a set of variables, Gibson and his colleagues found that there was a strong connecting thread throughout the responses to the surveys: respondents who tended to be pro-democratic on some items tended to be democratic on the entire democratic spectrum. This outlook consisted of support for competitive elections and personal liberty, as well as, though with a little less consistency, belief in the need for a free press, acceptance of the right of dissent, and support for political rights. Significantly, support for the value of tolerance for political opposition was not strongly related to the democratic syndrome. Gibson and Duch drew

---

[25]Gibson and Duch, "Emerging Democratic Values," p. 79.

two conclusions from these findings. First, support for democratic values was stronger when they are formulated abstractly, without specific reference to one's political enemies. Second, people are more willing to support democratic rights for themselves than for their opponents. Both points appear to be reasonable in the context of a society in which people were denied political rights for a long time—but where they were taught to fear the consequences of anarchy and disorder.

Our second question, whether democratic values are stable, is difficult to answer, given the very short window of time that we have to measure trends in the distribution of values and beliefs in Russian society. Were the findings of Gibson and other researchers who have found relatively high levels of support for democracy simply reflections of a fleeting moment in the early 1990s of optimistic enthusiasm for democratic rights and liberties? As James Gibson puts it, "Like religion, Levis, and Snickers, democracy became fashionable in the USSR."[26] If democracy was a fair-weather fashion, we might anticipate that support would soon wither in the face of social tension, widespread crime, and economic insecurity. Several studies have attempted to determine whether support for democratic values is stable, or whether it will fade as times get hard and democratic hopes are disappointed. The findings show that democratic values seem to hold up over time, while support for market institutions is more volatile. Gibson and his colleagues found, using panel data,[27] that between 1990 and 1992, respondents tended to maintain the same political views, while their views on economic institutions diverged sharply.[28] The major Russian public opinion survey institute, the All-Russian Center for the Study of Public Opinion (VTsIOM), has been asking respondents every two months since spring 1992 whether they believed that the only way out of the situation in which Russia finds itself is by the establishment of a strong dictatorship. The proportion responding affirmatively has fluctuated between 31 percent and 25 percent; it has never been higher than 36 percent nor lower than 19 percent. The proportion disagreeing has hovered around 50 percent—rising to 52 percent at its highest, and falling to 37 percent at its lowest. Thus there seems to be a certain stable core of agreement that dictatorship is not an acceptable answer to Russia's problems.[29]

On the other hand, however much Russians may believe in the principles of liberal democracy, they have little confidence in the present postcommunist regime. In contrast to the populations of most East European states, Russians consistently rate the old pre-Gorbachev communist regime more favorably than the current postcommunist one: in a survey in March 1995, Richard Rose and his associates found that two-thirds of the respondents gave a positive evaluation of the political system before perestroika began.[30] A 1993 survey distinguished between commitment to the principles of democracy and people's assessments of how Russia's cur-

---

[26]James L. Gibson, "A Mile Wide but an Inch Deep (?)," p. 397.

[27]A panel study is one which surveys the same sample of respondents at several different points over a given period of time. That way it is possible to judge whether the same people continue to hold the same views over time, or whether their opinions change.

[28]Gibson, "A Mile Wide but an Inch Deep (?)."

[29]*Segodnia*, August 27, 1994.

[30]Richard Rose, "Russia as an Hour-Glass Society: A Constitution without Citizens," *East European Constitutional Review* 4 (1995), p. 39.

———————————————————————TABLE 3.4———————————————————————
Trust in Institutions, 1993–95 (in percent)

	June 1993	July 1994	February 1995
Orthodox Church	48	46	47
Mass media	26	20	21
Armed forces	39	37	24
Security services	20	21	13
Local government	13	11	13
Regional government	10	8	13
Courts, police	16	14	9
Parliament	9	5	4
Government	18	7	6
President	28	16	8
Trade unions	13	8	8

Source: Stephen White, "The Presidency and Political Leadership in Post-Communist Russia," in Peter Lentini, ed., *Elections and Political Order in Russia: The Implications of the 1993 Elections to the Federal Assembly* (Budapest: Central European University Press, 1995), p. 215. Reprinted by permission.

rent political institutions are performing, and found a wide divergence. Around half the sample expressed support for democratic values, but only one-fifth gave favorable evaluations of the way these principles were realized in Russia.[31]

Consistent with this theme of acceptance of democracy in general and sharp antagonism toward the actual present-day regime are the findings of many surveys that Russians have lower confidence in present-day representative political institutions than in such structures as the army and the Orthodox Church. Surveys over the past few years conducted by the All-Russian Public Opinion Research Institute, have asked a battery of questions about which institutions respondents had confidence in.[32] (See Table 3.4.)

The results suggest much higher levels of confidence in the army (at least until the war in Chechnia) and Orthodox Church than in representative institutions. Asked in another large national survey in summer 1993 whether they believe that the government in Russia reflects the wishes of ordinary people, 69 percent of the respondents answered negatively; only 9 percent answered in the affirmative.[33]

In contrast to the mistrust expressed by citizens toward the structures of national government and the representative institutions nominally designed to link them to government, Russian citizens continue to maintain close friendship ties. These, in fact, remain vital for people who are trying to cope with the difficulties of the present. Rose found, for instance, that two-thirds of his respondents in a 1995 national survey believed that they could borrow up to a week's worth of wages from friends if

---

[31]Whitefield and Evans, "The Russian Election of 1993," pp. 46–47.

[32]Stephen White, "The Presidency and Political Leadership in Post-Communist Russia," in Peter Lentini, ed., *Elections and Political Order in Russia: The Implications of the 1993 Elections to the Federal Assembly* (Budapest: Central European University Press, 1995), p. 215.

[33]Whitefield and Evans, "The Russian Election of 1993," p. 59.

they were in great need.[34] By an equal margin, Russians believed that the central government had little influence on their daily lives.[35] Thus there continues to be a dense, rich nexus of social relations at the primary level, where people interact in the setting of family, circles of friends, and the workplace, but it is not closely related to the great choices over national policy made at the level of the central government. Between the distant power of the state and the network of associations making up most people's daily lives, there are, as in the past, still relatively few opportunities for people to identify with their country as citizens of a national political community. Richard Rose characterizes the situation as an "hour-glass society," with a large state bureaucratic society at the top, an extensive network of primary ties among private citizens, and few ties or institutions in the middle to connect top and bottom.[36]

Dual Russia

The separation between state and people is in fact an old problem in Russia, one which, clearly, the radical political upheavals of the last decade have not overcome. It is captured in the "image of dual Russia" which Robert Tucker described as a theme running through Russian culture over many centuries.[37] This was a cultural construct powerfully embedded in the consciousness both of state officials and the popular masses: the populace regarded the state as an alien power while state officials regarded the popular masses, as if across a great divide, as dark and distant, an alien force, as "cogs in the wheels of the great state apparatus," to quote Stalin in his famous toast to the Russian people at the great Kremlin victory banquet in 1945.[38] This dualism between the life of the state and the life of the society has taken many forms in Russian political culture; it was strongly felt in the Soviet period despite the heroic propaganda effort to portray the masses as the true masters of the state. At times in the pre-revolutionary and Soviet periods, the gulf separating those on top and those below broke down: the masses were invited to share in wielding the power of the state. These were usually moments of revolution or war, when established routines gave way to more spontaneous forms of popular mobilization and collective purpose. Most observers noted that World War II was such a moment in Soviet history. The enormous stresses of the war permitted a greater freedom and sincerity to improve relations between the authorities and the populace, but when the war ended, the state quickly reimposed tight political controls to prevent any lasting institutional effects.

After Stalin's death, Khrushchev sought to inspire greater popular identification with the regime through his denunciation of Stalin's crimes and liberalizing reforms in politics and economics. After Khrushchev, however, all attempts at serious system reform were halted, and the regime's performance began a long, slow,

---

[34]Rose, "Russia as an Hour-Glass Society," p. 38.

[35]Ibid., p. 41.

[36]Rose, "Russia as an Hour-Glass Society."

[37]Robert C. Tucker, "The Image of Dual Russia," in Robert C. Tucker, *The Soviet Political Mind* (New York: Norton, 1971), pp. 121–142.

[38]Ibid., p. 136.

steady decline. Economic growth fell to around zero by the beginning of the 1980s although secrecy shrouded public discussion of virtually all serious problems. The gulf between the state and populace grew deeper. The promise that the system was moving forward to a brighter socialist future rang hollow: almost no one pretended to take Soviet propaganda seriously by the end of the 1970s. And just as Soviet conservatives warned, as socialist consciousness waned, alternative ideologies spread. Among these were the pro-Western, liberal democratic views which became widespread among the younger, urban, educated strata.

Not least of these strands of alternative ideologies was a renascence of Russian national consciousness. One wing of the Russian nationalists emphasized the importance of Orthodox Christianity to Russian culture and identity, deploring the loss of spirituality that had occurred under Soviet rule. Another was a more authoritarian type of nationalism, which stressed the statist, imperial tradition in Russian history and believed that Russia's political system must return to monarchy or some other hierarchically ordered form.[39] For these latter nationalists, Stalin was a positive figure in Russian history, since he was regarded as having created a powerful, industrialized state that successfully defeated Hitler's armies. Both camps paid homage to the Russian Orthodox Church as an institution which had worked to unify Russia and guard its ethical principles over many centuries. In the post-Soviet period, Russian political leaders have been eager to associate themselves with the Orthodox Church as the embodiment of the continuity and cultural heritage of Russia.

We can infer from several pieces of evidence that the breakdown in popular support for the regime's ideology had begun to alarm the Soviet leaders by the late 1970s and early 1980s. One was the effort by the party leadership to undertake a major campaign of ideological revival in 1979. Another is their inconsistent response to the politicization of Russian national consciousness. Some senior party leaders evidently wished to give Russian nationalism a wider outlet; others were opposed on the grounds that the strengthening of nationalism in Russia would stimulate parallel movements for national sovereignty in other republics and in Eastern Europe. Although the regime had created safe, nonpolitical outlets for expression of Russian national sentiments in the 1960s, national feeling continually took threatening forms. In late 1972, Alexander N. Yakovlev, an official in the Propaganda Department of the Central Committee of the party, attacked the rise of anti-Marxist nationalist sentiments among intellectuals, for which he was punished by being sent as ambassador to Canada. Later, Yakovlev became the chief intellectual architect of the shift to democratic and humanistic values in Gorbachev's *perestroika* program.[40] Late in the 1970s, a new threat arose from within the regime-supported mass organization designed to channel Russian pride into safe and constructive outlets. A group of activists formed a society of book collectors that took the name *Pamyat'* (Memory) in 1982 and gained official recognition as a hobby association. Under Andropov, however, the group was subjected to fierce repression,

---

[39]John B. Dunlop, *The Rise of Russia and the Fall of the Soviet Empire* (Princeton: Princeton University Press, 1993).

[40]Some time in the 1980s, Yakovlev abandoned Marxism, and tried to push the Soviet system in the direction of a Western social-democratic society. A book he wrote at the time contains his reflections on the way Marxism was adapted to Russian conditions. Alexander Yakovlev, *The Fate of Marxism in Russia*, trans. Catherine A. Fitzpatrick (New Haven, CT: Yale University Press, 1993).

with the result that when it revived in 1984–85 it was more militant and political in orientation, voicing anti-Semitic, anti-Western, and anti-Marxist views.

The regime entered the 1980s amidst accumulating and undeniable evidence that the system was at or near a crisis point, but until Gorbachev came to power the leadership was unable or unwilling to choose a strategy of fundamental reform. The "extensive" growth model of the Stalin era had reached a point of negative returns, and the USSR was falling behind as the capitalist world was undergoing dramatic technological shifts and challenging the foundation of the Soviet Union's national security. But, rather than taking the steps necessary to reverse these trends, the Brezhnev leadership instead adopted conservative policies that simply staved off confrontation with its difficulties. A large professional, educated, urban elite had formed, but the regime's efforts to make it a loyal component of the system failed. Outside Russia, and to some degree in Russia as well, members of the intelligentsias of the national republics identified more with ethnic-national than with Soviet socialist causes.

As the gap between the regime and society widened, those elements of the Soviet leadership concerned with the long-range viability of the regime became worried that, if current trends continued, they would reach a point where massive popular unrest, possibly coupled with external military pressure, could result in a new revolution. But they had no way of estimating how far into the future that point lay. In the early 1980s, the triple succession intervened and eventually produced a new leadership committed to a major change of policy which it accompanied by an attack on the dangerous rift which had gathered between "words" and "deeds" in public life.[41] Its major weapon was *glasnost´*, or a policy of wider freedom in culture and communications.

Under the influence of *glasnost´*, the gap between the state and society narrowed in 1989–91. *Glasnost´* and elections stimulated a new generation of young and politically ambitious leaders to mobilize popular followings around the cause of reform. In this period the intelligentsia assumed the mantle of moral leadership. Figures such as Andrei Sakharov (whom we shall discuss further in the next chapter) became the symbolic leaders of a broad national movement for democratic change. A wave of hopes and expectations of democratic change encouraged many to take active part in the flood of popular rallies, strikes, elections, and new organizations. The gap between the state and society helps explain the fact that it was precisely the more educated strata, younger generations, people of higher income and status, and urban residents who were the most alienated from and mistrustful of the old Soviet regime in this period, and thus the most likely to become politically active in the new forms of participation that were opening up.[42] The mistrust felt by many citizens toward the Soviet regime thus helped to stimulate political involvement in the period of deep reform under Gorbachev, but also led to a sense of betrayal and

---

[41]Thomas F. Remington, "Gorbachev and the Strategy of Glasnost´," in Thomas F. Remington, ed., *Politics and the Soviet System: Essays in Honor of Frederick C. Barghoorn* (London: Macmillan, 1989), pp. 56–82; Thomas F. Remington, "A Socialist Pluralism of Opinions: Glasnost´ and Policy-Making under Gorbachev," *Russian Review* 48 (1989), pp. 271–304.

[42]Arthur H. Miller, "In Search of Regime Legitimacy," in Miller, Reisinger, and Hesli, eds., *Public Opinion and Regime Change*, pp. 95–123.

disillusionment with the successor regime in Russia, when many of those hopes and expectations were dashed.

Influences on Russian Political Culture in the Soviet Period

Given the great lengths to which the Soviet authorities went in molding the country's political culture, why did they fail to create a more supportive matrix of values and beliefs? Why despite the comprehensive controls over culture and communications that we have noted did dissident ideologies such as liberal democracy, religious faith, and ethnic nationalism nonetheless flourish? Indeed, did the Soviet indoctrination system leave any lasting impact on the country's political culture at all?

Although a definitive answer to these questions will probably not be available for years, some suggestions about the impact of different influences on Russian political culture can be offered. First, we should keep in mind certain institutional features of the old regime's system for shaping public values and beliefs. The Soviet political socialization machine never claimed or possessed full control over all possible influences on citizens. Even in the darkest years of Stalinist tyranny, a sphere of private life survived, formed through powerful family and friendship links. So too did something of the legacy of Russian and Western humanism through the great classic works of prerevolutionary literature and art which generations of Soviet schoolchildren were taught to know and respect. Throughout the Soviet Union, intellectuals, artists, and teachers preserved over a hundred different cultural legacies and national languages. The need for a powerful scientific and technological capability required the Soviet regime to accept a certain level of openness to outside influences: scientific and cultural exchanges of people and ideas, though closely monitored and directed, nonetheless kept open channels through which the diverse influences of the outside world filtered in and out of the Soviet Union. As the regime's own ideological machinery grew increasingly ossified and ineffectual in the 1970s and 1980s, these internal and external cultural influences assumed an ever-greater importance in shaping Soviet political culture and public opinion.

A second point to remember is that the discrepancy between the beliefs and values that the regime preached and the actual behavior of officials and citizens tended to weaken the credibility of regime propaganda. Nearly universal was the understanding that in public certain forms and observances needed to be respected: certain ritualistic words needed to be uttered and gestures made. One was to quote Lenin in a speech, article, or book. The vote taken at a meeting was to be unanimous; one would dutifully go to the polls to cast a ballot or attend a ceremony celebrating some official event. But these forms and observances had little bearing on one's ordinary, everyday life, both for officials and for citizens. They provided a certain stability and predictability in the forms of social interaction, which might have been comforting to people who had undergone the horrors of revolution, war, and terror in previous decades. These rituals and ceremonies also gave the authorities a convenient way to see whether anyone was bold enough to deviate from the accepted patterns. But few actually believed in the conventional doctrines and principles that were constantly echoed throughout the public domain. The actual rules governing behavior were quite different and diverged strongly among various groups.

Younger generations might be attracted to Western popular culture, while the thinning ranks of the older generation still wept each year at the ceremonies commemorating the Soviet victory in World War II. In Central Asia, traditional clan ties came to determine the real distribution of power and status, while in the Baltic states, citizens of all strata cherished the dream that they would once again regain national independence. Behind the ritual obeisances to Marxist–Leninist dogmas, Soviet political culture was extremely diverse. This diversity has contributed to the very different trajectories that the various republics have followed since the breakup of the union. Thus the incompleteness and weakening of the political socialization effort, combined with the sharp divergence between what was preached and what was practiced, meant that actual Soviet political culture was being shaped by a variety of home-grown and international influences.

Over time, Soviet political culture was also affected by three dynamic factors, the effects of which were cumulative over the decades of the Soviet regime's existence.

GENERATIONAL CHANGE

The first of these is the turnover of generations. A careful comparison by Donna Bahry of surveys taken at different times to determine how public opinion on fundamental political and economic values had evolved over the Stalin and post-Stalin years found that Soviet public opinion had not changed drastically over the past several decades. There was a considerable amount of support for political liberties and a mixed economy back in the 1930s and 1940s just as there is in the 1990s. But the structure and composition of public opinion changed.

To explain the change she observed in the passing of the decades, Bahry found that the single largest factor was the *turnover of political generations*.[43] She found that generational change had the greatest effect on Soviet public opinion of any of the factors she examined—education, income, or occupation. Whereas the Stalin-era population had shown relatively minor differences in opinion across generational and educational lines, the gap between generations widened substantially by the time of the Brezhnev-era and Gorbachev-era studies. Those of the older generation might be critical of some features of the Soviet system, such as collectivized agriculture, but were more inclined to accept some of the political and economic values associated with state socialism. Not so the younger generations, which were significantly more critical of living conditions and sympathetic to the loosening of political and economic controls. Thus, not age (and hence life-cycle effects), but genera-

---

[43]Donna Bahry, "Society Transformed?" Bahry reanalyzes data from three surveys taken at different times: the Harvard Project of refugees to Europe after World War II, which reflects attitudes, shaped in the 1920s, 1930s, and early 1940s; the Soviet Interview Project (SIP) data from the emigré survey in the United States in the late 1970s; and a Times-Mirror survey conducted in 1991. This method allows her to compare public opinion on comparable issues for the *same* generations across surveys taken at different times, and to track change and continuity in opinion *across* generations. She finds that both the earlier and later studies found an essential consistency in the values of the prewar generations, even though members of those generations had grown much older by the 1970s and 1980s.

tion, Bahry finds, affects the shift in public opinion: "Those born after World War II, and especially after 1950, had fundamentally different values from their elders."[44]

What were the differences in values? Later generations were more likely to see material shortages as unjust than had previous generations. More important, their standard of reference had shifted. They were less inclined to accept the egalitarianism characteristic of the Stalin-era generations, and more likely to express a resentment of *relative* deprivation. They were far more likely to express dissatisfaction with the same material conditions that the older generations had accepted. There was also a marked difference in views on political liberties. Stalin-era citizens tended to support a mixture of some liberties and some state limitations on individual freedom, while those from post-Stalin generations, "especially the ones with a college degree, were markedly more liberal across the board on individual rights."[45] The younger generations, and particularly those with higher educations, tended to be more consistent in their preference for more economic *and* political freedom, being more inclined to support private ownership of heavy and light industry and agriculture. In other words, while earlier generations might have supported a mixed economy and accepted a combination of state restrictions on liberty with some political freedom, later generations came to have a more ideologically consistent, individualistic, and liberal outlook on major policy questions. This important effect of changing generations was reinforced, in turn, by the cumulative effect of rising levels of educational attainment and other long-term social changes. And in turn, generational turnover and higher educational attainments generated a social base that supported political and economic reform.

Besides generational change, two other long-term social factors have powerfully affected contemporary Russian political culture: the rise in educational attainments in society, and the transformation of Russia over the last six decades from a predominantly rural to a predominantly urban society.

EDUCATIONAL LEVELS

Over the 1960s, 1970s, and 1980s, the proportion of the population who were 15 years of age and older and who had completed their secondary education rose to over 60 percent. Moreover, a significant part of this growth has occurred among those with higher education. By 1989, over 10 percent of Soviet citizens aged fifteen and older had higher educational degrees, approaching the U.S. level.[46] As various studies have shown, it is precisely the most educated strata of the society who were the most dissatisfied with the Brezhnev-era system. For example, the important study of Soviet immigrants to the United States in the 1970s, the Soviet Interview Project (SIP), found that critical and individualistic outlooks were strongest among the most highly educated

---

[44]Bahry, p. 544.

[45]Bahry, p. 540.

[46]In 1980, 66.3 percent of Americans aged 25 or over had completed secondary school, and 16.3 percent had four or more years of college. See Andrew Hacker, *U.S.: A Statistical Portrait of the American People* (New York: Viking, 1983), pp. 250–251.

groups.[47] Similarly, all the studies of contemporary Russian values and attitudes find variance in educational levels to be one of the strongest predictors of degree of commitment to democratic principles: the more highly educated, the more likely an individual is to support values and principles associated with liberal democracy.[48] Consequently, over time, as Russian society comprised more and more people with secondary and higher educational degrees, levels of support for democratic principles grew.

One other effect of education should be noted as well. Higher educational attainments are also associated with rejection of the authority and values of the Soviet system. Arthur H. Miller and his colleagues from the University of Iowa studied a syndrome of alienation from the old regime, which consisted of low confidence in Soviet leaders and institutions and a sense of personal powerlessness. Significantly, they found that alienation from the old regime was associated with support for democratic values, and was associated positively with educational level and inversely with age. These relationships held up even after controlling for income levels, religious affiliation, and occupation. Belief that the government was mismanaging the economy and a perception that the system was unfair were both related positively to alienation. Ethnic identification had a powerful effect: Lithuanians were significantly more inclined to express alienation than were Russians within Lithuania, and resentment toward Russians was very strongly associated with alienation from the regime. The study also sheds light on the surge of political participation that occurred in the late 1980s as Gorbachev opened opportunities for legal political expression and organization. Miller found that the alienated were four times as likely to join a political organization than were those low on the alienation scale. Other forms of nontraditional political activity were also significantly associated with high levels of alienation. Of course, as Miller observes, in some cases the organizations that the alienated joined were antidemocratic. One reason for the strength of democratic values in Russian society, therefore, seems to be that they are associated with rejection of the old regime and its values, a tendency which is stronger among the young and the better-educated.[49]

URBANIZATION OF SOCIETY

Although old village mentalities and habits have retreated slowly, Russian society has become predominantly urban in a very short span of time. By the late 1970s, more than two-thirds of the Russian population lived in cities; today, 73 percent of the population of Russia is classified as urban.[50] But as recently as the late 1950s, the

---

[47]Brian Silver, "Political Beliefs of the Soviet Citizen," in James R. Millar, ed., *Politics, Work, and Daily Life in the USSR* (Cambridge: Cambridge University Press, 1987), p. 127.

[48]Gibson and Duch, "Emerging Democratic Values," p. 86; William M. Reisinger, Arthur H. Miller, Vicki L. Hesli, and Kristen Hill Maher, "Political Values in Russia, Ukraine and Lithuania: Sources and Implications for Democracy," *British Journal of Political Science* 24 (1994), pp. 216–218; Jeffrey W. Hahn, "Continuity and Change in Russian Political Culture," in Frederic J. Fleron, Jr. and Erik P. Hoffmann, eds., *Post-Communist Studies and Political Science: Methodology and Empirical Theory in Sovietology* (Boulder: Westview Press, 1993), pp. 319–322.

[49]Arthur H. Miller, "In Search of Regime Legitimacy," in Miller, Reisinger, and Hesli, eds., *Public Opinion and Regime Change*, pp. 95–123.

[50]*Rossiiskaia federatsiia v 1992: Statisticheskii ezhegodnik* [The Russian Federation in 1992: Statistical Annual] (Moscow: Republikanskii informatsionno-izdatel'skii tsentr, 1993), p. 88.

society was half urban, half rural. From 1950 to 1980 the urban population of the Soviet Union increased by nearly 100 million people—most of them immigrants from the countryside, which suffers from a continuing flight of population. The growth of the urban population has had some significant but subtle effects on political culture, as the historian Moshe Lewin has argued. It has tended to focus the attention of policymakers on problems of individual personality and human needs more directly than when the society was composed of large, seemingly homogeneous social blocs such as "workers" and "peasants." Second, urbanization has facilitated the formation of informal and cross-cutting social ties that tend to nurture independent sources of public opinion and mediate the political messages sent out by the rulers.[51]

We should also note that urbanization affected different ethnic groups within Russia differently. The Russian ethnologist Mikhail Guboglo has pointed out that urbanization in the Soviet setting helped stimulate ethnic political mobilization. In the Russian republic, 1960s, 1970s, and 1980s, the *Russian* ethnic urban population grew by about 75 percent, but the urban population of autonomous (national) republics within Russia more than doubled. The rate of urbanization of non-Russian titular nationalities was twice that of Russians. The result, according to Guboglo, was the formation of a national intelligentsia that was unable to satisfy its demands for national cultural expression within the restrictive political climate of the Soviet regime. Moreover, the breakdown of traditional culture among the national minorities created a number of social pathologies and conflicts with the dominant Russian population. Guboglo compares the situation in a number of cities in the autonomous republics within Russia to the formation of black ethnic ghettos in American cities.[52]

Survey research since the end of the Soviet regime continues to find that education, generation, and urbanization have a strong impact both on political ideology and on political behavior in Russia. The evidence exists both in the form of *aggregate-level* behavioral data—patterns of voting across regions—and *individual-level* opinion data. For example, careful examination of the voting returns by district reveals a very strong association between the level of urbanization and support for reform. Vote shares for the democratic reform camp are highest in the largest cities and most heavily urbanized districts, and drop off monotonically as the size of a voter's area of residence diminishes.[53] All the regional analyses of Russian elections demonstrate that the single strongest determinant of the level of vote support that a region gives to democratic reforms is the level of urbanization. The largest cities

[51]Moshe Lewin, *The Gorbachev Phenomenon*, expanded ed. (Berkeley: University of California Press, 1991), pp. 63–71; see also S. Frederick Starr, "The Changing Nature of Change in the USSR," in Seweryn Bialer and Michael Mandelbaum, eds., *Gorbachev's Russia and American Foreign Policy* (Boulder: Westview Press, 1988), pp. 3–36.

[52]Mikhail N. Guboglo, Izmeneniia v natsional´nom sostave avtonomnykh respublik Rossiiskoi Federatsii v 1959–1989 gg.: K izucheniiu demograficheskoi osnovy sovremennykh etnopoliticheskikh protsessov. *Etnopoliticheskaia mozaika Bashkortostana. Ocherki, Dokumenty, Khronika, vol. 1.* M. N. Guboglo (Moscow: TsIMO, 1992), pp. 41–43.

[53]Jerry F. Hough, "The Russian Election of 1993: Public Attitudes toward Economic Reform and Democratization," *Post-Soviet Affairs* 10 (1994), pp. 1–37; Ralph S. Clem and Peter R. Craumer, "A Rayon-Level Analysis of the Russian Election and Constitutional Plebiscite of December 1993," *Post-Soviet Geography* 36 (1995), pp. 459–475.

and regional capitals are the bastions of electoral support for the cause of democratic and market-oriented change. In smaller towns, pro-opposition conservatism is stronger, and in villages it is strongest of all. The other factors we have identified as sources of differentiation in the political culture—generation and education—are also powerful predictors of people's voting preferences, but across regions, the single strongest factor affecting the strength of a reform candidate is the share of the urban population.[54] Educational levels and the age structure of a region are also strong predictors of the vote. All public opinion surveys point to the same finding: education, age (negatively), and urban residence are all significantly and independently correlated with support for democratic and market principles.

The Soviet regime's strategy, then, of creating a modern urban, industrial, educated society had an entirely different effect from that which was anticipated. Rather than strengthening the hold of socialist ideology in the consciousness of the populace, modernization resulted in the formation of a critically minded, alienated, and democratically oriented constituency for radical reform. Conceivably, had Soviet socialism yielded a more successful, prosperous model of development, a more supportive political culture might have resulted. But that is to argue not only from a counter-factual supposition about "what might have been," it is also to argue an impossibility, since the Soviet-type economic system has been unable to generate sustained growth anywhere.

The evidence shows that Soviet political culture developed in a way best predicted by the theory of social modernization: support for individual rights and freedoms rose over the decades and was strongest among the youngest cohorts of society, those with the greatest education, and those living in the largest cities.

Taken together, according to Gail Lapidus:

> The social and demographic changes from the mid-1950s to the mid-1980s transformed the passive and inarticulate peasant society of the era of Stalin into an urban industrial society with a highly differentiated social structure and an increasingly articulate and assertive middle class. . . . [B]y the mid-1980s, a large urban middle class, including a substantial professional, scientific-technical and cultural intelligentsia with new cultural as well as material requirements had emerged as a major actor on the Soviet scene. This urban middle class, moreover, occupied an increasingly important place in both the membership and the leadership of the Communist Party itself.[55]

These changes in society made the political transformation wrought by Gorbachev both necessary and possible. They expanded the numbers of citizens with aspirations influenced by Western values and living standards. Certainly the modernization of Soviet society helped prepare the way for its democratization. But some of its effects were neither anticipated nor desired by Gorbachev: having loosened central political controls, he could not prevent some republican leaders from employing

---

[54]Michael McFaul and Nikolai Petrov, *Russia Between Elections: What the December 1995 Results Really Mean* (Moscow: Carnegie Moscow Center, 1996), pp. 7–8; Michael McFaul and Nikolai Petrov, eds., *Politicheskii al'manakh Rossii 1995,* (Moscow: Carnegie Moscow Center, 1995), pp. 33–34; Clem and Craumer, "A Rayon-Level Analysis."

[55]Gail W. Lapidus, "State and Society: Toward the Emergence of Civil Society in the Soviet Union," in Seweryn Bialer, *Politics, Society, and Nationality Inside Gorbachev's Russia* (Boulder: Westview Press, 1989), pp. 125–127.

police tactics and violence to shore up their political power or others from embracing the tide of anti-Russian nationalism that impelled popular movements for republic independence. His goal of preserving overall communist party control over the political system while democratizing it proved impossible, with the result that the political evolution of the fifteen successor states has varied significantly. Some, such as Uzbekistan, are far less democratic than was the Soviet system in the 1980s, and others, such as Lithuania, are much more so. These differences reflect both the different distributions of political values and beliefs in the societies of each former republic, as well as the commitment on the part of their national leaders to democratic practice.

Cultural Diversity Within Russia

Much as the decay of the old regime combined with the modernization of society tended to stimulate alternative ideological movements in Russia and other national republics of the union, these changes also affected the self-awareness among ethnic minorities living in Russia's national republics and autonomous territories. The revival of nationalism among Russians and other Soviet peoples in the late 1980s, in response to the opening up of the media and the arts, gave this process a particularly strong impetus. Cultural centers, language revival movements, and political associations sprang up in many regions of Russia, including Tatarstan, Bashkortostan, Chechnia, Udmurtia, Tuva, and elsewhere.

A case in point is the Sakha Republic, formerly known as Yakutia.[56] Sakha occupies a huge territory in Northern Siberia, comprising 17 percent of Russia's landmass, an area three times the size of France. It is an extraordinarily rich area, containing vast reserves of gold, diamonds, and oil, as well as other mineral resources. Around 40 percent of the population is ethnically Sakha as of 1995, and around 50 percent is Russian. During the peak of ethnic political mobilization within Russia, in 1990, Sakha, like many other republics, passed a declaration of sovereignty, although signalling that it did not seek secession. Nonetheless, as in other ethnic republics, tensions between the republican leaders and Moscow increased, just as tensions increased between the Russian population of the republic and the population of the titular indigenous nationality. As elsewhere, these conflicts revolved around both redistributive economic issues (which side would get which share of the profits from the exploitation of native mineral wealth), as well as symbolic cultural-identity issues: what would be the language of instruction in the schools, and what would be the language of politics and administration?

In the case of Sakha, these tensions have been managed without reaching a critical point. The central Russian government has renegotiated the terms of profit-sharing from the mining of gold and diamonds, and the Sakha government has encouraged the revival of Sakha language and culture without seeking to expel the Russian population in the republic. Mutual mistrust and hostility sometimes flare

---

[56]The discussion of the Sakha Republic that follows is based on the article by Marjorie M. Balzer and Uliana A. Vinokurova, "Nationalism, Interethnic Relations and Federalism: The Case of the Sakha Republic (Yakutia)," *Europe-Asia Studies* 48 (1996), pp. 101–120.

up, but in the absence of some new russifying campaign, the movement to make the Sakha republic a cultural homeland for the Sakha people has been accommodated in the new model of Russian federalism.

The Sakha case is characteristic of a number of the ethnic republics in Russia in that demands for cultural autonomy and a greater share of economic sovereignty have been granted by the federal government in return for the preservation of Russia as a multicultural federal state. The center has shown a striking degree of flexibility, in fact, in handling the political implications of Russia's ethnic-cultural diversity. In Tatarstan, for example, a strong ethnic-nationalist movement (the leaders were not averse to citing the great victories of their illustrious forebear, Genghis Khan, over the Russians) subsided through adroit maneuvering by the republican and federal leadership which granted the republic a sufficient share of economic and cultural autonomy to satisfy all but the most irreconcilable separatists. The instrument for this accommodation was the bilateral treaty (see Chapter Two, "The Center and the Regions"). Although a treaty is a highly unconventional and extra-constitutional method for settling political relations between the federal government and the governments of its constituent territories, in the circumstances of post-Soviet Russia, it seems to have been successful, at least for now, in preserving the state's integrity.

The huge exception, of course, is the case of Chechnia. Here, as elsewhere, conflict between the indigenous people and the Russian center stemmed from a combination of cultural and economic causes. In Chechnia, however, the indigenous leadership unilaterally declared its independence of Russia, without submitting the matter to a referendum. After three years of attempts at negotiations alternating with heavy-handed pressure to overthrow the Chechen leadership, Russia invaded the small Caucasian republic with massive ground and air forces. Although its operations were extraordinarily brutal, they were unable to bring about a rapid defeat of the pro-independence Chechen forces. The war reached a stalemate, with neither side able to achieve its full objective, and federal forces were withdrawn in fall 1996. Certainly relations between Chechnia and the federal government will remain difficult, tense, and ambiguous for a very long time. Yet the Chechen case stands out not only for its exceptional destructiveness, but also for its uniqueness. In no other ethnic territory has the central government imposed its will by military force.

Contemporary Russian political culture has thus been influenced by many factors, among them the thousand-year heritage of Russian statehood, the ambitious program of the Soviet communist regime to remake society, and the effects of social modernization which the communist regime generally encouraged but tried, with little success, to direct to its ends. We have noted the major lines of cleavage in society associated with generation, education, urbanization, and ethnic-national identity. The tumultuous events of Soviet history have affected different generations differently. Among the older generation, for instance, Stalin is viewed much more favorably than among the younger generations.[57] And to a large extent, these dif-

---

[57]Reisinger, Miller, Hesli, and Maher, "Political Values in Russia, Ukraine and Lithuania," p. 200.

ferences are mutually reinforcing: members of the older generations tend to have lower levels of education and less exposure to the more cosmopolitan way of life in the cities. Many individuals combine democratic values in the abstract with support for state ownership and control over much of the economy and a very negative evaluation of contemporary political and economic institutions.

The alienation from the authorities—Russia's characteristic pattern of reciprocal detachment, mistrust, and misunderstanding that separates the state from the populace—which helped to undermine the old regime has returned again under the new regime. Many hopes that the gap would be closed have been dashed, leaving a bitter nostalgia for the past. Three quarters of the populace believe that Russia was better off five years ago: 56 percent believing it was *much* better off, and 23 percent saying it was *somewhat* better off.[58] There has also been a reaction against Western influence and models. Two 1993 surveys found a majority supporting the sentiment that the West has been trying to *weaken* Russia by meddling in its reforms.[59] These findings suggest that while democratic aspirations have been awakened, strongly shaping what Russians think *should* be in politics, they have also created standards of evaluation that existing institutions do not meet. The resulting frustration helps to explain, for instance, the nationalist backlash reflected in the 23 percent vote given to the extremist party of Vladimir Zhirinovsky in the December 1993 elections and the similar share of the vote won by the communists in the December 1995 election.

Russian political culture is a dynamic mixture of contradictory elements drawn from the prerevolutionary, Soviet, and post-Soviet periods, as well as from the interpenetrating medium of international influences. Even in Soviet times, behind the veil of apparent Marxist–Leninist solidarity, a variety of democratic, religious, and cultural values struggled for recognition. It is difficult to imagine how Russia's cultural diversity could ever be successfully reduced to the iron logic of a single ideology again.

---

[58]Ibid., p. 55.

[59]Whitefield and Evans, "The Russian Election of 1993," p. 52; Hough, "The Russian Election of 1993," p. 6.

Chapter 4

Political Participation and Recruitment

Directed Participation

A hallmark of the old Soviet regime was the emphasis the authorities put on ceremonial forms of mass political participation. Extremely high proportions of the population were recorded as taking part in voting, belonging to trade unions, and assuming volunteer responsibilities. Soviet citizens were encouraged to think of themselves, collectively, as owners of the state. However, they were not to question the basic values and principles of the regime. The authorities recruited a large number of citizen activists to help with such tasks as rallying workers to fulfill plan targets and to get out the vote. However, individuals who organized opposition groups were arrested. The authorities acted to maximize participation in the conventional channels established by the regime, as if the forms of popular participation were important but the reality of popular participation posed a potential threat to state security.

INTERLOCKING DIRECTORATES

Why did the communist regime place such emphasis on mass participation? One reason is that it contributed directly to the recruitment of leaders.[1] The numerous governing committees of social organizations created positions for activists and leaders who directed the participation of the general public in social, political, and productive activities. Leaders in these organizations, in turn, belonged to the governing bodies of other organizations. The Communist Party likewise formed its own party committees at every level: its members always included the ranking full-time

---

[1]See Bohdan Harasymiw, *Political Elite Recruitment in the Soviet Union* (New York: St. Martin's Press, 1984).

party officials in the given jurisdiction, as well as the heads of government and social organizations. For example, the party committee for a city typically included, besides its own top party secretaries, the heads of the city government, the chairman of the trade union council, the first secretary of the Komsomol branch, directors of major enterprises, the editor of the local newspaper, and other notables. Serving as the hub from which a series of membership ties extended into a locality's organized institutions, the party committee at each level of the hierarchy was a vehicle for the *horizontal integration* of elites by offering a common channel for the political participation of leaders at the same level of responsibility. At the same time such channels provided for the *vertical integration* of elites through the inclusion of heads of subordinate organizations on nominally elective collective bodies at higher levels. A good example would be the membership of the first secretaries of the most important regional party committees on the Central Committee of the Communist Party of the Soviet Union.

Integration of elites through organizational cross-representation helped overcome the danger of the dissipation of control and coordination across hierarchical levels and sectors of the political system. Although in practice, the old regime vested actual decision-making authority in administrative bodies such as the executive committees that ran local administrations and the party's secretariats that directed and coordinated the work of the party's salaried staff employees, it also preserved elements of the old Bolshevik model of "democratic centralism" and "soviet democracy." These were embedded in the electoral system, under which Soviet citizens voted for deputies to soviets which were given constitutional authority to decide any question of state life in their jurisdiction. Formal democracy prevailed within the party as well. Party members voted for representatives to governing bodies which were supposed to oversee the work of its own executive organs. These governing bodies included the Central Committee at the summit of the party hierarchy, as well as party committees at each level of the party organizational ladder. But the ceremonial authority of such committees, like that of the soviets which were the backbone of state power, was understood by all to be a formality, a tribute to principle, which must not be used in a way that could weaken the unity of command within state and party.

Cross-representation of institutions and hierarchical levels was facilitated by the bifurcation of executive and representative power. The party ensured that chief executives of party organizations from subordinate levels were represented on party committees at superordinate levels, as were the chief executives of important state institutions including government administrations. In keeping with this pattern, leading party and government officials were "elected" as deputies to soviets. The same single-candidate elections allowed the party to ensure representation for members of major social constituencies such as laborers, peasants, youths, veterans, and so on. Undoubtedly the interlocking of leaders from different sectors through their incorporation into the elective bodies of each agency eased the dilemma of coordination that a huge state bureaucracy required. Yet as the Soviet literature itself makes clear, each organization was run in fact by its full-time executive officials, not by the elective representative bodies to which the executives were theoretically answerable. Party secretaries and department chiefs ran party organizations; government officials dominated decisions in the soviets and executive committees;

full-time trade union officials ran the trade unions. Cross-representation across these bodies and vertical integration across hierarchical rungs in each organization may have alleviated some coordination problems, but did not solve the growing problem of nonaccountability by executive officials in each sector.

CHANNELS OF MASS PARTICIPATION

For most rank-and-file citizens, participation in membership organizations was mainly formal—a matter of attending required meetings, paying the monthly dues, and obtaining the benefits these organizations distributed. Trade unions administered social insurance funds and subsidized vacations. Youth groups provided recreational opportunities. For some individuals, however, and especially those who were keen on making political careers, mass organizations were an essential rung on a career ladder through which energetic activism, coupled with political reliability, could bring ambitious individuals to the attention of the party's personnel managers. They in turn could ensure that the individual received the right combination of political education, volunteer assignments, and job opportunities to allow him or her to rise through the ladder of promotions.

KOMSOMOL

The Komsomol, or Communist Youth League, which, at its height, enrolled some 40 million young people between the ages of 15 and 28, was the principal recruiting ground for the Communist Party. By the mid-1980s, three quarters of new party members entered directly from Komsomol, so that a good record as Komsomol member was a prerequisite to admission to the party. For many other people, however, to be put up for membership in various boards, councils, committees, and other elective and appointed posts was a ceremonial honor which came automatically as a result of achieving a certain status in society. Everyone understood that real power in mass organizations was in the hands of their full-time staff (who were appointed by local party officials) rather than their elected governing bodies.

SOVIETS

This was true as well for the country's *soviets,* the elected councils serving as representative and law-making bodies. As we have seen, elected deputies were expected to help their constituents with various problems, but not make policy decisions in their jurisdictions without the guidance of the Communist Party. In every territorial subdivision of the state—every town, village, rural district, city, province, ethno-territory, and republic—there was a corresponding soviet. (In the case of the union and autonomous republics, and at the level of the union government itself, it was called Supreme Soviet.) Soviets tended to be quite large: in 1987, 2.3 million deputies were elected to 52,000 soviets in all. (Some of these served in soviets at two different levels, but a deputy could not be elected to more than two soviets at the same time.) A deputy's calling was not full-time; soviets usually met on a quarterly or biannual basis, for a day or two at a time, hearing reports and approving the proposed budget and plan. Soviets were not deliberative, policy-making bodies, but were means of acquainting deputies and citizens with the policies and priorities of the regime at each level of the state, for giving deputies a feeling of personal responsibility for the well-being of the system, and for showcasing the democratic character of the state. This last function is particularly evident in the care taken to ensure a high level of participation by women, blue-collar workers, youths, nonparty members, and other groups of the populace who were severely underrepresented in more powerful organs. To this end, the party employed a quota system to select candidates to run, controlling the outcome of the nomination process to obtain the desired mix of social characteristics among the elected deputies.[2] Generally speaking, the party tried to select as candidates people who could serve as role models to society, leading citizens from all walks of life who were politically reliable and thought to enjoy a measure of popular esteem. Virtually all prominent Soviet citizens were deputies to soviets at one level or another, often being elected in districts far from their place of residence or work.

In addition to service as deputies, Soviet citizens were also brought into the work of local government and administration in other ways as well. Many served as volunteer members of the standing committees of local soviets monitoring the government's performance in housing, education, trade, catering, public amenities, and other sectors of community life. Still others joined residential committees and neighborhood self-help groups. These activities were not entirely ceremonial. Often they gave public-spirited citizens an outlet for their involvement in the community.[3]

PAROCHIAL CONTACTING

The habit of turning to deputies for help with private problems is characteristic of a larger pattern of "parochial contacting," which might be categorized as a kind of traditional citizen participation. The Soviet authorities have long encouraged citizens to transmit their ideas, grievances, hopes, and petitions to a wide range of official institutions, including soviets, newspapers and broadcast media, party committees, the procuracy, the KGB, and individual notables. The volume of such mail and personal visits was huge. For 1983 alone, it was estimated that Central Television received about 1.7 million letters; all-union radio over 600,000; Moscow radio, over 170,000; the central newspapers, around 500,000 each; provincial newspapers, 30,000–35,000 letters each; the trade unions, 2 million letters and personal visits; party organizations, 3.3 million letters and visits.[4] At the local level, ordinary citizens had some opportunity to influence government administration, pushing for improvements in the condition and availability of housing, for example, or for better provision of stores and cultural amenities. But these demands were generally

---

[2]See Stephen White's discussion of this process in *Gorbachev and After* (Cambridge: Cambridge University Press, 1991), pp. 27–29.

[3]Theodore H. Friedgut, *Political Participation in the USSR* (Princeton: Princeton University Press, 1979); L. G. Churchward, "Public Participation in the USSR," in Everett M. Jacobs, ed., *Soviet Local Politics and Government* (London: Allen & Unwin, 1983), pp. 38–39; Jeffrey W. Hahn, *Soviet Grassroots: Citizen Participation in Local Soviet Government* (Princeton: Princeton University Press, 1988).

[4]Thomas F. Remington, *The Truth of Authority: Ideology and Communication in the Soviet Union* (Pittsburgh: University of Pittsburgh Press, 1988), pp. 123–124.

nonpolitical in nature, not aimed at influencing basic policy or challenging the incumbents' right to rule.[5] Often this kind of contact between citizen and state generated a pattern of individualized, parochial participation, in which individuals became adept at "working the system" for their own private benefit rather than changing the allocation of resources for whole classes of people.[6] The regime in fact encouraged the *demobilization* of society, by giving people numerous opportunities to pursue private, particularistic demands but discouraging them from getting involved in the political system to satisfy generalized, policy demands.

VOTING

Voting for deputies to soviets was another example of the directed, formal aspect of political participation in the old system. The regime went to great lengths to ensure that everyone cast a ballot, and treated the massive turnout and near unanimous endorsement of the candidate as a sign of the unshakeable unity of regime and people, despite the fact that virtually every race was uncontested.[7] The act of voting was a matter of dropping a ballot with a single, preprinted name into a ballot box at a polling station, where, after the polls closed, officials would count the number of ballots cast for the candidate, and duly announce the candidate's election by an overwhelming majority. The campaign emphasized the ideological solidarity of society—there was no room for an "opposition platform"—but voters were encouraged to see the deputies they elected as go-betweens who could intercede with the bureaucracy for their particular needs. In this area, more than any other, we can see the ritualistic quality of much participation under the old regime. For the authorities, the *appearance* of mass support was evidently of great importance, while for much of the population, participation in such ceremonies was regarded as part of the harmless pageantry of everyday life.

---

[5]On popular participation in local government, see Theodore H. Friedgut, *Political Participation in the USSR* (Princeton: Princeton University Press, 1979) and Jeffrey W. Hahn, *Soviet Grassroots: Citizen Participation in Local Soviet Government* (Princeton: Princeton University Press, 1988).

[6]Wayne Di Franceisco and Zvi Gitelman, "Soviet Political Culture and 'Covert Participation' in Policy Implementation," *American Political Science Review* 78 (1984), pp. 603–621. These forms of "participation," if that is the right term, included many kinds of parochial contacting (e.g., letters and visits to influential officials and organizations) as well as the use of networks of favor-trading and influence-peddling.

However, Donna Bahry and Brian D. Silver take issue with this view of Soviet citizen participation. In their article, "Soviet Citizen Participation on the Eve of Democratization," *American Political Science Review* 84 (1990), pp. 821–848, they argue that there is a higher degree of continuity between Brezhnev-era mass participation and the explosive informal associational activity under Gorbachev than is commonly supposed. Analyzing data about attitudes toward and forms of citizen participation from the Soviet Interview Project (SIP), the large U.S. government-funded study of 3,000 emigrés to the United States during the 1970s, they show that some of the same attitudes (higher than average levels of interpersonal trust and a sense of personal political efficacy) characterize both within-system and extra-systemic ("dissent") political activists under the Brezhnev regime, and that citizen participation can be differentiated according to the types of individuals and types of activities in which people were engaged. They therefore refute the proposition that citizen participation was largely "for show" and devoid of all interest or benefit for ordinary citizens.

[7]On elections, see Victor Zaslavsky and Robert J. Brym, "The Functions of Elections in the USSR," *Soviet Studies* 30:3 (July 1978), pp. 362–371.

CONTROL OF SOCIAL ORGANIZATIONS

As time went on, the growth of repressed popular grievances far exceeded the slow growth of regularized opportunities for Soviet citizens to voice their demands. As a result the gap between approved gestures of participation and the actual realities of power widened. Those new public organizations which formed with official approval, such as the "Rodina Society," which was dedicated to defending Russia's cultural heritage, quickly grew into branches of the state rather than autonomous expressions of a public interest.[8] The Russian Orthodox Church had a quasi-official status as well, despite the constitution's declared separation of church and state, illustrated by the Communist Party's rule that senior ecclesiastical officials could only be named by approval of the party. And the KGB had a large network of informers and agents working within the Church for surveillance of believers and to guide the Church's social and political activity in directions congruent with the regime's purposes.[9] The party, in short, claimed a "licensing" power over organized social bodies through which it ensured control over their choice of leaders and the direction of their activity.[10] Because the nominally public (*obshchestvennye*—meaning formally nonstate) organizations in fact carried out state-set goals and operated under close political control, the boundary lines between state and society were never distinct.

DISSENT

Some nonstate organizations operated outside the limits of regime approval, of course, and incurred repression. Beginning in the mid-1960s, various groups pressed the regime to respect the civic and political rights that were granted by the Soviet constitution but were denied whenever the authorities found that a particular act violated the limits of permitted expression.[11] The movements for democratic, national, and religious rights established alternative normative frameworks to those propagandized by the regime and generated counter-elites whose prestige and authority drew on their willingness to risk arrest and prosecution for their beliefs. Some of the prominent figures of dissent became leaders of new political movements in the late 1980s, such as Andrei Sakharov, the most famous of the democratic dissidents, who became the moral leader of the democratic group of

---

[8]On the Rodina Society, see John B. Dunlop, *The Faces of Contemporary Russian Nationalism* (Princeton: Princeton University Press, 1983), p. 38. See also the article, published posthumously, by the late Soviet journalist Anatolii Agranovskii, "Sokrashchenie apparata," *Izvestiia,* May 13, 1984, which discusses the bureaucratization of the Rodina and other nominally public organizations.

[9]On the politics of the Church, see John Dunlop, "The Russian Orthodox Church as an 'Empire Saving' Institution," in Michael Bourdeaux, ed., *The Politics of Religion in Russia and the New States of Eurasia* (Armonk, NY: M.E. Sharpe, 1995), pp. 15–40; and Dimitry V. Pospielovsky, "The Russian Orthodox Church in the Postcommunist CIS," in ibid., pp. 41–74.

[10]John H. Miller, "The Communist Party: Trends and Problems," in Archie Brown and Michael Kaser, eds., *Soviet Policy for the 1980s* (Bloomington: Indiana University Press, 1982), p. 2.

[11]A comprehensive chronicle of such movements is Ludmilla Alexeyeva, *Soviet Dissent: Contemporary Movements for National, Religious, and Human Rights* (Middletown, CT: Wesleyan University Press, 1987). See also Frederick C. Barghoorn, *Detente and the Democratic Movement in the USSR* (New York: Free Press, 1976).

USSR deputies elected in 1989. Others include Father Gleb Yakunin, arrested for dissent in 1979 but who became a leader of the group of democratic deputies in the Russian republic parliament in 1990; Zviad Gamsakhurdia, who was arrested as a dissident in the 1970s (and who was also one of the few arrested dissidents to turn state's evidence and confess the error of his ways), but who became the acclaimed popular leader of the Georgian national movement in 1990 and 1991 until he turned in an authoritarian direction; Viacheslav Chornovil, imprisoned for his advocacy of Ukrainian national rights and in 1990 elected chairman of the city soviet of Lviv; and Sergei Kovalev, a close friend and collaborator of Sakharov's in the democratic movement who became chairman of the human rights committee of the Russian Republic's parliament in 1990. Thus, in many cases, it was past participation in political movements *outside* and *in opposition to* the regime that lent credibility to the new leaders during the democratization period under Gorbachev.

As a result of the pattern of state-directed mass participation in the old regime, few civic associations existed that were not developed either in opposition to the state, or were themselves extensions of the state's power.[12] Elimination of most forms of private property, the suppression of political and ideological opposition, and the spread of state control over social organizations left a vacuum of nonstate structures when the political regime fell apart. This vacuum in turn created opportunities for radical politics, particularly radical nationalism, because of the destruction of class and other cleavages that cut across national divisions.[13]

Rise of the Informals

In a famous comment on the fact that the minor reforms under Louis XVI in France not only failed to relieve the revolutionary pressure of mass discontent, but actually appeared to stimulate it, Alexis de Tocqueville noted that "the most dangerous time for a bad government is when it starts to reform itself." In our time there have been many examples when authoritarian regimes attempted to release the pressure of popular discontent by holding elections or legalizing opposition groups, only to find that the public's desire for radical, fundamental change was more powerful than they calculated.

Often, in fact, it seems that a positive feedback loop is set in motion. Limited measures of liberalization by the authorities are followed by an increase in the organized pressure from society for more rights and freedoms; this results in further concessions from above, which in turn leads to still more politicization and activation of mass politics. The dynamic soon acquires a momentum of its own that cannot be controlled by the regime except at the price of enormous bloodshed. The process of democratization results in a peaceful transition if the leadership is willing and able to concede power without suppressing its opponents. But its ability to do so depends on the civilian leadership's ability to preserve the support of the military

---

[12]Marcia A. Weigle and Jim Butterfield, "Civil Society in Reforming Communist Regimes," *Comparative Politics* 25:1 (October 1992), pp. 1–23.

[13]Zbigniew Brzezinski, "Post-Communist Nationalism," *Foreign Affairs* (Winter 1989/90), pp. 1–2.

and secret police *and* the ability of the opposition to remain sufficiently united as it pushes the regime to prevent popular demands from spilling out and provoking large-scale repression. Often in such revolutionary settings, mass frustrations and grievances, having accumulated over a long period, sweep away the more moderate and liberally minded leadership that could mediate between regime and opposition, and instead thrust forward maximalist or demagogic leaders, with the result that confrontation results in new violence and repression. A willingness and capacity to compromise on both sides is thus required if the transition is to be negotiated peacefully and to result in a democratic outcome.

In the case of the Soviet Union, new channels of participation and recruitment quickly sprang up in response to the opening that Gorbachev's democratic reforms provided. In 1986 and especially in 1987 and 1988, an explosion of associational activity occurred.[14] Much of this was not explicitly political in character, and took form in rock music groups, body-building and martial arts clubs, loose associations of pacifists, hippies, and religious mystics, and cultural and environmental preservation movements. Even groups like these, that have no political agenda as such, are *implicitly* political in a communist system, however, because they are outside the network of party controls over ideology and personnel selection. They may become nuclei of opposition ideas and organization. Moreover, in a rapidly changing environment, the clash between groups seeking to preserve their independence and the party-state bureaucracy often tends to politicize and radicalize society. With time, therefore, and particularly as opportunities opened up for forms of political expression, such as mass demonstrations, publication of independent newsletters and leaflets, and electoral campaigning, that did not incur repression from the authorities, more and more groups were drawn into politics. This process of politicization of the informal groups seems to have been given its greatest impetus in the spring of 1988, as society was drawn into the debate over democratization.[15] Broadly speaking, two processes occurred simultaneously over the 1987–89 period: the proliferation of independent social associations (Soviet authorities estimated that 30,000 unofficial groups had formed in 1988, and perhaps as many as 60,000 by 1989) and the aggregation of smaller groups into larger movements and organizations.

POPULAR FRONTS

One of the most common forms of independent, organized political activity in the 1988–89 period was the popular front. Typically the popular front was a broad movement with a democratic orientation that aggregated several overlapping causes: environmental preservation, expansion of political freedoms, and, for those operating in national republics, greater autonomy for the national homeland. The first to form were those in the Baltic Republics, Estonia, Latvia, and Lithuania, where over the 1988–89 period they quickly grew from loose groupings of the cultural and scientific intelligentsia into broad movements with mass followings and

---

[14]Vladimir Brovkin, "Revolution from Below: Informal Political Associations in Russia, 1988–1989," *Soviet Studies* 42:2 (April 1990), pp. 233–257; Judith B. Sedaitis and James Butterfield, eds., *Perestroika from Below: New Social Movements in the Soviet Union* (Boulder: Westview Press, 1991).

[15]Brovkin, "Revolution from Below," p. 234.

organized branches in every town. Their power to mobilize support from the population (including—significantly—substantial elements of the Russian minorities living in the Baltic republics) was demonstrated most impressively in the elections to the new Congress of People's Deputies in March 1989. In Lithuania, for example, the Popular Front (called Sajudis, or "movement," in Lithuanian) made a strategic decision to withdraw its candidates from the races against two Communist Party secretaries whom Sajudis considered moderate and acceptable, thereby allowing these two to win. Sajudis candidates competed against and defeated nearly all the other leaders in the Lithuanian party and government: the chairman of the republican council of ministers, the chairman of the Supreme Soviet, the minister of justice, and two party republican central committee members. Sajudis claimed victory in 36 out of 39 districts. The strength and cohesiveness of the popular front organizations in all three Baltic Republics—in the face of economic and other forms of pressure from Moscow—were important factors in Gorbachev's willingness to negotiate with the republican leaderships on republican independence from the Soviet Union.

STRIKES

Another important form of spontaneous collective action was strikes. Usually strikes by industrial workers were motivated by a set of grievances revolving around degrading living and working conditions, demands for meaningful workplace and regional autonomy, and resentment at the privilege and power of the ruling elite. In many regions, however, strikes were vehicles of ethnic-national protest, beginning in 1988 with strikes in Transcaucasia and the Baltic Republics.[16] The largest labor action was the strike by coal miners in July 1989, when at its peak, the strike was joined by 300,000 to 400,000 workers. The strikes ended when the government promised to make substantial concessions to the workers' demands for better living and working conditions and greater economic control over their mines and cities. In turn the miners' frustration with the government's failure to make good on these promises led to a new, smaller, but far more politically directed strike wave in November, centered in the minefields of Vorkuta, in the far north of the Russian republic. Generally, nationalism mobilized more strikes than did the labor movement. The evidence from the count of workdays lost to strikes and protest in 1989 indicates that far more downtime was caused by ethnically related movements than from economically inspired protest.[17]

The strike movements helped to generate new organizations and new leaders independent of the old party-state. In the coal fields, the strike movement of 1989 created a cadre of grass roots leadership as strike committees turned into permanent workers' committees. In turn, in May 1990, these workers' committees created an independent confederation of labor to compete with the official trade union structure for the loyalty of workers. However, it failed to rally the workers of other

---

[16]Peter Rutland, "Labor Unrest and Movements in 1989 and 1990," in Ed A. Hewett and Victor H. Winston, eds., *Milestones in Glasnost and Perestroika: Politics and People* (Washington, D.C.: Brookings Institution, 1991), p. 290.

[17]Elizabeth Teague, "Soviet Workers Find a Voice," *Report on the USSR,* Radio Liberty 302/90, 13 July 1990, pp. 13–17.

industries to its fold. Soon afterward, coal miners created an independent trade union which broke with the old Soviet practice of organizing trade unions vertically to include managers, technical personnel, and workers within a given industry, and instead excluded managers and service personnel.[18] These were not the only workers' organizations formed out of the great strike wave of 1989. In addition to efforts by the regime to co-opt the movement, regional organizations emerged as well, such as the Union of Kuzbass Workers, which sought to unite workers with peasants and intellectuals, as well as purely local workers' organizations.[19]

In 1991 a new wave of strikes erupted, again centered in the coal fields. Although it embraced fewer workers than the 1989 strikes, at its height, labor leaders estimated that around a third of the mines were down.[20] Coordination across regions was managed by a council formed of representatives of the major region strike committees (called the Interregional Council of Strike Committees) and it was this Interregional Council that drafted a list of demands supported by all the striking workers. Besides the demands for a general wage agreement and meaningful improvements in living conditions, the program included radical political points, including demands for the resignation of the entire structure of central power—including Gorbachev's resignation as president, the dissolution of the USSR Congress of People's Deputies, the resignation of the USSR Cabinet of Ministers, and the transfer of power to the republics. Moreover, smaller-scale work actions in other industries suggested that workers outside the coal industry were sympathetic to the miners and unwilling to be used by the government to oppose them. The strikes ended only after the Russian Republic government agreed in early May with the union government on the transfer of the coal mines to the Russian Republic's jurisdiction.

ANOMIC PROTEST

The strike committees, popular fronts, and other grass roots political organizations that sprang up in the 1987–90 period were generally peaceful channels of informal mass participation, even when they exceeded the limits of what the authorities were willing to tolerate. Some events, however, resulted in violence and bloodshed. A shocking incident occurred in Tbilisi, capital of the Georgian republic, in April 1989, when a peaceful rally for Georgian independence and sovereignty was broken up with brutal force by Soviet troops, leaving at least 19 people dead. The Tbilisi killings in turn fortified Georgian determination to achieve independence from the Soviet Union. A similar incident occurred in Kazakstan in December 1986, in one of the first nationality-related mass political demonstrations of the Gorbachev period. Moscow engineered the removal of the First Secretary of the Communist Party of Kazakstan, an ethnic Kazak named Dinmukhamed Kunaev, and replaced him with an ethnic Russian, Gennadii Kolbin. As news of the decision spread through the capital city of the republic, Alma-Ata (today called Almaty), thousands of people,

---

[18]Ibid.

[19]Sarah Ashwin, "The 1991 Miners' Strikes: New Departures in the Independent Workers' Movement," Radio Liberty Research Report, RL 283/91, August 7, 1991.

[20]Ibid.

most of them young Kazaks, gathered on the main square to protest. Although the Moscow authorities claimed that the crowd attacked the police who were there to maintain order, all eyewitnesses agree that the police moved in to break up the demonstration with violence and that as a result, dozens of people were killed and many hundreds seriously injured.[21] In the eyes of many Kazak people, according to Martha Brill Olcott, "the violent repression of the peaceful demonstration is seen as but another manifestation of official Russia's long history of harsh retaliation against the Kazaks' efforts at political self-expression."[22] Some inter-ethnic grievances were so intense that they spilled out into warfare, especially in the Transcaucasian region where Armenia, Azerbaijan, and Georgia are located. Undoubtedly the bloodiest is the dispute between Armenians and Azerbaijani over Nagornyi-Karabakh. The conflict between Armenians and Azerbaijani over the status of this enclave inside Azerbaijan has turned into a bitter and protracted war.

The informal, often anomic, character of much popular political participation in the late Gorbachev period had important effects on the subsequent development of Russian politics. The explosiveness of demands for decent living conditions, the end of bureaucratic privilege, autonomy for the national culture, and redress of other broad popular grievances substantially raised the costs to the regime of using force to suppress protest. This helped to bring about radical change, such as the acknowledgment of the right to strike, the legalization of opposition parties, and ultimately the breakup of the union. Since the Soviet regime had suppressed almost all forms of organized participation except those it controlled and directed, there were few independent associations able to channel popular protest in the *perestroika* period. Many informal organizations sprang up but quickly faded away. The regime attempted to co-opt others by drawing them under state sponsorship. Most organizations found it very hard to survive since the economy continued to be overwhelmingly state-owned and state-administered: new informal organizations struggled simply to obtain office space and equipment. In contrast to Central Europe, Soviet society lacked a network of civic associations that could assume responsibility for mobilizing and managing popular pressure for democratic change. In the Soviet case, the mass outpouring of popular protest in 1989–91 therefore tended to be followed by rapid demobilization. Still, the surge of popular participation in this period left two lasting institutional changes: regular democratic elections and the nuclei of a number of political parties and interest groups. In the next section we will discuss electoral participation. In Chapter Five we will turn to parties and interest groups.

Electoral Participation

YELTSIN AND ELECTORAL POLITICS

The mobilization of popular political participation had the effect of generating new leadership and new organizations around a variety of populist, democratic, and nationalist issues. In many areas it forced former communist party and government

---

[21]Martha Brill Olcott, *"Perestroyka* in Kazakhstan," *Problems of Communism* 39:4 (July–August 1990), pp. 66–67. Note that the preferred spelling is now *Kazak* and *Kazakstan* rather than the older forms, *Kazakh* and *Kazakhstan.*

[22]Ibid., p. 67.

executives to adapt themselves to a pluralized political environment that they could no longer control. Some were swept away, but most managed to hold on to their power, and a few have emerged as champions of reform. A prominent example of the latter is Boris Yeltsin. Yeltsin, born (like Gorbachev) in 1931, had a conventional political career for a provincial party boss. He graduated from the Urals Polytechnical Institute in 1955 with a diploma in civil engineering, and worked for a long time in construction. In 1961 he joined the Communist Party, and in 1968 was recruited into full-time party work. From 1976 to 1985 he served as first secretary of the Sverdlovsk oblast (provincial) party organization. Sverdlovsk oblast is a major center of heavy industry and defense production, and the first secretary of its party committee was traditionally a very powerful figure.[23] As first secretary, Yeltsin gained a reputation as a decisive and relatively effective provincial leader, hard-driving and imperious in style.

One month after Gorbachev's selection as party leader, Yeltsin was transferred to Moscow and early in 1986 was named first secretary of the Moscow city party organization—a vital and also highly visible post. Shortly afterward he was also brought into the party Politburo as a candidate (nonvoting) member. He lasted as Moscow party chief until he was formally removed in November 1987 for speaking out against Gorbachev at the October 1987 Central Committee plenum. Well before that, he had antagonized most of the leading party politicians by his heavy-handed, confrontational methods and radical policy line. Firing most of the district party committee leaders, he became an advocate of the cause of the long-suffering Soviet consumer and railed against the privileges of bureaucrats. Impatient with the slow pace with which *perestroika* was being implemented, he attacked conservative opponents of reform and criticized Gorbachev for failing to fight hard enough for change. The final straw was his demand that the party accept his resignation from the Moscow post at the Central Committee plenum in October 1987, which was supposed to be devoted to the more ceremonial business of preparing for the celebration of the seventieth anniversary of the October Revolution. This move provoked an outpouring of public criticism of Yeltsin by his colleagues in the party leadership, and he was removed from his position as Moscow city party chief and member of the Politburo, although he was given a position as deputy minister of construction and remained a member of the Central Committee.[24]

Political disgrace such as this would traditionally have ended a Soviet party politician's career; in Stalin's time it would also have ended his life. But, by skillfully positioning himself as a populist democrat who had been made a martyr by the party establishment, Yeltsin mounted a remarkable political comeback. In the 1989 elections to the Congress of People's Deputies, he ran as a candidate for a Moscow-wide seat, campaigning as an underdog and an outsider against the establishment. The fact that his opponent was the director of a major state industrial firm simply gave Yeltsin additional ammunition for his campaign, as did various machinations by the party bureaucracy intended to hinder his campaign. In a stunning landslide,

---

[23]Both the city and the oblast surrounding it were named Sverdlovsk in Soviet times, but the city took back its traditional name of Ekaterinburg in 1991 while the oblast retained the name Sverdlovsk.

[24]Seweryn Bialer, "The Yeltsin Affair: The Dilemma of the Left in Gorbachev's Revolution," in Seweryn Bialer, ed., *Politics, Society, and Nationality Inside Gorbachev's Russia* (Boulder and London: Westview Press, 1989), pp. 91–120.

Yeltsin won his race with nearly 90 percent of the vote. His victory gave him a new mantle of democratic legitimacy which none of the other top party leaders possessed: Gorbachev, in glaring contrast, had never subjected himself to a popular vote for a political job. Yeltsin's immense prestige and authority were further heightened the following year, when he ran as deputy to the Russian Congress of People's Deputies from his old political base of Sverdlovsk. Here he defeated a field of 12 rivals and won his seat with over 80 percent of the vote. Subsequently, when the Congress convened in June 1990, he was elected its chairman. This made him, in effect, the chief executive of the vast and powerful Russian Republic, and a rival to Gorbachev himself. Then, consolidating his power further, he called for creation of a Russian state presidency, and, when the proposal passed in a national referendum, he ran for and won the presidency in June 1991, receiving 57 percent of the vote in a field of six candidates. Thus, unlike Gorbachev, he had run in and won three major popular electoral races in three successive years.[25] Electoral success such as this would be extraordinary in any country.

His culminating electoral victory came in 1996 when he ran for reelection as Russian president. Despite the serious physical infirmities that had been evident in 1995, he rallied once again and mounted a vigorous campaign. Starting out with extremely low popularity ratings (less than 10 percent in March 1996), he made full use of the advantages of incumbency to rekindle popular confidence in his leadership and arouse fear of the consequences of a communist victory. Touring the country, issuing a torrent of edicts, promising an end to the war in Chechnia, and addressing the crisis of nonpayments of wages and pensions contributed to Yeltsin's steadily rising popularity over the months of the campaign. When the first round of the election was held on June 16, 1996, he received over 35 percent of the vote, the highest share of any candidate. Gennadii Ziuganov, his communist rival, received 32 percent.[26] (See Table 4.1.) These two candidates then faced each other in the runoff, scheduled for July 3. Yeltsin then made a dramatic and brilliant tactical maneuver. He named General Alexander Lebed´, who as a candidate in the first round had received 14.5 percent of the vote, as his national security advisor and secretary of the Security Council with a broad mandate to eliminate corruption, fight crime, and end the war in Chechnia. Lebed´, who had surreptitiously received assistance from the president's staff throughout the campaign, willingly embraced the offer and threw his support to Yeltsin. At the same time, Ziuganov's campaign seemed to collapse. Even the fact that Yeltsin then suffered another of his periodic bouts of exhaustion (later it was learned that he had suffered another heart attack), and made no public appearances between June 26 and election day, did not alarm the voters. In the second round, Yeltsin received almost 54 percent of the vote to Ziuganov's 40.3 percent.[27] (See Table 4.2.) The master of Russian campaigning had won once more.

---

[25]A vivid portrait of Yeltsin as a politician is Bill Keller, "Boris Yeltsin Taking Power," *New York Times Magazine,* September 23, 1990. Yeltsin has published two memoirs, both of which have been translated into English: Boris Yeltsin, *Against the Grain,* trans. Michael Glenny (New York: Summit Books, 1990); and *The Struggle for Russia,* trans. Catherine A. Fitzpatrick (New York: Times Books, 1994).

[26]Based on results published in *Rossiiskaya gazeta* on 22 June 1996, and taken from the OMRI Daily Digest of 25 June 1996. The percentages are calculated based on the number of voters participating in the voting (75,587,139), the method used in the 1995 Duma elections.

[27]*Segodnia,* July 10, 1996.

TABLE 4.1

First-Round Presidential Election Results, June 16, 1996

	Percentage / of Votes	Number of Votes
Boris Yeltsin	35.28	26,665,495
Gennadii Ziuganov	32.03	24,211,686
Alexander Lebed´	14.52	10,974,736
Grigorii Yavlinsky	7.34	5,550,752
Vladimir Zhirinovsky	5.70	4,311,479
Svyatoslav Fedorov	0.92	699,158
Mikhail Gorbachev	0.51	386,069
Martin Shakkum	0.37	277,068
Yurii Vlasov	0.20	151,282
Vladimir Bryntsalov	0.16	123,065
Aman Tuleev	0.00	308
Against all candidates	1.54	1,163,921

Registered voters: 108,495,023
Total valid ballots: 74,515,019
Total invalid ballots: 1,072,120
Turnout: 69.8 percent

Source: Rossiiskaya gazeta, June 22, 1996 and OMRI Daily Digest, June 25, 1996.

RADICAL DEMOCRATIC POPULISM

The elections of the all-union Congress of People's Deputies in 1989 and the republican and local soviets in 1990 illustrate the turn from the directed political participation characteristic of the old system to the new politics of competitive elections. The 1989 and 1990 elections were conceived by Gorbachev as ways of giving the wave of popular political participation stimulated by *glasnost´* a constructive outlet, one that would help weaken Gorbachev's conservative opposition while at the same time enable him to continue to set the country's basic policy direction. But the elections had much more far-reaching effects than he anticipated, by activating popular

---

TABLE 4.2

Second-Round Presidential Election Results, July 3, 1996

	Percentage of Votes	Number of Votes
Boris Yeltsin	53.82	40,208,384
Gennadii Ziuganov	40.31	30,113,306
Against both	4.83	3,604,550
Turnout	**68.89**	**74,815,898**

Source: Segodnia, July 10, 1996.

movements and generating new opposition leaders with large popular followings. The elections mobilized political participation around the major political cleavages that we reviewed in the last chapter: the demands for an open, democratic, market-oriented society from the educated urban strata, and the demands for autonomy and independence from the national communities living in the ethnic republics. Although the elections of 1989, 1990, and 1991 were not organized around competing parties for the most part, proto-partisan tendencies formed as candidates aligned themselves with competing political causes.

Thus these early elections often revolved around personalities rather than parties. In many cases they were understood both by authorities and voters as a referendum on the system rather than as a choice between alternative political programs. The electoral process enabled the populace to register their opposition to the old party and government elites, resulting in some dramatic upsets. In the 1989 elections of deputies to the new all-union Congress of People's Deputies, some 38 regional and district party secretaries lost their races; in Leningrad, the first secretaries of the regional party committee and city party committee were both defeated, as were the chairmen of the regional and city soviet.[28] All six of the most powerful officials in Leningrad lost their races: in fact, even though he was running unopposed, the first secretary of Leningrad's obkom (provincial party committee) was defeated because he failed to garner the required 50 percent + 1 of the votes cast. In the Russian and Ukrainian republics, around 40 leading party and government officials were defeated, and a group of 300 to 400 deputies identified with liberal democratic views were elected to the Congress. Upon election, they began organizing themselves as a parliamentary bloc called the "Interregional Group of Deputies." In some republics, however, particularly in Central Asia, the entrenched political elite was able to maintain its control in much the same way as it had done in the past. Altogether, 80 percent of the republic and obkom secretaries who ran did win their races, with bureaucratic dominance most evident in Central Asia; many officials found "safe" seats for themselves in outlying rural areas around the cities.[29] The same pattern was apparent in the 1990 elections as well: politicians from the apparat managed for the most part to win their races by avoiding direct confrontation with well-organized opposition movements, but, especially in major cities, new political movements succeeded in electing democratically minded candidates to the republican and local soviets.

Table 4.3 provides a breakdown of the social composition of the old and new corps of people's deputies for the USSR and the Russian republic. Several conclusions about elections in the transition period may be drawn from the table.

---

[28]White, *Gorbachev in Power*, pp. 45–47.

[29]Jerry F. Hough, "The Politics of Successful Economic Reform," *Soviet Economy* 5:1 (1989), p. 17. *Argumenty i fakty*, no. 21, 1989, reports that 191 regional and republican party secretaries ran but 126 succeeded in running without opposition. For most, noncompetitive races produced victories: of the 38 party secretaries who lost, 32 had faced opponents. On the other hand, in localities where the political environment permitted independent popular mobilization, uncontested races were widely condemned as antidemocratic. In Leningrad, Kiev, and certain other places, uncontested races backfired for the candidates and yielded spectacular defeats for prominent officials.

————————————————TABLE 4.3————————————————
Social and Political Composition of USSR and Russian Deputies, Selected Levels (in percentage)*

	Communist Party Members	Manual Workers	Women
1. USSR Supreme Soviet (1970) (N = 1,500)	72.3	31.7	30.5
2. USSR local soviets (1971) (N = 2 million)	44.5	36.5	45.8
3. USSR Supreme Soviet (1984) (N = 1,500)	71.5	35.2	32.8
4. Russian Republic Supreme Soviet (1985) (N = 975)	66.6	35.8	35.3
5. USSR Congress of People's Deputies (1989) (N = 2,250)	87.6	18.6	17.1
6. USSR Supreme Soviet (1989) (N = 542)	87.8	24.7	18.4
7. Russian Republic Congress of People's Deputies (1990) (N = 1,026)	86.3	5.9	5.4
8. Local Russian Republic soviets (1990) (N = 702,268)	49.1	24.9	35
9. State Duma of the Federal Assembly (December 1993) (N = 450)	10.0[a]	1.3	13.5
10. State Duma of the Federal Assembly (December 1995) (N = 450)	33.0[a]	2.4	10.2

*Note: Because categories overlap, figures add up to more than 100 percent in some rows.

[a]Figure refers to membership in the party faction of the Communist Party of the Russian Federation within the State Duma.

Source: Compiled by author.

DEMOCRACY AND THE END OF "DESCRIPTIVE REPRESENTATION"

First, voters generally rejected, where possible, the phony tokenism of the old system. This is reflected most dramatically in the sharp decline in the number of women, workers, and collective farm workers among the new deputies. Women fared poorly in the 1989 all-union elections, where they comprised only 17 percent of the candidates and an equal number of the winners (note that they were not disadvantaged once they had been nominated and registered as candidates). They were still more disadvantaged in the 1990 elections to the Russian Republic parliament, where they comprised 7.2 percent of candidates and 5.4 percent of winners. Workers suffered a similar drop in their representation. These changes in the social composition of the new deputy corps—and similar results for other groups, such as the young and the elderly—have fueled the arguments of antiliberal groups who claim that the very process of democratic elections in a competitive environment undermines the ideals of socialism and especially the interests of the working class.

A second pattern that strikes the observer is the increase in the representation of Communist Party members, from slightly over 70 percent in the old, quota-rigged USSR Supreme Soviet, two-thirds in the Russian Republic Supreme Soviet, and only 44 percent in the lower soviets, to 86–87 percent among deputies in the newly elected Congresses at the union and Russian Republic levels in 1989 and 1990. Does this fact mean that the Communist Party dominated the new parliaments? To understand why this is not so, we must distinguish victory by party members from victory by the party. Because many of the members of the intelligentsia were members of the party, and because the public showed a clear preference for articulate, educated, and potentially effective candidates, party members were disproportionately represented among the candidates and, therefore, among the victors. Party members were overrepresented for the same reason that women and workers were at a disadvantage: the existing patterns of social prestige and status tended to give an advantage to people with higher social status and higher education, and this category tended to be concentrated among men and party members.[30] During the campaigns Communist Party members divided along the same ideological and interest lines as the rest of society; there was no clear party line or ideological discipline among members. Party members were elected in many cases because as individuals they appealed to voters. As a result, the new Congresses at the all-union and republican levels were neither entirely one-party nor multiparty parliaments. Only in the 1993 and 1995 parliamentary elections did voters have a choice among something like real parties with ideologically distinct electoral organizations competing for shares of power over government. For the first time parties began to link the preferences of segments of the electorate with the policy-making processes of the state.

In fact, as in other countries undergoing a transition from communism to democracy, members of the "prestige" elite formed a large share of the first generation of elected politicians as voters looked to turn out the existing political establishment.[31] In the Russian Republic Congress of Deputies, nearly 20 percent of the elected deputies came from the sectors of health, education, journalism, and the arts. Another 35 percent were managers of enterprises, while 86 percent of the candidates and 93 percent of the winners had higher educational degrees. What was important to voters, therefore, was not whether a candidate was a party member or not, but whether he or she was a representative of the old political elite. Indeed, prior political experience was often a liability to candidates. Asked whether they regarded prior experience as a people's deputy as an asset, only 12 percent of respondents in one poll said experience was needed, and fully 42 percent saw no need for experience at all. A similar number said, in fact, that it was necessary to replace all the old deputies. And indeed in the new Congress of People's Deputies

---

[30]In this sense, the bias in favor of candidates from more privileged social origins and particularly those with higher educations resembles the pattern in the social recruitment of parliamentarians in West European democracies. See Joel D. Aberbach, Robert D. Putnam, and Bert A. Rockman, *Bureaucrats and Politicians in Western Democracies* (Cambridge, MA: Harvard University Press, 1981), pp. 46–62.

[31]Gerhard Loewenberg, "The New Political Leadership of Central Europe: The Example of the New Hungarian National Assembly," in Thomas F. Remington, ed., *Parliaments in Transition: The New Legislative Politics in the Former USSR and Eastern Europe* (Boulder: Westview Press, 1994), pp. 29–53.

in the RSFSR, fully 94 percent had not been deputies previously. In some cities, the percentage of turnover among deputies to the city soviet approached 100 percent.

More recent elections have witnessed a backlash against the antiestablishment politics of the 1989–90 period. This is because of the sharp disappointment that most people have experienced with the results of the change of regime. Now many voters prefer to elect individuals who have proven credentials as competent managers. Therefore, instead of counting against a candidate, prior experience as an official often is an asset in electoral contests, and the label of "democrat" is a term of scorn. Very often, this gives an advantage to members of the old communist hierarchy running on a platform of gradualism, defense of social welfare, and antagonism toward the wave of politicians elected on democratic platforms who brought down the old system faster than they could build up a new one. Such appeals have considerable attraction for citizens suffering from the trials of transition. They are strengthened by the unconstitutional actions taken by President Yeltsin who, in September 1993 decreed the dissolution of parliament and called for holding new elections in December, and who, when faced with an uprising by the extreme opposition to these decrees, suppressed it with heavy and demonstrative violence. These and other actions give the communist opposition grounds for charging that the first wave of democratically oriented politicians—whom they invariably call the "so-called democrats"—are in fact more power-hungry and unscrupulous than those they defeated in the 1989 and 1990 elections.

EBBING PARTICIPATION

Two effects of the backlash against the initial wave of democratic expectations may be observed in recent elections. First was a drop in electoral turnout. In 1989 total turnout for elections of deputies to the new all-union Congress of People's Deputies was 90 percent. In 1990, turnout for the elections of deputies to the new Russian Congress of People's Deputies was 76 percent. In 1991, 75 percent of the electorate took part in the presidential election in Russia, while 69 percent voted in the Russian referendum of April 1993 on approval of President Yeltsin and his government. However, at the end of 1993, after Yeltsin had forcibly dissolved the parliament and demanded new elections to a parliament whose structure he instituted by decree, turnout fell sharply. Yeltsin had dissolved parliament after failing to win its approval for a new constitution and after it refused to allow the draft worked out by Yeltsin's advisors to be put to a nationwide referendum for approval. In December Yeltsin demanded that Russian citizens vote up or down on the constitutional draft that he proposed for their adoption as well as elect new deputies to a parliament which was itself to be created by that constitution.

Anticipating that turnout would be low, Yeltsin decreed that elections of representatives to the parliament would be valid if turnout in a district was at least 25 percent, and that a candidate would be elected if he or she received more votes than any other candidate. For passage of the constitutional referendum, however, Yeltsin decreed that at least half of the registered voters in the country would have to take part in the voting, and that at least half of them would have to have approved it. President Yeltsin and his administration went to considerable lengths to ensure the constitution's passage. Regional heads of administration were placed under heavy pressure by President Yeltsin to achieve a 50 percent turnout and a majority for the constitution. In the end, the government declared that some 54.8 percent of the electorate had voted and that, of these, 58.4 percent cast their ballots in favor of the constitution. However, these official figures may overstate the actual level of turnout. According to estimates by a team of researchers headed by Alexander Sobyanin, actual turnout was probably closer to 46 percent, which implied that the constitution had, in fact, not been adopted.[32] While these charges were stoutly refuted by election officials,[33] the precipitous decline in electoral participation was a warning to all sides that many citizens no longer considered voting worth the effort.

Moreover, turnout in many regional and local races was still lower. In St. Petersburg (formerly Leningrad), an election for deputies to the local city council was called for March 20, 1994. Like the parliamentary elections in December, the elections were to be considered valid if at least 25 percent of the voters took part. On the day of the election, however, only 22 percent of the voters turned out. As the polls were closing on the evening of the twentieth, Mayor Anatolii Sobchak decreed that the polls would be held open another day so that voters would have another chance to cast their ballots; at the same time, he issued an order extending voting rights to soldiers, students, and other temporary residents of the city. Enough people then cast ballots the next day to enable Sobchak to declare that total turnout, at 25.6 percent, had met the necessary threshold for validity.[34] The situation in other cities was little better. On March 6, some 152 cities had held elections of city councils, and in 59, turnout was below the minimum necessary to be legally valid. In Yaroslavl, where electoral turnout exceeded 70 percent in the 1990 elections, participation fell to around 25 percent in the local elections of spring 1994.[35]

However, turnout, at least in national elections, began to rise again in 1995 and 1996. Perhaps because of the efforts by parties to mobilize voters for their leaders, voter turnout in the December 1995 parliamentary elections was 65 percent. This figure is all the more impressive when we realize that the elections took place in deep winter, did not coincide with a major referendum or presidential election, and were held simply to elect representatives to one chamber of parliament.[36] It may be

---

[32]V. Vyzhutovich, "Tsentizbirkom prevrashchaetsiia v politicheskoe vedomstvo" [The Central Electoral Commission Is Turning into a Political Agency] *Izvestiia,* May 4, 1994. While it is impossible to assess the validity of Sobyanin's charges, it is worth noting that the Central Electoral Commission reported that the total number of voters on the registration rolls in December 1993 was lower by 1.14 million voters than the number in April 1993. The lower figure, of course, eased the task of declaring that a majority of voters had turned out for the election. How a million voters had vanished between April and December was not indicated. Moreover, the Central Electoral Commission refused to publish a full tally of election results by electoral district, confining itself only to publishing a list of winners. No independent verification of the CEC's own conclusions was thus possible.

See Vera Tolz and Julia Wishnevsky, "Election Queries Make Russians Doubt Democratic Process," *RFE/RL Research Report* 3:13 (1 April 1994), p. 3.

[33]Iu. Vedeneev and V. I. Lysenko, "Vybory-93: Uroki i al´ternativy," *Nezavisimaia gazeta,* June 28, 1994.

[34]UPI, March 22, 1994.

[35]Jeffrey W. Hahn, "The Development of Local Legislatures in Russia: The Case of Yaroslavl," in Jeffrey W. Hahn, ed., *Democratization in Russia: The Development of Legislative Institutions* (Armonk, NY: M. E. Sharpe, 1996), p. 190.

[36]Michael McFaul, *Russia Between Elections: What the December 1995 Results Really Mean* (Moscow: Carnegie Moscow Center, 1996), p. 1.

that the vigorous campaigns mounted by the parties had the effect of persuading voters that their interests were at stake in the elections.[37] The turnout in the two rounds of the presidential election in summer 1996 was still higher, nearly 70 percent each time. It is likely that however disillusioned voters may feel with democratic politics, they see a link between their participation in the electoral process and the country's future. This inference is supported by the results of an opinion poll commissioned by the Central Electoral Commission immediately after the July 3, 1996, presidential runoff vote. Respondents in a nationwide sample of voters were asked what freedoms they valued most highly. Freedom of the press and free elections tied for the largest number of responses (18 percent each). Of the respondents, 59 percent expressed the view that leaders should be chosen by means of free elections, and 68 percent believed that elections could change the situation in the country for the better.[38]

POLITICAL BACKLASH

The other trend was the success of antireform parties and candidates in elections after 1990–91, a trend which was especially worrisome to President Yeltsin and his supporters. Yeltsin's political successes had always come about through his ability to appeal to the public at large for support. The results of the April 1993 referendum showed that his faith in his popular support was not misplaced: whatever the missteps and failures of the democratic reformers who came to power in 1990 and 1991, the public preferred Yeltsin to his communist opponents in parliament. He and his administration evidently underestimated, however, the extent of public dissatisfaction with the government. Both the December 1993 parliamentary elections and a series of regional and city elections in 1993 and 1994 showed that the day when democratic reformers could win elections with a platform calling for rejection of the old communist regime had passed. In several regional races in 1993, candidates running for the post of chief regional executive ("governor") won who were former party and government officials. In the parliamentary elections of December 1993, the reorganized Communist Party and its Agrarian Party all together took 20 percent of the party list vote, while the extremist Liberal Democratic Party of Vladimir Zhirinovsky, running on a demagogic and xenophobic platform, won 23 percent of the party list vote. The party associated with the radical economic reforms carried out by the government, Russia's Choice, only won 15.5 percent of the party list vote.[39] Most observers were surprised at the degree to which democratic reformers had been repudiated and were disturbed at the strength of support for antidemocratic parties.

The December 1995 elections produced an even higher share of votes for antireform parties although the total proportion of votes cast for reform-oriented parties

[37]Sarah Oates, "Vying for Votes on a Crowded Campaign Trail," *Transition* (1996) 2: 26–29.

[38]Cited in OMRI Daily Digest, August 2, 1996.

[39]The December 1993 elections employed a new electoral system which Yeltsin decreed into law. Half of the 450 seats in the lower, popular chamber of the new parliament would be assigned to parties running candidates on national party lists. The other half would go to candidates who won a plurality of the vote in 225 individual districts. The upper house would be made up of 2 deputies from each of Russia's 89 constituent federal regions (provinces as well as ethnic republics).

remained roughly similar to the 1993 results. Now, instead of Zhirinovsky winning 23 percent and the communists 12 percent of the party list vote, the communists won 22 percent and Zhirinovsky 11 percent. Most analysts concluded that the opposition parties were mainly competing for the same constituency while the pro-reform electorate tended to hold its own.[40] The core constituencies for basic ideological alternatives may therefore be relatively stable even though the party system is in flux. Moreover, the June–July 1996 presidential election, where Gennadii Ziuganov's support could not rise beyond a ceiling of about 40 percent, suggested that however unpopular President Yeltsin and the current postcommunist leadership was, the majority of voters were unwilling to endorse a return to communist rule.

RUSSIAN POLITICAL PARTICIPATION IN COMPARATIVE PERSPECTIVE

Over the past decade political participation in Russia has undergone enormous change. The old model of directed participation—where the rituals of lip-service to communist ideals were complemented by a modest undercurrent of unlicensed activity and a great deal of parochial, private interaction between citizens and state—underwent two great transformations. First was the mobilization of popular involvement in new forms of participation—informal organizations, rallies and strikes, and competitive elections. Then this wave passed, leaving fewer informal organizations behind but still giving citizens numerous opportunities to cast ballots in local and national elections. Over time, the choices posed for voters in the elections came to be associated more and more with ideologically distinct political alternatives.

Overall, how does contemporary Russian political participation compare with the patterns found in Western democracies? Surveys suggest that, in some respects, levels of participation in Russia are comparable with those in North American and European political systems. A set of surveys of Russian, Ukrainian, and Lithuanian citizens carried out by Arthur H. Miller of the University of Iowa and his colleagues in 1990, 1991, and 1992 found that around 15 percent of Russian citizens reported having contacted a newspaper or magazine at least once; around 20 percent had contacted an elected official; 30 percent had participated at least once in a rally or demonstration; and a third had signed a petition.[41] These rates were comparable to, and in some cases, higher than, those found in Western Europe and North America. On the other hand, they found that Russia was far lower than other democracies in the levels of membership in voluntary associations. Only 6 percent of Russian respondents in the 1992 survey reported having joined a social organization or initiative group and only 2 percent reported belonging to a political party or movement.[42] Moreover, the surveys showed a tendency for participation in various protest

---

[40]E.g., see McFaul, *Russia between Elections*, p. 4.

[41]William M. Reisinger, Arthur H. Miller, and Vicki L. Hesli, "Public Behavior and Political Change in Post-Soviet States." *Journal of Politics* 57 (1995): 941–970.

[42]Ibid., p. 959.

activities to fall off in 1992. As these scholars put it, "the 'defeat' of the old regime and the beginning of a new political phase occurs at the end of 1991."[43]

Low levels of organizational membership—the legacy of the imposition of state control over all voluntary associations in society and the suppression of all autonomous political activity—have very serious implications for the vitality of democratic institutions in the post-Soviet period. Studies by political scientist Robert Putnam indicate that both the actual performance of democratic government, and people's evaluations of government's responsiveness and effectiveness, are very strongly related to the density of membership in voluntary associations. These, as Putnam shows, need not be strictly political: extensive involvement in a variety of community bodies—choral societies, sports leagues, and civic improvement groups—is a powerful source of the "social capital" that enables individuals in a society to cooperate with one another for common purposes. Their "horizontally" formed social capital in turn carries over into their interactions with government. It enables more people to take on shares of responsibility for making decisions and monitoring the acts of government officials, thus holding government to higher standards than would otherwise be the case, and helping to check government abuses. In a setting where interaction in civic and social associations is low, people are more likely to turn instead "vertically" to powerful protectors for basic social needs such as order, even though such bosses may exact a high price in power and wealth for their services. This pattern of mutual dependence and alienation between patrons and clients, rulers and ruled, can last for many decades or even centuries, since it can be difficult for a process of mutual trust and cooperation to get started in a setting where mistrust and hopelessness prevail.[44] The gap between regime and populace that we have characterized as a feature of Russian political culture over many centuries has analogues in many other societies with tendencies to authoritarianism. The low and falling levels of political participation in the mid-1990s in Russia, following the surge of popular mobilization in the late 1980s and early 1990s, are evidence that it may be a long time before Russia overcomes that gap.

Another reason for pessimism is the high level of inequality in income and wealth, which has widened as a result of the economic changes occurring in Russia since 1991. As in other societies with great disparities in economic resources, the political system may act to deepen inequality rather than to offset it. Comparative studies generally show a stratified pattern of participation: in most countries, people with higher levels of education and income tend to be more active in politics.[45] However, in most societies *voting* reflects a somewhat different pattern than other forms of participation, such as joining political associations or taking part in campaigns. Voting requires much less effort than many other forms of political activity

---

[43]Ibid., p. 966.

[44]Robert D. Putnam, *Making Democracy Work: Civic Traditions in Modern Italy* (Princeton: Princeton University Press, 1993).

[45]Sidney Verba, Norman H. Nie, and Jae-on Kim, *Participation and Political Equality: A Seven-Nation Comparison* (Cambridge: Cambridge University Press, 1978); Samuel H. Barnes and Max Kaase, eds., *Political Action: Mass Participation in Five Western Democracies* (Beverly Hills, CA: Sage Publications, 1979).

and so tends to be more readily accessible to poorer, less mobile, and more marginal strata of a society. Participation in elections for individuals with low education and income levels greatly depends on the success of parties and interest groups in motivating them to take part. A competitive party system can offset some of the effects of inequality in social status which are reflected in other forms of political participation. Therefore, although participation in Russia lacks a sturdy foundation in organizational membership, the relatively high participation in elections contested by opposing parties is at least one bridge across the gap separating the populace from the regime.

Elite Adaptation and Replacement

NOMENKLATURA AND ELITE RECRUITMENT UNDER THE OLD REGIME

Chapter Two noted that in the Soviet system, the method by which political elites were chosen was carefully regulated by the Communist Party. The filling of any position which carried important administrative responsibility, or which was likely to affect the formation of public attitudes, was subject to party approval. The system for recruiting, training, and appointing individuals for positions of leadership and responsibility in the regime was called the nomenklatura system, and those individuals who were approved for the positions on nomenklatura lists were often called, collectively, "the nomenklatura." Many citizens thought of them as the true ruling class in Soviet society.

Members of the nomenklatura did enjoy certain privileges, minor ones in the case of lesser posts, substantial ones for positions carrying greater status and authority. For much of the post-Stalin era, their careers were relatively secure: only in cases of severe incompetence or malfeasance were they likely to be removed entirely from the ranks of the privileged. Some organizations, such as the trade unions, were considered "retirement homes" for older or less able officials, while postings to other organizations were considered necessary stepping stones for political advancement. Many officials, for instance, spent a tour of duty as a full-time functionary for the Communist Party itself before re-entering jobs in government or economic management.

The party used the nomenklatura system to enforce lower officials' accountability for their actions, although it was a relatively inefficient mechanism. Among other effects, the nomenklatura system fostered the formation of strong personal links among leaders and the entrenchment of patron–client relationships: a leader was often more interested in subordinates' political loyalty in party power struggles than in their merits as administrators. In a comprehensive survey of the phenomenon, Patrick Willerton estimated that as of 1981, one-third of the Politburo's members had clientelistic links to Brezhnev.[46] These networks evidently contributed to elite cohesion and coordination and helped stabilize the political regime in much the same way that corruption, to which patronage was often linked, helped to redis-

---

[46]John P. Willerton, *Patronage and Politics in the USSR* (Cambridge: Cambridge University Press, 1992).

tribute resources and iron out certain inflexibilities in the centrally planned economy. But this flexibility came at a very high price, which was ultimately paid by the political regime as a whole. The undermining of party policy and principles by the pursuit of private ends, the ubiquity of mediocrity and incompetence, and the impunity of corruption all corroded the foundations of the regime. Finally, as the entire Brezhnev-era political elite entrenched itself into power, growing older and older through the 1960s, 1970s, and 1980s, upward mobility ground to a near-halt, blocking the opportunities for advancement by succeeding cohorts of elites. Not the least of the reasons for the collapse of the Soviet system was the frustration of their aspirations for a larger share of power.[47]

CHANGING PATTERNS OF ELITE RECRUITMENT

The democratizing reforms of the late 1980s and early 1990s made two important changes in the process of elite recruitment. First, the old nomenklatura system crumbled along with other Communist Party controls over society. Second, although most members of the old ruling elites adapted themselves to the new circumstances and stayed on in various official capacities, the wave of new informal organizations and popular elections brought about an infusion of new people into elite positions. Thus the contemporary Russian political elite consists of some people who were recruited under the old nomenklatura system together with a smaller share of individuals who have entered politics through new democratic channels.

We can get an idea of the ways in which the opening of popular participation under Gorbachev and Yeltsin affected elite recruitment by comparing two typical political careers.[48] The first represents the old ruling elite, whose members made their careers after World War II. The second represents the newer generation of politicians who have come up through new representative and executive institutions.

The typical official of the older generation was born in the second half of the 1930s, often in a peasant family. He received only eight years of schooling, after which he went to work in a factory or collective farm, performing manual labor. After serving in the army, where he joined the Communist Party, he returned home and went into political work, typically starting out as a full-time Komsomol official. While working, he completed a higher educational institution as a correspondence student, receiving his degree from a pedagogical institute or an agricultural science institute. Gradually he climbed the ladder of party jobs: first as a low-level staff official, then as head of a department for a local party organization, then on the staff of the next higher party organization, and then as a full-time secretary of the party committee of the province. Along the way, he would have studied at a regional party school and received an advanced degree, or as a correspondence student through the Higher Party School in Moscow. Eventually he was assigned to work at the party's

[47]Boris Golovachev, Larisa Kosova, and Liudmila Khakhulina, "⟨⟨Novaia⟩⟩ Rossiiskaia elita: starye igroki na novom pole ?" *Segodnia,* February 14, 1996.

[48]This follows closely the discussion by Nikolai Petrov of the Institute of Geography of the Russian Academy of Sciences in an unpublished paper entitled, "Politicheskie elity v tsentre i na mestakh" [Political Elites at the Center and in the Localities], (Moscow: 1994), pp. 13–14. Dr. Petrov's permission to cite this study is gratefully acknowledged.

headquarters in Moscow, as an official of the CPSU Central Committee staff, before being sent out to one of the provinces as the first secretary of the regional party organization—the highest political official in the region, equivalent to the position of governor of an American state. Then, still only in his late 50s, he was caught up in the democratization wave. He survived the shakeups in the party and the elections of 1989 and 1990, but in the fall of 1991 he lost his job when President Yeltsin outlawed the Communist Party, disbanded its organization and confiscated its assets. However, he found a new job as chairman of the province soviet or as a senior official in the province government. He holds on, in part, because he is known as a capable and effective manager; he knows the province well and can get things done; and he is skilled at holding on to power. If elections are held in his region for chief executive, he has a good chance of winning. Politically, he would call himself a pragmatist, not an ideologue; he would favor the expansion of market relations in Russia, but would invariably caution that in view of Russia's traditions and economic makeup, the transition must be gradual and carefully managed. He is not likely to aspire to any further political advances, regarding the position of chief executive in the region as the pinnacle of his career.

Compare his career to that of a politician of the next generation, someone born in the late 1940s or early 1950s. He comes out of a city rather than the countryside. Instead of leaving school, he has completed his secondary degree and gone on to the local university studying a natural science such as physics, and then, after university, taking an advanced degree at a research institute. Along the way he enters the Communist Party. The sensational debates and disclosures of the *glasnost'* period in the late 1980s have a considerable impact on his political outlook. He joins an unofficial study group, perhaps devoted to the thought of an Old Bolshevik repressed by Stalin, or becomes active in a local youth group or environmental defense movement. He makes public statements calling for internal democracy in the Communist Party, and supports Gorbachev's *perestroika* program. In 1989, he gains his first electoral experience working in the campaign of one of the democratically oriented candidates running for USSR deputy; in 1990, he himself runs for deputy to the Russian Congress of People's Deputies and wins his seat. Going to Moscow, he is one of the young, radical, reform-minded deputies who align themselves with the democratic fractions, and vote for Yeltsin, sovereignty for Russia, and a decisive push for a market economy. After the August 1991 coup attempt and the dissolution of the Communist Party, Yeltsin appoints him as presidential representative or as chief of administration in one of the regions. More interested in politics than in economic management, he finds himself surrounded by older officials with strong local ties, and dreams of further career promotions that will carry him to Moscow.

These two portraits, which are based on a composite depiction of the career patterns of many different people rather than any particular individuals, illustrate the point that as a result of the upheavals of recent years, the political elite has not so much been replaced as it has been expanded to accommodate the influx of new, often younger, politicians who have come in to fill positions in representative and executive branches. In numerous cases, the old guard have successfully adapted themselves to the new conditions, and, drawing upon their experience and contacts, have found different high-status jobs for themselves. The new wave of young democrats, coming up through elections to local and national soviets, have often now found livelihoods in structures under President Yeltsin's appointment and control.

Some indication of the ways in which members of the old guard have accommodated themselves to the new political situation may be gained from the results of a survey conducted by President Yeltsin's administration in November 1992. Fifty provinces were surveyed to determine what their former top officials were now doing. Specifically, information was sought on the three highest officials in the region as of August 1991: the head of the provincial party committee (obkom first secretary); the chief executive of the provincial government (head of the oblast ispolkom); and the head of the party organization of the capital city of the province (gorkom first secretary). Information was returned on 141 of these individuals. Table 4.4 indicates the results.[49]

The figures suggest that most members of the old ruling elite remained in the regional elite; 88 percent of the sample reported here were still in their home regions, a majority in high political posts. On the other hand, party officials showed considerable adaptability, with 38 percent of the former first secretaries of the regions having gone into business.

The present-day political elite in Russia, then, is a mixture of old and new, in which the old guard still predominates. This is true at the national and regional levels. Russian geographer Nikolai Petrov has examined a pool of 343 individuals who, as of late 1993, were considered to be among the most influential politicians in national politics. We may regard these as a representative cross-section of the national political elite. One is immediately struck by the predominance of men in the group: only 10 (3 percent) were women. This is a reflection of the various filters and biases that restrict women's political mobility in the post-Soviet period, once the old regime's use of quotas and tokenism was gone, and it is comparable to the representation of women in the national political elite under the old regime. The proportion of women in the CPSU Central Committee (which comprised a cross-section of the membership of the Soviet Union's senior party, government, diplomatic, military, scientific, and cultural elite) was around 4 percent in the mid-1980s, and many of the women who were members were there as token representatives of heavily female occupations, such as farmworkers.

Another significant pattern among the members of the pool is that while only one-fifth were born in Moscow, over half received their higher educations there. This is explained by the traditional pull of Moscow for talented and ambitious young people from around the country, many of whom then stay in Moscow to work. One-fifth went to Moscow State University, the most prestigious of the country's universities. This fact illustrates the centralized nature of the old system, where Moscow dominated the country's political, educational, academic, and administrative life.

Recently the Russian public opinion research institute VTsIOM conducted a comprehensive study of Russia's contemporary social and political elite.[50] They compared a sample of over a thousand people who had held senior nomenklatura jobs in 1988 with an equivalent group holding leading positions in the state administration, politics, science, culture, and economic management in 1993. The results showed that the great majority of the 1993 elite had either held nomenklatura jobs

---

[49]Ibid., p. 21.

[50]See note 47, above.

TABLE 4.4
Regional Elite Circulation After 1991 (in percentages)

	August 1991 Position			
	Provincial Party Leader	City Party Leader	Provincial Chief Executive	Total
Status in November 1992:				
Remained in regional leadership	16	12	40	23
Entered state sector as government or economic manager	32	44	22	32
Entered private sector	38	32	28	33
Left the region	14	12	10	12
Total	100	100	100	100
	(N = 50)	(N = 41)	(N = 50)	(N = 141)

Source: Survey of presidential representatives, November 30, 1992.

---

in 1988, or came from positions that were in the "reserve nomenklatura"—positions such as deputy director of important institutions rather than director. Only 16 percent had entered elite positions without having had any administrative experience at all. By the same token, 57 percent of the old nomenklatura group had been able to stay in administrative positions in the state or economy; another 18 percent found reasonably high but not top-level positions. Most of those who failed to stay in the elite were over 60 years of age. Clearly the old elite has managed to survive in positions of power and influence.

One major reason for their success in staying in power was the value of their social connections. Among those of the current elite who were former communist party members, three-fourths were former full-time party officials, suggesting that their personal networks had helped them withstand the collapse of communist rule. Another factor, however, is education and youth. The new elite, on average, was 10 years younger than the old one, reflecting a generational turnover that had probably been over-long in coming. Over 20 percent had never been Communist Party members.

Turnover was least among the economic managers and greatest among those in politics. Seventy percent of those in economic elite positions in 1993 had held nomenklatura jobs in 1988 as enterprise managers or ministerial officials. But of those holding top government positions, only one-third had been in nomenklatura jobs in 1988. Still, even those holding jobs in the state and Communist Party bureaucracy in 1988 were often able to hold onto their elite status: one-third of state bureaucrats in 1988 were still in the state bureaucracy in 1993. Of party officials in 1988, 20 percent had taken top-level positions in the state bureaucracy and 40 percent were in high managerial jobs, such as executives in state firms and holding companies.

Continuity through adaptation thus accounts for a larger share of the members of the new Russian political elite than does turnover through democratic renewal. This is perhaps logical in view of the largely peaceful nature of the transition from communist rule in Russia. Quite clearly, the old nomenklatura—which comprised most of the people who possessed leadership and administrative experience at the time that the old system fell apart—had to be the principal pool from which political and bureaucratic officials in the post-1991 period were drawn. Thus, the degree to which various elements of the new political elite come out of the old nomenklatura is telling. According to a study by the Russian Academy of Sciences' Institute of Sociology, around three quarters of the officials in the federal government and a similar proportion of the officials working in the presidential administration come out of the old nomenklatura. An even higher share, 82.3 percent of the officials in the regional government elite are former nomenklatura officials. But among the new business elite, only 61 percent are former nomenklatura members, and still fewer (57 percent) of the leaders of political parties are from the old nomenklatura.[51] It is fair to conclude that party politicians are recruited from a more socially diverse pool than are government bureaucrats. This is indeed typical of other democracies.[52]

Thus, there has been a change in the patterns of political elite recruitment in Russia. Gone is the centralized mechanism of the nomenklatura system through which the circulation of elites between society and regime was managed by the party's personnel division. To make a career in the past in fields such as government or politics, industrial or farm management, culture, law, science, diplomacy, or the military, an individual had to stay in the good graces of higher-level party officials. In turn the party sought to recruit the most promising and ambitious leaders to its nomenklatura system, promising them bright career prospects in return for political loyalty. Today alternative routes to power and influence are available, particularly, as we have seen, through electoral politics and business. Even though the largest share of the present-day political elite is drawn from the old nomenklatura, today elections play an important part in bringing fresh political forces into power. In turn, election to representative bodies has grown increasingly important as a springboard into other elite positions. With time, therefore, fewer new officials will have risen through the nomenklatura system, and more will have entered local and national politics through competitive elections.

---

[51]Ol´ga Kryshtanovskaia, "Finansovaia oligarkhiia v Rossii," *Izvestiia,* January 10, 1996; Ol´ga Kryshtanovskaya and Stephen White, "From Soviet *Nomenklatura* to Russian Élite." *Europe-Asia Studies* (1996) 48: pp. 711–733.

[52]Joel D. Aberbach, Robert D. Putnam, and Bert Rockman, *Bureaucrats and Politicians in Western Democracies* (Cambridge, MA: Harvard University Press, 1981).

Chapter 5

Changing Patterns of Interest Articulation and Aggregation

Interest Articulation: From Statism to Pluralism

The changes of the last decade in Russia have had a powerful impact on the expression of interests and demands. Political liberalization has given many people an opportunity to organize freely for the advancement of long-held common interests, such as environmental protection and the rights of ethnic minorities, disadvantaged groups, and the disabled. At the same time, the shift from state socialism to a system of private property rights has altered people's interests, widening the gap between beneficiaries and victims of change. In the same family there may be one wage-earner who works in a private business and is benefiting from the spread of market relations and another employed by a state enterprise that has been idled by economic depression. Can any one party or interest group represent such households? A far more differentiated spectrum of interest associations has developed than existed under the old regime, corresponding to the wider diversity of interests in society. But though there is much more organized interest articulation than there was in the past, inequality in the political clout of weaker and stronger groups has also increased.

In all societies, public goods—that is, goods which anyone may enjoy whether they have expended any effort to obtain them or not, and the supply of which is not diminished as people use them—tend to be underproduced, as the famous theory of collective action by Mancur Olson demonstrates.[1] This occurs because few people

---

[1]Mancur Olson, *The Logic of Collective Action: Public Goods and the Theory of Groups* (Cambridge, MA: Harvard University Press, 1965).

are willing to take upon themselves the cost of organizing collective action for the common good of large groups of people if their own share of the benefit is worth less than the cost of the effort they make to achieve it. Those who do organize groups for collective benefit often are seeking some other private benefits for themselves by doing so. Some may have aspirations to become political leaders, for instance, and by going to the trouble of mobilizing followings around a common cause they win the reputation of effective leaders.

The difficulty in organizing a large group of people around a common cause varies. If there is already an organization in place that can facilitate communication with an existing membership group, collective action is made much more likely. If organizational entrepreneurs have to launch a new structure, and go around to people one by one to persuade them to sign a petition or contribute dues or turn out for a demonstration, large-scale collective action is much harder to produce. Consequently, when a regime changes, we would expect that interests which can be articulated through already-existing organizational structures will have an easier time being heard than interests which are not already organized.

The same logic applies to the political calculations of leaders. Leaders who can capture control of existing organizations, and make them vehicles for representing new groups of constituents, have an easier time winning influence than do leaders who must must start a movement or party from scratch. Therefore, even in a time of deep change in society, the way political and organizational resources were structured in the past will tend to bias the way interests are articulated in the new regime.

The other side of the coin is the fact that collective interests themselves change as societies change. In the case of the Soviet Union and Russia, these fundamental shifts in social interests have been profound. As the old state-socialist economy becomes more driven by commercial pressures, and property rights begin to be defined, most people in Russia are worse off materially than they were under the old regime, but a minority are better off, some considerably so. Meanwhile, regions are becoming more differentiated in their interests. Some causes are now linked more to cultural identities than to material well-being. The Gorbachev era witnessed an explosion of expression of "identity politics" as a number of groups linked to various causes formed and joined in asserting the right to a public voice.[2] Some of these causes have faded away—partly because they lack a firm footing in people's material needs—but others have become an important part of the political spectrum (such as those that seek to revive cultures suppressed under the old regime—Cossacks, Tatars, and so on).

Collective action therefore has both a demand side and a supply side. People's interests and identities create a potential for mobilization in the political arena, but whether that potential is realized depends a good deal on the existing distribution of organizational resources and the strategies of leaders who hope to build popular followings. As a consequence, in studying how interests in postcommunist Russia are articulated and aggregated, we face a twofold task. We seek to understand how structural change in politics and society has affected people's material and cultural

---

[2]Michael Urban, with Vyacheslav Igrunov and Sergei Mitrokhin, *The Rebirth of Politics in Russia* (Cambridge: Cambridge University Press, 1997), p. 115.

interests. We also need to examine the incentives that followers and leaders face when they organize to advance these interests.

SOCIALISM AND THE DOCTRINE OF "NONANTAGONISTIC INTERESTS"

The old regime did not tolerate the open pursuit of any interests except those authorized by the state. This was because communist doctrine held that socialism eliminated the class antagonism that dominated capitalism. According to the Marxist–Leninist ideology, under socialism there was no class of property owners to exploit the labor of propertyless workers. Soviet doctrine did recognize that there were diverse interests in society and encouraged the formation of a number of public organizations, such as labor unions organized by branch of the economy, professional unions for creative artists, and associations for particular groups of the population, such as youths, women, and veterans. But the regime required that organizations articulating interests do so in a way compatible with its goals. As we have seen, the regime treated such organizations as means of directing and controlling the participation of the population in public life. Stalin's classic formulation was often cited: public organizations were to be "transmission belts" connecting the state with society.[3]

Although the regime declared that the interests and organizations making up Soviet society existed in harmony, there was intense behind-the-scenes competition for power, especially within the state bureaucracy. In contrast to democratic societies, though, Soviet interest groups were unable to compete openly by appealing for public support. Nonetheless, branches of the state bureaucracy, regions, and sections of the political leadership vied for influence over policy and appointments. The expression of demands and ideas took other forms as well, some of them treated by the regime as illegal. Surveying Soviet interest articulation in 1973, Frederick C. Barghoorn identified three categories: factional, sectoral, and subversive.[4] Factional opposition was intra-elite competition for personal influence and took the form of alliances between patrons and clients. A good deal of research in the past went into discerning the networks of reciprocal loyalty and support that top Soviet leaders built up, since these were crucial to understanding their policy orientations and bases of power.[5]

The second type of articulation arose from the complex organization of the state itself. As Philip Roeder has argued, policymakers at the top depended upon the great agencies of state power to achieve their policy goals. Heads of ministries,

---

[3]According to Gregory J. Kasza, such "administered mass organizations" as Stalin-era trade unions and youth groups have been a characteristic feature of a number of the mobilizing regimes of the twentieth century. Gregory J. Kasza, *The Conscription Society: Administered Mass Organizations* (New Haven, CT: Yale University Press, 1995).

[4]Frederick C. Barghoorn, "Faction, Sectoral and Subversive Opposition in Soviet Politics," in Robert A. Dahl, ed., *Regimes and Oppositions* (New Haven, CT: Yale University Press, 1973), pp. 27–88.

[5]John P. Willerton, *Patronage and Politics in the USSR* (Cambridge: Cambridge University Press, 1992); T. H. Rigby and Bohdan Harasymiw, *Leadership Selection and Patron-Client Relations in the USSR and Yugoslavia* (London: Allen & Unwin, 1983).

state committees, and other branches of state power in turn needed the support of top party leaders for their institutional interests. Between the bureaucracies and the policymakers a kind of reciprocal dependency arose, which, according to Roeder, made it impossible to carry out any serious reform of the system.[6] Other lines of division were also apparent to close students of the regime, as professional groups struggled to increase their sphere of autonomy, regional groups attempted to win a greater share of resources for industrial investment, and environmental lobbies pressed for restrictions on pollution.[7] Recognition of within-system forms of pressure as various interests sought to influence policy led scholars to try to develop an appropriate framework for understanding how Soviet interest groups formed and operated.[8] Jerry F. Hough, for example, proposed the term "institutional pluralism" to refer to the competition for influence which went on among bureaucratic and occupational interests.[9]

The final form of interest articulation identified by Barghoorn was "subversive." Usually the Soviet regime labeled as subversive—that is, "anti-Soviet" and hence punishable under Soviet law—expression which challenged fundamental institutions and doctrines of the regime. Particularly after the Stalin era, when the authorities encouraged a certain amount of criticism of abuses associated with Stalin's "cult of personality," many writers, scholars, and other intellectuals began to formulate critiques of Soviet society that went considerably beyond the limits of what the regime could tolerate. The authorities cracked down on such dissent, often arresting or harassing those who produced or read dissent literature, and sending some dissidents to psychiatric hospitals. The regime was particularly concerned about contacts between dissenters and the democratic world, as well as efforts by dissidents to organize broader popular movements.[10]

Two of the most prominent Soviet dissidents were Andrei Sakharov and Alexander Solzhenitsyn. Sakharov, who died in December 1989, was one of the most brilliant of the group of Soviet physicists who developed the Soviet hydrogen bomb. At the age of only 32, he was elected a member of the Soviet Academy of Sciences, an extraordinary and unprecedented honor for so young a scholar. But Sakharov, like such American scientists as Robert Oppenheimer, became beset with doubts about the threat that atomic weapons could pose to mankind's peace and security. First cautiously, and later more publicly, Sakharov criticized regime policies first on issues such as education and science policy and then on the more sensitive question of nuclear weapons testing. In the late 1960s, as the more conservative climate of Brezhnev replaced the open and de-Stalinizing policies of Khrushchev, Sakharov

[6]Philip G. Roeder, *Red Sunset: The Failure of Soviet Politics* (Princeton: Princeton University Press, 1993).

[7]Thane Gustafson, *Reform in Soviet Politics* (Cambridge: Cambridge University Press, 1981).

[8]A major collection of essays on this question is H. Gordon Skilling and Franklyn Griffiths, eds., *Interest Groups in Soviet Politics* (Princeton: Princeton University Press, 1971).

[9]Jerry F. Hough and Merle Fainsod, *How the Soviet Union Is Governed* (Cambridge, MA: Harvard University Press, 1979), pp. 522–529.

[10]Major studies of dissent and the regime's treatment of it include Ludmilla Alexeyeva, *Soviet Dissent: Contemporary Movements for National, Religious and Human Rights*, trans. Carol Pearce and John Glad (Middletown, CT: Wesleyan University Press, 1987); Frederick C. Barghoorn, *Detente and the Democratic Movement in the USSR* (New York: Free Press, 1976).

began to play a leading role in the broader fight against restrictions on civic rights and freedoms.

In the 1970s, Sakharov became the most famous champion of the democratic movement in Soviet society and took up the cause of countless individuals and groups who had been repressed by the regime for peaceful political activity. In 1970, with two fellow physicists, he founded the Moscow Human Rights Committee, which inspired many later groups seeking to protect the cause of democratic freedoms and human rights in the Soviet Union. For his work he was awarded the Nobel Peace Prize in 1975; in response the Soviet regime mounted a campaign of denunciations and slander against him.

In 1980, after he had spoken out against the invasion of Afghanistan, the government forced him into exile in the closed city of Gorky, where he was almost entirely cut off from his friends and from Western sources of information. Nonetheless, despite harassment and privations, he continued his human rights work. Because of his reputation as the most outstanding symbol of the moral opposition to Soviet regime repression, Gorbachev's personal appeal to him in December 1986 to return to Moscow to resume his work in science represented a stunning vindication of Sakharov's position. Sakharov continued to press for democratization and freedom. In the radically changed climate of the late 1980s, his immense prestige enabled him to play a leading role in the democratization of Soviet society. He was elected to the Congress of People's Deputies in 1989, and soon assumed a position as de facto head of the group of democratically oriented deputies. The outpouring of public grief, affection, and admiration following his death in December 1989 was a powerful testimonial to Sakharov's stature as the embodiment of the spirit of humane and democratic values.

Alexander Solzhenitsyn, on the other hand, gained fame as the author of powerful, realistic literary works in the early 1960s based on his own experiences in camps and prisons during the Stalin era. His most famous work of that time, *One Day in the Life of Ivan Denisovich,* was published with the specific authorization of CPSU First Secretary Nikita Khrushchev. Soon the political climate changed, however, and Solzhenitsyn was unable to publish anything more in the Soviet Union, and was even expelled from the Writers' Union. He continued to publish his novels abroad, however, among them *The First Circle* and *Cancer Ward,* which were both powerful portraits of the moral climate of the Stalin period. In 1970 he was awarded the Nobel Prize for Literature. After his great nonfictional study of Soviet labor camps, *Gulag Archipelago,* was published in the West, Solzhenitsyn was forcibly expelled from the USSR. He lived in the United States in exile for 20 years until he returned to Russia in 1994, hailed both by the authorities and much of the populace as one of the greatest voices of moral principle of the Soviet era. Back in Russia, however, his public stature diminished quickly. When he was invited to address the State Duma, his speech, which denounced both the communists and the Yeltsin government, was received indifferently. A talk show on television that he hosted attracted little interest. Although he regularly denounced the current regime for its inability to reverse the trends of moral and material decline in Russia, he became politically isolated and no longer attracted much public attention.

Under the Soviet regime, since the articulation of interests was regulated by the Communist Party, and there could be no open, active competition among political parties or interest groups for membership or support, the Communist Party was the major institution for weighing alternatives and deciding policy. In the totalitarian atmosphere of the Stalin era, party policies such as the collectivization of private farms were carried out using enormous coercion: collectivization resulted in the loss of millions of lives through the killing, deportation, and starvation of peasants.[11] But in the post-Stalin era, as the system grew bureaucratized, corrupted, and weakened, entrenched bureaucratic interests grew adept at ensuring that the system served them. Any policy initiative that threatened to upset the existing distribution of resources was watered down before it was adopted, and often was further blunted, distorted, or forgotten as it was implemented. Paradoxically, policymakers at the top of this seemingly centralized political system lacked the authority to break through the mass of bureaucratic inertia, and frequently lacked the information necessary for an accurate appraisal of the real state of affairs in many areas.

GLASNOST' AND THE RELEASE OF GRIEVANCES

The statist model of interest articulation began to be upset once *glasnost'* gained momentum. For Gorbachev, the policy of *glasnost'* was an essential part of the leadership's strategy to restore the flow of information about the performance and problems of the system—and simultaneously to increase the accountability of officials both to higher authority and to the general populace.[12] *Glasnost'* stimulated an explosion of political expression. It is hard to realize how profound was the impact of the flood of startling facts, ideas, disclosures, reappraisals, scandals, and sensations that followed. One Soviet woman of the older generation commented that it was akin to being in a dark and closed room, when suddenly the doors and windows are flung open, and light and fresh air rush in. But if Gorbachev expected that *glasnost'* would result in expression generally favoring his own strategy of *perestroika,* or restructuring, of Soviet socialism, he must have been surprised at the range and intensity of new demands, grievances, ideas, and pressures that erupted. In loosening the party's controls over communication sufficiently to encourage people to speak and write freely and openly, Gorbachev also loosened the controls that would have enabled him to limit and halt political expression when it went too far.

Moreover, ideology and organization in the Soviet regime were so intertwined that by releasing controls over the ideological limits of speech, he was also giving up the party's traditional power to penetrate and direct public organizations. As people voiced their deep-felt demands and grievances, others recognized similar beliefs and values, and made common cause with them, sometimes forming new, unofficial organizations. The direct result of *glasnost',* accordingly, was the formation of a massive wave of "informal"—i.e., unlicensed and uncontrolled—public associations.

---

[11]Robert Conquest, *The Great Terror: A Reassessment* (New York: Oxford University Press, 1990). The terrible famine of 1932, which struck the Ukraine and certain other regions with particular force, was itself the product of deliberate policy as Stalin and his associates expressly prohibited sending relief to the affected areas, apparently in order to break any resistance to the collectivization campaign.

See also Robert Conquest, *The Harvest of Sorrow: Soviet Collectivization and the Terror-Famine* (New York: Oxford University Press, 1986).

[12]Thomas F. Remington, "Gorbachev and the Strategy of *Glasnost',*" in idem ed., *Politics and the Soviet System* (London: Macmillan, 1989), pp. 56–62; idem, "A Socialist Pluralism of Opinions: Glasnost and Policy-Making under Gorbachev," *The Russian Review* 48 (July 1989), pp. 271–304.

Simply by defending their rights to exist and articulate goals, these groups came to focus their attention more and more on the values and doctrines by which the Soviet system operated, and to press the regime for greater freedom to influence policy.[13] The authorities continued to try to limit, and often prohibit, independent organizations from forming, producing more frustration and protest. Thus the dynamic relationship between groups formed to articulate particular concerns and needs, and the state which still tried to establish some limits to the right of expression and organization, served to stimulate groups toward more radical political views, and thus to step up their confrontation with the state.

As Paul Goble observes, "Because the Soviet system both at the center and in the republics lack[ed] a mechanism for the advancement of interests outside formal politics, interest groups too have been forced into becoming or at least acting like political parties."[14] We have already seen how important this mobilization of large-scale political activity was in creating new outlets for popular participation in nationalist movements, independent labor unions, and electoral coalitions in 1990 and 1991. Some of these movements—which included new labor unions, women's groups, environmental protection groups, nationalist organizations, associations of cooperatives, farmers' groups, human rights and cultural groups—in turn evolved into channels of interest articulation and aggregation in the post-Soviet era.[15]

DEMOCRATS, "REDS," AND "BROWNS"

In Russia, as new organizations espousing political goals proliferated, two opposing tendencies became distinct. One espoused principles of individualism, liberal democracy, market economy, and the rule of law—and generally a Western orientation for Russia. This group adopted the label "democrats" or "reformers." The other group—often called the "opposition"—voiced an inconsistent mixture of principles drawn from two not entirely compatible sets of values. One source was Marxism–Leninism, whose advocates made up for their limited base of popular support with flights of extravagant rhetoric. They spoke in terms of a strong centralized state, an assertive foreign policy, a collectivist, centrally planned economy, and preservation of the Soviet Union. The other forces in the opposition coalition tended to draw on traditional Russian and Slavophile conservative nationalism. These included demands for a hierarchical and imperial state; restoration of traditional, patriarchal moral values; and rejection of Western materialism, individualism, and

---

[13]Marcia Weigle and Jim Butterfield, "Civil Society in Reforming Communist Regimes: The Logic of Emergence," *Comparative Politics* 25:1 (October 1992), pp. 1–23.

[14]Paul A. Goble, "Nationalism, Movement Groups, and Party Formation," in Judith B. Sedaitis and Jim Butterfield, eds., *Perestroika from Below: Social Movements in the Soviet Union* (Boulder: Westview Press, 1991), p. 173.

[15]Sedaitis and Butterfield, eds., *Perestroika from Below* is a valuable collection of articles about several such types of social movements. One major example of the moral impetus to many of the "informals" is Memorial, a movement dedicated to honoring the memory of the victims of Stalinist repression. See Nanci Adler, *Victims of Soviet Terror: The Story of the Memorial Movement* (Westport, CT: Praeger, 1993). A valuable overview of the emergence of nationalist movements in the Gorbachev period is Ch. 4, "Nationalism and Nation-States: Gorbachev's Dilemmas," in Ronald Grigor Suny, *The Revenge of the Past: Nationalism, Revolution, and the Collapse of the Soviet Union* (Stanford: Stanford University Press, 1993), pp. 127–160.

rationalism. In various hybrid forms, the combination of the "red" ideology associated with state socialism and the "brown" values associated with right-wing nationalism has fueled much of the opposition to the democratizing trends in Russia over
the past several years.[16]

One of the most prominent nationalist groups in the *glasnost'* period was a
movement called "Pamyat'," or memory. Pamyat' began in the late 1970s as an unofficial circle of people committed to reviving pride in historical Russian culture. As it
grew more active through *glasnost'*, it became more extreme and more explicitly
concerned with politics. Its activists disrupted meetings of the democratic movement and became skilled at attracting publicity through manifestos and demonstrations. Within a few years, Pamyat' splintered and faded from public view. Its place
was taken, however, by a number of other ultranationalist groups, generally advocating the revival of Russian absolutism, imperialism, social regimentation, and a
rejection of Western values.[17] Some of these nationalists saw in Russian communism—especially Stalin's rule—the embodiment of Russian virtues of strong state
power, imperialism, and social solidarity. Others rejected communism for having
ruined Russia's cultural and religious heritage, and instead called for a new synthesis of tsarist and Orthodox values.

The greater freedom for political expression under Gorbachev thus revealed
not only that there was sizable popular support for more radical democratization
and market reform, but also that there was an intense backlash among orthodox
socialists and extreme nationalists against the modest steps that had been taken.
The very loosening of the party's ideological controls governing what could be said
in public meant that Gorbachev could not prevent attacks on his restructuring program, both from the democratic and the conservative sides.

As liberalization proceeded, it became clear that the "red-brown" alliance had
good friends in high places. In March 1988, a lengthy article appeared in a prominent official newspaper which vehemently denunciated the ideological consequences of Gorbachev's restructuring program.[18] Accusing the Gorbachev leadership of betraying the socialist cause for which so many Soviet people had fought and
died, the author, Nina Andreeva, defended Stalin and linked Stalin's program of
building a powerful, industrial state in Russia to the heroic ambitions of Russia's
great state-building tsars. Her letter was a synthesis of many of the themes around
which Stalinist "reds" and extreme nationalist "browns" could unite: that there was
a Western, and particularly Jewish, conspiracy to weaken Russia; that powerful
authoritarian rulers such as Stalin, Ivan the Terrible, and Peter the Great had
increased the might and wealth of the state through the suffering of the people; that

---

[16]The labels "red" and "brown" are widely used to refer to these ideological tendencies in Russian dis-
cussions. "Red," of course, is the symbolic color of the Bolsheviks, of communism and revolution; it was
the dominant color of the Soviet flag. "Brown" represents extremist nationalism after the "brown shirts"
who were early Nazi followers of Adolf Hitler in Germany in the 1920s. Thus they are regarded as quasi-
fascist ultranationalists.

[17]Walter Laqueur, *Black Hundred: The Rise of the Extreme Right in Russia* (New York: HarperCollins, 1993),
pp. 204–271.

[18]Nina Andreeva, "Ne mogu postupat'sia printsipami [I Cannot Waive My Principles]," *Sovetskaia Rossiia*,
March 13, 1988. An English translation may be found in Alexander Dallin and Gail W. Lapidus, eds., *The
Soviet System in Crisis: A Reader of Western and Soviet Views* (Boulder: Westview Press, 1991), pp. 338–346.

Russia required a higher moral and spiritual principle to unite it, not an imported doctrine of individual freedom; and that Russia's economy must be state-owned and state-run in order to preserve it from the destructive aspects of market competition.

Conservative officials within the Communist Party apparatus immediately seized upon the Andreeva letter as a signal for a reversal of policy; party meetings to discuss it were held in various regions, and many local newspapers reprinted the piece.[19] Although Gorbachev and his reform-minded allies in the party leadership ended this mini-campaign 10 days later, and reasserted the official line of support for restructuring, the outpouring of official support for the letter was a powerful sign of high-level sympathy for the strange mixture of Stalinist and nationalist views which it contained.

TOWARD PLURALISM

The collapse of the Soviet regime ended the regime's ideological controls over political expression that Gorbachev's reforms had loosened. The transition created an opportunity for the rise of a variety of new groups that voiced a wide range of demands. But besides these fundamental political changes, the post-1991 period brought about another change of equal importance. The elimination of the state's monopoly on productive property resulted in the formation of new class interests, among them those of new entrepreneurs, commercial bankers, private farmers, and others interested in protecting rights of property and commerce. Another important category of interests was that of the managers of state-owned enterprises, who were facing a radically changed environment as state orders, credits, and sources of supply dried up, and as Yeltsin's privatization program took effect. Organized labor too found itself in a new position dealing with managers of privatized enterprises rather than, as in the past, with administrators of state property. Unions themselves were divided among competing labor federations. Also divided were the farmers: while private farmers were united in an association pressing for legal guarantees and state support for private farming, the collective farmers formed a powerful association and political party. Meanwhile new associations representing banks, consumers, deceived investors, city governments, disabled persons, soldiers' mothers, defense industries, and a host of other interests began to form.

As these new interest organizations have formed, they have entered into a variety of relationships with the state. Older statist forms of interest representation have survived in many instances, but are now combined with corporatist and pluralist elements. Among these, however, pluralism is the predominant pattern. The very rapidity with which new associations have formed has defeated efforts by both government and interest groups to form corporatist structures in which the state recognizes one encompassing association as the official voice of a particular interest. In most cases, there are too many rival associations competing for support for corporatism to succeed. The prevalent pattern is one of differentiation and even fragmentation of interest representation.

The rapid changes in the structure of social relations have meant that both old and new organizations have had a difficult time keeping a firm base of support.

---

[19]Remington, "A Socialist Pluralism of Opinions," pp. 287–288.

Some organizations that appeared influential at first have turned out to be little more than an empty shell. Other interest groups have proven to be very strong politically even though they are not formally organized. Some formerly cohesive groups have split. The diversification of interests has generated a wide range of opportunities for organizers and activists.

STATE INDUSTRIAL MANAGERS AND CIVIC UNION

The directors of state industrial enterprises are a group universally considered to be very powerful, but their *latent* influence is greater than is the influence of the organized associations that claim to speak for them. One reason for the difficulty of uniting them in a single interest group is the widening division among them with respect to market competition: some seek greater access to world and domestic markets, others want the state to protect them from competition. They share a set of common interests with respect to privatization; generally the directors want to maximize their ownership of the enterprises they manage. But on other issues, such as state fiscal and monetary policy and the desirability of foreign investment in Russia, they are divided. These divisions have weakened the organizations that purport to represent them, such as Civic Union. The case illustrates the difficulty for organizations of speaking for a constituency at a time when economic conditions in the country are changing so deeply and quickly that their membership divides over strategic goals.

. During the Gorbachev period, an association of the heads of state enterprises called the "Scientific-Industrial Union" was created.[20] Its leader, Arkadii Vol´skii, had made his career in the party apparatus, where he headed the Central Committee department overseeing industrial machine-building. The new organization was dedicated to preserving economic ties among enterprises to offset the breakdown of the old system of central planning. After the dissolution of the Soviet Union, the organization reformed as the Russian Union of Industrialists and Entrepreneurs (RUIE). Although the RUIE professed to have no explicit political goals, it did seek to defend the interests of state industry—including their interest in obtaining credits and production orders—as well as to prevent the interruption of supply and trade ties in the face of economic upheavals. Like other interest groups, Vol´skii's organization was drawn into politics. In spring 1992, Vol´skii entered the field directly, first forming a political arm of the RUIE, then allying it with other parties and political groups in a coalition called Civic Union. Civic Union consistently declared that its political outlook was "centrist" and indeed sought to stake out the center ground as opposing lines were hardening over the radical Yeltsin/Gaidar stabilization program. Centrism, for Civic Union, meant ending the "shock therapy" program, which sharply cut back government subsidies to state enterprises, and

---

[20]Information on Civic Union may be found in Stephen White, Graeme Gill, and Darrell Slider, *The Politics of Transition: Shaping a Post-Soviet Future* (Cambridge: Cambridge University, 1993), pp. 166–169. A more detailed study is Peter Rutland, "Business Elites and Russian Economic Policy" (London: Royal Institute of International Affairs, 1992). See also Michael McFaul, "Russian Centrism and Revolutionary Transitions," *Post-Soviet Affairs* 9:3 (July/September 1993), pp. 196–222. Wendy Slater, "The Diminishing Center of Russian Parliamentary Politics," *RFE/RL Research Report* 3:17 (April 29, 1994), discusses the fate of Civic Union through the 1993 elections.

opening up the country's borders to free trade. But Civic Union also claimed to back a gradual transition to a market system even though it allied itself with some nationalist groups whose opposition to the Gaidar program was far more extreme.

Many thought that Civic Union was a major force with which Yeltsin and Egor Gaidar had to contend, and for a time, it probably was. Some believe that the government's privatization program was significantly influenced by Civic Union and other allied interests: specifically, that one of the forms that the privatization of state enterprises could take was to allow the workforce of each enterprise to acquire 51 percent of its shares. Given the dominant position of the management within the workplace, this effectively meant that such a path to privatization turned a controlling share of ownership rights over to the managers. Not surprisingly, once this option was permitted, it became the most popular form: around three-fourths of privatizing enterprises in 1992 and 1993 chose this option.[21] Some think that the Civic Union also successfully pressured the government to remove certain objectionable figures from the cabinet, and to name as deputy prime ministers some prominent figures from state industry. These personnel decisions were made, but it is difficult to judge whether they were the products of Civic Union's lobbying, or whether instead the government attempted to anticipate the desires of state directors in order to preserve its freedom of action in more important areas.

A test of the clout of Civic Union came in December 1992 during the confrontation between Yeltsin and his political opponents at the Seventh Congress of People's Deputies. Despite a reported agreement with Yeltsin on a modified economic program, Civic Union proved unable to carry a majority at the Congress or broker a compromise agreement between the deputies and the president. Civic Union's leaders diverged sharply over whether Gaidar was acceptable to them as prime minister: some considered him an unrepentant champion of "shock therapy" who must be removed, while others thought that by ensuring a majority for his confirmation, they could acquire a decisive say over his future policy program. When Civic Union failed to deliver a deal, Yeltsin concluded that the group was a paper tiger. Calling the organization's power "mythical," Yeltsin's media representative explained that there was no need any longer to bargain with Civil Union since it could not swing a majority of the Congress to back a compromise program.[22] Yeltsin proceeded to nominate Egor Gaidar as prime minister anyway despite indications that the nomination would fail. When it did, he proposed Viktor Chernomyrdin, a much more agreeable figure from the standpoint of the industrial lobby. The nomination was confirmed by the Congress, and Chernomyrdin went on to begin an unexpectedly long term of service as head of government.[23]

---

[21]McFaul, "Russian Centrism," p. 206; Michael McFaul, "State Power, Institutional Change, and the Politics of Privatization in Russia," *World Politics* 47 (1995), pp. 229–230; Pekka Sutela, "Insider Privatization in Russia: Speculations in Systemic Change," *Europe-Asia Studies* 46:3 (1994), p. 420. The other variants include one giving a greater share of stock to outside interests, and one requiring insiders to bid for the right to restructure the enterprise.

[22]RFE/RL Daily Report, December 7, 1994.

[23]On Chernomyrdin's low-key but politically effective tenure as prime minister, see Anders Åslund, "Russia's Success Story," *Foreign Affairs* 73:5 (September/October 1994), pp. 58–71. Initially considered a faithful member of the state industrial lobby, Chernomyrdin turned out to pursue a forceful line for fiscal discipline and free trade.

Political scientists have observed that interest groups generally pursue either "inside" or "outside" strategies for influencing policy. That is, either they tend to concentrate their resources on cultivating close, friendly relations with key policy-makers, or they seek to build large public followings and membership bases that can apply pressure on policymakers through elections, demonstrations, letter-writing campaigns, and media attention.[24] The effectiveness of insider strategies depends on establishing relations of trust, which generally requires that the group's representatives and the policymakers keep each others' confidences. For this reason it can be difficult to judge from the outside how powerful an "insider" group is. Civic Union tried to work both ways. Unable to derail Yeltsin's economic reform program in 1992 by its "insider" strategy, it switched over to an "outsider" strategy of running for parliament in December 1993 and again in December 1995. Both times, it was markedly unsuccessful.

In 1993, after its inability to broker a compromise between Yeltsin and the opposition, part of the Civic Union coalition split off. Vol´skii reorganized what remained into a new political party called the Civic Union for Stability, Justice, and Progress, which put forward a list of candidates in the December 1993 parliamentary election. Civic Union campaigned as the party of moderation, gradualism, and experience. It received less than 2 percent of the vote, however, well below the 5 percent threshold required for representation of its party list candidates in parliament. Once more, Civic Union failed to demonstrate actual strength.

Civic Union tried yet again to appeal for voter support in the December 1995 parliamentary election. This time Vol´skii reorganized Civic Union as the Russian United Industrialists' Party and allied it with the main official trade union federation in an electoral bloc called the "Trade Unions and Industrialists of Russia: the Union of Labor." Their appeal was pragmatic and centrist, calling for cooperation between industrial management and labor. But despite the seemingly huge social base for this alliance—the trade union federation claimed over 50 million members—it was crushed at the polls, receiving only 1.63 percent of the national list vote.

Why did Civic Union turn out to be so weak when it appeared so strong? The reason seems to be that notwithstanding the stature of its leaders, Civic Union was deeply divided internally. When forced to commit to a positive program it was unable to speak with a common voice. Some of its members were closely allied with the hard-line socialist opposition, while others were far more positive toward the market reforms associated with the policies of the Yeltsin/Gaidar government. This division reflects the fundamental divergence of interests among the enterprises that formed the backbone of Civic Union. Some, especially those that were more competitive in the marketplace, came to oppose government protectionist policies that simply fueled inflation and cushioned inefficient enterprises. They favored a more open, internationalist trade policy, and the reduction of state subsidies and credits which interfered with the marketplace. Other enterprises, especially those least ready to adapt to the pressures of competition (and these included a sizable share of defense-related plants), supported a more conservative, backward-looking program. As one enterprise director explained, with every day that passed, the government's economic program furthered the transformation of society, and the divisions

---

[24]Steven S. Smith, *The American Congress* (Boston: Houghton-Mifflin, 1995), pp. 330–336.

within the ranks of Civic Union's membership grew wider. There simply was less and less common ground between those enterprise directors operating in a competitive and commercial environment, and those still tied to the system of state life support.

Moreover, the industrial association that has been Civic Union's core, the RUIE, faces rivalry from other lobbies competing to represent the interests of state industry. One leading competitor, Yuri Skokov's Federation of Manufacturers of Russia, also formed an electoral bloc for the December 1995 elections with the highly popular army general Alexander Lebed´. Defense industries are represented by yet another organization, the League in Support of Defense Enterprises. This group has shunned the "outsider" strategy of party and electoral politics, preferring to use an "insider" strategy, which has been quite effective.[25]

This is not to say, however, that the state industrial lobby as such has been weak. By all accounts, "the directors' corps" has been the single most powerful interest group in Russian politics. Evidence of this may be found in the way the privatization program was adjusted to the benefit of enterprise management. Although a massive privatization of state property occurred over 1992–94, ownership of most of the large enterprises that have been privatized has passed to their own workforces with the result that management has wound up with a controlling packet of stock shares. The pattern is sometimes called "insider privatization" and it contradicts the avowed intention of the Yeltsin/Gaidar program, which was to spread ownership rights as widely as possible among the population. One result, for example, is that almost no enterprises have been allowed to go bankrupt, despite the fact that many are highly inefficient. By giving enterprise managers a privileged position in privatization, however, the government has weakened the industrial ministries which had been an essential prop of the communist regime. It has also ensured that the massive de-nationalization of state property has met with virtually no resistance. This is a key to understanding why the extraordinary transformation of Russia from the communist regime has been accomplished without a new revolution.

Was there a strong, organized state enterprise directors' lobby pulling strings behind the scenes, or were the policymakers strategically devising privatization policy in such a way as to anticipate the political interests of the enterprise managers? There is some evidence for the latter interpretation. Three of the architects of the privatization program wrote about their reasons for a decentralized program:

> Privatization had to start on a voluntary basis, with managers of companies who wanted to privatize leading the way. Moreover, managers had to have some control over when their company was privatized and what fraction of shares was offered for vouchers. In addition, local officials demanded control over voucher auctions, particularly of companies of regional importance. To get the consent of the managers and the local officials, voucher auctions had to be decentralized and pushed to localities. Once this was done, managers of many companies realized that they could profit from privatization and did not need to fear the immediate takeover of their company. As a result, many

[25]Julian Cooper, "Defense Industries in Russia and the Other Post-Soviet States," in Bruce Parrott, ed., *State Building and Military Power in Russia and the New States of Eurasia* (Armonk, NY: M. E. Sharpe, 1995), p. 76.

more consented to putting their company through the program, and even pushed local (and Moscow) officials to accommodate them. Privatization took off.[26]

Thus as a *latent* interest group, the state industrial directors have benefited from state privatization policy, which has been framed as if in anticipation of their preferences. But when called upon to act collectively in behalf of common *positive* goals, their efforts have been ineffective and incohesive. Their disunity reflects the widening division between winners and losers in economic reform. Note that the policymakers made a conscious effort to accommodate yet another set of interests as well: regional and local governments.

ORGANIZED LABOR

Why, we might wonder, has the economic upheaval since 1992 provoked so little protest from manual workers? Workers are threatened by several effects of the economic transformation of the country: frequent long delays in receiving their monthly pay; widespread layoffs and forced leave; price inflation; the privatization of many previously subsidized or state-provided services, such as education, children's daycare, health care, and vacations; and the heavy burden of uncertainty about their own and the country's future. In a society in which unemployment previously had been almost unknown, unemployment stood at around 10 percent (7 million people) of the economically active population as of the end of 1996. Of these, around half were on unpaid leave or forced to work short hours.[27] As in other societies undergoing a transition from state socialism to a market economy, the layoffs affected men and women differentially: many more women have lost their jobs than men. According to the labor and employment department of the Moscow city government, 70 percent of the registered unemployed are women.[28] The arrangement that once had been termed a tacit "social contract" between regime and working class—which guaranteed certain social benefits such as secure employment to the workers in return for their acceptance of the regime—had vanished.[29]

How has organized labor responded to this enormous social change? To date, there has been less political protest on the part of workers than might be expected. Attempts by the leadership of the Federation of Independent Trade Unions of Russia (FITUR), the main umbrella organization of trade unions, to call a general strike in October 1993 failed utterly. Strikes in the first part of 1992 actually declined, despite the rapid rise in prices, compared with 1991.[30] In summer 1992, after the initial effects of the "shock therapy" program had begun to be felt, only 10 percent of

[26]Maxim Boycko, Andrei Shleifer, and Robert Vishny, *Privatizing Russia* (Cambridge, MA: MIT Press, 1995), p. 90. The authors were associates of Anatolii Chubais in designing and implementing the privatization program in Russia.

[27]OMRI Daily Digest, 12 March 1997; *Segodnia*, February 17, 1997.

[28]OMRI Daily Digest, 5 March 1997.

[29]Linda J. Cook, *The Soviet 'Social Contract' and Why It Failed: Welfare Policy and Workers' Politics from Brezhnev to Yeltsin* (Cambridge, MA: Harvard University Press, 1993).

[30]Elizabeth Teague, "Russian Government Seeks 'Social Partnership,'" RFE/RL Research Report, June 2, 1992.

workers surveyed by the FITUR said that they would support a strike against the Gaidar government program, although 86 percent said that they were willing to participate in other forms of protest, such as rallies and demonstrations.[31]

Since then, there has been a rise in the incidence of strikes, stemming above all from the growing problem of unpaid wages. In the first five months of 1994, about as many workers went out on strike as did in all of 1993, and the major reason was wage arrears.[32] As of the beginning of August 1994, some 3.5 trillion rubles—equal to about 1.75 billion U.S. dollars—were owed to workers in unpaid back wages: in some areas, workers had not received wages for an entire year, and throughout the country, delays of one to two months were common.[33] In September 1994, the board of the FITUR met to discuss its action program for the fall. The chairman of the FITUR, Mikhail Shmakov, agreed that as layoffs and wage arrears spread, labor must act to protest, but he refused to agree to the demands of some member unions to call for strikes.[34]

Strikes grew more numerous in 1995 and even more in 1996: again the main reason was late payment of wages. In 1994 a total of 514 strikes were recorded, while in 1995 there were nearly 9,000 strikes. By February 1996, over 2,000 workplaces were experiencing strikes, nearly all of them among teachers; many were hunger strikes.[35] A particularly large-scale strike was called by coal miners on February 1, 1996: almost half a million miners went out to protest enormous wage arrears, amounting to some $200 million. Two days later, they called the strike off when Prime Minister Chernomyrdin promised to find the funds to pay them.[36]

Clearly coal miners represent a powerful as well as politically sensitive group. Their massive strikes in 1989 and 1991 helped to undermine the old regime by demonstrating how high the costs of repression would be if the authorities attempted to suppress popular demands for reform. Although the coal industry is unprofitable, backward, and depressed, with production having declined by one-third from 1988 to 1995, the industry still requires heavy state subsidies. The government recognizes that a number of mines must be closed but has been reluctant to pay the high short-term political and financial costs of doing so. Miners are well organized and radicalized, and the government is usually quick to respond to their periodic threats to strike, even though it also appears to be helpless to solve their most basic grievance—the chronic nonpayment of wages.

As the total bill for unpaid wages in Russia reached 50 trillion rubles (nearly 10 billion U.S. dollars), the FITUR mounted a nationwide protest on March 27, 1997. Between one and two million people participated. This figure was well below the organizers' predictions that 20 million would turn out, but it was the largest labor action that had yet occurred, and it comprised nearly 1,000 different rallies in 73

---

[31]RFE/RL Daily Report, August 19, 1992.

[32]RFE/RL Daily Report, July 13, 1994.

[33]RFE/RL Daily Report, August 1, 1994.

[34]*Segodnia,* September 8, 1994.

[35]OMRI Daily Report, February 29, 1996.

[36]OMRI Daily Reports, February 1, 2, 5, 1996; Alessandra Stanley, "Miners in Russia and Ukraine Strike for Back Wages," *New York Times,* February 2, 1996.

different regions.[37] In the first three quarters of 1996, the State Statistical Administration estimated, over 350,000 workers took part in strikes, causing a total loss of
some two billion work hours in over 3,700 different firms and organizations. The
largest number of strikers were teachers and coal miners.[38] Labor protest, it is clear,
is becoming more widespread with time as grievances accumulate and labor organizations gain greater ability to mobilize followings.

Still, why has there not been more protest? Why have there not been general
strikes on the scale of the strikes of 1989 and 1991? The FITUR debated whether to
demand the resignation of the government among its slogans for the national day
of protest on March 27, 1997, and ultimately decided against doing so: it concentrated on the single demand of receiving the unpaid wages.[39] Why have workers not
mobilized to bring down the government?

One reason is workers' dependence on the enterprises where they work for a
variety of social benefits which are administered through the enterprise; often these
include basic subsistence goods, such as food and housing.[40] A survey found that in
1992, two-thirds of urban workers received fringe benefits, usually in the form of
paid vacations, medical care, and child care.[41] The change in the economic environment has, in many cases, deepened this dependency, as directors gain greater
autonomy vis-à-vis their enterprises.[42] It becomes more difficult to organize workers
of a single industry across enterprises, as individual enterprises are positioned differently with respect to their sources of supply and sales revenues. Evidence for this
is found in the fact that at different enterprises, workers choose to affiliate with any
of a number of competing labor unions and federations.[43] Once again, where the
interests of the members of formerly unitary membership associations begin to
diverge as a result of economic reform, it becomes increasingly likely that the organization will split.

As with the industrial directors, where rival associations now compete for members
and support, so too is organized labor represented by multiple competing associations.
Besides the largest, the FITUR, there are now Sotsprof (the Union of Socialist Trade
Unions); the All-Russian Confederation of Labor; the Confederation of Labor of Russia; the Congress of Trade Unions of Russia; and various unaffiliated branch unions.

The FITUR is the successor to what used to be the single, monopolistic former
trade union federation under the Soviet regime.[44] Its membership is by far the

---

[37]OMRI Daily Digest, 28 March 1997.

[38]OMRI Daily Digest, 31 October 1996.

[39]*Segodnia*, March 20, 1997.

[40]Stephen Crowley, "Barriers to Collective Action: Steelworkers and Mutual Dependence in the Former
Soviet Union," *World Politics* 46:4 (July 1994), pp. 589–615.

[41]Richard Rose, "The Value of Fringe Benefits in Russia," *RFE/RL Research Report* 3:15 (15 April 1994), p.
19.

[42]Michael Burawoy and Pavel Krotov, "The Rise of Merchant Capital: Monopoly, Barter, and Enterprise
Politics in the Vorkuta Coal Industry," *Harriman Institute Forum* 6:4 (December 1992).

[43]Dmitrii Semenov and Vladimir Gribanov, "Grozit li nam proletarskaia revoliutsiia? [Is a Proletarian Revolution Looming?]" *Nezavisimaia gazeta*, August 21, 1993.

[44]This was called the All-Union Central Council of Trade Unions, or VTsSPS for its Russian initials.

largest of any of the union federations; it claims around 50 million members, or 95 percent of all organized workers, as compared with a total of at most 5 million for all the rest. Until 1993, FITUR retained a key power that its predecessor had exercised: the right to collect workers' contributions for the state social insurance fund. This fund allows the official unions to distribute benefits such as disability pay and sick pay, but it also is used to pay union dues. Control of this fund has enabled the official trade unions to acquire enormous income-producing property over the years, including hotels and resorts. These assets and income streams give leaders of the official unions considerable advantages in competing for members. But the FITUR lacks the degree of centralized control over its regional and branch members that it once had, as is evidenced by the failure of member unions to heed the leadership's strike calls in the fall of 1993. Many of the member organizations of the FITUR considered the central leadership too closely allied with the anti-Yeltsin opposition and preferred a strategy that concentrated on bread-and-butter material issues.[45] The various branch and regional members within FITUR have pursued very different political lines. In the 1993 and 1995 parliamentary elections, for instance, member unions formed their own political alliances with parties.[46] Meanwhile, as we saw, the FITUR alliance with Vol'skii's association of industrial directors brought no political rewards to either side.

In 1993, after the FITUR leaders failed to give Yeltsin full support in his suppression of the parliamentary opposition, the government stripped the union of the right to administer the social insurance fund. Instead, local state offices were set up around the country to handle payments and disbursements. The evidence suggests, nonetheless, that in many regions the old system continues; the local branch of FITUR continues to act as an extension of the state, giving it a powerful means to discourage rival labor unions from forming.[47]

A second reason for the relatively low level of strike activity is the fact that organized labor and employers do meet at the national level to discuss general wage and economic policy, giving unions at least a nominal voice in social policy. In 1991, in anticipation of the implementation of the radical reform program, Yeltsin called for a "social partnership" between government, employers, and labor. He promised that organized labor would be consulted on major economic policy decisions concerning wage levels and working conditions. Since 1992, the government has met with representatives of organized labor and managers in a loose framework called the "Tripartite Commission." This quasi-corporatist institution has had little influence over government economic policy, but has demonstrated that labor unions have more to gain by joining enterprise directors in seeking state support for industry than by taking a position opposed to management. Government has agreed to grant substantial wage increases and other social benefits under the annual "General Agreement" reached among the three sides. Under the first such agreement,

[45]RFE/RL Daily Report, October 28, 1993.

[46]Viktor Khamraev, "Byvshaia ⟨⟨shkola kommunizma⟩⟩ v novom politicheskom kontekste," *Segodnia,* October 26, 1995.

[47]On the material incentives facing would-be rivals to the official trade unions, see the Ph.D. dissertation of Susan F. Davis of Emory University, *Re-forming Leviathan? State-Society Relations in Ukraine and Russia: The Case of Trade Unions* (Emory University, Political Science Department, 1997).

signed in March 1992 by representatives of government, trade unions, and various employers' associations, each side made commitments. The government promised to create safety nets for workers such as unemployment benefits and retraining programs; the employers promised not to slash workforces; and the unions agreed not to call strikes. To some extent, each side has made good on its part of the bargain; the catch is that there is no way the agreements can be enforced. Yet each year the three sides meet and sign an annual General Agreement, and perhaps the bargaining process itself enables each side to ensure that certain of its interests are met.[48]

It is difficult to discern alignment patterns in the Tripartite Commission, but they scarcely resemble corporatism. For one thing, neither labor nor employers speak with a single voice. Rival labor associations compete with FITUR for seats on the commission. Private and state firms divide over government policy. The division line seems to be at least as much one of state industrial managers in alliance with official trade unions against market-oriented industries and independent trade unions as that of labor against capital. In any case, the fragmented arena gives government a freer hand to set national policy than it would if it confronted unified peak associations representing industry and labor.

THE AGRICULTURAL SECTOR

Few areas of social life display more vividly the effect of economic change on interest representation than agriculture. Under the old Soviet model of socialism, there was no private farming. Although both city and country residents could maintain small fruit and vegetable gardens for their own use and to sell surpluses, the size of such plots was closely regulated, and they could not be bought or sold or used for commercial purposes. Large-scale farming was organized in two forms, state farms and collective farms. State farms were agricultural enterprises wholly owned by the state, the employees of which were wage laborers with a legal status similar to that of factory workers. Collective farms were legally organized as cooperatives, with the land and equipment collectively owned by the farmers; but they were so closely controlled by the state, which even dictated the prices at which the products were sold to the state's own procurement agencies, that they were effectively equivalent to state property and the farmers to state employees.

Since 1991 an intense battle over property rights in land has raged. On one side are those opposing private property rights in land, including the communists and the state and collective farm lobby. On the other side are those committed to the spread of market and property relations, including many urban residents and the small body of private farmers. It is an unequal contest. The collective and state farm lobby is far larger and more powerful thanks to its organizational base: over 90 percent of cultivated land still belongs to collective and state farms, of which there are some 26,000 in all. These operate in much the same way as in the past although nearly all have been reorganized on paper as joint stock companies. They depend heavily on favorably priced state procurement, state credits, and tariff protection

---

[48]For a discussion of the creation of the Tripartite Commission, see Walter D. Connor, *Tattered Banners: Labor, Conflict and Corporatism in Postcommunist Russia* (Boulder: Westview Press, 1996), pp. 23–63.

against foreign competition, which serve to protect highly inefficient, costly practices. Meanwhile the number of private farms remains flat: after a surge of creation
of private farms in 1991–93, since mid-1993 few new ones have formed, and the total
number of private farms has remained level at fewer than 300,000. Attempts to form
private farms fail more often than not due to the enormous difficulty private farmers face in finding suitable land, equipment, credit, and customers.[49]

The state-oriented farm lobby wields decisive leverage over agricultural policy.
First of all, it speaks for a compliant and dependent population of peasants, many of
whom would be unable to survive in a competitive market environment; most have
little choice but to support the continuation of the existing system. It is notable that
in each election, reported rural turnout is much higher than urban turnout, despite
the vast distances and dismal roads connecting villages to polling stations. The rural
vote also leans very heavily toward the Agrarian Party, the Communist Party, and the
ultra-nationalists. There are strong reasons to suspect that, in many cases, farm leaders and rural government officials gladly spare their constituents the trouble and
inconvenience of traveling to the polls and casting ballots themselves. Instead, in
many rural areas, local authorities drive the ballot boxes around to villages themselves and supervise the voting process. In other cases, they simply report the results
they think proper. All studies of the geography of vote fraud in Russia agree that it
is greatest in rural areas, where voters are most easily cowed, election monitors are
scarce, and local authorities can most readily resort to techniques such as ballot-
stuffing or deliberate misreporting of tallies.[50]

The state-oriented farm lobby also has a lock on "its" committee in both chambers of parliament. In fact, in each parliament, the Russian Supreme Soviet of
1990–93, the 1994–95 Duma, and the new Duma that convened in January 1996, the
agriculture committee has been dominated by representatives of the state-oriented
agrarian lobby and its associated political party, the Agrarian Party of Russia.
Indeed, this party, more than any other major party, is nearly indistinguishable from
an interest group. Although the Agrarian Party of Russia is allied with the Communist Party of the Russian Federation, it is better understood as the political arm of a
highly organized, highly specific sector of interest. For this reason, the agrarian
lobby has not been willing to take a fully oppositional stance toward the government. Two members of the agrarian party entered the Chernomyrdin cabinet and
one, Victor Zaveriukha, went so far as to break with the party after the 1995 elections while staying on as deputy prime minister in charge of agricultural policy. In
parliamentary voting, the agrarians sometimes have been willing to support the government in return for specific promises of support for the farm sector and for dominant influence on shaping state policy on land relations. This lock on lawmaking

---

[49]Figures from European Bank for Reconstruction and Development, *Transition Report 1995: Investment
and Enterprise Development* (London: EBRD, 1995), p. 55; *Nations in Transit: Civil Society, Democracy and
Markets in East Central Europe and the Newly Independent States* (Washington, D.C.: Freedom House, 1995),
p. 120. An analysis of the hurdles facing private farmers is provided by Stephen K. Wegren, "The Politics
of Private Farming in Russia," *Journal of Peasant Studies* 23 (July 1996), pp. 106–140.

[50]On the prevalance of vote fraud in the rural areas, see Nikolai Petrov, "Elektoral´nyi landshaft," Ch. 2
of M. McFaul and N. Petrov, *Politicheskii al´manakh Rossii* (Moscow: Carnegie Moscow Center, 1995), pp.
40–44; A. A. Sobianin and V. G. Sukhovol´skii, *Demokratiia, ogranichennaia fal´sifikatsiiami: vybory i referen-
dumy v Rossii v 1991–1993 gg.* (Moscow: Proektnaia gruppa po pravam cheloveka, 1995), pp. 59–65.

has given them the opportunity to block legislation that would legalize full private ownership of agricultural lands. Instead, through the Land Code and other laws, they qualified and regulated the right of land ownership in such a way as to prevent agricultural lands from being subject to free purchase and sale.

The influence of the state and collective farm lobby over land and farm policy is countered by the commercial farm sector lobby and, more effectively, by presidential power. Private, market-oriented farmers have far fewer political resources in the struggle for influence in land and agriculture policy than do the well-organized state and collective farm officials. They are represented by two major interest associations, the Association of Peasant Farms and Cooperatives of Russian (AKKOR) and the Union of Landowners. The first formed in 1991 to voice the interests of private farmers and commercially oriented cooperatives while the second, formed in 1994, has moved more directly into the political arena as a quasi-party.[51] The Union of Landowners, for instance, joined Viktor Chernomyrdin's Our Home is Russia electoral bloc in the December 1995 parliamentary elections, and in spring 1996 came out strongly in support of President Yeltsin's reelection. Still another organization representing private farmers is the Peasant Party headed by Yuri Chernichenko, but its influence has been quite limited.

More powerful in the struggle for policy influence is presidential power. As we saw in Chapter Two, under Yeltsin's 1993 constitution, the president has the power to issue decrees (*ukazy*, or edicts) that carry the force of law. These do not need to be confirmed by parliament, but they may not violate existing law. Parliament cannot directly counter a presidential edict with a countermanding law (so ruled the Constitutional Court), but it may pass a law "clarifying" a presidential decree, or filling in legislative gaps. Parliament has used that power to block some presidential actions just as President Yeltsin has used the combination of his veto power and his decree power to make major policies. Land policy is a prime example of this contest for power between parliament and president. Yeltsin's 1993 constitution enshrined the right of citizens to own land as private property.[52] But it did not specify that all land should be made subject to free purchase and sale, and it provided that the "conditions and procedure for the use of land" are to be established through law. Thus, like other open-ended constitutional rights, land rights need to be specified by law, and here the agrarian lobby's iron grip on the legislative process means that parliament has refused to allow farmlands to become subject to market competition.

Still, Yeltsin's decrees have shaped land relations to some degree. Three in particular have attempted to create a right of private property in land. In December 1991 Yeltsin decreed that farmers on state and collective farms could leave their farms with rights to shares of the farmland; these shares could be used to obtain land through leasehold or purchase. A second decree in October 1993 went somewhat further, giving the members of state and collective farms a right to a share of

---

[51]Wegren, "The Politics of Private Farming in Russia."

[52]Article 36 states:

1. Citizens and their associations are entitled to hold land in private ownership.

2. Owners freely possess, utilize and dispose of land and other natural resources provided that this does not damage the environment and does not violate the rights and legitimate interests of others.

3. The conditions and procedure for the use of land are defined on the basis of federal law.

the land itself of the farm in the form of a negotiable certificate. They could use this share to create their own private farm, or sell or lease it back to the parent farm, or use it as security for a bank loan.[53] Both urban and rural dwellers could also purchase or lease land from the local district governments to start private farms, but relatively few people have done so. In fact, very few people used their shares to start their own farms. Ambiguity surrounded the rights created by these decrees, and enormous local resistance inhibited their enforcement. For instance, the October 1993 decree stipulated that if a farmer sought to sell his land share, the collective or state farm had a priority right to buy it back from him. In March 1996 Yeltsin issued yet another decree restating the right of individuals who wished to use their land shares to create farms, or, alternatively, to sell or mortgage their shares, and that they should be able to do so without legal hindrance from collective and state farm managers and local government authorities. But parliament countered with a law "clarifying" this right, ensuring that the owner of a land share was free to sell it back to the collective farm, or to lease it from the collective farm for agricultural use, but not to sell it freely to outsiders.[54]

Even more than the legal struggle between parliament and president over land rights, the unfavorable economic environment stifles the incentive for private farms: private farmers find it extremely difficult to obtain fuel, fertilizer, affordable credit, storage, transportation and distribution facilities, and small-scale and affordable farm machinery. The land parcels they are able to obtain are often remote and unfavorable; the prices they are offered by state procurement agents are often low and late in being paid. The hostility of local authorities and the inability of the central government to make good on its promises of support for the private agricultural sector have discouraged all but the most determined private farmers.[55] Their economic weakness translates into political vulnerability in the great national battle over land and agricultural policy. The state and collective farm lobby has been far more effective politically because of its comprehensive control over state and collective farmers and the officials of rural district governments; its near-monopoly position through the agriculture committee in parliament on legislation on land and agricultural issues; and its willingness to trade support of other government policies, such as the budget, in return for their lock on land policy.

Within the agrarian lobby, however, more ideological, hard-line forces compete for influence with more moderate elements. The more ideological wing would align the party more closely with the Communist Party of the Russian Federation, take a position more sharply opposed to President Yeltsin and the Chernomyrdin government, and fight any form of private property in land. The more moderate wing would distance itself from the communists, maintain a cooperative relationship with the government so as to keep the flow of subsidies and cheap credits coming, and tolerate certain forms of private land ownership—in urban areas, for instance. The party's poor showing in the December 1995 election increased the pressure on it to

---

[53]Stephen K. Wegren, "The Development of Market Relations in Agricultural Land: The Case of Kostroma Oblast," *Post-Soviet Geography* 36:8 (October 1995), pp. 497–498.

[54]On the 1996 decree, see *Segodnia*, March 23, 1996 and April 5, 1996.

[55]Wegren, "The Politics of Private Farming in Russia."

choose between two roles: interest group or political party. The dilemma illustrates a fundamental point about Russian politics: interest groups often tend to act as if they were political parties, seeking to capture a share of governing power rather than to influence those in government. Perhaps this is because in the transitional environment, in which the state still monopolizes a number of scarce resources, merely possessing the abstract freedom to organize may not suffice to allow interest groups to obtain benefits. To solve their own organizational dilemmas, interest groups often seek a statist or corporatist relationship with the state in which they hold an exclusive "license" on policy-making in their domain.

NEW SECTORS OF INTEREST

We have seen that in a time when people's interests themselves are changing rapidly as a result of social change, both old and new organizations—whether they have an exclusive "license" to represent a sector of interest or not—find it hard to stay united. Overall, the pattern is clearly one of a shift from a statist pattern to a pluralist pattern of interest organization. The statist inheritance continues to be significant, as shown by the survival of the old trade union association and the agrarian lobby. There are also certain limited developments in the direction of a corporatist pattern of interest articulation, as illustrated by the "tripartite commission." But, for the most part, the prevailing pattern is pluralist, as is indicated further by the formation of new associations speaking for interests that had never been organized in the past.

These include organizations that speak for the common interests of cities and regions, such as the Union of Governors, an association of the chiefs of administration in the oblasts and krais first formed in 1992. Most of the chiefs are appointed by Yeltsin, and they have generally been willing to support Yeltsin in national politics at the price of demanding substantial autonomy in their own territories. They meet periodically to discuss issues of center-regional relations, such as the legal status of regional and local government. Also included are organizations representing groups of contiguous provinces, such as "Black Earth," which voices the demands of Voronezh, Lipetsk, Kursk, Belgorod, Tambov, and Orel oblasts, where agriculture is vital to the economy. Some others are the "Urals Interregional Association," "Central Russia," "Northwest," "Siberian Accord," and "Great Volga." Most concentrate their efforts on strengthening the legal powers of oblast-level governments, lobbying for the interests of their areas, and resolving problems of intraregional trade.

These regional associations are a significant political force. The leaders of both chambers of parliament signed an agreement with eight regional associations in July 1994 promising to submit any proposed law that concerned the rights of regions to the regional associations for their views.[56] Representatives of the associations meet regularly with the government and parliament to press for the needs of their areas. Moscow views the rise of strong regional associations as a useful way in which the interests of regions can be aggregated and channeled to policymakers,

---

[56] *Segodnia,* July 15, 1994.

while checking some of the more radical aspirations of individual territories.[57] At the same time, in order to keep such associations from gaining too much strength, Moscow has played one territory off against another, signing bilateral treaties with individual republics and oblasts in order to undercut collective action among them.[58]

In the past, some associations and some individual provinces have been tempted to move beyond lobbying and to declare themselves "republics" with the same status as the ethnic-national republics. In the fall of 1993, the 11 oblasts of Central Russia considered reconstituting themselves a "republic." Soon afterward, the leadership of Sverdlovsk oblast adopted a formal decision to declare itself the "Urals Republic" with its own constitution. President Yeltsin put an immediate end to the effort, however, using a combination of carrots and sticks. He issued a decree annulling the decision and firing the local chief of administration, Eduard Rossel´. Yeltsin also sweetened the federal government's subsidies to one of the neighboring oblasts, leading its governor to denounce the "Urals Republic" scheme as a power grab by Rossel´. Later, however, Yeltsin granted Sverdlovsk oblast the right to hold elections for governor—in effect giving Rossel´ a chance to return to the position from which Yeltsin had fired him, in return for abandoning his ambitions for a "Urals Republic."[59] Rossel´ ran and won, and became part of Yeltsin's political support base.

The range of new interest organizations is wide. One rapidly growing type of organization is women's groups, hundreds of which have sprung up in recent years. Some run health care and maternity centers, family planning centers, or foundations for the care of abused women and children. Others operate charitable institutions for indigents or for the families of discharged servicemen. Still others promote the development of small businesses owned by women. Newspapers, research and public policy centers, and professional associations oriented principally to women's concerns have formed. In the city of Novosibirsk, a group called the "Disabled Parents' Association," most of whose members are women, created a program to lobby for social services for disabled people and to enable them to discuss common problems.[60] A prominent women's group enjoying widespread public sympathy is the "soldiers' mothers" movement, which presses for an end to the often cruel hazing practices in the Russian army that have led to the deaths of many recruits.

The majority of the new women's organizations are based in cities, most often Moscow. Unlike the Soviet Women's Committee or the "women's soviets" that were a

---

[57]Meeting with the Urals Association in September 1994, for instance, the Minister of Nationality Affairs, Nikolai Egorov, called regional associations "a model of [a] healthy federal constitutional system" and promised that the government would "support the development of associations in every way possible," *Segodnia,* September 17, 1994.

[58]Steven L. Solnick, "The Political Economy of Russian Federalism: A Framework for Analysis," *Problems of Post-Communism* 6 (1996), pp. 13–25.

[59]Ibid., p. 22.

[60]Marc Krizack, "Disabled Women Form Coalition for Change in Novosibirsk," *Initiatives in the New Independent States,* World Learning, Inc., Issues II & III (Spring/Summer 1994), p. 15. This publication is a valuable source of information on women's organizations in the former Soviet states and their contacts with organizations in the United States.

visible feature of the statist system of public organizations under the old regime, they are autonomous of the state and can focus their attention on the issues with which they are most concerned. And, in sharp contrast to the past, now many women's and other groups have established direct ties with counterpart groups abroad.

Some groups have formed to protest the absence of effective legal protection for economic actors in the poorly regulated marketplace. The Association of Russian Banks, representing some 900 banks, demanded that the government protect them against the wave of contract killings by organized crime against bankers and members of their families, which has taken over 30 lives since 1992.[61] Over 50 women's organizations joined in an appeal to parliament in spring 1996 to take action to protect women's economic rights, pointing out that women make up 62 percent of registered unemployed and face discrimination in hiring, firing, promotion, and wages.[62] Another example is the "deceived investors" movement. Lacking clear understanding of the risks attendant upon investment in dubious get-rich-quick schemes, unprotected by any effective legal requirements of disclosure of records, and operating in a fast-moving, often bewildering, new commercial environment, many Russians invested their privatization vouchers and their money in banks, mutual funds, stock companies, and other financial vehicles which collapsed. Some were simply Ponzi schemes. Because depositors and investors have had almost no recourse to the courts, as has so often been the case with groups in the private sector, they have turned to political action. Two associations representing the interests of deceived investors, the United Congress of Investors and Shareholders and the All-Russian Movement of Investors, were founded in October 1995 and have demanded that the government find ways to compensate citizens who were defrauded. Evidently in response to their demands, President Yeltsin decreed in November 1995 that the government must find a way to compensate deceived investors.

In several fields new professional associations have formed. These act to set guidelines for professional practice, seeking to fend off onerous government restrictions and to regulate entry into their fields. For instance, three associations of defense attorneys (*advokaty,* who will be discussed further in Chapter Seven) united in September 1994 under an umbrella association to press government to increase their autonomy to regulate legal practice.[63] Television broadcast companies founded a National Association of Television Broadcasters on August 31, 1995, to seek the expansion of private ownership of television facilities and tax relief for broadcasters.[64]

The opportunity to gain publicity and influence by running candidates for parliament drew a large number of interest groups into party politics in the fall of 1995. Many of the electoral associations which attempted to run party lists in the December 1995 election were interest groups or amalgams of interest groups, rather than parties. Among those which gathered the necessary number of signatures to put up candidate lists were the following. The share of the vote they received is indicated in parentheses:

---

[61]RFE/RL Daily Report, April 5, 1995.

[62]OMRI Daily Report, March 5, 1996.

[63]RFE/RL Daily Report, September 13, 1994.

[64]RFE/RL Daily Report, September 1, 1995.

- The bloc including the heads of the Party for Defense of Pensioners and Veterans; the Party for Eliminating Crime—for Law and Order; the Party for Defense of Health Care, Education, Science and Culture; the Party for Defense of Youth; the United Free Trade Unions; the Party of Justice; and the Party for Defense of Nature (.48 percent)
- The Association of Lawyers (*advokaty*) of Russia (.35 percent)
- The Association "League of Employees of the Communal Services and Housing Industry of Russia" (.15 percent)
- The bloc including the heads of the Party for Defense of Children; the Party "Russian Women"; the People's Christian-Monarchist Party; the Party of the Orthodox; the Party for the Union of the Slavonic Peoples; the Party of Rural Toilers "Land-Matushka"; the Party for Defense of Invalids; the Party of Those Suffering from the Authorities and of the Unfortunate (.21 percent)

Together, these groups received a total of just over 1 percent of the vote. It is instructive that the leaders of these groups considered it more useful to organize separate electoral organizations than to put their resources behind supporting existing parties or lobbying government for their interests. They chose a form of "outsider" strategies for interest associations by attempting to publicize their cause through an election campaign. Merely winning the theoretical freedom to organize may not suffice to allow civic associations to operate effectively. Since such basic material necessities as meeting and office space and communications equipment and the like are still not readily available except by order of a government organization, many groups—particularly outside the capital cities—depend upon the state to obtain what they need through official allocations. In this case the election campaign was a low-cost way for an interest group to publicize its cause.

Clearly, the degree of associational pluralism today is far greater than in the late Soviet period. Formerly monopolistic associations have divided and split, but many rival groups seek to unite around common demands for regulatory protection or for autonomy from it—for credits, tariff protection, tax relief, and subsidies, or for speedier privatization of state resources. A deep division separates groups interested in the deepening of market and property relations in society, and groups demanding the restoration of state ownership and control. Yet within each of these camps are divergent interests as well. Among pro-market reformers there is a difference in perspective between those more interested in short-term rewards than long-term opportunities. Those with shorter time horizons, for instance, include the "cheap ruble" lobby, which welcomes the devaluation of the ruble against the U.S. dollar in order to make the export of Russian raw materials still more profitable. These include many in the oil, coal, and gas industries and the officials from export-oriented regions.[65] Those with longer time horizons would prefer the ruble to grow stronger in international currency markets so that ruble-denominated assets in Russia will be more valuable as time passes. Among those pressing for continued state control over much of the economy are avowed communists, while others would not

---

[65]Interview with President Yeltsin's economic advisor Alexander Lifshits in journal *Vek*, October 20–26, 1996, as cited in OMRI Economic Report, November 2, 1995.

go so far as to restore the communist system. Vol´skii's RUIE, for instance, preferred Yeltsin to Ziuganov in the 1996 presidential race.

The new competitive environment for interest articulation has made parliament an important site for interest group pressure. Much lobbying concerns fiscal policy. For example, in countless cases ranging from the military's intense pressure for greater budget allocations, the agrarians' constant demands for new credits and tariffs, the regions' desires to reduce the fiscal burden on them, the defense industry's demands to increase arms exports, and the coal industry's need for subsidies, lobbies make demands on the budget. The process of budget approval has come under parliament's control, requiring that interests press their case not only in the corridors of executive power, but openly in parliamentary debate. The politics of budgetary policy has produced some unexpected coalitions, but, most significantly, it has required open deliberation on setting national policy priorities. The zero-sum politics of the budgetary game has produced a more pluralistic policy-making process. Parliament is also pressured in the struggle over basic regulatory policy, particularly over property rights, but also over such matters as restrictions on foreign religious missionaries, whose activities the Russian Orthodox Church has lobbied successfully to limit.[66] Russia's hybrid constitution, combining presidentialism with parliamentarism, encourages organized interests to choose whether to push for legislation or a presidential decree, depending on which is likely to be a more advantageous channel of influence. The president has been broadly sympathetic to the spread of market relations, but to affect the specific details of legislation and for leverage over the state budget, interest groups must lobby parliament. This brings interest groups immediately into the new arena of Russian party politics.

Interest Aggregation: Toward a Multiparty System

We saw that in the *glasnost´* era, many new organizations were politicized as they struggled with the state for legal registration, and began to articulate a broader, often more radical, political program. Some allied themselves with the democratic movement, others with the hard-line wing of the communist party, and still others with extreme anti-Western nationalists. All three tendencies—democratic reformers, communists, and ultranationalists—are represented in the spectrum of Russia's political parties. Although specific party names and organizational identities continue to evolve rapidly, the ideological position of most parties can be located on a spectrum between the liberal, democratic parties at one end, and the anti-reform socialist and nationalist groups at the other. In between are a number of parties which seek to stake out the elusive center ground.

---

[66]Harold J. Berman, "Religious Freedom and the Rights of Foreign Missionaries under Russian Law," *The Parker School Journal of East European Law* 2:4/5 (1995), pp. 421–446.

We have noted that the line between interest groups and parties continues to be unclear in the present, since some parties tend to concentrate on interests of concern to a single occupational group while some interest groups represent broader ideological movements. Many contemporary Russian parties grew out of the "informal" groups and movements that mobilized during the *glasnost'* period.[67] Others came out of the CPSU, which fractured into hard-line and more liberal wings. The greatest impetus to the development of political parties as electoral organizations, however, were the elections of 1989, 1990, 1993, and 1995. Each round of elections stimulated a burst of organizational activity.[68]

The elections of USSR deputies in early 1989 produced the first efforts by like-minded activists to elect candidates sympathetic to their views, as democratically oriented intellectuals organized to elect Andrei Sakharov and other champions of the democratic movement. Then, when the USSR Congress of People's Deputies convened in May 1989, Sakharov and other newly elected deputies formed the first independent legislative caucus in Soviet history: the "Interregional Group of Deputies." In turn, it became the organizational nucleus for the formation of a still broader coalition of democratic candidates running for the Russian Congress of People's Deputies and for seats in lower soviets in the March 1990 elections; this coalition was called "Democratic Russia." After the election, Democratic Russia's deputies in the Russian parliament divided up into several parliamentary factions which sought to coordinate their actions and press for support of economic and political reform. But the creation of the presidency and the growing strength of the anti-Yeltsin opposition in the parliament weakened the democratic forces. Dozens of deputies left parliament to take jobs in the presidential administration.[69]

Yeltsin's decrees of September and October 1993 dissolving parliament and calling for new elections in December radically changed the incentives affecting political parties. Most important was the fact that the electoral law that he enacted by decree introduced a strong proportional representation element into the election of new deputies. Elections in the past had used a single-member district system exclusively: the country was divided into electoral districts equalling the number of seats mandated in parliament, and the winning candidate had assumed that district's seat. As discussed previously, the new 1993 system divided the seats in the lower house of parliament, the State Duma, into two categories. Each voter would have two votes, one for a candidate running for that electoral district's seat, the other for one of the registered parties putting up candidates on party lists. Half, or 225, of the seats in the Duma would be filled by the winners of single-member dis-

---

[67]Vera Tolz, *The USSR's Emerging Multiparty System* (Washington, D.C.: Center for Strategic and International Studies, 1990); Marcia A. Weigle, "Political Participation and Party Formation in Russia, 1985–1992: Institutionalizing Democracy?" *The Russian Review* 53 (April 1994), pp. 240–270.

[68]Good accounts of the political campaigns surrounding the 1989 and 1990 elections include Brendan Kiernan, *The End of Soviet Politics: Elections, Legislatures, and the Demise of the Communist Party* (Boulder: Westview Press, 1993); and Michael McFaul and Sergei Markov, *The Troubled Birth of Russian Democracy: Parties, Personalities, and Programs* (Stanford: Hoover Institution Press, 1993).

[69]On the growing confrontation between Yeltsin and the Congress of People's Deputies/Supreme Soviet over the 1990–93 period, see Thomas F. Remington, "Ménage à Trois: The End of Soviet Parliamentarism," in Jeffrey W. Hahn, *Democratization in Russia: The Development of Legislative Institutions* (Armonk, NY: M.E. Sharpe, 1996), pp. 106–139.

trict seats. The other half of the seats would be filled by candidates nominated on party lists, according to the share each party received in the proportional representation ballot.

The electoral law had been discussed and debated for well over a year before Yeltsin enacted it, and there was a widespread consensus among both pro-Yeltsin and anti-Yeltsin groups that a mixed election system would combine the advantages of a single-member district model (particularly the individual ties between a deputy and a district) with those of a proportional representation system (the stimulus the law gave for the formation of national political parties as a means to stabilize and channel political activity in the country). For party leaders, whether they were opposition, centrist, or reformist, the law provided real benefits. The fact that the party leaders could choose the order in which the candidates running under that party's label were listed on the ballot (the voter could not mark a preference for one candidate on the list over another—the voter simply chose which list he or she preferred) gave the leaders incentives for attracting other politicians to their organization. The electoral law therefore served the political ambitions of party leaders of all ideological camps. Perhaps that is the reason that there was little protest over the details of Yeltsin's electoral law.

The new institutional setting had a strong impact on the outcome of the elections. For one thing, Yeltsin's law set very high requirements on registration of parties.[70] Only 21 parties submitted lists to the Central Electoral Commission by the deadline, and only 13 of these were approved.[71] For another, the PR (proportional representation) portion of the electoral system created one Russia-wide district in which aggregate shares of parties' votes would be tallied, rather than a larger number of multimember districts. This was done to reduce the chances that parties with a strong regional or ethnic appeal might win seats and weaken the state's unity. A third factor was the short time the parties had to organize and mount campaigns. A fourth was the fact that many voters formed their opinions about the parties based on the televised images of their leaders' personalities. The vivid television presence of Vladimir Zhirinovsky, therefore, was converted through the PR system into a large share of seats for his party in parliament.[72] Finally, the law specified that only parties exceeding 5 percent of the party list vote were eligible to receive seats. Again, this was done to filter out potentially destabilizing fringe parties. This feature also had a considerable impact, since 5 of the 13 parties competing for the list vote failed to clear the 5 percent hurdle. These features of the electoral law therefore had a very substantial effect: of dozens, if not hundreds, of organizations which might

---

[70]First, parties and electoral associations had to have been registered by the Ministry of Justice to form lists. Second, they had to collect 100,000 signatures nominating petitions, of which no more than 15 percent could be obtained in any one province. And third, they had to gather the signatures and submit them to the Central Electoral Commission by November 6.

On the way in which the design of the electoral law affected the campaign, see Michael Urban, "December 1993 as a Replication of Late-Soviet Electoral Practices," *Post-Soviet Affairs* 10:2 (1994), pp. 136–139.

[71]The CEC disqualified eight on the grounds that some of the signatures were invalid or too many were collected in one region.

[72]Peter Lentini and Troy McGrath, "The Rise of the Liberal Democratic Party and the 1993 Elections," *Harriman Institute Forum* 7:6 (February 1994), pp. 8–9. Zhirinovsky's party won almost 23 percent of the party list vote, the highest share won by any party in the race.

have attempted to field candidates, only eight succeeded in entering parliament through proportional representation.

Table 5.1 indicates the strength of political factions in the lower house of parliament, the State Duma, as of spring 1994.

The balance of seats by faction is a product of the outcome of the voting in the two ballots. As the table indicates, eight parties which ran candidates on party lists won seats. Five failed to clear the threshold and did not receive seats. Nearly all of the deputies who won single-member district seats joined one or another faction. Some joined one of the eight party factions (often because they had run in their districts with that party's support). Others, rather than joining existing parties, formed groups oriented toward single-member district deputies. Three such deputy groups were created: New Regional Policy; Russia's Path; and the Liberal-Democratic Union of December 12.

Notwithstanding the restrictive conditions in which the elections were held, the eight party factions and three deputy groups that formed in parliament covered a wide ideological spectrum. They fell into three political families, loosely called "opposition," "democrats," and "centrists." Let us examine these groups more closely.

OPPOSITION PARTIES IN THE STATE DUMA

The Liberal Democratic Party of Russia (LDPR)—Zhirinovsky's party—differs from the communists and agrarians in certain important respects. Zhirinovsky's party stresses the national theme, even more than they do, appealing to feelings of injured ethnic and national pride. Zhirinovsky calls for aggressive foreign policies and harsh treatment of non-Russian ethnic minorities. However, his economic policy is much fuzzier. While demanding that the government relieve the distress of Russians who have suffered under market reforms, he also distances himself from the socialist economic system of the past and poses as a "third force," which is neither tied to the old communist regime nor to the new order under Yeltsin.[73] Finally, he also sends a clear message that he is seeking the presidency, the powers of which he will use dictatorially to right wrongs and settle accounts with Russia's enemies.

The Communist Party of the Russian Federation (CPRF) is the major successor party to the old CPSU. Other splinter groups are more militantly Stalinist; the CPRF has cautiously embraced certain elements of the market and has declared that it no longer believes in violence and revolution as means to achieve its policy goals.[74] But the party vehemently opposes the Yeltsin and Gaidar stabilization and privatization programs and demands immediate restoration of state ownership and planning in industry. Given its history and hostility to Yeltsin's policies, it may seem surprising that the CPRF decided to take part in the elections of 1993 at all. But it has evidently decided to make use of the rules of the parliamentary game to influence national policy, trying to show that, unlike Yeltsin who violated the constitution in dissolv-

---

[73]Many of Zhirinovsky's writings, including an autobiography, have been collected and published by the party in a volume entitled *O sud'bakh Rossii* (n.p., 1993).

[74]Wendy Slater, "The Russian Communist Party Today," *RFE/RL Research Report* 3:31 (12 August 1994), p. 4.

TABLE 5.1
Results of December 1993 Parliamentary Elections

Party	Party List Vote Percentage	List Seats Received	Affiliated District Deputies	Total Seats (April)	As Percentage of Duma (450 Seats)
Reform Parties					
RC	15.51	40	33	73	16.22
PRES	6.73	18	12	30	6.67
Yabloko	7.86	20	8	28	6.22
Dec 12	0	0	26	26	5.78
RDDR	4.08	0	0	0	0.00
Total	34.18	78	79	157	34.89
Centrist Parties					
DPR	5.52	14	1	15	3.33
WOR	8.13	21	2	23	5.11
NRP	0	0	66	66	14.67
KEDR	0.76	0	0	0	0.00
BRNI	1.25	0	0	0	0.00
Civic Union	1.93	0	0	0	0.00
DiM	0.7	0	0	0	0.00
Total	18.29	35	69	104	23.11
Opposition Parties					
APR	7.99	21	34	55	12.22
CPRF	12.4	32	13	45	10.00
LDPR	22.92	59	5	64	14.22
RP	0	0	14	14	3.11
Total	43.31	112	66	178	39.56
Against All Lists	4.22				
Total	**100**	**225**	**214**	**439**	**97.56**

Legend

RC: Russia's Choice. This was the pro-market reform party led by Egor Gaidar. **PRES:** Party of Russian Unity and Accord. This party, led by Sergei Shakhrai, positioned itself as a moderately pro-reform force, which also sought to articulate the concerns of regional governments in national policy-making.

Yabloko: The name, which is also the Russian word for apple, is an acronym made up of elements of the names of the initial three leaders, Grigorii Yavlinsky, Vladimir Lukin, and Yuri Boldyrev. **Dec 12:** The Liberal-Democratic Union of December 12. This was a parliamentary group which formed from among deputies elected in single-member districts who shared a reformist orientation but chose not to join one of the party-based factions. **RDDR:** Russian Movement for Democratic Reform: coalition headed by the prominent Moscow and St. Petersburg politicians, Gavriil Popov and Anatolii Sobchak.

DPR: Democratic Party of Russia, initially headed by Nikolai Travkin. **WOR:** Women of Russia. **NRP:** New Regional Policy. This was a deputies' group which formed after the election to unite single-member district deputies who were politically close to state industrial directors. **KEDR:** The "Constructive Ecological Movement 'Cedar.'" This was a movement loosely affiliated with the environmental protection cause which arose out of the state public health service. **BRNI:** Future of Russia/New Names. This group advertised itself as the voice of youth. **Civic Union:** The political wing of the Russian Union of Industrialists and Entrepreneurs, and a voice for the interests of state industrial directors. **DiM:** Dignity and Mercy.

APR: Agrarian Party of Russia. **CPRF:** Communist Party of the Russian Federation. **LDPR:** Liberal Democratic Party of Russia (Vladimir Zhirinovsky's party). **RP:** Russia's Path. This was a deputies' group principally made up of single-member district deputies who shared a nationalist, pro-USSR, anti-Yeltsin political orientation.

ing parliament in 1993, it respects the principle of constitutionalism. The CPRF also attacks Western influence in Russia: this writer heard its leader, Gennadii Ziuganov, declare at a press conference in June 1994, having just returned from a tour of the provinces, that the process of "Americanization" of Russia had advanced to the point of "vampirization." As evidence for this, Ziuganov cited his observation that in every town and village one could now see Russian children wearing baseball caps. In addition to anti-Westernism, Ziuganov has also worked hard to align the party with the religious and spiritual traditions of Russian culture, overlooking Marx's and Lenin's militant enmity toward religion. Ziuganov frequently invokes the traditional mutual support between the Russian state and the Russian Orthodox Church. So far, however, the Patriarch has refrained from endorsing the Communist Party.

The Agrarian Party of Russia (APR) is closely allied with the CPRF on most issues, but, as we have seen, its political activity is almost entirely focused on agricultural issues. The APR staunchly and effectively opposes the privatization of land in Russia and persistently and successfully lobbies for credits and subsidies, including price supports, to the country's collective and state farms. The APR is often considered to be more a lobby for collective and state farm managers than a political party aggregating interests across sectors. For that reason, its interests sometimes diverge from those of the communists. Not only are the APR's interests focused specifically on the agricultural sector, but it also has been willing to support the government's position on some issues where the communists were not.[75] As mentioned, the agrarians did poorly in the 1995 election, failing to take any party list seats, and winning only 20 district seats. Appealing to other single-mandate district winners, and "borrowing" members from the large communist party faction, they managed to enroll 35 members and thus to register as a recognized faction in the Duma in January 1996. Registration is important, since it enables a faction to hold a seat on the governing committee of the parliament, the Council of the Duma, to acquire office space and other organizational resources, and to have priority rights to recognition in debate on the floor of the chamber.

When the first Duma convened in January 1994, another opposition-minded parliamentary faction formed of deputies from single-member districts who preferred to organize a group of their own rather than enter any of the existing party factions. This group, called Russian's Path (or Russian's Way), was led by the capable, articulate, young legal scholar, Sergei Baburin. One of its members was Anatolii Lukyanov, who used to be Gorbachev's closest associate in the old USSR Supreme Soviet, but who became a bitter opponent of Gorbachev and Yeltsin and was jailed on suspicion of involvement in the August 1991 coup. Another was the flamboyant young television producer, Alexander Nevzorov. Members of this group prized their independence of party ties despite the fact that their numbers were too few to qualify for registration as a parliamentary faction. They did not enjoy the material and procedural rights that registered factions were given. In the 1995 parliamentary election, elements of this faction organized a party list of their own called "Power to the People." Although it failed to clear the 5 percent hurdle, a number of its mem-

---

[75]An example was the passage of the 1994 state budget. In the Duma's vote on the bill on June 8, 95 percent of the members of the APR faction supported the budget, while only 73 percent of the communists did so.

bers were elected in district races. They then proceeded to form a parliamentary group and to seek registration as a faction, but fell short of the 35-member minimum required; the communist party "lent" them some members and thus enabled them to register.

DEMOCRATIC PARTIES

The democratic forces in the Duma include both party factions and factions comprising deputies elected in single-member districts. In the 1994–95 Duma, Russia's Choice was the largest democratic faction. It comprised some politicians and activists of the old Democratic Russia movement as well as prominent figures from the government. Egor Gaidar headed the party's list, and the party was widely seen as the government party despite the fact that Prime Minister Chernomyrdin had nothing to do with it. President Yeltsin kept his distance from Russia's Choice, indicating that it was the party closest to him politically, but never campaigning for it. The power and prominence of its leaders gave it certain advantages, but many fewer than observers suspected or it expected. Moreover, the party was itself divided over strategy between its government wing and its old, more radical Democratic Russia wing.[76] And observers believed that Gaidar himself proved to be an ineffective campaigner who projected a somewhat aloof, even arrogant television image.[77]

In 1995, Prime Minister Chernomyrdin led a political movement called "Our Home Is Russia," which had a broadly reformist, pro-government position, and won 10 percent of the party list vote. Our Home is less an ideologically defined political movement than it is a coalition of officeholders, particularly regional governors. Our Home is often called "the party of power" because many believe it is united more by the desire of those in power to hold on to power than by any particular set of political principles.

The only democratic party to win parliamentary representation on the list vote both in 1993 and 1995 is Yabloko, led by Grigorii Yavlinsky. Yabloko regards itself as the "democratic opposition" to the president and government and espouses a socially oriented market economy. It regularly votes against the government in parliament even when its faction members work closely with the government in preparing legislation.

Fragmentation has cost the democratic parties dearly. Many pro-reform votes are wasted when the parties fail to clear the 5 percent threshold. Thus in 1993, the Russian Movement for Democratic Reform, which won 4 percent of the party list vote, won no seats. Similarly, in more than 90 single-member electoral districts in 1993, two or more of the democratic parties ran candidates against each other, in some cases splitting the democratic vote so greatly than an opposition candidate won the seat.

In both the 1994–95 and post–1995 Dumas, a number of reform-oriented deputies elected in single-member districts decided not to affiliate with any of the party factions. In the first Duma such deputies formed a group called the "Liberal-Democratic Union of December 12" and, in the second Duma, a group called

---

[76]Urban, "December 1993," pp. 131–132.

[77]Michael McFaul, "Explaining the Vote," in Symposium, "Is Russian Democracy Doomed?" *Journal of Democracy* 5:2 (April 1994), pp. 5–8.

"Regions of Russia." These groups served the interests of members with reform leanings who wish to remain independent of the main parties. In both cases, they tended to support the government position on major issues.

THE PARLIAMENTARY CENTER

Finally, there is a set of factions which avoid clear identification with either the democrats or the opposition, and strive to occupy the political middle ground. One is a party which did much better in the 1993 elections than anyone expected, Women of Russia. A movement resisting ideological definition, and certainly not feminist in orientation, Women of Russia was more a product of the old regime's official women's groups than of the new autonomous women's organizations which had arisen in the past several years. It was formed as a coalition of three public organizations: the League of Women of Russia (which was the successor to the former Soviet Women's Committee); the Association of Women-Entrepreneurs of Russia; and the League of Women of the Navy.[78] It ran on a platform stressing the need for more defense of social welfare, and it appealed particularly to voters tired of existing party politics and politicians. Women of Russia drew votes from men as well as women by skillfully building an outsiders' image and promoting itself as a mediating and balancing force rather than a political party staking out a platform of its own. Most observers expected it to hold its place in the 1995 elections, but the bloc only took 4.7 percent of the vote.

The Democratic Party of Russia, on the other hand, worked hard to establish itself in the electorate's mind as *the* party of the center, which seeks gradual, sensible, and moderate reform. One of the oldest of the new parties, it was founded in 1990 by a number of prominent figures of the democratic movement. But it split repeatedly, eventually expelling its own leader, Nikolai Travkin, and splintering into multiple rival organizations.

In the 1994–95 Duma, another centrist faction, called New Regional Policy, represented a large number of deputies from single-member districts who shunned any party identification. Their leader was president of the League of Oil Industries of Russia and their general orientation was sympathetic to the interests of factory directors and other powerful local officials. Lacking any clearly defined set of issues or policies or a common electoral base, it split into separate factions in 1995, and did not form again after the 1995 elections.

PARTIES AND THE 1995 ELECTIONS

As time passed, some factions lost members, and other factions formed. The basic division of deputies into these three camps remained constant, however, and the major party factions retained their influence and identity throughout the life of the 1994–95 Duma. Each faction in turn then developed a campaign organization and list of candidates to compete for seats in the new Duma that was to convene in Jan-

---

[78]Grigorii Belonuchkin, ed., *Federal'noe sobranie: Spravochnik* [The Federal Assembly: A Reference Guide] (Moscow: Panorama, 1994), p. 96.

uary 1996. Altogether 400 (90 percent) of the deputies ran for reelection to the Duma and 158 (40 percent) were successful.

The December 1993 elections, Yeltsin decreed, were to elect only a transitional Duma. Elections were to be held again two years later, in December 1995, for a new Duma that would have the right to serve out its full, constitutionally mandated four-year term unless it was dissolved prematurely. The elections were duly held on schedule on December 17, 1995, under an election law that was passed by both chambers of parliament and signed into law by the president.[79] The election law was similar in most respects to the law under which the 1993 elections had been held.[80] Once again, there were two ballots: one to choose candidates competing for seats in 225 single-seat districts; the other to choose one of the parties and electoral associations running lists of candidates, which would be given the right to fill the 225 parliamentary seats reserved for them in proportion to the share of the national vote they received. A voter thus cast two votes, one for a district candidate, and the other for a party.

This time an immense array of political groups competed to elect deputies—far more than could possibly be accommodated given that the same 5 percent threshold rule was kept. Some 43 organizations succeeded in registering and winning a spot on the ballot (see Figure 5.1). Serious observers worried that it was entirely possible that no party at all would win representation on the party list ballot. For example, if the 21 most popular parties each won just under 5 percent, no party would win seats in the PR vote. There were last-minute efforts to have the Constitutional Court annul the election law but there were no constitutional grounds for such an action, and the court rejected the petition.

In the end, only four parties crossed the 5 percent threshold: the communists, Zhirinovsky's LDPR, the "Our Home Is Russia" bloc formed around Prime Minister Chernomyrdin, and the Yabloko bloc led by Grigorii Yavlinsky. Of these, the communists were by far the most successful, with 22.7 percent of the party list votes. Zhirinovsky's party won 11.4 percent; Our Home Is Russia (NDR, in its Russian initials) took 10.3 percent, and Yabloko 7.0 percent. The proliferation of reform-oriented parties associated with prominent personalities split much of the pro-reform vote among them, with the result that 8.2 percent of the votes went to four small democratic parties that failed to cross the 5 percent barrier. One of these was Egor Gaidar's party, Russia's Democratic Choice, which had been the major reform faction in the previous Duma. It had received over 15 percent of the party vote in 1993, but in 1995 it failed to receive even 4 percent.

Another 11.5 percent went to centrist groups which also failed to clear the threshold. Altogether, half of the votes were cast for parties which failed to win any

---

[79]On the politics of the 1995 election law, see Thomas F. Remington and Steven S. Smith, "Political Goals, Institutional Context, and the Choice of an Electoral System: The Russian Parliamentary Election Law," *American Journal of Political Science* 40:4 (1996), pp. 1253–1279.

[80]One difference was that parties and electoral associations running lists for the proportional representation ballot were required to divide their candidate lists in such a way that no more than 12 could run on a Russia-wide, central portion of the list. The rest had to run in regional lists. They would be allocated seats according to the share of the vote for that party in the particular region where they ran. Each party was free to delineate its regions as it chose. In practice this did not greatly hinder parties from making up lists in the way they chose.

ИЗБИРАТЕЛЬНЫЙ БЮЛЛЕТЕНЬ

для выборов депутатов Государственной Думы
Федерального Собрания Российской Федерации второго созыва
по федеральному избирательному округу
17 декабря 1995 года

ГОРОД МОСКВА

РАЗЪЯСНЕНИЯ ПОРЯДКА ЗАПОЛНЕНИЯ ИЗБИРАТЕЛЬНОГО БЮЛЛЕТЕНЯ

- *Поставьте любой знак в пустом квадрате справа от наименования **только одного** избирательного объединения, избирательного блока, за которое(ый) Вы голосуете, либо в квадрате справа от строки "Против всех федеральных списков кандидатов".*
- *Избирательный бюллетень, в котором любой знак проставлен более чем в одном квадрате, либо не проставлен ни в одном из них, считается недействительным.*
- *Избирательный бюллетень, не заверенный участковой избирательной комиссией, признается бюллетенем неустановленной формы и при подсчете голосов не учитывается.*

---

1 "ПОЛИТИЧЕСКОЕ ДВИЖЕНИЕ "ЖЕНЩИНЫ РОССИИ""
Федулова Алевтина Васильевна, Лахова Екатерина Филипповна, Климантова Галина Ивановна
региональная группа :
Маркина Людмила Николаевна, Абдурахманова Эльмира Гусейновна, Айвазова Светлана Григорьевна ☐

2 "СОЦИАЛ-ПАТРИОТИЧЕСКОЕ ДВИЖЕНИЕ "ДЕРЖАВА""
Руцкой Александр Владимирович, Кобелев Виктор Васильевич, Душенов Константин Юрьевич
региональная группа :
Макушок Иван Викторович, Федоров Андрей Владимирович, Телушков Александр Николаевич ☐

3 "ОБЩЕСТВЕННО-ПОЛИТИЧЕСКОЕ ДВИЖЕНИЕ "ДУМА-96""
Буренин Владимир Арсеньевич, Симонов Михаил Петрович, Кондратьев Георгий Григорьевич
региональная группа :
Лаптев Николай Иванович, Зотов Александр Алексеевич, Лырщиков Петр Константинович ☐

4 "ПРЕОБРАЖЕНИЕ ОТЕЧЕСТВА"
(Общероссийская общественная организация "Преображение Отечества", Свободная демократическая партия России, Всероссийская партия безопасности человека)
Россель Эдуард Эргартович, Якимов Виктор Васильевич, Салье Марина Евгеньевна
региональная группа :
Канаев Сергей Федорович, Нуждин Владимир Николаевич, Шаркин Сергей Алексеевич ☐

5 "ТИХОНОВ-ТУПОЛЕВ-ТИХОНОВ"
(Партия консолидации, Лига кооператоров и предпринимателей)
Тихонов Александр Анатольевич, Туполев Алексей Андреевич, Тихонов Виктор Васильевич
региональная группа :
Андрухович Анатолий Антонович, Дожин Анатолий Иванович, Василевич Николай Степанович ☐

6 "РОССИЙСКОЕ ОБЩЕНАРОДНОЕ ДВИЖЕНИЕ"
Баженов Александр Васильевич, Мошняков Валерий Владимирович, Платонов Владимир Константинович
региональная группа :
Морокин Владимир Иванович, Нестеров Виктор Андреевич, Обидин Александр Александрович ☐

7 "ОБЩЕРОССИЙСКОЕ МУСУЛЬМАНСКОЕ ОБЩЕСТВЕННОЕ ДВИЖЕНИЕ "НУР" ("СВЕТ")"
Яхин Халит Ахметович, Яруллин Вафа Сейтбатталович, Шагидулин Анвер Галлямович
региональная группа :
Агишев Харис Анверович, Ибатуллина Гюльнара Ренатовна, Юсипов Сяид Рашидович ☐

8 "ФЕДЕРАЛЬНО-ДЕМОКРАТИЧЕСКОЕ ДВИЖЕНИЕ"
Новиков Олег Иванович, Калугин Олег Данилович, Казакова Римма Федоровна
региональная группа :
Иванов Александр Александрович, Усов Александр Арсентьевич, Михайлов Андрей Леонидович ☐

Figure 5.1

The 1995 Parliamentary Election Ballot

The party list ballot used in the 1995 State Duma election listed 43 different political parties and organizations. Voters were to choose one and place a mark in the box corresponding to that party. Each party or electoral association is represented by its official name, its logo if it had one, the names of the top three candidates on its central list, and the top three candidates on the list for the region where that precinct was located. Note that in a few cases, election officials have crossed out some candidates' names as a result of last-minute withdrawals. For instance, on Vladimir Zhiri-

9 ДЕЛО ПЕТРА I
ПРЕДВЫБОРНЫЙ БЛОК, ВКЛЮЧАЮЩИЙ РУКОВОДИТЕЛЕЙ ПАРТИИ ЗАЩИТЫ ДЕТЕЙ (МИРА, ДОБРА И СЧАСТЬЯ), ПАРТИИ "РУССКИЕ ЖЕНЩИНЫ", ПАРТИИ ПРАВОСЛАВНЫХ (ВЕРЫ, НАДЕЖДЫ, ЛЮБВИ), НАРОДНОЙ ХРИСТИАНСКО-МОНАРХИЧЕСКОЙ ПАРТИИ, ПАРТИИ ЗА СОЮЗ СЛАВЯНСКИХ НАРОДОВ, ПАРТИИ СЕЛЬСКИХ ТРУЖЕНИКОВ "ЗЕМЛЯ-МАТУШКА", ПАРТИИ ЗАЩИТЫ ИНВАЛИДОВ, ПАРТИИ ПОСТРАДАВШИХ ОТ ВЛАСТЕЙ И ОБЕЗДОЛЕННЫХ"
(Туристско-спортивный союз России, Российский профессиональный союз работников телевидения и радиовещания, Общество потребителей автотехники России)
Дикуль Валентин Иванович, Воеводин Вадим Алексеевич, Колтунов Ян Иванович
региональная группа :
Родионова Валентина Николаевна, Заржицкий Георгий Юрьевич, Шевцова Елена Евгеньевна

10
"МЕЖНАЦИОНАЛЬНЫЙ СОЮЗ"
(Конгресс гражданского согласия России, Российская Христианско-Демократическая партия, Ассоциация корейцев России)
Микитаев Абдулах Касбулатович, Гареев Махмут Ахметович, Зайцев Александр Николаевич
региональная группа :
Шаинский Владимир Яковлевич, Сиверцев Михаил Андреевич, Пряхин Георгий Владимирович

11 СТАБИЛЬНАЯ РОССИЯ
ОБЩЕСТВЕННО-ПОЛИТИЧЕСКОЕ ДВИЖЕНИЕ "СТАБИЛЬНАЯ РОССИЯ"
Петров Олег Вадимович, Быстрицкая Элина Авраамовна, Горлов Александр Викторович
региональная группа :
Моисеев Владимир Константинович, Бондарев Борис Иванович, Кожанов Дмитрий Александрович

12 МОЛОДЕЖНЫЙ БЛОК
"ПОКОЛЕНИЯ РУБЕЖА"
(Общественно-политическое движение молодежи (Союз), Общественное объединение Союз эмжековцев России (Союз МЖК России))
Солонников Дмитрий Владимирович, Пилипешин Николай Анатольевич, Барнев Марат Мансурович
региональная группа :
Редько Сергей Витальевич, Ивлиева Елена Валерьевна, Монастырева Галли Германовна

13
"МОЕ ОТЕЧЕСТВО"
Громов Борис Всеволодович, Шаталин Станислав Сергеевич, Кобзон Иосиф Давыдович
региональная группа :
Титов Юрий Александрович, Архипов Виктор Алексеевич, Кирюшин Владимир Васильевич

14 ЗА РОДИНУ!
"ЗА РОДИНУ!"
(Российский Союз ветеранов Афганистана, Народно-патриотическая партия, Общественно-политическое движение "Новая Россия")
Полеванов Владимир Павлович, Подколзин Евгений Николаевич, Балтин Эдуард Дмитриевич
региональная группа :
Сухоруков Петр Петрович, Разумов Александр Николаевич, Макаров Сергей Васильевич

15 ОБЩЕЕ ДЕЛО
"ВНЕПАРТИЙНОЕ ПОЛИТИЧЕСКОЕ ДВИЖЕНИЕ ИЗБИРАТЕЛЕЙ "ОБЩЕЕ ДЕЛО"
(Объединение "Общее дело", Союз "Живое кольцо")
Хакамада Ирина Муцуовна, Быков (Ролан Быков) Роланд Анатольевич, Джанибеков Владимир Александрович
региональная группа :
Маслюков Виктор Федорович, Динес Игорь Юрьевич, Диордийчук Александр Тимофеевич

16
"БЛОК НЕЗАВИСИМЫХ"
(Объединенный демократический центр, Всероссийский татарский культурно-просветительский центр)

региональная группа :
Комчатов Владимир Федорович, Ключников Виталий Алексеевич, Ремигайло Александр Всеволодович

17 НАШ ДОМ РОССИЯ
"ВСЕРОССИЙСКОЕ ОБЩЕСТВЕННО-ПОЛИТИЧЕСКОЕ ДВИЖЕНИЕ "НАШ ДОМ - РОССИЯ"
Черномырдин Виктор Степанович, Михалков Никита Сергеевич, Рохлин Лев Яковлевич
региональная группа :
Ресин Владимир Иосифович, Шохин Александр Николаевич, Гребенников Валерий Васильевич

18 ПАМФИЛОВА
"ПАМФИЛОВА-ГУРОВ-ВЛАДИМИР ЛЫСЕНКО (РЕСПУБЛИКАНСКАЯ ПАРТИЯ РОССИЙСКОЙ ФЕДЕРАЦИИ)"
(Республиканская партия Российской Федерации, Союз "Молодые Республиканцы")
Памфилова Элла Александровна, Гуров Александр Иванович, Лысенко Владимир Николаевич
региональная группа :
Порфильев Александр Борисович, Гулимова Валерия Вячеславовна, Шаталов Юрий Михайлович

19 ЯБЛОКО
"ОБЩЕСТВЕННОЕ ОБЪЕДИНЕНИЕ "ЯБЛОКО"
Явлинский Григорий Алексеевич, Лукин Владимир Петрович, Ярыгина Татьяна Владимировна
региональная группа :
Щекочихин Юрий Петрович, Аверчев Владимир Петрович, Борщев Валерий Васильевич

20 ВПЕРЕД, РОССИЯ
"ОБЩЕСТВЕННО-ПОЛИТИЧЕСКОЕ ДВИЖЕНИЕ "ВПЕРЕД, РОССИЯ!"
Федоров Борис Григорьевич, Денисенко Бэла Анатольевна, Владиславлев Александр Павлович
региональная группа :
Ходжаев Андрей Закирович, Адарченко Игорь Михайлович, Нестеренко Андрей Николаевич

novsky's party, the Liberal Democratic Party of Russia (number 33 on the ballot), two of the three top candidates for this region have dropped out.

The order of parties on the ballot was chosen at random. The bloc "Women of Russia" is number 1. The Communist Party of the Russian Federation is number 25. Our Home Is Russia is number 17 and Yabloko is number 19. The Beer-Lovers' Party is represented by the frothy logo of number 37. The space after number 43 allows a voter to cast a ballot "against all lists," an option chosen by almost 3% of voters.

21 **БЛОК 89 РЕГИОНОВ РОССИИ** **"89" (89 РЕГИОНОВ РОССИИ)"**
(Общероссийское политическое движение "Выбор России", Всероссийское общественно-политическое движение "Ассоциация независимых профессионалов")
региональная группа :
Медведев Павел Алексеевич, Желнин Вадим Алексеевич, Пузырев Эдуард Игоревич ☐

22 **"ЭКОЛОГИЧЕСКАЯ ПАРТИЯ РОССИИ "КЕДР"**
Панфилов Анатолий Алексеевич, Якубович Леонид Аркадьевич, Тарасов Артем Михайлович
региональная группа :
Покровский Вадим Валентинович, Киселев Алексей Иванович, Пивоваров Олег Николаевич ☐

23 **ВЫБОР** **"ДЕМОКРАТИЧЕСКИЙ ВЫБОР РОССИИ - ОБЪЕДИНЕННЫЕ ДЕМОКРАТЫ"**
(Партия "Демократический выбор России", Крестьянская партия России, Российская партия социальной демократии, Конгресс национальных объединений России)
Гайдар Егор Тимурович, Ковалев Сергей Адамович, Шукшина (Федосеева-Шукшина) Лидия Николаевна
региональная группа :
Юшенков Сергей Николаевич, Улюкаев Алексей Валентинович, Радзиховский Леонид Александрович ☐

24 **"ПАРТИЯ РОССИЙСКОГО ЕДИНСТВА И СОГЛАСИЯ"**
Шахрай Сергей Михайлович, Быков Валерий Алексеевич, Иванков Владимир Иванович
региональная группа :
Бурлацкий Федор Михайлович, Чернов Владимир Михайлович, Карпухин Виктор Васильевич ☐

25 **"КОММУНИСТИЧЕСКАЯ ПАРТИЯ РОССИЙСКОЙ ФЕДЕРАЦИИ"**
Зюганов Геннадий Андреевич, Горячева Светлана Петровна, Тулеев Аман-гельды Молдагазыевич
региональная группа :
Губенко Николай Николаевич, Мельников Иван Иванович, Куваев Александр Александрович ☐

26 **БЛОК СТАНИСЛАВА ГОВОРУХИНА** **"БЛОК СТАНИСЛАВА ГОВОРУХИНА"**
(Всероссийское объединение профсоюзов, Российское общественно-патриотическое движение "Народный альянс", Российское Христианское Демократическое Движение)
Говорухин Станислав Сергеевич, Румянцев Олег Германович, Аксючиц Виктор Владимирович
региональная группа :
Краснов Александр Викторович, Семенов Тимур Ервантович, Соломатина Тамара Борисовна ☐

27 **АДВОКАТ-ВАША ЗАЩИТА** **"АССОЦИАЦИЯ АДВОКАТОВ РОССИИ"**
Малаев Алексей Никифорович, Мирзоев Гасан Борисович, Федосеев Анатолий Михайлович
региональная группа :
Вицин Сергей Ефимович, Шушаков Виктор Пивлович, Руднев Олег Александрович ☐

28 **"НАЦИОНАЛЬНО-РЕСПУБЛИКАНСКАЯ ПАРТИЯ РОССИИ (НРПР)"**
Лысенко Николай Николаевич, Павлов Николай Александрович, Овчинников Константин Николаевич
региональная группа :
Чижевский Владимир Сергеевич, Латышев Валерий Александрович, Бабенко Олег Георгиевич ☐

29 **"СОЦИАЛ-ДЕМОКРАТЫ"**
(Социал-демократический союз, Политическое движение "Молодые социал-демократы России", Российское Движение Демократических Реформ)
Попов Гавриил Харитонович, Липицкий Василий Семенович, Богомолов Олег Тимофеевич
региональная группа :
Кудюкин Павел Михайлович, Рывкин Альберт Анатольевич, Федосов Петр Анатольевич ☐

30 **"ВЛАСТЬ - НАРОДУ!"**
(Российский общенародный союз (политическая партия), Движение матерей "За социальную справедливость")
Рыжков Николай Иванович, Бабурин Сергей Николаевич, Шувалова Елена Анатольевна
региональная группа :
Трушин Василий Петрович, Уваров Борис Иванович, Кодин Михаил Иванович ☐

31 **КОНГРЕСС РУССКИХ ОБЩИН** **ОБЩЕСТВЕННО-ПОЛИТИЧЕСКОЕ ДВИЖЕНИЕ "КОНГРЕСС РУССКИХ ОБЩИН"**
Скоков Юрий Владимирович, Лебедь Александр Иванович, Глазьев Сергей Юрьевич
региональная группа :
Дондуков Александр Николаевич, Кутафин Олег Емельянович, Щербина Андрей Владимирович ☐

32 **СТ** **"ПРОФСОЮЗЫ И ПРОМЫШЛЕННИКИ РОССИИ - СОЮЗ ТРУДА"**
(Российская объединенная промышленная партия, Общероссийское общественное движение "Профсоюзы России - на выборы")
Щербаков Владимир Иванович, Шмаков Михаил Викторович, Вольский Аркадий Иванович
региональная группа :
Пономарев Геннадий Семенович, Артюх Игорь Григорьевич, Шулунов Алексей Николаевич ☐

33 **ЛДПР** **"ЛИБЕРАЛЬНО-ДЕМОКРАТИЧЕСКАЯ ПАРТИЯ РОССИИ (ЛДПР)"**
Жириновский Владимир Вольфович, Абельцев Сергей Николаевич, Венгеровский Александр Дмитриевич
региональная группа :
Жуковский Александр Иванович, Дунец Михаил Иванович, Лебедева Галина Александровна ☐

Figure 5.1 *(continued)*

seats on the party list ballot. These votes were redistributed to the parties that did clear the threshold, as is usual in proportional representation systems. As a result, each of the four winners gained about twice as many seats as they would have been entitled to had there been no wasted votes.

Moreover, the communists were quite successful in winning district seats, taking more than 50. Combined with the seats they won through the party list vote, they

34	**ПРЕДВЫБОРНЫЙ БЛОК, ВКЛЮЧАЮЩИЙ РУКОВОДИТЕЛЕЙ ПАРТИИ ЗАЩИТЫ ПЕНСИОНЕРОВ И ВЕТЕРАНОВ, ПАРТИИ ИСКОРЕНЕНИЯ ПРЕСТУПНОСТИ - ЗАКОННОСТИ И ПОРЯДКА, ПАРТИИ ЗАЩИТЫ ЗДРАВООХРАНЕНИЯ, ОБРАЗОВАНИЯ, НАУКИ И КУЛЬТУРЫ, ПАРТИИ ЗАЩИТЫ МОЛОДЕЖИ, ОБЪЕДИНЕНИЯ СВОБОДНЫХ ПРОФСОЮЗОВ, ПАРТИИ СПРАВЕДЛИВОСТИ, ПАРТИИ ОХРАНЫ ПРИРОДЫ"** (Ассоциация военных журналистов, Ассоциация формирования здоровья подрастающего поколения, Ассоциация духовного возрождения науки, Российская Конфедерация Свободных профсоюзов) Даванташвили Евгения Ювашевна (Джуна), Волков Андрей Романович, Панкратов-Черный Александр Васильевич региональная группа : Лебедь Александр Иванович, Захаров Юрий Евгеньевич, Кедочников Алексей Алексеевич	□
35	**"ПАРТИЯ САМОУПРАВЛЕНИЯ ТРУДЯЩИХСЯ"** Федоров Святослав Николаевич, Казанник Алексей Иванович, Пороховщиков Александр Шалвович региональная группа : Малыхин Владимир Павлович, Кузнечевский Владимир Дмитриевич, Мариночкин Виктор Павлович	□
36	**"КОММУНИСТЫ - ТРУДОВАЯ РОССИЯ - ЗА СОВЕТСКИЙ СОЮЗ"** (Российская коммунистическая рабочая партия, Российская партия коммунистов) Тюлькин Виктор Аркадьевич, Крючков Анатолий Викторович, Анпилов Виктор Иванович региональная группа : Слободкин Юрий Максимович, Глаголева Наталия Олеговна, Хорев Борис Сергеевич	□
37	**"ПАРТИЯ ЛЮБИТЕЛЕЙ ПИВА"** Калачев Константин Эдуардович, Шестаков Дмитрий Юрьевич, Пальчевский Андрей Иванович региональная группа : Сапунков Александр Анатольевич, Калашников Сергей Федорович, Полянский Эдуард Иванович	□
38	**"БЛОК ИВАНА РЫБКИНА"** (Общественно-политическое объединение "Народное движение - Россия" (Союз), Общественное объединение "Регионы России", "Российский Союз Молодежи", Общественно-политическое движение "Согласие", Общественно-политическое движение "Союз реалистов") Рыбкин Иван Петрович, Петров Юрий Владимирович, Чилингаров Артур Николаевич региональная группа : Пальчиков Юрий Дмитриевич, Ильинский Игорь Михайлович, Печенев Вадим Алексеевич	□
39	**"ПАРТИЯ ЭКОНОМИЧЕСКОЙ СВОБОДЫ"** Боровой Константин Натанович, Некрасов Леонид Васильевич, Шпигель Леонид Теодорович региональная группа : Тарасенко Олег Алексеевич, Сороко-Цюпа Андрей Олегович, Федоров Евгений Аверьянович	□
40	**ПАРТИЯ "НАРОДНЫЙ СОЮЗ"** Лукьянов Владимир Николаевич, Галагин Дмитрий Андреевич, Миронов Геннадий Анатольевич региональная группа : Зайцева Екатерина Михайловна, Вялов Юрий Леонидович, Соколова Татьяна Сергеевна	□
41	**"АГРАРНАЯ ПАРТИЯ РОССИИ"** Лапшин Михаил Иванович, Назарчук Александр Григорьевич, Стародубцев Василий Александрович региональная группа : Бошляков Владимир Никанорович, Лучко Клара Степановна, Арцибашев Александр Николаевич	□
42	**"ПОЛИТИЧЕСКАЯ ПАРТИЯ "ХРИСТИАНСКО-ДЕМОКРАТИЧЕСКИЙ СОЮЗ - ХРИСТИАНЕ РОССИИ"** Савицкий Виталий Викторович, Иванова Татьяна Борисовна, Киселев Александр Николаевич региональная группа : Семченко Александр Трофимович, Пчелинцев Анатолий Васильевич, Мишина Валентина Васильевна	□
43	**"СОЮЗ РАБОТНИКОВ ЖИЛИЩНО-КОММУНАЛЬНОГО ХОЗЯЙСТВА РОССИИ"** Чернышов Леонид Николаевич, Суров Петр Сергеевич, Авдеев Валерий Валентинович региональная группа : Гончаров Владимир Борисович, Цветнов Андрей Викторович, Киселев Сергей Валерианович	□
•	**ПРОТИВ ВСЕХ ФЕДЕРАЛЬНЫХ СПИСКОВ КАНДИДАТОВ**	□

wound up with one-third of the seats in parliament, the highest share that they or any party had held in the previous Duma. The results of the elections produced the distribution of parliamentary mandates shown in Table 5.2.

The election results were unexpected in several respects. The communists' strong showing was greater than most observers had expected, as was Zhirinovsky's share; Yabloko and Our Home did worse than many expected, and the failure of the

---TABLE 5.2---

Party Factions and Deputy Groups in the State Duma, January 16, 1996

	Vote Share in PR Ballot (in Percentage)	PR Seats Won	District Seats Won	Total Seats Held	Share of Seats (in Percentage)
CPRF	22.7	95	54	149	33.1
LDPR	11.4	50	1	51	11.3
Our Home Is Russia	10.3	45	20	65	14.4
Yabloko	7.0	31	15	46	10.2
Regions of Russia	—	0	41	41	9.1
Agrarian	—	2	33	35	7.8
People's Power	—	2	35	37	8.2

Note: The Regions of Russia, Agrarian, and People's Power factions were formed after the new Duma convened in order to represent deputies elected from single-member districts, many of whom had been nominated by parties which failed to receive seats in the PR ballot.

Russia's Choice party to cross the 5 percent threshold disappointed its supporters. A radical, hard-line communist party, Working Russia, received 4.6 percent of the vote, much more than most observers had anticipated. Altogether, opposition forces received about 53 percent of the list vote in 1995, about 10 percent more than they had received in 1993.[81]

Examined more closely, however, the election produced less of an upset than appeared at first glance. For one thing, the communists' success mainly came not at the expense of democratic parties, but by taking votes from other opposition parties. The Agrarians had won 8 percent of the party list vote in 1993 and had run well in rural districts, taking 34 single-member district seats. This time they failed to clear the 5 percent threshold, taking only 3.8 percent of the vote, and they only won 20 district seats. Zhirinovsky's LDPR fell to 11.4 percent of the party list vote, still a strong showing, but only half its 1993 total; and, as in 1993, it did extremely poorly in district races, winning only one district seat. Two other parties representing the nationalist opposition to Yeltsin also did considerably worse than expected; former Vice-President Alexander Rutskoi's Derzhava (Great Power) Party, winning 2.6 percent; and the Congress of Russian Communities (KRO), with the highly popular General Alexander Lebed´ occupying the second spot on the list, receiving only 4.4 percent—far less than polls had predicted. Splintering of parties affected the opposition no less than it did the democratic camp. In the end, of the 43 electoral associations that attempted to cross the 5 percent threshold to parliamentary representation, only four succeeded in winning seats. Two are associated with the democratic and market reform cause, and two are associated with the opposition wing. Other

---

[81]McFaul, "Russia Between Elections," p. 5.

partisan forces won representation by taking district seats but they were gravely disadvantaged by parliament's strongly party-oriented governance system.[82]

PARTY STRATEGIES AND THE SOCIAL BASES OF PARTY SUPPORT

The outcomes of Russia's elections are the product of multiple factors, among them the political interests and preferences of voters, the means by which the parties and politicians sought votes, and the rules for translating votes into political representation. The runoff system used in the presidential election in 1996, together with the polarization of political forces in the country between pro- and antireform camps, produced a stark choice in the second round between communist leader Gennadii Ziuganov and Boris Yeltsin as champion both of the status quo and of the reform cause.

Similarly, the mixed electoral system used for Duma elections in 1993 and 1995 allowed a wider array of political forces to gain representation in the lower chamber of parliament thanks to the proportional representation portion of the ballot. The electoral rules encouraged parties to find niches of social and ideological support—albeit rather large niches, in view of the 5 percent cutoff for representation in the Duma, not to mention the extravagant proliferation of electoral groups that won a place on the ballot. Parties therefore worked to find their electorates and to associate themselves with particular social interests. In 1993, polls of voters taken before and after the elections show that each major party strengthened its support among a particular constituency in the course of the campaign.[83] Zhirinovsky, for example, benefited from a substantial surge in support: he kept a strong base of popularity among workers in state, and especially defense, industries; and to these he added support among voters in small towns and cities (where as many as 40 percent of the voters cast ballots for his party). He also raised his support among younger voters, including students, as well as among women, middle-aged, and lower-educated voters.[84]

The communists attracted the votes of older people, running very poorly among the young, and hardly at all among the industrial working class. But they drew very strongly among retired persons, leading many to conjecture that the communists are a party with a brighter past than future.

Not surprisingly, the agrarians appealed heavily but almost exclusively to the rural population.

The two most successful reform-oriented parties, Russia's Choice and Yabloko, ran well among residents of larger cities, managerial and professional strata, and

[82]On the party domination of parliamentary structure and procedure, see Thomas F. Remington and Steven S. Smith, "The Development of Parliamentary Parties in Russia," *Legislative Studies Quarterly* 20:4 (November 1995), pp. 457–489; and idem, "The Early Legislative Process in the Russian Federal Assembly," *Journal of Legislative Studies* 2:1 (Spring 1996), pp. 161–192.

[83]Wyman, Miller, White, and Heywood, "Parties and Voters in the Elections," p. 131.

[84]Ibid., p. 129.

TABLE 5.3
Party Support Among Social Groups (in percentages)

As percentage of all voters		KPRF	RW	Yabloko	DVR	NDR	KRO	LDPR	Other
100	All Russians	26	7	11	5	11	4	11	24
Sex:									
45	Men	26	4	10	4	10	5	16	25
55	Women	25	10	12	6	13	3	8	24
Age:									
19	18–29 years	11	7	17	9	13	3	13	27
48	30–54 years	24	7	11	5	11	6	13	24
33	55 years and up	37	7	8	3	10	2	9	22
Income:									
	Lowest quartile	28	8	8	3	9	3	14	28
	Middle quartiles	29	7	10	3	11	4	12	23
	Upper quartile	18	6	15	10	14	5	9	23
Residence:									
40	Big city	22	7	13	8	12	4	8	25
35	Small city	24	7	13	4	9	4	12	27
26	Rural	32	6	7	2	12	4	17	20
Occupation:									
3	Independent entrepreneur	10	0	16	16	13	10	7	29
5	Manager, bureaucrat	19	5	18	8	18	5	11	18
15	Professional	14	9	16	11	12	6	4	28
3	Military, Ministry of Internal Affairs, procuracy	20	0	9	0	6	14	20	31

the most highly educated segments of the population. But Yabloko's voters tended to have lower incomes on average than those of Russia's Choice: Yabloko appealed to students and younger people more than did Russia's Choice, which tended to be the party for those who had benefitted from economic and political reform.[85]

Likewise, the survey data on support for parties in 1995 show a pattern of social support for the main political parties. Table 5.3 shows how voters in various social groups distributed their votes among parties in 1995.[86]

---

[85]Ibid., pp. 130–131.

[86]Note that the table reads horizontally: each social group's vote totals approximately 100 percent (because of rounding, the total may be slightly more or less than 100 percent). Also, since this was a post-election opinion survey and voters sometimes misremembered or misreported their actual vote, the totals differ slightly from the actual vote.

As perecentage of all voters		KPRF	RW	Yabloko	DVR	NDR	KRO	LDPR	Other
7	Routine white-collar	13	6	17	1	15	5	8	35
26	Worker	29	5	9	2	10	5	21	20
4	Student	5	7	23	12	12	0	5	37
32	Pensioner, housewife	38	8	7	4	11	2	8	21
6	Unemployed	22	13	10	2	8	2	13	30
Education:									
17	Higher, incomplete higher education	17	4	21	15	13	4	3	23
45	Secondary	21	8	11	4	13	5	11	27
37	Elementary	36	6	8	2	9	3	16	20
	N =	299	80	130	58	131	48	135	290

Legend

KPRF: Communist Party of the Russian Federation

RW: Women of Russia

DVR: Russia's Democratic Choice

NDR: Our Home Is Russia

KRO: Congress of Russian Communities

LDPR: Liberal Democratic Party of Russia

Source: Matthew Wyman, "Developments in Russian Voting Behaviour: 1993 and 1995 Compared," *Journal of Communist Studies and Transition Politics* 12(3) (1996), p. 282. Data originally collected by a nationwide sample survey conducted by VTsIOM (the All-Russian Center for Public Opinion Research) immediately following the election. The number of respondents was 1606. The interviews were conducted in the week following the December 17 election, were carried out at sampling points in 20 regions and republics, and have been weighted by age, income, education, rurality, and sex. Reprinted by permission from *Journal of Communist Studies and Transition Politics,* Vol. 12, No. 3, published by Frank Cass & Co., Ltd. Copyright Frank Cass & Co. Ltd.

As the table shows, Russia's parties differed markedly in their sources of support in society. As in 1993, the elderly and least-educated were much more favorable to the communists than were the younger and better-educated, who were more likely to vote for Yabloko. Men were twice as likely to support Zhirinovsky's LDPR than were women. Industrial workers and rural voters supported the communists and LDPR. Administrators and managers were about equally likely to support the communists, Yabloko, and the government party, Our Home Is Russia.

Still, Russia's politics and society are highly fluid, and politicians must work hard to find successful electoral strategies. A case in point was the effort by aides to President Yeltsin in the spring of 1995 to create two broad electoral blocs, one center-left and the other center-right. They were looking ahead both to the upcoming parliamentary elections in December and to the presidential elections the following June. The formation of two broad blocs, they hoped, would channel much of the organizational energy of Russia's numerous small parties into larger, consolidated coalitions. In part, they hoped to marginalize extremists, and in part, they hoped to form a broad coalition of centrists and reformists to support Yeltsin's reelection. The left-center bloc would be broadly socialist or social-democratic in orientation, and would take a stance of moderate, responsible opposition to the Yeltsin/Chernomyrdin government. The other would be somewhat right of center, oriented toward moderate market reform, and would unite the government with the old democratic movement. Undoubtedly the strategy was intended to split the communists and the agrarians, drawing moderates into the center-left bloc while leaving more hard-line elements outside, and to marginalize the more rabid nationalists.[87]

Acting on this strategy, President Yeltsin urged Prime Minister Chernomyrdin to enter the electoral fray and form a center-right coalition. Previously Chernomyrdin had remained outside party politics, much as Yeltsin himself had done. But Chernomyrdin agreed to head an electoral coalition called "Our Home Is Russia" and to rally a bloc of supporters around themes associated with his own policies of moderate reform, stability, compromise, and managerial pragmatism. Soon, however, his bloc came to be associated with the interests of national and regional power-holders rather than with any distinct policy line. Not an enthusiastic or active campaigner, Chernomyrdin himself did not define a clear partisan identity for the voters. Almost immediately Our Home came to be called "the party of power," and regarded by many as an instrument for those in power to keep it. Another quip was that the real name of the party was "Our Home is Gazprom," a reference to the fact that before entering government, Chernomyrdin had headed the hugely influential natural gas monopoly, Gazprom, and was still close to it. To be sure, despite the image of self-serving authority that surrounded it, Our Home attracted the votes of many supporters of democratic reform on the grounds that only Chernomyrdin's party could preserve a firm political base for market institutions. But it was relatively ineffective at converting the substantial bureaucratic resources of its natural support base of state and managerial officials into a broader electoral constituency.[88]

President Yeltsin asked Duma Chairman Ivan Rybkin to head the center-left bloc. Rybkin had been a leader of the communist faction in the 1990–93 parliament and was elected to the Duma on the Agrarian Party ticket. As chairman of the Duma, Rybkin proved to be moderate in his political views and temperament, and had been able to broker a number of compromises that enabled parliament and president to reach agreement on divisive issues. However, Rybkin found himself unable to attract any major organizations to his side, and did little to mobilize a popular base of support. Although widely respected in Moscow for his political skills, he was little known in the country at large. Moreover, the dismal reputation of the parliament in most voters' minds added no luster to his image. President Yeltsin further undercut him by predicting offhandedly at a press conference that Rybkin's bloc was unlikely to make it into parliament. Indeed, the

---

[87]A document summarizing this strategy leaked out and was published in the newspaper *Nezavisimaia gazeta* on May 20, 1995 under the title "Dvublokovaia terapiia."

[88]Grigorii V. Golosov, "Russian Political Parties and the 'Bosses,'" *Party Politics* 3:1 (1997), pp. 5–22.

fact that the president's staff had created the entire two-bloc structure gave it a somewhat contrived, artificial character. Ultimately Rybkin's bloc only took 1.1 percent of the party list vote. The strategy of constructing a two-party system from above had failed.

Nonetheless, there are signs that the party system is beginning to settle into certain predictable patterns. This can be understood more readily if we distinguish among three aspects of political parties. These can be called "the party in the electorate," "the party as organization," and "the party in public office."[89] The first is the way parties interact with voters and local activists; it includes the way voters regard parties and the ability of parties to reach voters and attract their support. The second is the formal structure of parties, including their procedures for devising their programs and selecting candidates, the relations between their national offices and local branches, and the rules regulating the flow of revenues and expenditures. The third is the way the party affects and is affected by the activities of its members who hold public office, both in the legislative and executive branches. It includes the organized factions that parties maintain in parliament as well as the way government officials behave in relation to their parties.

Parties vary in the degree to which each of these elements predominates: in a centralized party, the headquarters may impose strict discipline on members, including those who hold office. Other parties may be loose and decentralized, with local branches determining who runs for office and how campaign resources are gathered and used. Other parties may be little more than loose collections of electoral machines that enable ambitious politicians to gain and keep power. These patterns sometimes reflect historical differences in party development but they also reflect distinct political strategies for winning votes. Some parties, especially those dominated by a central executive office, seek to mobilize a particular constituency that they see as their primary base of support. Their main strategy for winning elections is therefore to maximize the turnout of their voters by persuading them that their vote is essential. Other parties offer a broad, general appeal, seeking to win votes from across the social spectrum. Individual membership and party discipline are deemphasized in favor of a role for the party as broker among a variety of potential constituencies. Finally, in parties dominated by their office-holders, politicians develop personal campaign organizations, with their own fund-raising channels and individualized programs. Such politicians are usually unwilling to be too closely tied to a party central office.[90]

Russia's parties reflect much of this diversity of party types. The communists exemplify a party dominated by its central organization: its office-holders tend to be highly disciplined in their voting behavior and programmatic positions, personality is downplayed, and their campaigns are characterized by intense get-out-the-vote

---

[89]David W. Brady, *Critical Elections and Congressional Policy Making* (Stanford: Stanford University Press, 1988); Richard S. Katz and Peter Mair, "The Evolution of Party Organizations in Europe: The Three Faces of Party Organization," *American Review of Politics* 14 (Winter 1993), pp. 593–617.

[90]Katz and Mair, "The Evolution of Party Organizations in Europe," pp. 601–605.

efforts among their followers. Similarly, the Agrarian Party has concentrated its effort on a particular segment of society, using its strong base among collective and state farm managers, and a relatively strong central organization. Our Home Is Russia, LDPR, and Yabloko have relatively weak electoral organizations and are dominated by their office-holders at the central level, in parliament and in government. Russia's Democratic Choice has a relatively extensive network of local branches and supporters, but a weak and fragmented central organization. As Steven Fish has argued, the very fact that Russia's Choice was formed from among those who held government office may have encouraged its leaders to depend too heavily on their access to state power and too little on building up a network of supporters throughout the country.[91]

The fact that President Yeltsin has refused to identify himself with any party or to create a party organization to link his own electoral fortunes with those of candidates and office-holders in parliament and regional governments means that the pro-reform forces continue to splinter and divide among multiple personal followings. In the December 1995 election, where the fragmentation of democratic forces was particularly severe, several prominent parliamentary leaders of the reform camp formed their own separate electoral associations and party lists instead of uniting in a single democratic bloc. Many observers believed that they did so less in the hope of crossing the 5 percent threshold and entering parliament than in obtaining free access to television air time and thus promoting their own parallel campaigns in their district races. Whether that was the intent or not, the result was that each succeeded in winning their district races but collectively they prevented each other from winning seats in the party list race.

PARTY FRAGMENTATION OR CONSOLIDATION?

Given the extensive fragmentation in Russia's party system, are there any signs that it is settling into a more stable pattern? There are three reasons to believe that it is. First is the effect of the rules of party competition. The electoral law has a powerful filtering effect on the party system. Many parties and party-like organizations exist, but only a few have the capacity to enter parliament and shape policy-making. Those that succeeded in winning seats both in 1993 and 1995 have developed a combination of political resources—whether emphasizing an appealing national leader, cohesive organization, or broad electoral base—that enable them to win substantial national support and thus tie a particular electoral constituency with a policy program. Only three parties succeeded in winning seats in the party list race both in 1993 and 1995, and they represented the three major ideological tendencies that we have discussed: the communists; Zhirinovsky's nationalistic LDPR; and Yavlinsky's reform-oriented Yabloko bloc. But the parties fought hard and successfully to ensure that half the seats in the Duma would be occupied by candidates elected pro-

---

[91]M. Steven Fish, "The Advent of Multipartism in Russia, 1993–95," *Post-Soviet Affairs* 11 (1995), pp. 361–362.

portionally from party lists, and this has provided a powerful impetus to the maintenance of separate identities for multiple parties.

Another institutional factor is the way parliament is organized. Above we noted that members of parliament have an incentive to unite in parliamentary factions that have at least 35 members, because by doing so they acquire a voice on the powerful Council of the Duma which directs the work of the Duma. The Council is made up of the leaders of all registered factions, which include the factions representing any party that cleared the 5 percent threshold as well as any groups gaining registration. It hammers out the details of much of the legislation that is passed by the Duma, and it ensures that parties as such are favored in Duma deliberations. Thus if a party wants to use the parliament to showcase a favored bill or investigation or resolution, to hold a press conference or parliamentary hearings, to force a vote or to prevent a vote, the Council of the Duma allows it to do so. *Parties thus use parliament for their policy and electoral purposes,* with the Council of the Duma as their mechanism for doing so. It is desirable, therefore, for individual members of parliament who want to further their political careers or to shape policy to affiliate with one or another parliamentary faction.

Second, as in other presidential or semi-presidential systems, the presidential election encourages the coalescence of partisan forces around rival candidates for president. This is especially true, as in France, between the first and second round of the voting, since in the second round, the two candidates who receive the most votes in the first round face off. This encourages them to broaden their electoral base by forming alliances with other candidates and blocs. In the June 16, 1996 Russian presidential election, President Yeltsin employed many of the organizers, activists, and strategists who had run the parliamentary election campaign for the "Our Home Is Russia" movement headed by Prime Minister Chernomyrdin. The organizational resources of Our Home, including a national network of storefront campaign offices, were given a new purpose by the Yeltsin campaign staff. After the presidential election, the same organizational structure was further developed in order to assemble a nationwide list of candidates whom Yeltsin and Chernomyrdin supported in the 50-odd races for governor held in the fall of 1996. Thus, Our Home and several associated organizations became the nucleus of a moderately center-right political party embodying the political legacy of President Yeltsin. Despite the weakness of voter support for Our Home, it continues to be held together by the shared interest of federal and regional office-holders in hanging on to power.

The communists also used the presidential election to create a broad national alliance of communist and nationalist forces serving as the main opposition bloc to Yeltsin. Gennadii Ziuganov, the communist candidate, was nominated by a newly constructed electoral coalition with a general, populist, and nationalistic program; this strategy was intended to emphasize Ziuganov's broadly populist and nationalist credentials rather than his position as head of the Communist Party of the Russian Federation. After his defeat in the presidential election, this coalition reorganized itself as the "Popular-Patriotic Union of Russia" and announced that it would field a list of candidates for the upcoming gubernatorial elections and future federal elections. It also declared that it would deemphasize the influence of the communists in the organization in favor of more moderate and more nationalistic groups. Thus the presidential election produced a tendency for the forces of the opposition to coalesce around Ziuganov in a new nationalistic bloc, and the reformers to unite around Yeltsin and the government. Remaining outside both coalitions, however, were Vladimir Zhirinovsky and his Liberal Democratic Party of Russia, and Grigorii Yavlinsky, head of the Yabloko party.

Third, although there is still relatively low individual voter identification with parties, there are indications that campaigns stimulate voters to identify their interests with particular party leaders and labels.[92] There is evidence on this point from the surveys of Russian voters in the course of the 1993 and 1995 parliamentary election campaigns. How do citizens choose which parties to support? It appears that television plays a crucial part in conveying images of parties to voters, particularly impressions of their leaders. According to Sarah Oates,

> Preference for the leader as an individual and the party as an organization played fairly equal roles in the party-list vote in the [1995] Duma elections. . . . About 30 percent of the respondents who voted named the party leader as the most important factor in voting for a certain party. Roughly another 30 percent who voted chose a particular party because it 'expresses the interests of people such as myself.'[93]

The electoral campaign thus stimulated a certain amount of voter identification with parties; voters could articulate preferences that linked their interests with the platforms and leaders of particular parties. Of the three faces of political parties—in the electorate, central offices, and office-holders—we see the beginnings of alignments in the electorate that link voters to particular parties. And we see office-holders working to construct electoral machines that will enable them to gain and hold on to power. Recall that 90 percent of the deputies in the Duma ran for reelection. Of these, half ran simultaneously in a district and on a party list and almost a hundred more ran only on a list. Therefore legislative office-holders identify themselves with political parties, some for the organizational and financial resources they can gain, some because they have no chance of winning election unless they are on a party list, and some out of ideological conviction. The complementary interests of voters in supporting a particular organized political entity, on the one hand, and of office-holders in affiliating themselves with a particular party organization to win power and influence policy, on the other, are thus influencing the development of Russia's nascent democracy in the direction of a competitive party system.

Still, Russian parties suffer from two severe disabilities, both of which raise grave doubts about Russia's ability to develop into a consolidated constitutional democracy. First, parties remain highly Moscow-centric. Second, the voters are still strongly alienated from the parties. Let us briefly consider each point.

In Russia, as in many countries, the capital city tends to dominate political life. And as in other countries, there is considerable resentment on the part of people elsewhere in the country toward the self-serving pursuits of politicians "inside the beltway" (Moscow's equivalent of the beltway around Washington, D.C., is called the "ring road"). Russia's parties historically tended to develop in Moscow as part of the political struggles surrounding radical reform, and their links to other parts of the

---

[92]Sarah Oates, "Vying for Votes on a Crowded Campaign Trail," *Transition* 2:4 (February 23, 1996), p. 26.
[93]Ibid., p. 29.

country remain weak and tenuous. Political competition outside Moscow is not closely tied to the party system. This is a reflection of the enormous centralization of social and economic life that is a legacy of the Soviet era. There simply is too little autonomous political and social power outside Moscow to encourage strong party competition.[94] To be sure, the gubernatorial races of 1996 displayed a certain amount of partisanship, as candidates aligned with the Yeltsin–Chernomyrdin forces were opposed by candidates aligned with the communist–nationalist opposition. In fact, however, both the "party of power" and the opposition coalition claimed victories whenever a competent, middle-of-the-road figure won an election. Parties as such had little to do with selecting candidates or running their campaigns.

Moreover, in the Federation Council, the heads of the executive and legislative branches of government in each of the 89 constituent territories of the federation have resolutely rejected aligning along party lines. As the newly elected governor of Leningrad oblast put it, "there will never be factions in the Federation Council."[95] Parties, in short, are doing little to aggregate the interests of ideologically similar constituencies across the regions. They are not equipped, as a result, to maintain that balance between competition and cooperation in the relations between the central government and regional units that stable federalism requires.[96]

The other problem is the deep alienation of ordinary Russian citizens from the play of party politics. In a survey of the population to determine which Russian institutions ordinary citizens feel some level of confidence in, Richard Rose and his colleagues discovered that Russians had less confidence—by far—in political parties than in any other institution. Almost 80 percent of the population fails to identify with any party (in the United States and Britain, around 90 percent of the society identifies with a party). The only party that commands much confidence is the communist party![97]

In these conditions, what motivates Russians to vote at all? White, Rose, and McAllister argue that the strongest impulse in Russian elections is the urge to *vote against:* against the communist past (for supporters of democratic values), or, more commonly, against the current authorites for the sorry state of the economy. Rarely do voters feel much more than a resigned or tepid acceptance of the party or politician for whom they vote.[98] Voters are beginning to be able to link their interests with particular political tendencies, labels, and personalities, but the party system, as a whole, lacks a firm or stable foundation in society. Few voters or politicians feel much loyalty to particular parties. This helps explain the fact that, almost a decade after the first open parliamentary elections in Russia, the party system remains fragmented and fluid.

---

[94]Fish, "The Advent of Multipartism," pp. 356–357.

[95]*Segodnia*, December 6, 1996.

[96]Peter C. Ordeshook, "Russia's Party System: Is Russian Federalism Viable?" *Post-Soviet Affairs* 12 (1996), pp. 195–217.

[97]Stephen White, Richard Rose, and Ian McAllister, *How Russia Votes* (Chatham House, NJ: Chatham House, 1997), pp. 52–53, 132, 135.

[98]Ibid., p. 230.

Overall, Russia's political spectrum remains basically bipolar. Since 1990, though they continually change their organizational identities, most Russian politicians have tended to identify with either the democratic or opposition camp.[99] Efforts by politicians to claim the center ground tend to founder as they are drawn to ally themselves for support with one side or the other. Both camps are divided among themselves, and neither has a stable majority in parliament. This situation has tended to favor the executive branch by leaving the legislative branch weakened and divided. Neither the pressure of a presidential election nor President Yeltsin's strategy of constructing two broad, opposing political blocs succeeded in overcoming the desire on the part of party politicians to preserve their separate organizational structures. Yet Russia's emerging political system possesses certain features that produce incentives for politicians to form up into stable parties based on their programs and on the personalities of their leaders. The politicians themselves have shaped both the electoral law and the governance of parliament in such a way as to further the parties' influence over policy-making and elections in Russia. These rules motivate the politicians to try to rally the voters behind party banners: slowly the politicians are learning to adapt the *supply* of party candidates, programs, and policies to meet the voters' *demands* for a better life. They structure the choices that voters face on election day. Parties have a reason to try to overcome the alienation ordinary Russians feel toward national politics.

SUMMING UP

In this chapter we reviewed the nature of interest articulation and aggregation in contemporary Russian politics. We observed that while political systems require organized channels that link people's needs and desires with the policy processes of government, the availability and effectiveness of such means is not guaranteed. What sorts of interest groups and political parties operate in a particular political system at a particular time depends considerably on the distribution of organizations and the resources needed by organizations. In a time of great political upheaval, the inherited parties and associations may correspond poorly to people's actual needs and wishes. An association such as Civic Union may find itself unable to deliver much support despite a reputation for being a powerful insider group, while government may find it prudent to bow to the interests of groups such as enterprise managers and regional officials who are too numerous and diverse to take *positive* action for themselves, but who have enough *negative* power to block the implementation of government policy simply by ignoring it. The old official trade unions have turned out to be weak and uncohesive as representatives of Russian labor's political demands, but continue to exist due to their lock on the collection and distribution of state social funds. In Russia's transition, both interests and the

---

[99]Thomas F. Remington, Steven S. Smith, D. Roderick Kiewiet, and Moshe Haspel, "Transitional Institutions and Parliamentary Alignments in Russia, 1990–1993," in Thomas F. Remington, ed., *Parliaments in Transition: The New Legislative Politics in the Former USSR and Eastern Europe* (Boulder: Westview Press, 1994), pp. 159–180. A similar view is offered by Michael McFaul, *Russia Between Elections.* McFaul argues that Russia is undergoing a protracted social revolution over the basic shape of the country's political and economic institutions.

organizations articulating them have changed. Old organizations have either adapted to the new environment or have fallen away, and new organizations have formed. Some groups have long-standing interests that could not be effectively represented under the communist regime; others represent new interests that have been created as a result of the economic and political liberalization of the society.

Still, as in most societies, Russia's interest groups tend to be more organized and more effective when they serve constituencies whose members have more resources. The most disadvantaged categories of the populace, such as the elderly and women and children, are those least served by interest groups. Industrial labor's interests are divided between the traditional dependency on state enterprises for a host of social benefits, such as housing, medical care, and disability and retirement insurance, and the new opportunities to earn much higher incomes in the private sector. The center has also worked to prevent the formation of powerful coalitions of interest that could challenge its power, attempting to satisfy the demands of some important claimants, such as the agrarian lobby or particular regions, in order to win their support of its policies on other issues. Thus, interest articulation in Russia is not clearly statist, as it was in the old regime, while efforts to put it on a corporatist footing were half-hearted and unsuccessful. If a pluralist political arena is emerging, it is as much by default as by design.

We observed as well that political parties operate in a similar environment of change: out of the old ruling communist party have come several successor parties, most importantly the CPRF, but the eruption of new interests and identities that occurred in the *glasnost'* period also left behind it some proto-parties that have adapted themselves to the new rules and institutions of post-Soviet Russia. Partisan politics continues to be strongly bipolar, oriented around the struggle between the forces favoring market reform and liberal democracy and the forces seeking to reestablish state socialism. Devotees of the complex of values linked to Russian nationalism tend to ally themselves with the state-socialist opposition. Other political forces try to stake out the elusive center ground.

Despite the voters' indifference and hostility toward parties, party leaders have themselves made use of the resources at hand to create a kind of party system. Generally, the parties are heavily focused on Moscow, and their roots outside the capital are feeble. But the structure of the national representative institutions—especially the large PR component of the Duma—forces politicians to line up with one or another party in order to seek and hold elected office. Interest aggregation through political parties at present owes far more to the "top-down" and "supply-side" strategies of ambitious politicians than to the "bottom-up," "demand-side" processes of social mobilization. Whether Russia will succeed in producing a healthy, competitive party system remains to be seen. There can be little doubt, however, that if democracy is to become consolidated in Russia, a working party system will be essential.

Chapter 6

The Politics of Economic Reform

The Dual Transition

Like other countries undergoing the transformation from communism to democracy, Russia is remaking both its *political* and *economic* institutions. Some would say that Russia's transition is not only dual, but even triple, since it is also remaking itself as a new national state following the disintegration of the union. The relationship between the political and economic dimensions of this transformation is complex. Given the tensions it generates, is the painful passage to a market economy even possible under democracy? Is it possible *without* also moving toward democracy?

Often Russia's transition is contrasted with the paths of development of Asian countries. The "Asian way," some have argued, emphasizes growth before distribution, order before democracy, the rights of the society before the rights of the individual. Because of China's remarkable record of high economic growth rates in the 1980s and 1990s, many believe that China offers a model that can be emulated elsewhere. Certainly China's thriving economy is all the more impressive when compared to the spectacle of breakdown and decline seen in Russia over the last decade. China—where a communist leadership retained control over political power while setting the country firmly on the path toward market-oriented growth and prosperity—raises difficult questions indeed about the relationship between economic and political liberalization.

There are important lessons to be drawn from comparing Russia and China regarding about the relationship between political and economic reform. It is important to bear in mind, however, the tremendous differences in the structure of the two economies at the point that reforms began. China's economy was overwhelmingly agrarian, poor, and far less centralized. Still, the differences in economic performance are marked, as Table 6.1[1] indicates.

---

[1]World Bank, *World Development Report 1996: From Plan to Market* (New York: Oxford University Press, 1996), p. 21.

———————————————————TABLE 6.1———————————————————
Economic Performance in Russia and China

	Russia		China	
	1990	1994	1978	1994
Structure of employment (as percentage of total)				
Industry	42	38	15	18
Agriculture	13	15	71	58
Services	45	47	14	25
Total	100	100	100	100
Total employment in the state sector	90	44	19	18
Output				
GDP per capita (U.S. dollars)	4110	2650	404	530
At PPP (purchasing power parity)	6440	4610	1000	2510

Source: From *World Development Report 1996* by World Bank. Copyright © 1996 by The International Bank for Reconstruction and Development/The World Bank. Used by permission of Oxford University Press, Inc.

The table makes clear some dramatic changes in both countries since the onset of their reform programs, changes which are all the more notable when we remember the size of each country and the short time spans involved. In China, there has been a substantial increase in the proportion of the workforce employed in industry and a still larger increase in the number of people employed in services. In Russia, industrial employment has declined sharply while employment in services and agriculture have both increased their shares. In Russia, output has declined while in China it has risen rapidly, but from a very low base. China's reforms have been far more successful in raising economic productivity.

We could also contrast Russia to South Korea, Singapore, and Taiwan, where anticommunist authoritarian regimes pursued capitalist growth strategies over several decades before beginning to share power with their political rivals. Is there any necessary relationship between democracy and economic development? As economist Nicholas Lardy notes, "Over the long run, a competitive, market-oriented economy must be paired with a pluralistic political system. In the short run, however, this linkage can be quite loose, as the experience of countries in East Asia reminds us."[2]

As we consider how economic reforms have affected Russia's postcommunist development, we need to recognize that there is a difference between the short-term and long-term implications of radical economic reform for political institutions. Radical economic reform in the form of stabilization programs, structural adjustment, or austerity regimes have certain elements in common: they must restore a macroeconomic balance between what society spends and what it earns. They give the national currency real value, which requires eliminating chronic sources of inflation. Usually they require drastic cuts in state spending, increases in

---

[2]Nicholas Lardy, "China: Sustaining Development," in Gilbert Rozman with Seizaburo Sato and Gerald Segal, eds., *Dismantling Communism: Common Causes and Regional Variations* (Washington, D.C. and Baltimore: Woodrow Wilson Center Press and Johns Hopkins University Press, 1992), p. 220.

taxation, the end of price controls, and an open foreign trade regime so that foreign products can compete with domestic ones. Structural reform of this kind always lowers the standard of living for some or most groups of the population, at least in the short run. Therefore, unless and until living standards begin to rise again for most strata, such reform creates powerful political opponents. These are usually the groups which formerly had enjoyed the benefits of state-controlled wages and prices, high state spending to subsidize priority sectors of the economy, protection from competition from foreign industries, and welfare entitlement programs. Often these groups are well organized, voicing their opposition to reform through strong trade unions, associations of state-dependent firms, and political parties whose primary constituencies are among those most vulnerable to reform.

The thinking of the "growth before distribution, order before democracy" school holds that a country needs a different mix of institutions in the early stages of its economic development from those it needs after prosperity has come. In the short run, economic development is viewed as the first priority. To achieve successful development of the economy, the political influence of parties and interest groups must be forcibly restrained until economic growth has reached a certain point. Prosperity will then have begun to benefit enough people to create a new political base of support for the regime. In the long run, according to this point of view, limits on political freedom should and will be lifted as a growing number of people who are benefiting from the market economy seek political rights. They will demand the right to articulate their political interests and want to check the arbitrary power of the political authorities. After all, economic security for the general population requires the rule of law, which cannot be achieved until the rulers of the state can be restrained in their exercise of power. Economic success will build a base of social support for democracy. But this point, say the defenders of China's or Singapore's model, is still far off.

In the meantime, these voices say, a strong "developmental bureaucracy" is needed to prevent particularistic interests from squandering the resources needed for investment. In launching economic reform aimed at putting the economy on a path of growth and prosperity, government must not liberalize politically until well after it has liberalized economically. If it fails to retain control over policy-making, it will end up with a system that is neither economically successful nor democratic. If political resistance results in slow or hesitant economic reform, opposition will build up and bring further reform to a halt; therefore it is necessary to seize the moment that history presents, and to act quickly and decisively.[3] The more intense the political resistance to it, the greater the resolve of the reformers to prevent their opponents from derailing it.

Although this theory is compelling, there are strong arguments against it. One is a cultural argument. What works in the cultures of Asia, with their traditions of

---

[3]One of the Russian economists who helped devise and carry out the radical economic reform program put the issue this way: "Any obstacle to economic activity, especially one which assumes the existence of a discretionary choice, will be circumvented in Russia, and therefore this country has to be more liberal than any other." Quoted in Anders Åslund, *How Russia Became a Market Economy* (Washington, D.C.: Brookings Institution, 1995), p. 151. Åslund reformulates the observation in still more general terms: "strong states can liberalize slowly, weak states cannot" (p. 151).

powerful family and workplace cohesiveness, may not work in Western societies where individualism has stronger roots. Indeed, some in Asia say precisely this: do not impose your Western materialism, individualism, and liberalism on us, the West with its crime and social exploitation is no model for Asia. [4]

A second argument relates economic development to the political conditions needed for economic stability. Capitalism, after all, runs on credit, and credit is trust. Economic actors have to have reasonable confidence that loans will be repaid, that investments will not be confiscated, and that money will retain its value tomorrow. Credit, and hence trust, is the lifeblood of market systems. What is the source of confidence in economic institutions? Is credit more secure under dictatorship or democracy? The "no development without democracy" school holds that, since the foundation of a capitalist economy is faith in its institutions, both the rulers and the major interests of society must be limited in their power to undermine it. Only political democracy, this school believes, can ensure that both private interests and state officials play by the rules. Without political stability guaranteed by limits on the power of government officials to confiscate the citizens' wealth, economic agents cannot be sure that their present efforts will be rewarded with future returns.[5] Indeed, a similar argument was recently made by one of Russia's wealthiest and most prominent capitalist entrepreneurs, Kakha Bendukidze, who argued that for Russia's financial system to begin developing adequately, "a political regime is needed that is elected from start to finish. There is no other way to ensure confidence." He draws this conclusion, he says, "not from his own feelings, but from conversations with managers of funds."[6]

Thus the objection of this point of view to the "growth before distribution" model of social development is that under it, society has no way to check predatory, corrupt, or inefficient state officials. Only economic competition can restrain the appetites of rulers who seek private gain from control over public goods. Only if major economic actors have a say in making policy by holding government accountable through elections will they have confidence that the government is serving the larger interests of society.

Likewise, however difficult it may be for a government which seeks to liberalize economically to sustain its policy in the face of resistance, it can only succeed if it also opens up politically, since market reform and democratic reform are interdependent. Some of those whose short-term welfare is harmed by economic reform may only be willing to accept it if they have a voice in the political arena and secure political rights.

Both schools would agree that there is a short-term trade-off between economic liberalization and political liberalization, but both would agree that in the long

---

[4]Lee Kuan Yew, the former prime minister of Singapore, has often made this argument in his speeches both at home and abroad.

[5]See, for instance, Barry R. Weingast, "Constitutions as Governance Structures: The Political Foundations of Secure Markets," *Journal of Institutional and Theoretical Economics* 149/1 (1993), pp. 286–311; and Douglass C. North and Barry R. Weingast, "Constitutions and Credible Commitments: The Evolution of the Institutions of Public Choice in 17th Century England," *Journal of Economic History* 49 (1989), pp. 803–832.

[6]Kakha Bendukidze, "Finansovaia katastropha i kak s nei borot´sia," *Segodnia,* June 19, 1996.

run they are also mutually dependent as changes in public confidence in the legitimacy of the political regime exert a feedback influence on the effectiveness of economic institutions that require faith, such as financial institutions. Especially in the longer run, stable market institutions require the legitimacy in the political sphere that only democracy can provide. But if in the short run, economic development is strangled by political disorder, there may be no long run. Likewise, if state rulers hold on to power in the face of pressure for political liberalization, democracy may be very long in coming.

Because of the communist legacy, this short-run trade-off between democratization and market reform is deeper in Russia and in other former communist states than it is in Latin America and Southern Europe. Communist regimes carried out a far more sweeping destruction of autonomous economic and cultural institutions in their societies than did other authoritarian regimes.[7] In the post-authoritarian states of South America and Southern Europe, the economic dimension of transition consists more in liberalizing the foreign trade regime and privatizing state and parastatal enterprises than in creating a capitalist economy from scratch.[8] In the communist world, many fundamental features of a market-oriented economy were absent: a coherent set of enforceable legal rights to ownership and control of capital assets; a system of prices that approximated equilibrium between demand and supply; a set of financial institutions buying and selling debt at market prices; and regulatory institutions enforcing the rules of the game. As far as Russia was concerned, the conversion of the world's largest state socialist economy into a market-oriented economy would have been extraordinarily difficult regardless of the policy instruments chosen. In the short and intermediate run, the process would create winners and losers, depending on how particular enterprises, classes, age groups, ethnic groups, regions, industrial branches, and other actors were positioned. Some would benefit by the opening up of competition, others would suffer. Liberalizing prices meant that the elderly and others on fixed incomes would suffer a severe drop in living standards and people would see a lifetime of savings wiped out.

Communist systems differed from other authoritarian regimes in ways that made their economic transitions more difficult. But the Soviet Union possessed certain features that have made its successor states' transition to a capitalist economy even more painful than it has been for other communist societies. For one, the economic growth model followed by Stalin and his successors tended to seek economies of scale by concentrating large shares of the production of particular goods in particular enterprises. Consequently, many large enterprises entered the new era with near-monopolies in their line of production. In 1988, a small number of giant enterprises with more than 2,000 employees, a group comprising only 9

---

[7]Juan J. Linz and Alfred Stepan, *Problems of Democratic Transition and Consolidation: Southern Europe, South America, and Post-Communist Europe* (Baltimore: Johns Hopkins Press, 1996).

[8]On the economic policy dilemmas facing new democratic regimes in Latin America, see John Sheahan, "Economic Policies and the Prospects for Successful Transition from Authoritarian Rule in Latin America," in Guillermo O'Donnell, Philippe C. Schmitter, and Laurence Whitehead, eds., *Transitions from Authoritarian Rule: Comparative Perspectives* (Baltimore: Johns Hopkins University Press, 1986), pp. 154–164.

percent of all enterprises, produced over 60 percent of all output.[9] This meant that with state price and production controls freed, these enterprises could raise prices with impunity and collect monopolists' rents. Their dominance of the market in their sectors raised the barriers to entry for new enterprises after the system of central planning ended.[10]

In the economic sphere, some of the consequences of the state's monopoly over resource allocation are becoming clearer with time. The central planners tended to concentrate capital in a relatively small number of relatively large industrial enterprises, facilitating hierarchical control and aiming to capture advantages of scale. Alfred E. Kahn and Merton J. Peck cite data comparing the degree of monopolization in the U.S. and Soviet economies in the 1980s that give a rough guide to the order of magnitude of the difference (see Table 6.2).[11]

The concentration of production in a relatively small number of relatively large enterprises meant that many local governments are entirely dependent on the economic health of a single employer: almost half of Russian cities have only one industrial enterprise, and three-fourths have no more than four.[12] Since Russian industrial firms were traditionally responsible for a broad range of social welfare functions—building and maintaining housing for their workforces, and managing health, recreational, educational, and similar facilities—such cities are heavily dependent on these firms for the provision of basic social services as well as being the mainstay of employment. Therefore, economic transition has created severe problems for maintaining social welfare since local governments are unable to assume financial responsibility for these functions.

A second problem facing Russia was the enormous commitment of its economic resources to military production. According to a respected Swedish economist, the real level of Soviet Gross National Product (GNP) per capita was less than one-third that of the United States by 1985. This means that the actual share of gross economic output devoted to the military sector was around 25 percent, not 14–15 percent, as most Western analysts previously believed.[13] In some regions, at least half

---

[9]Roman Frydman, Andrzej Rapaczynski, John S. Earle et al., *The Privatization Process in Russia, Ukraine and the Baltic States* (Budapest, London, New York: Central European University Press, 1993), p. 7.

[10]There is a school of thought holding that the problem of monopolization in the Russian economy is not severe: that in comparative perspective, the Russian industrial economy is less dominated by monopolies and oligopolies than many Western economies, but that there are also many fewer small-scale firms than in the West. This argument misses an important point, however. In the absence of a working capital market—including a free flow of capital in and out of the country—Russian industrial firms tend to be price-setters more than they are price-takers. That is, they are rather free to set prices because they face such limited competition.

See the discussion of this point in Anders Åslund, *How Russia Became a Market Economy* (Washington, D.C.: Brookings Institution, 1995), pp. 152–156.

[11]Alfred E. Kahn and Merton J. Peck, "Price Deregulation, Corporatization, and Competition," in Merton J. Peck and Thomas J. Richardson, eds., *What Is To Be Done? Proposals for the Soviet Transition to the Market* (New Haven, CT: Yale University Press, 1991), p. 65.

[12]Åslund, *How Russia Became a Market Economy*, p. 154.

[13]Anders Åslund, "How Small is Soviet National Income?" in Henry S. Rowen and Charles Wolf, Jr., eds., *The Impoverished Superpower: Perestroika and the Soviet Military Burden* (San Francisco: Institute for Contemporary Studies, 1990), p. 49.

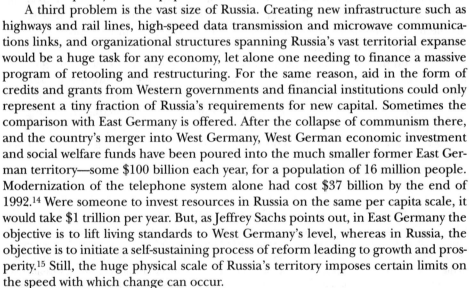

————————————TABLE 6.2————————————
Distribution of Concentration Ratios: Soviet Product Groups and U.S. Manufacturing Industries

	Soviet Groups: Share of Single Largest Producer (1988)	U.S. Industries: Share of Four Largest Producers (1982)
Market share (in percentage)		
0–50	39.2	72.6
50–75	24.1	21.3
75–100	36.6	6.1
Total	100.0	100.0

Source: Alfred E. Kahn and Merton J. Peck,"Price Deregulation, Corporatization, and Competition," in Merton J. Peck and Thomas J. Richardson, eds., *What Is To Be Done? Proposals for the Soviet Transition to the Market* (New Haven, CT: Yale University Press, 1991), p. 65. Reprinted by permission.

the work force was employed in defense plants. The end of the Cold War and the cutback in military spending hit such plants very hard and it was often impossible for them to quickly retool equipment, retrain workers, and find new markets.

A third problem is the vast size of Russia. Creating new infrastructure such as highways and rail lines, high-speed data transmission and microwave communications links, and organizational structures spanning Russia's vast territorial expanse would be a huge task for any economy, let alone one needing to finance a massive program of retooling and restructuring. For the same reason, aid in the form of credits and grants from Western governments and financial institutions could only represent a tiny fraction of Russia's requirements for new capital. Sometimes the comparison with East Germany is offered. After the collapse of communism there, and the country's merger into West Germany, West German economic investment and social welfare funds have been poured into the much smaller former East German territory—some $100 billion each year, for a population of 16 million people. Modernization of the telephone system alone had cost $37 billion by the end of 1992.[14] Were someone to invest resources in Russia on the same per capita scale, it would take $1 trillion per year. But, as Jeffrey Sachs points out, in East Germany the objective is to lift living standards to West Germany's level, whereas in Russia, the objective is to initiate a self-sustaining process of reform leading to growth and prosperity.[15] Still, the huge physical scale of Russia's territory imposes certain limits on the speed with which change can occur.

---

[14]Robert W. Campbell, "Economic Reform in the USSR and its Successor States," in Shafiqul Islam and Michael Mandelbaum, eds., *Making Markets: Economic Transformation in Eastern Europe and the Post-Soviet States* (New York: Council on Foreign Relations), pp. 131–132.

[15]Jeffrey Sachs, "Western Financial Assistance and Russia's Reforms," in ibid., pp. 145–146. Sachs is a Harvard University economist who was the principal Western architect of the strategy of macroeconomic stabilization that was applied in Poland in 1990 and partly in Russia in 1992, and he developed a similar strategy for Latin American economies in the 1980s. His prescription for rapid, anti-inflationary measures that achieve fiscal stabilization as a precondition of other reforms has been the target of tremendous controversy.

The final problem is that of human capital. It is not that the Soviet population was uneducated: literacy was nearly universal and educational attainment levels were among the highest in the world. Russia's state enterprise managers were highly capable at coping with the demands on them under the system of planned production targets. Rather, the incentive system built into state and social institutions encouraged skill in working in a heavily hierarchical, state-centered economy but discouraged the kinds of risk-and-reward-centered behavior that a market system requires. For example, the directors of Soviet state firms were rewarded for meeting output targets under difficult conditions, such as uncertainty about whether needed inputs would be delivered in time and in the right assortment. As noted, they were also responsible for a broad array of social welfare functions for their employees and their families, and the population of the towns and regions where they were located. Profitability and efficiency were well down the list of priorities of Soviet managers.[16] Almost no Soviet employees or managers had had firsthand experience with decision making in the conditions of a market economy.

However, to the extent that it meant incurring risk and investing effort in a venture for private gain, entrepreneurship was certainly not unknown in the USSR, but rather, it was highly illegal. Indeed, the criminal code prescribed the death penalty for large-scale economic crimes, such as currency speculation. A great deal of private enterprise existed, but as part of the black market. Many citizens, both those who viewed profit-making enterprise with the deepest suspicion and those who risked prosecution and became black marketeers, took it for granted that any profit-making business was illegal and immoral. Many who accepted the risk and went into illicit business viewed the law as an inconvenience to be circumvented. There was no pool of managers and entrepreneurs, therefore, immediately ready to take advantage of new opportunities for legal gainful enterprise when the political regime changed. For this reason, a high proportion of the first generation of new Russian entrepreneurs were young scientific and technical employees in state institutes and universities.[17]

These conditions sharpened the contradiction between economic and political reform in Russia by making economic transition more painful than it would have been had conditions been more favorable. However, economic and political liberalization need not collide if the populace of a country understands and accepts the necessity of belt-tightening in order to give the country's currency a sound basis and to redirect resources away from wasteful ends. But moments of consensus that market reform is necessary whatever the cost are historically rare. Such a national consensus probably existed in Poland at the end of 1989. It allowed the Solidarity government to launch a "big bang" program under which spending was drastically cut and prices soared before leveling off. A similar consensus seems to have existed as well in the Czech Republic, but not in Slovakia, and differences between the two

---

[16]Two useful studies of Soviet managers are Paul Lawrence and Charalambos A. Vlachoutsicos, eds., *Behind the Factory Walls: Decision Making in Soviet and US Enterprises* (Cambridge, MA: Harvard Business School Press, 1990); and Sheila M. Puffer, ed., *The Russian Management Revolution: Preparing Managers for the Market Economy* (Armonk, NY: M. E. Sharpe, 1992).

[17]An interesting portrait of 40 such individuals based on interviews is provided in the book edited by Igor Bunin, *Biznesmeny Rossii: Sorok istorii uspekha* (Moscow: OKO, 1994).

countries' national political climates toward radical reform directly fed the separatist movement in Slovakia which resulted in the division of Czechoslovakia into two countries.

"SHOCK THERAPY"

Did Russia have a moment of national consensus about the need for radical economic reform? The available evidence suggests that in 1990–91, around half the adult population expressed support for radical economic reform to bring about a rapid transition to a market economy. Two qualifications must be made. First, Russians had little experience with market principles. Many undoubtedly associated them with the prosperity of Western societies rather than with the problems of transition. Second, public attitudes about the market have proven to be more volatile than have attitudes about political democracy. That said, it is important to recognize the degree to which the Yeltsin/Gaidar team did have a solid foundation of public support for their stabilization program in 1992.

In July 1990, the Soviet Center for the Study of Public Opinion conducted a survey of 1,489 people in 10 regions of Russia asking a variety of questions on political and economic topics. One asked how respondents felt about the prospect of moving the country from a planned to a market economy over the next year or two. Responses were as follows:

- 21 percent were definitely positive
- 29 percent were more positive than negative
- 20 percent were more negative than positive
- 20 percent were definitely negative
- 10 percent found it hard to say.[18]

A May 1990 survey conducted in 20 regions of the European portion of the USSR by a team of researchers from the University of Houston in the Texas and the Soviet Institute of Sociology in Moscow (N = 1,510) found that 53.5 percent of the respondents believed that the country should carry out radical economic reform to bring about a market economy; only a quarter opposed the introduction of a market economy. Various other measures in the survey suggested, however, that the actual degree of support for a market economy lay somewhere between 30 and 40 percent.[19]

Two surveys conducted among Moscow residents in the spring of 1990 found even higher levels of support for the market, and a readiness to begin an immediate, rapid dismantling of the former state economic controls. A study in May 1990 compared residents of Moscow with residents of New York City with respect to their views of market principles, such as the nature of fairness in economic transactions, the use of money in personal relations, the place of economic incentives, the nature of inequality, and how a market economy works. Although the sample sizes were

---

[18]*Argumenty i fakty*, no. 34 (1990), p. 3.

[19]Gennady M. Denisovsky, Polina M. Kozyreva, and Mikhail S. Matskovsky, "Twelve Percent of Hope: Economic Consciousness and a Market Economy," in Miller, Reisinger, and Hesli, eds., *Public Opinion and Regime Change*, pp. 225–227.

small and the Moscow respondents were restricted to those who could be reached by telephone, the results were striking. The Moscow and New York populations expressed very similar attitudes about the market, particularly as pertains to their understanding of fairness, inequality, and the importance of incentives, although the Russians were less favorably disposed toward business.[20] Another 1990 Moscow survey found that a majority of respondents supported the transformation of the Soviet economy into a market economy.[21] The following year, a June 1991 survey of 3,000 citizens from across the Soviet Union found widespread support for radical economic reform.[22]

Another development further fueled support for radical reform. This was the August 1991 coup, which rallied support for Yeltsin against the communist opposition that attempted to seize power. Among the deputies in the Russian Congress and in public opinion, the response to the coup was a surge of support for Yeltsin and his radical reform program. Addressing the Russian Congress of People's Deputies on October 28, 1991, Yeltsin demanded special powers to enact radical reform by decree and on November 1 received them by a decisive margin. He named himself prime minister and head of government, and formed a cabinet of young, radically-minded intellectuals drawn from academic institutes. Gennadii Burbulis, a close associate of Yeltsin's, became First Deputy Prime Minister. Egor Gaidar, then 35 years old, became Deputy Prime Minister and overall architect of the reform program. Sergei Shakhrai became deputy prime minister in charge of legal policy. Alexander Shokhin was named deputy prime minister in charge of social policy. Yeltsin proceeded to issue a set of decrees liberalizing foreign trade and the circulation of hard currency.[23] On January 2, 1992, under Yeltsin's political protection, the new government undertook a major initiative to push Russia toward a market system by abolishing most controls on wholesale and retail prices and cutting government spending sharply.

Almost immediately, opposition to the new program began to form. Within two weeks of the introduction of the program, Ruslan Khasbulatov, then chairman of the Russian Supreme Soviet but previously Yeltsin's deputy as head of the parliament, came out strongly against the program and called on the government to resign. Since Yeltsin formally was head of government, this was a direct attack on him. Quickly Vice-President Rutskoi sided with Khasbulatov and the conservative opposition in parliament. Economists and politicians took sides. It became virtually impossible to get dispassionate analysis of, and even basic information about, the

---

[20]Robert J. Shiller, Maxim Boycko, and Vladimir Korobov, "Popular Attitudes Toward Free Markets: The Soviet Union and the United States Compared," *American Economic Review* 81 (1991), pp. 385–400. The survey's validity is weakened by the fact that a lower proportion of Moscow citizens own telephones than of New York citizens, and by the unrepresentativeness of the Moscow population compared with Russia generally. Moreover, the sample sizes were rather small: 391 in Moscow, 361 in New York.

[21]John P. Willerton and Lee Sigelman, "Perestroika and the Public: Citizens' Views of the 'Fruits' of Economic Reform," in Miller, Reisinger and Hesli, eds., *Public Opinion and Regime Change*, p. 219.

[22]Ibid.

[23]Hard currency is the term used for the U.S. dollar, German mark, Japanese yen, and other national currencies which are freely traded on world markets. Soft currencies are those where governments set a value and then protect that value against foreign currency markets.

effects of the stabilization program—quickly dubbed "shock therapy." Criticism of the program was legion, because even though there was no consensus among critics about what should be done, both hard-line communists and moderates alike could agree that it was deeply misguided. Opponents demanded that the pace of reform be slowed so that Russians would have more time to adjust to the new conditions; they complained that the Gaidar team might be capable theorists but had no idea how to run a government; they demanded creation of a safety net to cushion the blow of the transition for the indigent, the elderly, and the displaced. It became commonplace to say that the program was all "shock" and no "therapy."

Under the terms of the constitutional amendments passed by the Fifth Congress in late 1991, Yeltsin's special powers to issue decrees expired at the end of 1992. But Yeltsin demanded to keep them, as well as the power to name the government. As the stabilization program proceeded, however, the balance of forces within the parliament began to shift away from support for Yeltsin. The Sixth (April) and Seventh (December) Congresses in 1992 saw displays of passionate resistance to Yeltsin and the government on the part of many elected deputies. Last minute bargains averted more serious confrontations. In April, the Congress agreed to a resolution calling for an "adjustment" of the reform program instead of its complete reversal, and in December, Yeltsin and the Congress agreed to hold a national referendum to resolve the issue of whether the parliament or the president would have the final say over the makeup and policy of the government. However, in March 1993 the Congress met and decided not to hold a referendum. Yeltsin then threatened to dissolve the Congress. The deputies quickly convened again and voted on a motion to remove Yeltsin from office. The motion narrowly failed. The Congress then agreed to hold a referendum, not on constitutional issues, but on approval of Yeltsin and of the government. Four questions were posed: approval of President Yeltsin; approval of the government and its policies; support for holding early presidential elections; and support for holding early parliamentary elections. In the April 25 voting, Yeltsin proved to be far more popular than parliament. Responding to the Yeltsin camp's appeals to vote "da, da, nyet, da," the citizens turned out in large numbers (69.2 percent voted) and generally supported the Yeltsin positions: 58.7 percent, 53 percent, 49.5 percent and 67.2 percent.[24] As had been the case in the elections of 1989, 1990, and 1991, when Yeltsin posed the choice as one between his reform policies and a return to communism, a majority of the electorate preferred Yeltsin.

Through the summer Yeltsin sought a way to give the mantle of constitutional legitimacy to his demands for the power to enact policy by decree. The constitutional formula he sought, which would have created a presidential system with a relatively weak parliament and a powerful executive presidency, could not win the approval of the opposition-dominated parliament. Under the existing constitution, only the Congress was entitled to amend or replace the constitution. Yeltsin finally chose to act extra-constitutionally by abolishing parliament on September 21, 1993,

---

[24]There is serious reason to believe that these results understate the Yeltsin vote: many rural voting precincts recorded significantly higher turnout than was typical for such districts, with the surplus votes nearly all voting against the Yeltsin position.

and decreeing that elections to a new parliament would be held in December, together with a referendum to approve the draft constitution enshrining a political order with a powerful presidency.[25]

Thus the severe constitutional crisis of 1993 grew directly out of President Yeltsin's demands to preserve the powers to implement his radical economic reform program by decree, without needing to obtain parliamentary consent. He used a combination of force and plebiscitarian appeals to the populace to win his case. For all the criticism of his government's policies, no opposition force proved stronger than Yeltsin. Were the events that unfolded over 1992–93 confirmation of the theory that only an authoritarian leader could implement a harsh macroeconomic stabilization policy in Russia? Was Yeltsin following in the footsteps of someone like General Augusto Pinochet of Chile, who after suppressing the democratically elected socialist government of President Salvador Allende in 1973, and harshly repressing the opposition, carried out a program of economic stabilization that put Chile's economy back on a firm footing again? Russians made bitter jokes about the prospect of a leader named "Adolf Vissarionovich Pinochet."[26] Yeltsin's powers under the new constitution to issue decrees so long as they do not contravene existing law may lead to another conflict with parliament, so a crisis may arise again.

A program of drastic macroeconomic measures to restore a balance between aggregate demand and supply is generally termed "stabilization," because it is designed to end the situation in which far too much money is being created, chasing far too few goods. For those advocating programs of rapid "shock therapy"-style stabilization, the great enemy is hyperinflation.[27] Once inflation is under control, then the economy can be restored to health, this school argues. But high inflation will wreck both democracy and productivity because it undermines all faith in the currency and in the future. They regard inflation as a far worse ill than the recession that stabilization causes. By cutting government spending, letting prices rise, and raising taxes to squeeze inflationary pressure out of the economy, stabilization aims at stimulating production by building confidence in the government, the currency,

---

[25]In the scheme proposed by Matthew Shugart and John Carey, Yeltsin's model was of the "president-parliamentary" type, where the president is popularly elected and appoints and dismisses members of the government, but the government also must enjoy the confidence of parliament, and the president has either the power to dissolve parliament, or to enact laws by decree, or both. Such a system is considered by political scientists to be less stable than other dual-executive systems where the president does not also serve as chief executive. See Matthew S. Shugart and John M. Carey, *Presidents and Assemblies: Constitutional Design and Electoral Dynamics* (Cambridge: Cambridge University Press, 1992), pp. 23–24.

[26]The quip refers to the improbable combination of Adolf Hitler, Joseph Vissarionovich Stalin, and Augusto Pinochet. Needless to say, both Hitler and Pinochet were targets of vehement hatred and contempt in Soviet propaganda, while Stalin represented Russia's own totalitarian legacy. In this connection, it is interesting to consider the results of a 1994 poll of urban residents of Russia, which asked whether they believed that Russia today needs such a leader as Augusto Pinochet. One quarter responded favorably, while one half disagreed. See *Segodnia*, August 27, 1994. These findings are consistent with poll data over the last few years, which find that around one quarter of the population would support the idea of a strong leader to introduce order, while between 40 and 50 percent would not.

[27]Economists generally say that once prices start rising by 50 percent a month and more, the economy is in a state of hyperinflation.

and the future. This creates incentives for producers to increase output and encourages them to look for new niches in the marketplace where they can make and sell products for a profit. Increases in production should in turn bring prices back down. If producers respond slowly, society suffers from a sharp, sudden loss in purchasing power. People go hungry; bank savings vanish.

Moreover, state enterprise managers, accustomed to assured sources of supply and credit, find it extremely difficult to begin producing for new markets. Directors of top-priority defense plants which produced missiles that could deliver payloads to destinations anywhere in the world find it unthinkable to be told to develop new product lines. Factories cut back on production, reduce workforces, and stop paying their bills and taxes. The economy goes into a severe recession. How severe depends on the ability of both state enterprise managers and the new entrepreneurs springing up to adapt to the new situation, and to begin producing goods for the market or importing goods from abroad. Even if directors of state or private enterprises decide they want to retool or expand operations, however, they face a severe credit crunch. The state cuts back on the supply of easy money in an effort to get inflation under control. Organized crime rackets prey on any firm enjoying even a little success in the market.

Small wonder then that one line of criticism directed against the Yeltsin/Gaidar government, its Western advisors, and the international financial organizations that were supplying loans, was that they were seeking to "de-industrialize" Russia—i.e., trying to destroy the great industrial plant which had been built up at such cost over many years. Some of the critics went further, and said that the West was deliberately trying to sabotage Russia by forcing it to follow the "shock therapy" prescription. Communists and nationalists got a rise out of audiences by depicting Gaidar and the other radical members of the 1992 government as the traitorous hirelings of a malevolent, imperialist West. The Gaidar government and its Western supporters, however, were convinced that Russia would never progress economically if it remained wedded to a Stalin-era industrial system where defense and heavy industries received the lion's share of capital resources, and consumer goods and services were perennially starved of investment. Indeed, many Russian and Western economists take the view that some of Russia's industrial production actually drains value from the economy by using up resources that could have been put to productive purposes in other ways, but which were sold at such artificially low state prices that there was no incentive not to overuse them. In such a case, the finished product actually is worth less than the sum of the resources needed to make it.

Much of the commentary on Russia's economic reforms in 1992 has been misdirected, because it assumes that the government's policies actually had the effects they intended. Certainly the program is a tempting target for political polemics which attribute Russia's post-1992 economic successes and miseries to the "shock therapy" program enacted by the Gaidar government. Critics blame the deep and lasting economic depression which followed on Gaidar, while the defenders of the policy credit it with sparing Russia economic breakdown and even civil war. In fact, it is by no means clear how much impact the Gaidar program had. National policies in Russia frequently are accompanied with considerable publicity and attract intense controversy, but rarely are they implemented in a way intended by their sponsors, and still more rarely do they achieve their objectives. In the case of the "shock therapy" program, not all resistance was visible. Many officials simply circumvented the policies. Directors of important industries wheedled credits from the Central Bank (which was not under the government's control) or persuaded ministries to place orders for products simply to keep production going.[28] Rather than respond to the new financial austerity, many directors simply continued to turn out and ship their products without being paid, allowing inter-enterprise arrears to mount. The Gaidar government lacked full control over the government, so it could not completely shape the structure of incentives to which enterprise managers responded. As a result, the relationship between *policy* and *outcome* was far from direct.

The Gaidar team also had a very limited choice of policy instruments with which to achieve the goals of setting Russia on a self-reinforcing path toward economic liberalization. During 1991, as traditional lines of control via the Communist Party and state bureaucracy weakened, regional and local governments even began erecting barriers to interregional trade. Some set tariffs, others erected roadblocks preventing the "export" of goods from their territories. Moscow and other big cities introduced identity cards with residents' photographs to prevent out-of-towners from coming in and purchasing goods from their relatively better stocked stores. The networks of internal wholesale and retail trade were breaking down. Administrative measures probably would have failed to restore them, short of martial law (which Prime Minister Valentin Pavlov repeatedly urged Gorbachev to declare through the spring and summer of 1991). But the drastic price liberalization of January 2, 1992, which allowed producers and retailers to set any price that the market could bear for most goods and services, did immediately eliminate the internal trade wars and restored the circulation of goods, albeit at high and often ruinous prices.

PRIVATIZATION

Stabilization was followed shortly afterward by another, equally important program—the privatization of state assets. In contrast to the "shock therapy" program, privatization enjoyed considerable public support, at least at first, and offset the unpopularity of stabilization. Privatization is the transfer to private owners of the legal title to state enterprises (firms). Market theory holds that under the right conditions, private ownership of productive assets is more efficient than is monopoly or state ownership, because in a competitive environment owners are motivated to maximize their property's ability to produce a return. Whereas a monopolist does not care if the firm he or she owns is inefficient, the owner of the firm in a market system wants to increase the productivity and therefore the market value of the firm. For this reason, most economists consider it essential to transfer ownership of state assets from the state to private owners as part of the transition from socialism to a market economy in order to stimulate growth and productivity. In short, a system of private property benefits not only the individual owners, according to market theory, but also benefits the whole society.

The theory is generally valid. But, as is often true of good theories, many circumstances can interfere with its application to the real world.

---

[28]Joseph R. Blasi, Maya Kroumova, and Douglas Kruse, *Kremlin Capitalism: Privatizing the Russian Economy* (Ithaca, NY: Cornell University Press, 1997), p. 171.

We must distinguish the privatization of state-owned firms in Russia from the creation of new, private start-up businesses. Although private entrepreneurs and foreign interests have created a large number of new, independent businesses, these are usually small in scale. The fate of Russia's state enterprises has profound political importance because the overwhelming majority of the population is tied to them for their livelihoods as well as the wide circle of social benefits which, as we have noted, are supplied through jobs at state enterprises. The form privatization should take also has major political repercussions. One method is simply to give away state assets to the public as a democratic gesture that quickly turns the entire population into property holders and gives them a stake in the reform process. An alternative is to require auctions in which groups and individuals submit competitive bids to purchase assets, thereby creating real value that can be used as investment capital, but also allowing rich or corrupt elements of the population to capture control of state enterprises. Russia combined these two methods, distributing free vouchers to all citizens, who were then able to use the vouchers to bid for shares of privatized firms at special auctions.

The legal right to start a private company is much less politically controversial than was the design of the privatization program. As early as 1986 Soviet law was changed so as to permit individuals and family members to start their own businesses, as well as to allow groups of people to start private commercial businesses organized as cooperatives.[29] As of 1996, Russia had around 900,000 small private businesses. Of these, just over 100,000 were small state establishments that had been privatized, and around 800,000 were start-up businesses.[30] Most of these small firms work in the service sphere. Altogether they account for only around 9 percent of total employment.

Of greater political significance, therefore, is the problem of privatization of larger state firms. Privatization programs are usually politically sensitive, since someone must decide how to set a value on state enterprises in the absence of capital markets; whether to privatize enterprises for cash, or for government-provided coupons; how much to favor the workers and managers of the enterprise in gaining control over their own workplace; whether to allow foreigners to buy privatized enterprises; and which levels of government can privatize which assets. Disputes over these issues have often stalled privatization programs in countries undergoing the transition from communism.

In Russia, parliament gave Yeltsin and his government the authority to enact privatization by decree. Even so, disagreements within the government produced fits and starts in the policy. Some in the government wanted to use auctions as much as possible to sell off state enterprises, especially retail and service establishments where it was reasonable to think that purchasers might have sufficient resources to buy them. Others believed it was more just to distribute some sort of coupon or bank account to every citizen which they could use to bid on and buy enterprises. Although the government generally agreed that both fairness and the interests of social stability demanded that workers have some priority in acquiring title to the enterprises in which they worked, there were two objections to taking this idea too far. One was that not every citizen worked in an enterprise that could be privatized.

---

[29]In a cooperative, all the employees are co-owners of the business, and share in its profits.

[30]Blasi et al., *Kremlin Capitalism*, p. 189.

Retired people, military personnel, ballerinas, scientists, teachers, and many government employees, for instance, might still be unable to share in the privatization program. Another was that if workers were able to gain control over their enterprises, the managers would be able to use their power within the enterprise to gain both ownership and control over the workplace—a pattern increasingly prevalent elsewhere in postcommunist countries.

The Russian Supreme Soviet had approved legislation on the privatization of state enterprises in July 1991. In December, Yeltsin issued a decree stepping up the pace of privatization and changing the procedures envisioned in the July laws.[31] Privatization of thousands of small and medium-sized enterprises, and a smaller number of large firms, proceeded under the methods that the laws and decrees laid out. One method was for workers and managers who had leased their firms simply to buy them. Another was to hold an auction or to invite bids from investors proposing alternative reorganization plans. A third was to reorganize the firm into a joint-stock company and issue shares, in which case the workers and managers could acquire a fixed proportion of the shares at a discount.

In the forms of privatization used in 1991 and the first half of 1992, buyers used cash rather than state-issued vouchers. Auctions and the sale of shares were supposed to serve the end of efficiency, by creating a material interest on the part of an investor in the value of the newly acquired assets. It was hoped that investors, be they the workers of the firm themselves or outside buyers, would be interested in maximizing the return on their investment by seeing that the firms were run profitably and efficiently. But when efficiency became the principal objective of cash privatization schemes, fairness was jeopardized. Cash privatization had the effect of making the rich richer, and giving ownership of enterprises to the officials who had run them before. Ordinary citizens often were excluded from the most profitable opportunities as insiders acquired the stock of the most promising firms. And the poor, of course, had no chance at all to buy shares.

In the interests of dispersing ownership rights as widely as possible, parliament's law had envisioned that all citizens would be given special bank accounts to buy shares of privatized enterprises. Yeltsin's December 1991 decree promised that eventually everyone would be issued a voucher to buy shares, while deciding that this would not take effect for a year. Meanwhile the process of transforming state firms into stock companies and issuing shares would be stepped up, and the cash buyouts of leased and transformed enterprises would continue. In April 1992, however, as opposition to the stabilization program was gaining force, Yeltsin changed course again, and decreed that a program of vouchers would begin in the fourth quarter of 1992. Under the program, every citizen of Russia would be issued a voucher with a face value of ten thousand rubles. People would be free to buy and sell vouchers, but they could only be used to acquire shares of stock in privatized enterprises or shares of mutual funds investing in privatized enterprises. The program was intended to ensure that everyone became a property owner instantly. Politically the aim was to build support for the economic reforms by giving citizens

---

[31]Lynn D. Nelson and Irina Y. Kuzes, *Property to the People: The Struggle for Radical Economic Reform in Russia* (Armonk, NY: M. E. Sharpe, 1994), pp. 28, 44.

a stake in the outcome of the market transition. As far as the program's economic aims were concerned, even though the voucher privatization program would not generate any new investment capital, it would eventually spur increases in productivity by creating meaningful property rights, according to its designers.[32]

Therefore, beginning in October 1992, 148 million privatization vouchers were distributed to citizens. A citizen could sell the voucher to someone else, or invest it directly in enterprise stock or in an investment fund. The program established three ways in which vouchers could be exchanged for stock shares. These differed according to how much stock could be acquired by employees of privatized enterprises and on what terms. Each method balanced the demands of managers and workers of state enterprises for control over their own enterprises against the demand of outsiders for the right to bid freely for shares. Each mixed the objective of letting citizens acquire stock for free with that of creating a real capital market where stock had tradable value. The State Privatization Committee and its regional and local offices oversaw the entire privatization process, organizing auctions and approving privatization plans drafted by enterprises. This powerful agency, and its chairman, Anatolii Chubais, became targets for vehement criticism from all sides—from those accusing the committee of selling off assets too cheaply and not protecting enterprises to those distressed at the way in which state managers usually wound up with the controlling share of stock. With Yeltsin's protection, however, Chubais carried out the program over the objections of all critics.

In principle, the government opposed simply giving away Russia's vast capital stock to the powerful state enterprise directors. Instead it wanted to diffuse ownership rights as broadly as possible. The political realities, however, dictated that the government allow enterprise directors certain advantages. In the short run, at least, the consent of the directors to the program was essential to maintaining economic and social stability in the country. The managers could ensure that labor did not erupt in a massive wave of strikes. As we have seen, they also represented one of the most powerful collective interests in the country. The government, therefore, did not strenuously resist the tendency for voucher privatization to turn into "insider privatization," as it was termed, in which senior enterprise officials acquired the largest proportion of shares in privatized firms. Of the three options, the second, under which employees could acquire majority stakes in the enterprises, proved to be the most widely used. Three-quarters of privatized enterprises opted for this method, most often using vouchers. On average, only 22.5 percent of shares of enterprises were sold at voucher auctions, where the public could bid for them. Real control wound up in the hands of the managers.[33]

Around 18,000 medium- and large-scale firms were privatized by 1996. Privatization for most of them has not resulted in major changes in the way they are run.

---

[32]The goals of the privatization program are laid out in a volume of essays by its chief Russian designers and their Western advisors. See, in particular, Anatoly B. Chubais and Maria Vishnevskaya, "Main Issues of Privatisation in Russia," and Maxim Boycko and Andrei Shleifer, "The Voucher Programme for Russia," in Anders Åslund and Richard Layard, eds., *Changing the Economic System in Russia* (New York: St. Martin's Press, 1993), pp. 89–99 and 100–111.

[33]Pekka Sutela, "Insider Privatization in Russia: Speculations on Systemic Changes," *Europe-Asia Studies* 46:3 (1994), pp. 420–421.

Figure 6.1

A privatization voucher

Above is one of the privatization vouchers that were distributed to all Russian citizens in 1992 in order to enable them to acquire shares of ownership in the state firms that were being auctioned off as part of the privatization campaign. The nominal value of each voucher was 10,000 rubles. Vouchers could be bought and sold or exchanged for shares of stock until the program ended in June 1994.

One reason is that privatization did not bring an infusion of new investment capital to modernize their plant and equipment. This is due in part to managers' strenuous resistance to allowing their firms to be taken over by outside investors. In one major survey when enterprise directors were asked whether they would be willing to sell a majority of the shares of their enterprise to an outside investor who would bring the capital needed to invest in modernizing the firm, two-thirds said they would not be willing. In other words, they would rather remain majority owners of an unprofitable enterprise than the minority owners of a much more profitable one.[34] Very few firms have experienced much management turnover and even fewer have engaged in extensive restructuring of their operations to make them more productive or efficient.

All vouchers were to have been used by December 31, 1993, but President Yeltsin extended the expiration date until June 30, 1994. By that time 140 million vouchers had been exchanged for stock out of the 148 million originally distributed, according to Anatolii Chubais.[35] Some 40 million citizens had become property owners. Some 70 percent of large and medium-sized firms and 80 percent of all small businesses had been privatized. The next phase was to consist of the privatization of most of the remaining state enterprises, but by means of direct cash auctions. The voucher privatization phase had ended.

Overall, as of January 1, 1996, 122,000, or 53 percent of Russia's enterprises, had been privatized.[36] The great majority of these are small and medium-sized enterprises, although they were usually privatized without building or equipment. Some 60 percent of Russia's GNP is now produced in private firms.[37] Although it is premature to offer a general assessment of the results of privatization, a few observations can be made.

First, the actual transfer of ownership rights was far less impressive than it appeared. The dominant pattern was acquisition through "insider privatization," rather than through open competitive bidding. Some theorists said that in the long run, what mattered is that property rights had been created and these would eventually lead to a competitive market economy. Others countered by saying that nothing had really changed—the people who were powerful officials under the old regime came out on top under the new one. Meanwhile, the state continued to hold packets of shares in the great majority of large-scale enterprises often because it could not find buyers for the shares it sought to sell. It is also the case that regional officials were able to set the timing and conditions under which auctions of enterprises in their regions were held. Privatization thus created a number of regional markets, making it difficult for citizens to acquire title to firms outside the regions where they lived. Finally, many firms have not changed in the way they are managed—they continue to be closely tied to state life-support systems such as cheap loans and subsidies.[38]

---

[34]Blasi et al., *Kremlin Capitalism*, pp. 179–180. The authors have conducted a major national annual survey of the managers of privatized enterprises in Russia.

[35]Radio Free Europe/Radio Liberty Daily Report, July 1, 1994.

[36]Evgenii Saburov,"Privatizatsiia ili kolkhozizatsiia?" *Segodnia*, April 19, 1996.

[37]*Segodnia*, February 21, 1995.

[38]Michael McFaul, "State Power, Institutional Change, and the Politics of Privatization in Russia," *World Politics* 47 (1995), pp. 210–243.

2)   Second, for all its faults, the program probably could not have been carried out if Yeltsin had not assumed authoritarian powers. Given the strong position of opponents of reform in parliament in 1992–93, parliament would certainly have gutted the program if it had had the power to do so; it attempted directly to block Yeltsin's privatization policy in 1993 until Yeltsin dissolved parliament by force. Privatization remained a contentious issue in relations between Yeltsin and the new parliament in the 1994–95 period as well, although much less than before. In the summer of 1994 the parliament and government very nearly succeeded in agreeing on the terms under which the next phase of enterprise privatization would proceed; by a few votes the parliament failed to give the plan its approval, so the president put the program into effect by decree instead, but he modified it to take into account some of parliament's reservations. After the 1995 elections brought the communists to a position of much greater power in parliament, it again threatened to reverse some of the major privatization deals that had been made in 1994 and 1995, but the communist candidate, Gennadii Ziuganov, was curiously silent about the issue of enterprise privatization during his presidential election campaign. It may be that a common ground of agreement about privatization is emerging between government and its parliamentary opposition: the communists may be willing to tolerate some of the government's plans for privatization since many of the communists' major financial backers benefit from the transactions.

3)   Third, the program allowed a great many unscrupulous wheeler-dealers to prey on the public through a variety of financial schemes. Some investment funds promised truly incredible rates of return; most investors in Western companies would have regarded these claims as outrageous and fraudulent. But in a country lacking experience with capitalism, hope triumphs over caution more readily. Many people lost a great deal of money by investing in funds that went bankrupt or turned out to be simple pyramid schemes, where the dividends to the early investors were simply fueled by the contributions of later investors. Because the Russian government lacked the capacity to protect the investors, many people were disenchanted with the entire program as a result.

4)   Fourth, the privatization program contributed nothing to the urgent task of modernization and retooling of the economy. Vouchers, the dramatic instrument used in the first phase for mass privatization, were not inflationary, because they could not be used as legal tender for other transactions.[39] But neither were they forms of productive capital, as stocks and bonds are in countries with established financial markets. So the vouchers did not expand the pool of resources enterprises could use to increase productivity and efficiency. They were intended as an impetus to a process that would end in the consolidation of a market economy. The policymakers believed that mass privatization would establish an interest on the part of new property owners in increasing the value of their assets, which they would achieve by investing in the modernization and retooling of the firms. In turn, it was hoped that the need for capital would create a healthy capital market, but so far, the capital market in Russia remains extremely weak. The policy's failure to achieve this

---

[39]They were backed by the federal government's share of the proceeds of the sale of stock from state enterprises. Each enterprise had to offer at least 35 percent of its stock for vouchers. This corresponded to the share of ownership that the federal government claimed for itself. The federal government's share in the sale of privatizing enterprises was thus distributed to the citizens in the form of vouchers.

crucial outcome can be explained in part by a competing goal of government policy: that of raising revenues for the government through "cash privatization."

Under the current, cash phase of privatization, the government seeks to realize revenues by selling off state-owned shares of stock in privatized firms from the shares it still owns. While federal budget for 1995 anticipated revenues of nine trillion rubles from the privatization of such shares, only two-thirds of that amount was realized.[40] The weak market for shares in privatized enterprises is due to the "crowding out" of investment capital by the sale of state treasury obligations (GKOs), which promise far higher rates of return.[41] One government policy goal—that of financing budget expenditures by issuing bonds—is directly in competition with another—that of accelerating private ownership of state-owned enterprises. For this reason privatization has not brought a viable capital market into being: the mechanism for converting private savings into investment in Russian companies works very poorly. Enterprises that are starved for working capital are failing to pay their taxes; the government responds by issuing still more GKOs, further squeezing out private investment. The government continues to set unrealistic goals for raising revenues from privatization in its annual budgets. Meanwhile, Russian firms are starved for investment capital because of the extremely high interest rates they face on private capital markets.[42]

 Fifth, privatization has not extended to land, because of the concerted and effective opposition to allowing property rights in land by the communist–agrarian–nationalist forces which we discussed in the preceding chapter. Their opposition has been particularly effective in blocking any movement toward a market in agricultural land, over 90 percent of which continues to be owned by the old collective and state farms.[43] Almost all of these have been legally transformed into joint stock companies, but continue to be run as in the past. Many of the institutional forms necessary for capitalist development are lacking, particularly the legal right to use land as a security to guarantee a loan: despite repeated attempts by reformers to pass a law establishing mortgages as a legal form of secured debt, the communists and their allies have defeated them. As a result, it is impossible to secure a loan to buy personal or commercial real estate property with a deed to the property itself. The absence of such a legal institution inhibits the development of market relations in land and other real property.

 Finally, despite the goal of encouraging widespread property ownership through the mass privatization program, capital is becoming more highly concen-

---

[40]Most of the proceeds in fact came from a controversial policy at the end of the year by which the state auctioned off the rights to control shares of state enterprises to major banks and other firms in return for loans to the government. Some of these have since been investigated for suspected legal irregularities.

[41]In spring 1996, when the presidential election campaign was at its height, Russian state treasury obligations were selling at ruinously high interest rates—over 200 percent effective annual yields on six-month bonds. Little wonder that investors were uninterested in the stock market. Because of the instability of the political climate and the fear of default, the great bulk of this paper was short-term.

[42]Saburov, "Privatizatsiia"; Stephen S. Moody, "Decapitalizing Russian Capitalism," *Orbis* 40:1 (Winter 1996), pp. 123–143; Bendukidze, "Finansovaia katastropha."

[43]European Bank for Reconstruction and Development, *Transition Report 1995: Investment and Enterprise Development* (London: 1995), p. 55.

trated; financial capital is merging with industrial capital, in a manner reminiscent of Marxist caricatures of "monopoly capitalism." A small number of powerful "financial–industrial groups" are acquiring a growing hold over Russian industry. Financial–industrial groups are holding companies in which a leading bank owns controlling shares in a number of enterprises in a particular branch. In a few cases, a former ministry dissolved itself in such a way that its financial department formed a bank to service the enterprises that once were administered hierarchically by the ministry; thus the ministry recreates itself as a holding company with its own financial base. In other cases the government created a holding company to replace a ministry, and set up a bank to finance the company's operations. The most prominent form, however, are empires created by new, nominally private banks which were initially established with the participation of Communist Party, Komsomol, or other state-derived financial resources. In turn, these new banks have steadily built up their holdings in the economy.[44]

By June 1996 these financial–industrial groups numbered 34 and owned nearly 1,500 enterprises which together accounted for 10 percent of Russia's Gross Domestic Product (GDP), a figure which represented an increase of 2 percent over the previous year.[45] Both parliament and president have officially encouraged the spread of this form of ownership. Conservative elements in the government and parliament view them as a means of keeping the old state-owned industrial sector afloat by staving off competition from the foreign or domestic market. Industrial managers in these groups welcome an assured source of financing. The new entrepreneurial class gains greater opportunities to collect rents and finance profitable lines of activity, while forcing the Central Bank or Finance Ministry to cover their losses from the less profitable areas. In some cases, control over governance through a financial–industrial group allows a bank to force firms to become more efficient and productive in the domestic and international markets. However, this form of ownership also restricts open competition for financing in the capital and debt markets, a goal directly contrary to the liberal precepts of Russia's government and president. Nonetheless, the de facto strength of a coalition of bureaucratic industrialists and newly ascendant business interests has allowed them to take root and flourish.

Moreover, the intertwined financial–industrial groups are gaining strategic control over some of Russia's major media outlets. A financial group controlled by Vladimir Gusinskii which owns the powerful Most bank also owns the influential nonstate Russia-wide television company NTV as well as the important national newspaper *Segodnia*. Another prominent bank, Oneximbank, headed by former First Deputy Prime Minister Vladimir Potanin, owns a sizable share of the stock of the newspaper *Izvestiia* and has acquired substantial blocs of shares in some of the country's most important industrial firms. These giant conglomerates are frequently accused of trading on their connections to the president and government and their power over the media.

---

[44]Ol'ga Kryshtanovskaia, "Finansovaia oligarkhiia v Rossii," *Izvestiia*, January 10, 1996, p. 5. The author is a respected sociologist who heads the sector for the study of the elite of the Institute of Sociology of the Russian Academy of Sciences. Also see Blasi et al., *Kremlin Capitalism*, pp. 155–157.

[45]OMRI Daily Digest, June 21, 1996.

Overall, then, privatization has had a much greater political than economic impact. It has not yet made Russia's economy more productive, but it has widened the circle of groups benefiting from the demise of the communist system.

Evaluating Outcomes

The troubled results of the two prongs of the economic reforms begun in 1992—radical macroeconomic stabilization and the privatization of state enterprises—illustrate the dilemma of pursuing democracy and a market economy simultaneously. As we saw, the politically divisive nature of the reforms led to the rapid breakdown of leadership consensus once they began to be implemented in 1992. Recall that President Yeltsin used the decree-making power that the parliament granted him in late 1991 to create the legal basis for both the stabilization and privatization programs. President Yeltsin acted both as lawmaker and chief executive. When parliament tried to revoke his decree-making powers, he refused to accept limitations on his power, but he did make changes in the composition of the government. Following the clashes with parliament at the April 1992 Sixth Congress, Yeltsin added three new deputy prime ministers with backgrounds in industrial administration who were of a decidedly nonradical bent. But Yeltsin then balanced these appointments in June 1992, when he named Egor Gaidar acting prime minister. In December 1992, when the Congress of People's Deputies asserted its constitutional authority to vote on the president's nominee for prime minister, Yeltsin proposed Gaidar and the Congress rejected him. The president then submitted the name of one of the first deputy prime ministers, Viktor Chernomyrdin, and parliament confirmed him. Then, after forcibly dissolving parliament in September 1993 and mandating new elections, the president succeeded in gaining popular endorsement of a constitution embodying his conception of the presidency as the principal source of policy direction for the country.

President Yeltsin's actions reflected the view he and a great many other Russians hold that it is imperative that there be a single center of political power in the state. Many of President Yeltsin's bitterest political enemies and many who argue in favor of radical economic reform share this view.

Yet, in the end, what may be most conducive to success in economic policy in a new democracy is "not so much a *strong* hand as a *steady* one," to quote Arend Lijphart.[46] If the emergence of a pluralistic political system in which organized parties and groups compete for influence is a minimum condition of democracy, then a stable framework of rules for their competition is essential, along with the commitment by all major political actors to honor those rules. The same point applies to economic reform. Faith by economic actors that contracts will be enforced and that their ownership rights will be secure is an important condition for economic development. Without it, the mere transfer of formal ownership rights to private

---

[46]Arend Lijphart, "Democracies: Forms, Performance, and Constitutional Engineering," *European Journal of Political Research* 25 (1994), p. 12.

persons does not give them a strong incentive to maximize the productive value of their assets and therefore does not lead to a more productive economy overall.[47]

Moreover, the Russian president, for all his constitutional power, is in a surprisingly weak position to ensure that the policies he adopts will be implemented by the multiple layers of state officials under his authority. President Yeltsin has often expressed frustration that his directives are not carried out. (Some, in fact, are simply lost, as decrees get buried in a mass of paperwork awaiting his attention. Sometimes they are quietly misplaced by officials who oppose them. Russian state bureaucrats are extremely adept at getting their way.) Therefore simply centralizing nominal authority is often the worst possible way of increasing actual control. *Policy* may often have little direct relationship to actual *outcomes*. We have examined two of the principal policies that Russia's postcommunist government pursued. Now let us consider the actual state of Russia's economy.

From State Planning to State Capitalism

Some of the changes which have occurred in the Russian economy are the consequence of policies adopted before the "shock therapy" policy began. Under Gorbachev the Soviet regime pursued policies intended to make enterprises more responsive to the market and to reduce the burden of state subsidies for inefficient industries. In 1991 the old state planning system ended. Coupled with the drastic cuts in state spending in 1992, increases in taxation, elimination of price controls, and drastic reduction in easy credit, these policies did alter the economic environment for Russian firms substantially. Many firms found it difficult to maintain production because their suppliers could no longer send them inputs or their customers could no longer pay them. The breakup of the Soviet Union, and the collapse of the "ruble zone" among the former Soviet republics as each republic introduced its own national currency, disrupted former relationships among enterprises located in different republics. As a result, industrial production has fallen sharply and began to recover only in 1997. According to official figures, in 1995 industrial output stood at half its 1991 level. Agricultural output had declined by one quarter. Overall, Gross Domestic Product (GDP) had fallen 40 percent.[48] Occasionally there are indications that the depression has bottomed out and national income has begun to rise again. But, each time, the economy sinks further behind.

---

[47]Readers may recognize the reference here to the important theorem developed by Ronald Coase, to the effect that if the costs of transactions are low (including such costs as ensuring that other economic actors will respect contracts and guaranteeing that property rights are secure), then, regardless of the initial allocation of ownership rights, private property will lead to a socially optimal outcome because the market will efficiently redistribute ownership rights until they reach their most efficient aggregate level. The key here is the "if." In Russia, and in many other real-world societies, transaction costs are very high. Insecurity and uncertainty severely impede the working of the market. An initial distribution of ownership rights can keep society on a path of inefficiency and backwardness for a long time.

Douglass C. North, *Institutions, Institutional Change and Economic Performance* (Cambridge: Cambridge University Press, 1990).

[48]OMRI Daily Digests for January 18, February 17, and March 13, 1995.

---TABLE 6.3---

Russian Economic Performance, 1991–96
(percentage change over previous year)

	1991	1992	1993	1994	1995	1996
GDP[a]	−5.0	−14.5	−8.7	−12.6	−4.3	−6.0
Manufacturing and construction	−7.0	−21.0	−13.6	−20.0	−5.3	−5.0
Gross domestic investment	−2.3	−39.3	−29.4	−29.6	−9.4	−18.0
Consumption	−6.1	−5.3	−1.0	−2.1	−4.9	n.a.
Inflation[b]	138.0	2323.0	844.0	202.0	131.0	21.8

[a]GDP is measured in constant market prices.
[b]Inflation figures refer to the percentage change in the consumer price index from December of one year to December of the next.

Russia is suffering from a severe and protracted depression. Table 6.3[49] shows this clearly.

The figures in Table 6.3 almost certainly overstate the depth of the decline. Consumption, as we see, has declined much less than production. Sometimes observers skeptical of recent statistics about production point out that whereas in the past, industrial managers had every reason to overstate their actual levels of output, since they were under pressure to fulfill the production plan, now they were more likely to understate their actual output in order to evade taxation. As evidence, the skeptics point to figures on the consumption of electric power. Electricity consumption has fallen much less than has reported industrial production, yet there is no reason to think that it takes commensurately more electric power to produce each unit of output. Power consumption dropped by only around 20 percent, suggesting that industrial output may not have fallen as steeply as is reported.

Moreover, the very structure of national income has shifted. Much more of Russia's economic activity is occurring in the sphere of services, which is poorly captured in output statistics. There also continues to be a large volume of unrecorded economic activity taking place, not measured in the official statistics, and also outside the tax inspectors' scrutiny. A conservative estimate of the scale of output of unregistered goods and services is 20 percent of GDP, but it could well be greater.[50]

Still, the fact remains that Russia's economy is in deep depression. To attribute it, as critics invariably do, to the effects of the "shock therapy" program and the restrictive conditions imposed by international financial institutions in return for loans and credits may be politically gratifying, but squares poorly with the facts.

---

[49]Figures on production, investment, and consumption are taken from World Bank, *Statistical Handbook 1996: States of the Former USSR*, vol. 21 (Washington, D.C.: World Bank, 1996), p. 386. Inflation data for 1991–1996 are from the Russian State Statistics Committee, as reported in Blasi et al., *Kremlin Capitalism*, p. 190 and RFE/RL Newsline, April 3, 1997. I am grateful to Timothy Heleniak of the World Bank for 1996 figures on growth in GDP, manufacturing and construction, and gross domestic investment.

[50]OMRI Daily Digests for April 20 and May 30, 1995.

Poland, to take another postcommunist society which launched radical reform with a similar shock, quickly recovered and resumed rapid economic growth (GDP grew 7 percent in 1995, over 4 percent in 1994, and 2–3 percent in each of 1992 and 1993). It would be more accurate to say that real economic reform was never tried in Russia since it was quickly subverted by actors outside the government's control, such as the Central Bank, ministries, regional governments, and industrial managers, who preferred tacitly to preserve as much of the old system as possible, even if it led to piling up enormous unpaid obligations. Other problems undermined the reform program as well, among them a level of taxation that crushed initiative and almost demanded high levels of evasion; a monetary system that starved enterprises of working capital; and enterprises' inability to transfer responsibility for managing social funds to territorial governments. In turn, the economic depression has created critical problems for the government because tax collections have fallen well behind planned levels. In order to finance its operations, as a result, the government has issued high-interest-bearing short-term obligations; as noted above, these state bonds are so attractive that they soak up capital that might otherwise be available for investment in industry. Thus the government weakens its own present and future tax base. Such policies are unsustainable: if not altered, they would lead to a collapse of the financial system.

Although Russia's industry has descended into a profound depression, not all sectors of the economy are affected in the same way. Retail trade is flourishing, as are branches of the economy oriented to the export of raw materials, particularly gas, oil, coal, nonferrous metals, and timber. Firms tied to the extraction, marketing, and servicing of these sectors have become prosperous and have contributed to the formation of a sizable class of wealthy businesspeople. Both recorded and unrecorded foreign trade has risen amidst the general economic decline, in part fueled by the profits from the large raw materials export sector. In many categories of food and consumer goods, imported goods account for over half of retail sales. Analysts estimate that over $8 billion per year—an amount roughly equal to about one-sixth of the total volume of officially recorded imports per year—is generated by small-scale sales transactions on the part of "shuttle traders." "Shuttle traders" are the private dealers who cross the borders into other countries, purchase consumer goods there, and bring them back for sale in Russia without paying customs duties.[51]

While some people have become wealthy, and others have improved their lot modestly, most, however, have suffered a net loss in living standards as a result of unemployment, lagging income, and nonpayment of wages and pensions. A much larger share of the population lives in poverty than was the case in the Soviet era.

Estimates of the incidence of both poverty and unemployment have varied widely. In January 1995, Russia's Minister for Labor and Employment reported that actual unemployment was much higher than the level reported by official statistics: while the number of registered unemployed persons was 1.5 million, he declared that the actual number was 5.1 million. Moreover, he reported, another 4.8 million people were either underemployed or on forced unpaid leave from their jobs. Therefore the total rate of unemployment, he said, was around 13 percent of the

---

[51]OMRI Daily Digest, April 12, 1996.

working age population.[52] This rate—comparable to the levels of unemployment in France, Italy, Germany, and Belgium—was extremely high for a country accustomed to nearly full employment. However, survey researchers reported that around one quarter of the unemployed were in fact working, although usually not on a full-time basis. Around a tenth of these were earning three times or more than the average employed worker.[53] The actual unemployment rate is probably slightly under 10 percent—still high and rising steadily.[54]

As elsewhere in the former communist East European region, unemployment has affected women and youths much more severely than men: in Russia two-thirds of the unemployed are women and young people (and these are, of course, over-lapping categories).[55] Women are less likely than men to find offsetting employment, as are residents of small towns and people with lower educational levels.[56] Since the vast majority of single-parent households are headed by women, rising unemployment has pushed more women and children into poverty.[57]

Particularly vulnerable to the economic trends of the past few years have been groups whose incomes are paid directly out of the state budget, such as those living on pensions and disability payments, as well as teachers, scientists, and health care workers. Although they have received periodic increases in their earnings levels, these often have been insufficient to keep up with increases in prices. The propor-tion of pensioners living in poverty rose from 11.8 percent in 1959 to 18.5 percent in 1989 to 20.2 percent in 1995, according to a government report cited in a Moscow newspaper in early 1996.[58]

Wages in state industry have also lagged behind price increases, particularly in the early stages of the liberalization program, when prices rose rapidly. In 1992, when the price index for consumer goods rose 26 times over the course of the year, average real per capita incomes fell three times. Incomes rose gradually thereafter more quickly than prices. However, real incomes in money terms still have not caught up with their pre-reform level; according to the All-Russian Center for the Study of Public Opinion, average real incomes in mid-1995 stood at only 60–70 per-cent of their 1991 levels.[59] However, two other changes tended to offset this sharp net decline in living standards. First, in-kind and unreported forms of income (such as enterprises paying workers in the goods they produced, or people's consumption of products they grew themselves on garden plots) were rising. So were unreported

[52]OMRI Daily Digest, January 5, 1995.

[53]Ekaterina Khibovskaia, "Rossiiane stali bol´she opasat´sia poteriat´ rabotu," *Segodnia*, July 26, 1995.

[54]The rate rose from around 8.8 percent at the end of 1995 to 9.3 percent at the end of 1996. *Segodnia*, February 17, 1997.

[55]OMRI Daily Digest, January 12, 1995.

[56]Khibovskaia, "Rossiiane stali," *Segodnia*, July 26, 1995.

[57]Gail Kligman, "The Social Legacy of Communism: Women, Children, and the Feminization of Pover-ty," in James R. Millar and Sharon L. Wolchik, eds., *The Social Legacy of Communism* (Washington, D.C.: Woodrow Wilson Center Press and Cambridge University Press, 1994), p. 261; Mary Buckley, "The Poli-tics of Social Issues," in Stephen White, Alex Pravda, and Zvi Gitelman, eds., *Developments in Russian and Post-Soviet Politics*, 3rd ed. (London: Macmillan, 1994), pp. 192–194.

[58]OMRI Daily Digest, February 19, 1996.

[59]Tat´iana Zaslavskaia, "Rossiiskoe naselenie postepenno snizhaet svoi zhiznennye standarty," *Segodnia*, August 2, 1995.

earnings from off-the-book employment, often second and third jobs. As much as 40 percent of real earnings were not registered and taxed. Second, whereas in the pre-reform period, goods were scarce at the official state prices, people spent long hours standing in line at stores, and prices on the black market were high, after the 1992 radical reform, consumer goods became available in all major cities and lines disappeared. Since the cheap prices on basic subsistence goods set by the Soviet authorities had often been purely hypothetical—what use is a cheap price if the good is unavailable?—many people's living standards have improved.

Nevertheless, a high proportion of the Russian population has fallen into poverty. Again, figures vary because of the political sensitivity of the subject and the difficulty of measuring poverty objectively. In May 1995, the state statistical committee reported that between January and April, 30 percent of the population, or 44 million people, had monthly incomes below the subsistence minimum—i.e., the minimum level of income necessary to sustain a person's life—of 385,000 rubles, or 45 U.S. dollars.[60] The Russian government's own Working Center for Economic Reform, however, estimated that by September 1995, the proportion of the population living in poverty had declined to 34 million, or 23 percent.[61] Another estimate, by Branko Milanovic of the World Bank, gives the proportion of the population living in poverty in 1993 as 21 percent, as compared with 2 percent in 1987–88. Milanovic estimates aggregate inequality in Russia to be slightly less than in the United Kingdom, but higher by 50 percent than the Russian level in 1987–88.[62]

Some idea of how the lag of incomes behind prices has affected people may be conveyed by this example. A resident of Moscow receiving the subsistence minimum who wanted to buy a monthly transit pass permitting unlimited rides on public transportation would spend half of her income: 180,000 rubles of the 360,000 rubles considered necessary to sustain life in the capital.

Against the background of high unemployment, poverty, and inequality levels, the stabilization of price levels and of the ruble's exchange value is a mixed blessing. As Tables 6.4[63] and 6.5[64] show, by the end of 1995, inflation rates had fallen to low monthly levels, and the government had succeeded in sustaining the ruble's value against convertible Western currencies.

Low price inflation meant that producers and consumers could act with more confidence in the future value of their resources. However, stabilization came at the expense of a deep depression exacerbated by a severe shortage of economic liquidity. The export-oriented sector is insulated to a considerable degree from the

---

[60]OMRI Daily Report, May 17, 1995.

[61]Cited in OMRI Economic Report, November 2, 1995.

[62]Branko Milanovic, "Poverty, Inequality, and Social Policy in Transition Economies," Russian Littoral Project of the University of Maryland at College Park and The Johns Hopkins University SAIS, November 1995, Table X.1. His measure of aggregate inequality, a Gini coefficient, is estimated at 36 for Russia in 1993 and 24 in 1987–88. For the United Kingdom in 1993 it is 37; for the three Baltic states and the Central Asian states it is 34.

[63]Figures measure month-to-month change in the consumer price index. Those for 1992 and 1993 are reported by Joshua Chadajo, "The Independence of the Central Bank of Russia," *RFE/RL Research Report* 3:27 (8 July 1994), p. 28; 1994 and 1995 figures are from reports of the State Statistics Committee.

[64]Calculated by the author. Figures represent approximate value in rubles of one U.S. dollar at legal exchange points in Moscow. In January 1998, the government redenominated the ruble. The new ruble was pegged at 6 to the dollar rather than 6000 to the dollar.

―――――――――――――――――――――TABLE 6.4――――――――――――――――――――
Monthly Inflation Rates in Russia, 1992–95
(percentage change in consumer price index over previous month)

	1992	1993	1994	1995
January	245.0	26.0	21.0	17.8
February	38.3	25.0	10.0	11.0
March	29.8	20.0	9.0	8.9
April	21.6	19.0	10.0	8.5
May	12.0	18.0	8.0	7.9
June	18.6	20.0	5.0	6.7
July	11.0	22.0	5.0	5.4
August	9.0	26.0	4.0	4.6
September	12.0	23.0	8.0	4.5
October	23.0	20.0	15.0	4.7
November	26.0	16.0	14.0	4.5
December	25.0	13.0	16.4	3.2

depression by virtue of Russia's almost limitless supply of marketable natural resources, thanks to which a large stratum of well-to-do people has formed. The retail sector is also strong, but heavily dependent on imported goods. One study found that over 70 percent of the packaged food products sold in Russian grocery stores and city kiosks were imported.[65] But the sector of the economy that produces intermediate goods—goods used by other manufacturers—is profoundly depressed: manufacturers of intermediate goods are operating at only around 30 percent of capacity.[66]

Many firms try to cope with the crisis by delaying the payment of taxes and of wages. The nonpayment of taxes has created an increasing crisis of public finance: in the first two months of 1996, state budget revenues only reached 56 percent of the planned level.[67] The problem of nonpayment of wages is also severe. Even in 1994, according to a survey by Richard Rose, more than half of Russian workers report that they were not paid on time or at all for at least one month in 1994.[68] By early 1996, the total sum of unpaid wages had reached $5 billion, and unpaid pensions amounted to $1.2 billion.[69] A presidential economic advisor estimated that the sum of all unpaid wages, tax arrears, and inter-enterprise debt in 1996 had reached 719 trillion rubles, or around $150 billion.[70] President Yeltsin addressed himself energetically to the wage arrears problem in March and April 1996 as he launched his presidential election campaign, and the problem subsided somewhat. But the root causes of the general crisis of liquidity in the economy had not been eliminated.

――――――――――

[65]Stephen S. Moody, "The Crash of Kiosk Capitalism," p. 7.

[66]Ibid.

[67]OMRI Daily Digest, April 15, 1996.

[68]Richard Rose, "Russia as an Hour-Glass Society: A Constitution without Citizens," *East European Constitutional Review* 4:3 (Summer 1995), p. 37.

[69]OMRI Daily Digest, February 29 and April 3, 1996.

[70]Moody, "Kiosk Capitalism."

TABLE 6.5

Ruble Exchange Rate Against the U.S. Dollar ($1.00 =)

December 1990: 25 rubles
December 1991: 170
December 1992: 415
December 1993: 1240
December 1994: 3500
December 1995: 4650
December 1996: 5600
December 1997: 6000

THE 1997 OFFENSIVE

In March 1997 President Yeltsin launched a major new policy offensive aimed not only at eliminating the chronic lack of liquidity in the economy—the vicious circle of nonpayment of taxes, nonpayment of wages, and inter-enterprise arrears—but also at achieving a new set of structural reforms that would make the economy more competitive and productive. To lead the effort he turned, as he had done in 1991–92, to young and vigorous liberals, and he gave them strong support. He moved Anatolii Chubais from the post of head of the presidential administration into the position of first deputy prime minister. Viktor Chernomyrdin was retained as prime minister, largely as a shield behind whom Chubais could reconstruct the government and formulate a major new policy program. Chubais acquired far greater control over the executive branch than Gaidar had ever had in 1992.

The new team under Chubais quickly made its policy priorities clear. Chubais formulated a radical presidential message to parliament. On March 7—the same day Chubais was made first deputy prime minister—President Yeltsin delivered the address. His vigorous delivery demonstrated his own return to health following his long recovery from heart surgery. Although this was less noticed at the time, Yeltsin's address served notice that he was now about to launch a new wave of radical economic reforms. The message's theme of order in fact was related to a profoundly liberal outlook: that the many forms of bureaucratic control in Russia, through privileges, exemptions, and regulations, were stifling initiative. It specified the policy directions that the reformed government would emphasize. Yeltsin called for a radical overhaul of social spending so as to cut back on the numerous blanket entitlement programs that prevented targeted support to the truly needy. He also called for reform of the housing and utilities sector, so as to create incentives for maintenance and conservation on the part of residents. He demanded liberalization of the tax system and the system of industrial regulation.

The government's subsequent legislative initiatives were consistent with the president's message. Among Chubais's top priority requests for parliamentary action were reductions in spending on blanket social entitlement programs and a new, simplified tax code with lower marginal rates. The single most unpalatable pill that he demanded the parliament to swallow was a sharp reduction in budget appropriations for 1997. Appearing before the Federation Council on April 17, Chubais declared bluntly that federal revenues were running at scarcely more than half the planned level (and tax revenues at less than 40 percent of the expected amount), and that consequently a cut of some 100 trillion rubles in budgeted spending was essential. This amount is roughly $17 billion, or about 20 percent of the budget. Chubais played to the upper house's disdain for their counterparts in the lower house by lavishing praise on the senators' "realism" and urged them to resist the politicized policy-making characteristic of the Duma.

Chubais threatened the Duma with dissolution if it failed to pass the sweeping policy package that he proposed: radical budget cuts, changes in social benefits programs that would make entitlements contingent on household need, and a new tax code. The Duma balked and refused to pass most of Chubais's proposals. Through the rest of the year, the president and government used a combination of carrots and sticks to try to win the parliament's support for its fiscal reforms. Meantime the government worked to persuade the governors that more realistic tax and social policies would benefit the regions' economies as well.

The 1997 offensive displayed an invigorated president who had turned again toward market-oriented reform, but the strength of the opposition prevented him from achieving all of his objectives. Nonetheless, the campaign had some positive results. Tax collections rose and wage arrears fell as the government paid off its back wages to many groups of employees. Parliament passed some of the government's proposals. The slide in industrial production ended, and economic growth turned positive for the first time since 1989. However, Chubais's efforts to reduce profiteering by private bankers and state officials turned many of his former allies against him, and scandals involving some of his close associates weakened his political standing. Yeltsin responded by reducing Chubais's power. As in 1992, the impetus for market-oriented policy change in Russia remained dependent on the president's willingness to provide political shelter to a small team of appointed officials ready to take on powerful established interests in order to enact painful economic reforms.

Russia's economic reform policies thus have had some desirable and expected outcomes, and many undesirable and unexpected ones. These were only in part the consequence of policy choices by the central government over taxation, monetary policy, credit, and financial policy. They resulted as well from the loosening of legal restraints over regional and local governments, which often continued to impose confiscatory fiscal and social burdens on enterprises. To some extent, the human factor helps account for enterprises' unwillingness or inability to seek out new markets and new lines of production. And, as we noted at the outset, the heavily unfavorable conditions with which Russia had begun its difficult transition to a market economy further complicated the economy's response to the central government's reform policies. The situation strongly resembled that of those developing economies where economic growth is crippled by a perverse structure of incentives for investment, wealthy capitalists flaunt their riches in conspicuous consumption and send their profits to safe havens abroad, social inequality widens, and political pressures for government intervention to preserve living standards through indexed wages and secure employment in state-controlled firms become irresistible. Such economies do not escape the dilemma posed by the cycles of stagnation and inflation until economic incentives are restructured in such a way as to encourage growth-inducing behavior by society. While democratic institutions cannot guarantee that such a positive, self-reinforcing "virtuous cycle" of economic prosperity will result, their absence offers no assurance that economic conditions will improve.

Chapter 7

Toward the Primacy of Law

The Law-Governed State

One of the most important goals of reform in Russia is to establish a "law-governed state" *(pravovoe gosudarstvo)*. This is understood to mean a state in which both rulers and ruled would obey the law. Its opposite would be a condition where the rulers exercised power arbitrarily, freely violating the state's own constitutional and statutory rules. In the Soviet regime, Communist Party, KGB, and other officials commonly ignored constitutional and legal norms in exercising their power. When Mikhail Gorbachev declared the "law-governed state" to be one of the cardinal objectives of his reform program, therefore, it was a significant gesture.[1] Since 1991, the ideal has continued to attract lip service from Russian leaders even when they took actions violating the constitution. However, reforms of the constitutional and judicial systems have strengthened legal institutions by making them less subject to political abuse. The judicial system has grown more independent and effective. The legal principles essential to a democratic and pluralistic society have begun to be established. One of the most significant changes at the constitutional level is the creation of a Constitutional Court empowered to adjudicate disputes arising between the branches of government and between the federal level of government and the constituent territories. An important statutory change is the adoption of a body of law guaranteeing the right to private property.

Still, legal reform has confronted certain limits. For example, as of mid-1997, the Constitutional Court still had not seriously challenged presidential authority on any issue, and the right to private property remains bounded by numerous restrictions and exceptions: for instance, most land cannot be freely bought and sold. Law enforcement bodies were unable to reverse the huge increase in the volume and

---

[1]On the legal reforms of the Gorbachev period, see Donald D. Barry, ed., *Toward the "Rule of Law" in Russia? Political and Legal Reform in the Transition Period* (Armonk, NY: M. E. Sharpe, 1992); and Alexandre Yakovlev with Dale Gibson, *The Bear that Wouldn't Dance: Failed Attempts to Reform the Constitution of the Former Soviet Union* (University of Manitoba, Canada: Legal Research Institute, 1992).

impunity of crime, particularly organized crime. Some state officials were continuing to flout the law and constitution. Nonetheless, notwithstanding these problems, there were signs that in the centuries-long contest between law and arbitrary power, the sphere of law was expanding at the expense of that of state power. The slowness and difficulty of these changes indicated how deep were the political divisions among the population, and how lasting was the continuing imprint of the old regime's subordination of the legal system to its political interests.

As reformers defined it, the ideal of a law-governed state emphasized two basic objectives: individual rights should take precedence over the power of the state, and judicial power should be separated from legislative and executive power. Thus in a truly law-governed state, the judicial branch would guarantee the observance of citizens' rights by the state. Achievement of these two goals would represent a large step toward greater respect for law and away from the many abuses of law that the Soviet state committed in the past. For instance, the Bolshevik Revolution held that since "revolutionary justice" was higher than any written law, the rights and obligations of rulers and citizens must be subordinate to the political interests of the regime.[2] But this instrumental view of the law was not held by the Bolsheviks only. Many in and outside of President Yeltsin's administration have expressed the similar view that the goal of eliminating the foundations of communist rule took precedence over observance of the letter of the law: the populace must obey the law—but the authorities ("*vlast´*") could choose when to observe it and when not to, according to their judgements of expediency.

Not only the decades-long subordination of the legal system to the political interests of the communist regime impeded judicial reform. Law enforcement in Russia had weighted the scales of justice in favor of the *procuracy*—the agency charged with supervising the justice system, investigating crimes, preparing and prosecuting cases, and ensuring that the rights of *both* state *and* individuals were upheld—in comparison with both the judiciary and the defense attorneys (called the *advokatura*). Judicial reformers long had urged that judges be given greater authority with which to supervise pretrial investigations and court proceedings, and that individuals suspected or accused of criminal acts have more effective means to defend themselves.

The movement to reform legal institutions began well before Gorbachev.[3] After Stalin, Soviet political leaders and members of the legal profession attempted with

---

[2]Eugene Huskey identifies three competing influences on Soviet theory of law over the years: nihilism, statism, and legalism. Nihilism refers to the view that with the withering away of the state under full communism, law will disappear along with the agencies of state coercion. This doctrine, widespread in the early years of the revolution, was denounced with the rise of Stalin's machinery of state administration and terror in the 1930s, when the law was needed to give a framework of procedural regularity to the state's activities, and was replaced with a doctrine which held that the socialist state represented the highest stage of the development of law. The third idea, that of legalism, has tried to assert that law is a fundamental principle of society independent of either capitalism or socialism, and must serve as a constraint on the state in its relations with citizens. As Huskey notes, legalism will require widespread popular acceptance of the primacy of law, implying a long-term shift in political culture. See Eugene Huskey, "A Framework for the Analysis of Soviet Law," *Russian Review* 50:1 (January 1991), pp. 53–70.

[3]A seminal study of the influences on the development of law in the Soviet Union is Harold J. Berman, *Justice in the U.S.S.R.*, rev. ed. (Cambridge, MA: Harvard University Press, 1963).

mixed results to effect both institutional and statutory changes designed to make the rights of citizens somewhat more secure. One of the most important institutional changes made in the late 1950s was to place the secret police under stricter legal control. Extra-judicial trials, judgements, and sentences, which were a common practice in the time of Stalin's terror, were prohibited, and criminal defendants were granted important rights. New codes of criminal law and criminal procedure were adopted in the union republics, and official policy promoted a concept of "socialist legality." Like many slogans of the post-Stalin period, this was a formula meant to paper over contradictory policy goals. The idea was that the legal system should be less subject to political caprice than under Stalin, but still uphold socialist principles and practices. In fact, under the post-Stalin regime, the party and police could still use legal procedures as a way of legitimating actions taken in the interests of the regime's power and security. The criminal codes themselves contained articles providing legal penalties for "anti-Soviet agitation and propaganda" and for "circulation of fabrications known to be false which defame the Soviet state or social system." In the post-Stalin period these were frequently used against individuals whom the regime considered to be political dissidents.[4] Alternatively the authorities sometimes resorted to the practice of declaring a dissident mentally incompetent and forcibly incarcerating him in a mental hospital, where he could be further punished by being administered mind-altering drugs.[5] The continuation of these practices for political repression until the late 1980s attests to the inability of the law to protect the rights of individuals whom the party and KGB for any reason decided to suppress.

The struggle for legal reform continued even in the Brezhnev era, although results were meager, and accelerated in the Gorbachev and post-Soviet eras. As early as 1977, the new Brezhnev constitution included a principle that individuals had the right to sue state officials if the latter had violated their legal rights through an official action. As is common in Soviet and Russian constitutional practice, however, the constitutional text provided that the procedure for exercising this right would be prescribed by a statute to be enacted in the future.[6] The statute specifying the procedure for taking state officials to court, however, was long in arriving, and when it was finally adopted, at the end of the 1980s, it restricted the right in a subtle but significant way: the law made it impossible to go to court over the action of a "collective" body (such as a ministry, local government, or communist party committee), only for the action of an "individual." Since officials normally cloak their actions behind a veil of collective responsibility, the right to redress through lawsuits against officials was effectively nil. In April 1993, however, after the USSR collapsed, the Russian parliament passed a new statute providing that individuals whose rights had

---

[4]Full texts of these articles of the RSFSR Criminal Code together with commentary will be found in Harold J. Berman, ed., *Soviet Criminal Law and Procedure: The RSFSR Codes,* 2nd ed. (Cambridge, MA: Harvard University Press, 1972). Analogous articles were contained in the criminal codes of other republics as well.

[5]Sidney Bloch and Peter Reddaway, *Psychiatric Terror: How Soviet Psychiatry Is Used to Suppress Dissent* (New York: Basic Books, 1977).

[6]Alexander M. Yakovlev, *Striving for Law in a Lawless Land: Memoirs of a Russian Reformer* (Armonk, NY: M. E. Sharpe, 1996), p. 201.

been violated by state officials could sue for remedy regardless of whether the action had been taken by individual officials or organizational entities. In principle, at least, this represents a highly significant normative change.[7] As with other innovations in statutory law, however, its effectiveness will depend upon the willingness of judges and procurators to enforce it. The new federal criminal code which came into force in January 1997 makes it a criminal offense for state officials to withhold information from citizens concerning their rights; President Yeltsin singled this provision out in particular in his message to parliament in March 1997, calling on law enforcement bodies to uphold it.[8]

JUDICIAL REFORM

Full establishment of a law-governed state would mean that the abuses of the past would end and that no arm of the state would be able to bend or violate the law for political ends. In turn, this would require that the judiciary be independent of political influence. Through much of the Soviet period, however, judges were readily influenced by political pressures, some direct, some indirect. One of the most notorious forms of political influence was called "telephone justice." This referred to the practice whereby a party official or some other powerful individual would privately communicate advice or instructions to a judge on a particular case.[9] "Telephone justice" was symptomatic of a prevalent pattern in which the law was held in relatively low repute and legal institutions possessed little autonomy of the policy-implementing organs of government. The party might direct judges to be especially harsh in passing sentences on a particular class of criminals if it was attempting to conduct a propaganda campaign against a social problem, such as alcoholism, hooliganism, or economic crimes. A party official might direct prosecutors to crack down on some previously tolerated activity, or to gather incriminating evidence on someone it wished to punish. As Robert Sharlet has noted, in the past, pressures such as these often pushed adjudication over the line from full and vigorous enforcement of the law into abandonment of the law in pursuit of political ends.[10] By the same token, an unwritten but firmly observed norm made it impossible to prosecute a high-ranking member of the political elite without the party's consent. Even where

---

[7]Ibid., p. 202.

[8]*Poslanie Prezidenta Rossiiskoi Federatsii Federal'nomu Sobraniiu* (Moscow: n.p., 1997), p. 23.

[9]One of the early products of *glasnost'* was the exposure of "telephone justice" as a prevalent practice. See, for example, Arkadii Vaksberg, "Pravde v glaza," *Literaturnaia gazeta,* December 17, 1986, p. 13.

[10]Robert Sharlet, "The Communist Party and the Administration of Justice in the USSR," in Donald D. Barry et al., eds., *Soviet Law After Stalin, Part III: Soviet Institutions and the Administration of Law* (Alpen aan den Rijn, The Netherlands and Germantown, MD: Sijthofff and Noordhoff, 1979), pp. 321–392. In another article, Sharlet details several ways in which the regime acted to repress individuals for political acts, including administrative penalties such as job dismissal, officially sponsored acts of hooliganism, psychiatric internment, forced emigration, and criminal trials. See Robert Sharlet, "Party and Public Ideals in Conflict: Constitutionalism and Civil Rights in the USSR," *Cornell International Law Journal* 23:2 (1990), pp. 341–362.

improper political influence was not involved, many judges routinely accepted the prosecutor's case for a defendant's guilt, a reflection of the advantage of the procuracy over the defense in criminal proceedings.

Judicial reform is a good example of an area where the political reforms under Gorbachev set in motion—but did not bring to completion—significant policy changes. The legislative system comprising the USSR Congress of People's Deputies and Supreme Soviet (remember that it was in existence only from the spring of 1989 through the fall of 1991) enabled a group of newly elected deputies to bring about several significant changes in the principles of legal procedure. The Supreme Soviet's Committee on Legislation brought together a number of leading legal specialists who were eager to use the new legislative structures to enact liberalizing innovations in the judicial system; some of these changes had been discussed and advocated by legal reformers for a long time but had been blocked by conservative opponents. In 1989, in keeping with their aim of bringing the legal system closer to the ideal of a law-governed state, legal reformers succeeded in winning adoption of several symbolic and institutional changes in legal procedure that strengthened the rights of defendants. Among these were declaring that a defendant was to be considered innocent until proven guilty, giving a defendant the right to consult a defense lawyer from the moment that the preliminary investigation of his or her case began, and authorizing union republics to mandate jury trials in certain categories of cases.[11] These principles were intended to reduce the possibility of political abuses and to counteract the tendency for legal procedings to be biased in favor of the prosecution.

Alexander M. Yakovlev was one of the most prominent of the legal reformers who were newly elected to the parliament in 1989. Yakovlev wrote that when he presented the work of the Legislation Committee to the Supreme Soviet in the fall of 1990, proposing a change to the code of criminal procedure that would allow a person charged with a crime to hire a defense attorney from the moment the preliminary investigation began, rather than, as in the past, only when charges had been presented, Anatolii Lukyanov (chairman of the Supreme Soviet) presided over the proceedings. Although he was a leading member of the Communist Party and close to the conservative wing of the party establishment, Lukyanov's attitude toward this reform was favorable. The reform passed, although it was watered down under pressure from the procuracy. One year later, Lukyanov himself stood accused of participating in the conspiracy to overthrow state power that culminated in the August 1991 coup attempt by the "State Committee for the Defense of State Power." As soon as the criminal investigation began, he was granted access to an attorney.[12]

This incident points to a more fundamental observation about judicial reform. Because it serves ultimately to protect all citizens, regardless of their political persuasions, from the arbitrary exercise of political power, a fair and impartial judicial

---

[11]Donald D. Barry and Carol Barner-Barry, *Contemporary Soviet Politics: An Introduction,* 4th ed. (Englewood Cliffs, NJ: Prentice Hall, 1991), p. 160.

[12]Yakovlev, *Striving,* pp. 211–212.

system is an ideal that both right and left can agree upon. The obstacles to achieving it have less to do with the struggle between reformers and conservatives than with the struggle between change itself and the self-interest and inertia of existing state agencies. Often a consensus between legal experts of very different ideological camps emerges on the principles of judicial reform, but is opposed by the interest groups whose power would be threatened by reform, such as the procuracy and regional executives.

The new, short-lived USSR legislative bodies succeeded in enacting several important principles of judicial reform, but generally left it up to particular republics to decide on specific legislation to implement them. Accordingly, the Russian Supreme Soviet took up the work of drafting and adopting institutional changes. In the case of the right to counsel, it passed a new law which removed the limitations that had been set by the USSR legislature. Now accused persons could hire defense counsel immediately upon arrest and discuss their case with their attorney in confidence at any point during the investigation. The Russian parliament also adopted a law in July 1993—shortly before Yeltsin dissolved the parliament—providing that a defendant in a criminal case could request a jury trial. Below we will discuss the introduction of jury trials in more detail.

Another example of a reform enacted in a partial and tentative way in the 1989–91 period at the level of the federal, USSR government, and adopted more fully at the level of the Russian Republic by the transitional Russian parliament, is the creation of a constitutional court. While the USSR legislature only summoned enough political willpower to create a "Committee on Constitutional Supervision"—an entity somewhat stronger than an advisory council but not yet an actual court—the RSFSR legislature in 1991 adopted a law creating a regular Constitutional Court. This act was in accordance with a previously adopted constitutional amendment that provided for such an institution. The court was given the power to adjudicate the constitutionality of acts of the legislative and executive branches of state power, as well as of actions of the governments of the constituent regions, and of decisions of other courts. Although Yeltsin suspended the activity of the Russian Constitutional Court among his other actions of September–October 1993, he did not dissolve it. The new 1993 Russian Constitution preserved the institution of a Constitutional Court, and the new parliament passed a law defining its structure and powers. In 1995 the newly organized Court resumed its functioning. Below we will review the record of its decision-making.

There is a clear direction to the changes enacted in Russia's legal system since 1989. They have gradually expanded the effectiveness and independence of judicial institutions and strengthened individual legal rights. These institutional and statutory changes have not always pitted democrats against communists, but have met the firm resistance of powerful agencies of the state which lose a measure of arbitrary power when the sphere of social relations governed by law expands. After the first stabs at legal reform made by a nucleus of reform-minded specialists in the newly elected USSR parliament in 1989, successive Russian parliamentary bodies—the 1990–93 RSFSR Congress and Supreme Soviet, the 1994–95 Federal Assembly, and the post-1995 Federal Assembly—have continued to work on judicial reform. Parliament passed and the president signed a far-reaching reform of the judicial system. In addition, a number of important revisions to the criminal code, code of criminal procedure, and criminal corrections code have been adopted. It is fair to say that, together with the budget, judicial reform is one of the most important domains in which parliament has set national policy.

Let us now consider in more detail the nature of recent changes in five areas of the legal system: the procuracy; the judiciary; the *advokatura;* the Constitutional Court; and the reform of legal and procedural codes.

THE PROCURACY

Russia's legal system traditionally vested a great deal of power in the procuracy: the procuracy was considered to be the most prestigious branch of the law. A procurator is an official corresponding to a prosecutor in U.S. practice, but has wider powers and duties. Procurators are given sweeping responsibilities for fighting crime, corruption, and abuses of power in the bureaucracy, and for both instigating investigations of criminal wrong-doing by private citizens and responding to complaints about official malfeasance. The procuracy, more than the judiciary, has traditionally been seen as the principal check on illegal activity by officials and abuses of power. One of the procuracy's assigned tasks is to supervise all state officials and public organizations to ensure that they observe the law. In addition, the procuracy is responsible for overseeing the entire system of justice, including the penal system. Finally, the procuracy has the primary responsibility for bringing criminal cases to court. It supervises the investigation of the case, prepares the case for prosecution, and argues the case in court.

The procuracy has a difficult time coping with the comprehensive tasks that the law assigns to it, because of the difficulty of effectively supervising the vast economic bureaucracy and overcoming the entrenched political machines of central and regional governments. Lacking independence of the state which it is called upon to supervise, it is not an effective substitute either for full marketplace competition in the economy or for democratic accountability by office-holders to the citizenry.

The procuracy does have substantial political influence, which it exercises to protect its institutional prerogatives. Complaining that its resources leave it grossly underequipped to meet even the most elementary demands placed upon it, such as investigating the most serious violent crimes and bringing the offenders to justice, the procuracy's representatives plead for more resources rather than fewer responsibilities. The procuracy has even lobbied vigorously in defense of its institutional prerogatives when it believed that a proposed reform would weaken its power. For example, it has staunchly opposed such changes as introducing the right of an arrested person to consult with an attorney at any time during the pretrial investigation; it stubbornly opposed the adoption of the jury trial system; it fought reforms giving the courts the right to review procurators' decisions on the pretrial detention of criminal suspects; and it has battled successfully to retain the responsibility to supervise criminal investigations. The procuracy has won some of its fights, and in others it has succeeded in watering down reforms intended to strengthen other legal institutions. Both Russian statist tradition (including the experience of legal institutions in the Soviet and prerevolutionary eras) and Russia's use of a continental, or inquisitorial, system of legal procedure,[13] make it unlikely that reform would jeopardize the procuracy's central role in the legal system any time soon.

Because of the centrality of the procuracy in the Russian legal system, the position of Procurator General—who directs the procuracy throughout the country—is of enormous political sensitivity. Under the 1993 constitution, the president nominates a candidate for Procurator General to the Federation Council (the upper house of parliament), which has the power to approve or reject the nomination. Likewise, the president must receive Federation Council approval to remove the Procurator General. Only rarely in postcommunist Russia has the Procurator General taken a position directly opposing the president, but in one important precedent-setting instance at least, the procuracy did demonstrate its political independence. In February 1994, the State Duma approved an amnesty for several categories of persons, including those who were in jail awaiting trial for their participation in the attempted coups d'état of August 1991 and October 1993. The Duma was exercising the power of amnesty that the newly adopted Constitution had granted (although no law had yet been adopted specifying how this power was to be exercised). However, President Yeltsin expressed outrage at the decision and his advisors presented a variety of legal opinions purporting to demonstrate that the Duma's action was unlawful. Nonetheless, the Procurator General, Aleksei Kazannik, although believing that the Duma had exceeded its constitutional powers, complied with the Duma's decision, and ordered the release of the prisoners. When President Yeltsin pressured him to halt the release, Kazannik refused to comply and resigned instead. The release was duly carried out. Then, for several months afterward, the Federation Council refused to confirm Yeltsin's nominee for a successor to the position of Procurator General.[14]

---

[13]Inquisitorial procedure is contrasted with the adversarial model used in Anglo-American judicial proceedings. In the inquisitorial system, the presiding officer (judge, magistrate) actively seeks to determine the full truth of the case at hand rather than serving as an impartial referee in a contest between an accuser and a defendant. In Soviet and Russian tradition, the powerful procurator is the central figure in the proceeding; the judge may actively participate in questioning witnesses and ruling on matters of law, but the procurator is expected to serve the higher cause of justice and not simply to present the state's best case against the accused. From the standpoint of the Anglo-American tradition, this puts the procurator in a potentially contradictory position: while the procurator is required to ensure the legality of the entire proceeding (including, as appropriate, the obligation to defend the accused's rights), he or she must also seek to prosecute and win the case. Since the procurator has already overseen the pretrial investigation and concluded that there is sufficient evidence to proceed with the trial, it is extremely rare for a procurator to decide that the case lacks merit and should be dropped. From the standpoint of the Anglo-American criminal process, it is as though the procurator were wearing the hats of prosecutor, defender, judge, and jury all at the same time. In any case, in Soviet times, judges tended to be highly deferential to the procurators. As a result of the procuracy's power and prestige, very few criminal cases in the Soviet period resulted in acquittal, although in some cases, a higher court set aside a questionable conviction or remanded it for further investigation, effectively reversing a lower court's verdict.

For a discussion of the Soviet procuracy that places it in the context of both Western continental models and earlier, Russian historical precedents, see Berman, *Justice in the USSR*, pp. 238–247.

[14]Donald D. Barry, "Amnesty under the Russian Constitution: Evolution of the Provision and Its Use in February 1994," *Parker School Journal of East European Law* 1:4 (1994), pp. 437–461.

THE JUDICIARY

In contrast to the clout that the procuracy has traditionally wielded in Russia, the bench has been relatively weak and passive. Traditionally judges have been the least-experienced and lowest-paid members of the legal profession, and the most vulnerable to external political and administrative pressure.[15] Successful judicial reform, however, requires greater independence and discretion on the part of courts and less on the part of other institutions, including both law enforcement and extra-judicial bodies. If judges are to supervise the legality of arrests, ensure fair trials, and render just decisions in the face of intense external pressure, they will need greater legal training, experience, and social esteem. As Eugene Huskey observes, "independent courts are more difficult to create and nurture than representative institutions."[16] Judges are being called upon to raise their standards of professionalism, moreover, at a time of rapid change in law, legal procedure, and social conditions. In a few instances, judges have been murdered when they attempted to take on organized crime. Many judges have left their positions to take considerably higher paying jobs in other branches of the legal profession, but caseloads have risen substantially as a result of the widening of judicial power.

Policymakers recognize the importance of an independent judiciary: this is one of the points on which reformers and conservatives tend to agree. They disagree, however, on the conditions needed to achieve it. In the past, judges were formally elected by the local soviet of the jurisdiction in which they served; in actuality they were part of the Communist Party–controlled nomenklatura system and thus were appointed to their positions by the party staff. Reforms beginning in the late 1980s attempted to increase judges' independence of local political forces by lengthening their term of office and placing their election into the hands of the soviet at the next-higher level to that of the jurisdiction in which they served. But this still allowed powerful regional executives to sway judicial decision-making. Therefore reformers pushed a law through the Federal Assembly which put the power of appointment of all federal judges into the president's hands, although the president was to choose from among candidates screened and proposed by the Russian Supreme Court and Supreme Commercial Court.[17] The president was also obliged to take into account the suggestions of the legislatures of the regions where federal judges would serve.

The judicial reform law passed at the end of 1996 takes a significant step in the direction of establishing a single legal order throughout the Russian Federation.[18] Over the objection of some of the heads of the national republics and other regions,

---

[15]Eugene Huskey, "The Administration of Justice: Courts, Procuracy, and Ministry of Justice," in Eugene Huskey, ed., *Executive Power and Soviet Politics: The Rise and Decline of the Soviet State* (Armonk, NY: M.E. Sharpe, 1992), pp. 224–231.

[16]Ibid., p. 224.

[17]Peter H. Solomon, "The Limits of Legal Order in Post-Soviet Russia," *Post-Soviet Affairs* 11:2 (April–June 1995), pp. 96–97.

[18]Eugene Huskey, "Russian Judicial Reform after Communism," in Peter Solomon, ed., *Reforming Justice in Russia, 1864–1994* (Armonk, NY: M.E. Sharpe, 1997).

both chambers of parliament and the president agreed that all courts of general jurisdiction would be federal courts and would be guided by federal law, the federal constitution, and the instructions of the federal Supreme Court. The law establishes an institution of local justices of the peace *(mirovye sud'i)*, which had existed in Russia in the prerevolutionary era, but they may only consider the most minor cases. Thus in contrast to the United States' multi-tiered system of justice, Russia's law establishes a common federal judiciary throughout the country.

Until very recently, all judicial decisions in Russian courts in criminal cases were rendered by a judge and two "lay assessors." Lay assessors are ordinary citizens who are given paid leave from their place of work for a period of time in order to serve as co-judges in presiding over criminal trials; rather like juries in the Anglo-American legal system, their participation is a form of community service for citizens designed to bring the justice system closer to the values and interests of the public. The judge and lay assessors have equal votes in deciding on the verdict and sentence, but, in practice, lay assessors tend to defer to the superior legal knowledge and experience of judges. More recently, a serious practical problem has arisen with the system of lay assessors. Fewer and fewer citizens are willing to leave their jobs to serve as lay assessors, and many trials must be conducted without them.

A number of legal reformers have pushed to replace the old system of judges and lay assessors with a jury trial system in criminal justice. Those supporting the jury trial believe that it will help make citizens feel themselves to be part of the legal system, and, by extension, the political system, rather than passive and helpless objects of its will. Jury service would allow people to experience directly the responsibilities associated with civic self-government. Reformers assert that jury trials will also make the legal system more honest and effective, since it will be more difficult for police, investigators, prosecutors, and judges to get away with abuses and misconduct. Finally, they argue that the jury trial will redress the bias of criminal procedure by countering the strong advantages presently possessed by the procuracy and establishing a more level playing field between accuser and accused. As Alexander M. Yakovlev wrote:

> The introduction of jury trials into the Russian system of justice marked an important step from the inquisitorial principle to the accusatorial one. The jury represented the real third party, the umpire before whom the defendant and the prosecutor became equal. This meant a great deal in a country where the prosecutor personified the omnipotence of the state and the defendant was considered just a despised transgressor of the laws prescribed by the state, where the presumption was not of innocence but of guilt, and where to be accused meant mostly to be sentenced and punished.[19]

Trial by jury certainly is not a *necessary* condition of a democratic polity: other judicial fact-finding procedures are also perfectly consistent with democratic principles. But in Russia, where there are long traditions of local self-government and strong if latent norms of egalitarianism and communalism, the jury trial may indeed have subsidiary effects that reinforce democratic values. Moreover, it is an institution with substantial roots in Russian society. It was introduced and widely used in Russia as

---

[19]Yakovlev, *Striving*, p. 208.

part of the great reforms of the 1860s, and juries became an important instrument of civic participation.[20] Following the October 1917 revolution, however, the Bolsheviks eliminated the jury trial.

The reformers succeeded in winning parliamentary adoption of a law in 1993 which authorized the introduction of the jury trial in Russia. With help and advice from distinguished legal specialists in Moscow as well as the American Bar Association and other outside organizations, an experiment was launched in a number of regions in Russia to employ the jury trial in criminal cases when the defendant requested it. The details were based on the prerevolutionary Russian model more than on the Anglo-American system. For example, a Russian defendant can request a jury trial even if he or she admits guilt, hoping that the jury will recommend a lenient sentence. Preliminary reports indicate that juries seem to be somewhat more sympathetic to defendants than judges would be, a tendency noted also in Britain and America; and that the system may be having the desired effect of improving the quality of the judicial process. Acquittal rates have risen substantially. This is not surprising because although a majority of 7 votes out of the 12 jurors suffices to decide on a conviction, only 6 votes are needed to acquit.[21] The institution has since spread to more regions.

Generally, after many initial misgivings, legal experts in Russia and abroad have rated the experience of trial by jury favorably. Judging from the experience of the nine regions where it was introduced on a trial basis, the new system seems to be having a positive impact. Prosecutors are being forced to prepare their cases more carefully and defense attorneys have gained greater equality in judicial proceedings with the prosecution. In turn, the system is making the judges into neutral arbiters rather than participants in the prosecution.[22] Finally, as is the case in other countries using jury trials in criminal proceedings, it appears that juries are more lenient than would be judges. The initial fears that Russian juries would render harsh and vindictive verdicts against their fellow citizens are unfounded.[23]

Regional and republican courts serve to hear appeals from lower-level courts, as well as hear certain cases as courts of the first instance. Presiding over the entire judicial system is the Russian Supreme Court, which hears cases referred from lower courts and also issues instructions to lower courts on judicial matters. The Supreme Court does not have the power to challenge the constitutionality of laws and other normative acts adopted by legislative and executive bodies. That power is assigned by the constitution to the Constitutional Court. Under the constitution, judges of the Supreme Court are nominated by the President and confirmed by the Council of the Federation. There is a similar system of courts hearing cases arising from civil

---

[20]In one of the most famous trial verdicts in Russian history, Vera Zasulich, a young Russian revolutionary who had attempted to assassinate the chief of police of St. Petersburg in 1878, was acquitted by a jury following a fiery speech by her lawyer which scathingly denounced the injustices of the Russian government.

[21]Solomon, "Limits," p. 103.

[22]Stephen C. Thaman, "The Resurrection of Trial by Jury in Russia," *Stanford Journal of International Law* 31 (1995), p. 130. This is a very comprehensive survey of the new Russian jury system.

[23]Ibid., pp. 135–138.

disputes between firms or between firms and the government; these are called "commercial courts" *(arbitrazhnye sudy)*.[24] Like the Supreme Court, the Supreme Commercial Court is both the highest appellate court for its system of courts, as well as the source of instruction and direction to lower commercial courts. Also, as with the Supreme Court, the chairman of the Supreme Commercial Court is nominated by the president and confirmed by the Council of the Federation. Supervising all the courts, and providing for their material and administrative needs, is the Ministry of Justice. Its own influence over the justice system is limited, however, because it lacks any direct authority over the procuracy.

THE CONSTITUTIONAL COURT

Because there was no legal institution to ensure that legislative and administrative acts of the state conformed with the Soviet constitution, legal reformers in the Gorbachev period called for creating a constitutional court, equivalent to such bodies as the Constitutional Council in the French Fifth Republic or the Constitutional Court in Germany, which would rule on the constitutionality of laws and would adjudicate disputes between the union and the republics. As a cautious initial experiment with such a body, a constitutional amendment creating a "committee on constitutional supervision" *(komitet konstitutsionnogo nadzora)* was passed in December 1988. The committee's 23 members were elected in 1989 and it came into being on January 1, 1990. One of its early decisions was that there would be no communist party organization within it—a small symbolic indication that the committee's members considered the law superior to the dictates of the party. The committee's first official decision, in September 1990, found that Gorbachev had acted unconstitutionally when he had decreed earlier in the year that as president he had the power to forbid or allow demonstrations within Moscow. Gorbachev did not challenge the committee's ruling. But the committee found itself powerless to overcome the paralyzing effects of the "war of laws" between union, republican, and local government authorities. Moreover, since it was not a court, the committee could not adjudicate cases. Nevertheless, the committee's creation, and the care it exercised to avoid making decisions that would be flagrantly ignored, indicated that an important precedent had been established.

The committee dissolved along with the rest of the union government in December 1991. Russia, however, had established a constitutional court by a constitutional amendment in July 1991. The 15 members of the Constitutional Court were elected by the Congress of People's Deputies for life terms. The Congress elected a relatively young legal scholar, Valerii Zor´kin, as chairman.

The Russian Constitutional Court made several significant decisions in its first year of existence. Among them was a finding in December 1991 that an action of President Yeltsin merging two state ministries into a single body was unconstitutional; the president complied with the decision, establishing the precedent of effective

---

[24]It is misleading to call these "arbitration" courts, since they use judicial procedure, not arbitration, to adjudicate disputes. They arise out of the "arbitration boards" used in Soviet times to resolve disputes among economic entities such as enterprises and ministries, but now form a separate branch of the federal judiciary.

judicial review. Another very important decision concerned Yeltsin's decrees in the fall of 1991 outlawing the Communist Party and nationalizing its property. Reviewing the constitutionality of his actions, the court held in November 1992 that Yeltsin acted within his rights when he banned the Communist Party's executive organs but that he had no right to prohibit members of the party from forming primary organizations (PPOs or cells). With respect to the seizure of the party's property holdings, the court said that the state had the right to confiscate party property, but that in cases where the title of an asset was unclear or disputed, only the Supreme Commercial Court could rule on the state's rights. This decision was widely regarded as juridically sound and politically shrewd, in that it allowed both the communists and the president's side to claim victory. The court also, perhaps wisely, avoided taking sides on the president's assertion that the CPSU was itself unconstitutional. The court thus positioned itself as a politically neutral institution. This was no mean achievement in the tense, polarized environment of the time.

A final success for the court in the 1991–93 period was the intervention by its chairman into the severe confrontation which arose between President Yeltsin and the Congress of People's Deputies in December 1992 over the rightful powers of the president and the legislature. Chairman Zor´kin proposed a resolution of the crisis which both sides accepted: that a national referendum be held to decide on the basic constitutional principles to govern Russia. Here the chairman of the court came close to entering the political fray directly, but, unfortunately for the court, he did not stop there. Zor´kin soon came to agree with the chairman of the Supreme Soviet, Ruslan Khasbulatov, that the referendum should not be held after all, and supported the Congress's decision in early March 1993 to cancel it. When Yeltsin immediately thereafter appeared on television to declare his intention to suspend the Congress and impose special presidential rule, Chairman Zor´kin quickly issued a condemnation of Yeltsin's statement: but he did so without having reviewed the text of Yeltsin's proposed decree and on his own authority, rather than as a decision of the full membership of the court. When Yeltsin's decree was finally published a few days later, it had dropped the legally offensive provisions about declaring a special form of presidential rule and suspending the activity of the Congress. Perhaps Zor´kin's condemnation had helped to deter Yeltsin from taking such authoritarian steps. But it was clear that Zor´kin had acted precipitously, revealing a zeal more political than judicial.

Soon Zor´kin began supporting Khasbulatov's political positions routinely and thus forfeiting the court's claim to be politically neutral. In October 1993, following Yeltsin's decrees dissolving parliament and calling for new elections and a constitutional referendum, Yeltsin also suspended the operation of the Constitutional Court until the new constitution was ratified, new judges elected to fill vacancies, and a new law governing its activity was enacted by parliament. Under the new law on the Constitutional Court passed by parliament in summer 1994, there were to be 19 members and the members themselves would elect their own chairman. Thirteen of the original members of the court remained members (including Zor´kin, whom Yeltsin removed as chairman of the court but who continued to be a full member of it). The president then nominated six new justices to fill the vacancies on the court and presented them to the Council of the Federation for confirmation. The Council refused to confirm three and the stage was set for a new round of political bargaining between the president and parliament in order to find mutually acceptable candidates. Over the next 8 months, the president proposed 14 different candidates altogether, and the Federation Council rejected 8, until finally the full complement of 19 judges was confirmed. Thus for a year and a half, from October 1993 to March 1995, Russia lacked a functioning Constitutional Court. The accumulation of unresolved disputes between the executive and legislative branches and between the federal government and lower governments ensured that once the court did begin to operate again, it would face a heavy workload.

When the newly configured Court resumed work in March 1995 it quickly established its right to interpret the constitution in a variety of areas. It ruled on several ambiguous questions relating to parliamentary procedure (it found, for instance, that the constitution's provision that passage of a law required a majority "of the total number of deputies" in fact meant a majority of the total number of seats envisioned for that chamber, regardless of whether or not all the seats in the chamber were currently filled). It overturned some laws passed by ethnic republics within Russia, and struck down a provision of the Russian Criminal Code that limited individual rights. Generally, in cases involving disputes between individuals and state authorities, the court found in favor of individuals, thus widening and reaffirming the sphere of individual legal rights.

A major issue area in which the court has been active is in delineating the powers of territorial subjects of the federation and the federal government. Here it has generally steered a moderate course between the demands of the territories for autonomy and the interests of the unity of the country. A case in point is its January 1997 decision in the Udmurtia case. The legislature of the Udmurt Republic (an industrial territory located in the western part of the Urals area), passed a law in 1996 which dissolved the elected governments of the cities and districts throughout the republic, and required that the executive branch instead be headed by officials appointed by the republic government. The mayor of the capital city, joined by President Yeltsin and the Russian State Duma, took the matter to court and sought a ruling from the Constitutional Court. In January 1997 the Court ruled that while the Udmurt legislature was within its constitutional rights to pass a law on local government for the republic, it did not have the right to nullify the authority of previously elected government officials without taking into account the will of its citizens. An interesting outcome of the decision was that both sides claimed that they had won. For several weeks the regional legislature ignored the court's requirement that it reinstate the officials it had removed from office. Twice President Yeltsin went so far as to issue an edict demanding the region's compliance with the court's decision. After temporizing briefly, the region finally backed down.[25] Observers hailed this as an important precedent in establishing the court's legitimacy in adjudicating disputes arising from ambiguities in the rules of Russian federalism.

Of course, the most important challenge for the court has been the huge domain of presidential authority. Here the court has shown a politically prudent reluctance to challenge the president. One of its first and most important decisions concerned a challenge brought by a group of communist parliamentarians to the president's edicts launching the war in Chechnia. The court ruled that the presi-

---

[25] *Segodnia,* January 30, 1997; OMRI Daily Digest, March 10 and March 11, 1997.

dent had the authority to wage the war through the use of his constitutional power to issue edicts with the force of law. However, in other, less highly charged issues (which did not touch directly on national security), the court has established legal limits to the president's authority. For instance, the court ruled that the president may not refuse to accept a legally valid change of name adopted by one of the constituent subjects of the federation. And while the president, according to the court in another ruling, may exercise the power that he claimed for himself to appoint and dismiss the governors of the regions, he may not overturn laws adopted by regional legislatures calling for elections of their legislative and executive authorities. The court, it appeared, was gradually establishing its status as a legitimate source of judicial review power which could one day check potential abuses of presidential power.

Like its predecessor bodies—the USSR Committee for Constitutional Supervision and its own immediate 1991–93 precursor—the Constitutional Court proceeds by deciding whether to accept a case or inquiry. Usually if it does so, it has determined that a challenge to an existing law, decree, or official action has legal merit. It then holds hearings where parties and experts representing both sides of the issue make statements to the court. Each side listens to the arguments presented by its opponents, and seeks to counter them with superior arguments. The court then takes the information presented under advisement and renders its judgement. Dissenting opinions are published separately.

As presently constituted, the court tends to favor President Yeltsin in disputes with his political opponents. But because the new law on the court sets a 12-year limit to terms of membership (rather than, as in the 1991–93 phase, lifetime appointments), the political complexion of the court will likely evolve in response to changes in public opinion and the political tendencies of future presidents and parliaments. With time, the court's stature is likely to increase to the extent that it can steer the difficult narrow course between the Scylla of excessive zeal in upholding constitutional law that brings it into unwinnable confrontations with powerful state officials, and the Charybdis of excessive caution which may render it a passive instrument of the rulers.[26]

THE ADVOCATES

Change of another sort has been occurring among members of that branch of the legal profession who represent individual citizens and organizations in both criminal and civil matters: "advocates" *(advokaty)*. Comparable to defense attorneys in the U.S., Soviet advocates often oppose procurators and other state bodies in judicial proceedings, both in criminal and civil cases. As the volume of commercial transactions has grown, so has their activity in this area, as well as their opportunities for material gain.

---

[26]A thorough examination of the recent history and legal status of the court is the article by Herbert Hausmaninger, "Towards a 'New' Russian Constitutional Court," *Cornell International Law Journal* 28 (1995), pp. 349–386. Also see Robert Sharlet, "Transitional Constitutionalism: Politics and Law in the Second Russian Republic," *Wisconsin International Law Journal* 14:3 (1996), pp. 495–521.

The advocates have long enjoyed a certain corporate autonomy through their self-governing associations, called "collegia," through which they elect officers and govern admission of new practitioners. In the Soviet era, when they were supervised by the Ministry of Justice and the Communist Party, their ability to make effective use of the rights given them was limited. But in recent years, their independence and prestige have risen markedly, partly as a result of the new emphasis on legality under Gorbachev and the rapid growth of the private economic sector in the early 1990s. They have begun organizing their own professional association and codifying corporate ethical standards, often struggling with the Ministry of Justice to free themselves of interference from the state.

One of the most telling indicators of a change in the status of advocates was the revision of the previous rules limiting their earnings. As of September 1988, an advocate was theoretically free to take on as many cases as he or she wished and to charge any fee agreed upon with the client. With the new freedom to form cooperatives, some lawyers have begun forming legal cooperatives and competing with the collegia of advocates in dispensing legal assistance to citizens; the collegia of advocates have begun to organize their own for-profit legal cooperatives in response. Advocates have become popular guests on national television programs and have contributed a number of articles on legal subjects to mass periodicals, suggesting widespread popular interest in learning about the law.[27] New collegia of advocates, outside the old official collegia, have formed and have begun to compete with one another. Moreover, many advocates operate outside the structure of collegia, working in commercial firms licensed by local governments. The legal profession has become highly attractive to many young people for its opportunities to gain status and high incomes.

Like other features of the justice system, the status of the *advokatura* has been an object of intense controversy. For several years parliament has debated legislation that would regulate the profession of advocates. One thorny issue is whether the state should require that in any given jurisdiction, one and only one collegium of advocates be permitted to exist. Opponents argue that a monopoly on the provision of legal defense services would perpetuate the old system of state power and privilege and restrict the benefits of competition. Proponents argue that the system of a single, state-licensed collegium would ensure adherence to high standards of professionalism and probity in legal practice. Finally the presidential administration, the government, pro-government deputies in parliament, and the communists worked out the outlines of a system that they could all agree on. In any given region, a single collegium of advocates would have a monopoly on legal representation. Advocates themselves would be free to join the national professional association of advocates or not, and regional authorities could adopt their own laws and regulations on legal practice in their territories.

---

[27]An informative article about the advocates, based on interviews in the winter of 1988–89, is Michael Burrage, "*Advokatura:* In Search of Professionalism and Pluralism in Moscow and Leningrad," *Law and Social Inquiry* 15:3 (Summer 1990), pp. 433–478. An article analyzing the statute of the Russian Republic that governs the activity of the advocates is Harold J. Berman and Yuri I. Luryi, "The Soviet *Advokatura:* The 1980 RSFSR Statute with Annotations," *Soviet Union/Union Sovietique* 14:3 (1987), pp. 253–299.

STATUTORY REFORMS

In addition to these changes in judicial institutions, reformers have begun to make equally far-reaching modifications to legal codes and statutes. The objectives here are broadly consistent with those we have outlined and with the general goal of a "law-governed state" in Russia: they establish the legal principles needed for the protection of private property and the functioning of market institutions such as banks and stock markets; they extend individual legal and civil rights; they create legal conditions for the existence of civil society through laws on social and public organizations such as religious communities, political parties, charitable associations, labor unions, and business enterprises; and they have begun to lay the foundation for meaningful federalism through the adoption of laws such as that on local self-government. To a surprising degree, this statutory foundation of a democratic society has been achieved by the laborious process of bargaining and consensus-building among interested opposing groups rather than by decree or dictate. The area of consensus is larger than might be imagined, given the deep division between those who want to advance Russia toward a democratic, market-based society, and those who want to preserve the state-dominant, socialist character of Russia. As has been emphasized, the goal of a "law-governed state" is one that both reformers and conservatives can support. They can also agree that Russia requires a mixed economy in which both market institutions and state administrative power have a place. On other basic legal issues, however, reformers and conservatives cannot agree. The most important is the status of property in land.

Communists and their agrarian allies unite in opposition to the principle that individuals would be free to own, buy, sell, or securitize land. As we have seen in Chapters Five and Six, they have succeeded in blocking any real transformation of land relations in Russia. Under the Code of Land Law that they have been moving through parliament, the only land that an individual could own and freely dispose of would be the small plots used for gardens, garages, and country cottages—not agricultural land. At most, agricultural land could be subject to a lifetime, inheritable leasehold. Even though President Yeltsin has issued a number of decrees granting and redefining the rights of individuals to acquire and own farmland, local officials under the influence of the collective and state farm interests have prevented their implementation. Real change will require both an act of parliament and a concerted effort by the government to implement it. This will not occur until the communists and their allies lose their power to control parliamentary decisions on the issue.

Nevertheless, aside from this central and contentious matter, a number of other major legal questions have been decided through the parliamentary process. The first two parts of an entirely rewritten Civil Law Code have been passed by parliament and signed into law; the third and final part, dealing with property in land, remains mired in controversy. But it was notable that communists and reformers alike could agree on a set of legal principles defining a new body of civil law, because it enshrines the legal status of the private sector in the economy. Another important achievement was the new Criminal Code, finally signed into law by President Yeltsin in June 1996 following a year and a half of negotiations and deliberations among specialists, concerned state bodies, the presidential administration, and members of parliament. The new code brought the criminal law into closer conformity with the demands of the post-Soviet, postcommunist environment. It reduced the number of crimes subject to capital punishment, differentiated closely among crimes accord-ing to their seriousness, emphasized the need to protect individual legal rights as opposed to the state's interests, decriminalized some activities that had been illegal in the Soviet era, and at the same time introduced definitions of new types of crimes that had been previously unheard of, such as money-laundering and unfair compe-tition. "On the whole," Peter Solomon remarked about an earlier version of the draft, "the new code represented a moderate consensus document that promised to de-Sovietize and modernize Russian criminal law."[28]

Obstacles to the Primacy of Law

How close has post-Soviet Russia come to realizing the ideal of a "law-governed state"? While substantial change in legal institutions has occurred, the reforms have not yet succeeded in fully checking the arbitrary use of state power by executive authorities. Moreover, the severity of the problems of corruption and organized crime indicates how weak law enforcement is in the face of power and determined criminal interests. Rampant crime and corruption in turn discourage the spread of respect for the law and legal institutions.

The problem of crime and corruption is so serious that it requires separate attention. First let us note three other weaknesses in the capacity of the law and legal institutions to restrain the arbitrary exercise of power by the state. These are the extra-legal powers of the successor bodies of the KGB; the prevalence of sub-legal administrative rules and regulations issued by executive bodies; and the inclination of the president to wield his decree power in order to circumvent constitutional lim-its on executive power.

THE CONTINUING POWER OF THE KGB'S SUCCESSORS

Under Soviet rule, the Committee for State Security (KGB) had exercised very wide powers, including responsibility for both domestic and foreign intelligence. It also conducted extensive surveillance over society to prevent political dissent or opposi-tion, and in its exercise of power, it often operated outside the law. In October 1991, following the August 1991 coup (when the KGB chairman was one of the principal organizers of the seizure of power), Yeltsin dissolved the Russian republican branch of the KGB and divided it into two new agencies: the Ministry of Security, which was to guard the state's security in domestic matters, and the Foreign Intelligence Ser-vice, which took over the KGB's foreign espionage and intelligence functions. The reorganization altered the structure and mission of the successor bodies, but never were they subjected to a thorough-going purge or turnover of personnel. Like Gor-bachev, Russian leaders have preferred to cultivate a close political relationship with the security agencies rather than to antagonize them. Although many of the

---

[28]Solomon, "Limits," pp. 93–94.

archives containing documents on the past activities of the secret police[29] have been opened to inspection, thus exposing many aspects of the Soviet regime's use of terror, no member or collaborator of the security service has ever been prosecuted legally for these actions. None of the KGB's informers have been exposed to public judgement. The position taken by the KGB under Gorbachev and its successor agencies under Yeltsin is that the security police were themselves a victim of arbitrary rule and terror under Stalin, and therefore that today they strongly uphold the rule of law. Whether this position is credible is another matter. For example, the archival documents turned over by the Ministry of Security to the Sakharov Foundation detail the KGB's close surveillance of the distinguished scientist and human rights activist right up until his death in December 1989.

Through the 1990s the successor bodies were further reorganized. In 1993 the Ministry of Security was reorganized as the Federal Counter-Intelligence Service, and in 1995 President Yeltsin reorganized it yet again into the Federal Security Service (FSB), assigning it comprehensive duties and powers. Some idea of how wide-ranging its powers are is suggested by the description of the new body's mandate given by a senior Russian government official to the press. The new FSB, he stated, would "be able to infiltrate foreign organizations and criminal groups, institute inquiries, carry out preliminary investigations, maintain its own prisons, demand information from private companies, and set up special units and front enterprises." Its duties would include foreign intelligence activities to boost Russia's "economic, scientific, technical, and defense potential" and "to ensure the security of all government bodies."[30]

The FSB was only one of the successor bodies to the KGB demonstrating an inclination to aggrandize its power. Among the others were the Foreign Intelligence Service, which inherited the KGB's mandate for collecting and analyzing foreign intelligence, and the Federal Administration for the Protection of State Information (FAPSI), which is responsible for ensuring the security of state telecommunications. FAPSI is believed to provide telecommunications services to a number of governmental and commercial organizations, giving it unusually privileged intelligence-gathering opportunities.

In addition, there were two services responsible for providing security for state buildings and state officials. One of these, the presidential guard service, was headed by a close friend of President Yeltsin, Alexander Korzhakov, until Yeltsin fired him from that position in June 1996. Korzhakov had shown an alarming eagerness to offer advice, commentary, and demands on a number of policy matters—urging

---

[29]The KGB is the institutional successor to the powerful instruments of coercion that the regime has used since the revolution to eliminate its political enemies, including the Cheka (created within six weeks of the October Revolution), the GPU, and the NKVD. Today, according to its press representatives, the KGB has nothing in common with these predecessor organizations, and is dedicated to upholding the law while carrying out its mission of defending the security of the state and its citizens. Often KGB press representatives discuss the modern efforts of the organization in combating drug trafficking and terrorism. Evidently keen to be portrayed in a positive light in the media, the KGB promoted itself in the 1980s as a heroic organization, a body performing its difficult duties with scrupulous respect for the law as well as ingenuity and courage.

[30]OMRI Daily Digest, April 7, 1995.

Prime Minister Chernomyrdin to slow down economic reform, for instance, and floating an opinion that presidential elections were a needless source of tension and expense and should be cancelled. Leaning heavily on his close relationship with the president, Korzhakov engaged in various Kremlin plots and intrigues to advance the interests of a coalition of antireformers. After firing Korzhakov, Yeltsin then merged the two state protection services into a single agency.

The activities of the various successor organs of the KGB, therefore, have indicated that by dividing up the KGB into separate federal agencies, Russia has not necessarily increased their subordination to the law.

SUB-LEGAL ADMINISTRATIVE ACTS

The second impediment to the primacy of law is of a different order, reflecting less the repressive extra-judicial legacy of a once-revolutionary regime than the immense inertia of a heavily bureaucratized state. As Eugene Huskey has shown, the lawmaking authority of parliament is frequently vitiated by the practice of administrative agencies to issue normative acts—decrees, regulations, instructions, orders, directives, circular letters, and many other kinds of official and binding rules—applying not only to subordinates in the same agency but, often, to other governmental agencies and to Soviet citizens generally. Some indication of the magnitude of this practice is suggested by the fact that over the first 70 years of Soviet power, the USSR legislature adopted fewer than 800 laws and decrees, whereas over the same period, the union-level government issued hundreds of thousands of decrees and other normative acts.[31] In 1985, according to one estimate, there were 27,000 legal norms enacted by the USSR Council of Ministers that were still valid.[32] Tens of thousands more binding rules issued by particular government ministries and state committees also remained on the books. The profusion of rules and regulations, complementing, interpreting, and often contradicting one another, creates ample opportunities for evasion, as well as generating pressures for intervention through the authority of powerful individuals to cut through the jungle of red tape. Patronage and protection often serve to compensate for the paralyzing effects of anonymous bureaucratic power.

Moreover, as Huskey shows, two other features of the Russian rulemaking system reduce still further the subordination of state power to law: the tendency for much of the rulemaking by bureaucratic agencies to be secret, and the fact that rulings issued by lower levels of the bureaucracy often take precedence over the law. As he observes, the bureaucratic hierarchy "may also be conceived of as an iceberg. A small portion is visible but obscured from view is that vast body of departmental instructions that gives direction to Soviet life. As one goes further down the pyramid, *glasnost´* lessens. There is, to put it in an American context, no *Federal Register.*"[33] Most regulations are issued in numbered copies to a small list of authorized personnel, with most of these being classified "for internal use only." Even the procuracy, which is given official

---

[31]Eugene Huskey, "Government Rulemaking as a Brake on Perestroika," *Law and Social Inquiry,* 15:3 (Summer 1990), p. 421.

[32]Ibid., p. 422.

[33]Ibid., p. 424.

responsibility for ensuring the legality and consistency of governmental regulations, lacks full access to all legal acts of the bureaucracy.[34] The other element of government rulemaking, according to Huskey, that undermines legality is the tendency for laws passed by the parliament to remain dead letters until they are "interpreted" and given concrete, binding content by bureaucrats in state agencies. Although the rules and regulations that the departments issue are supposed to be consistent with both the language and spirit of the law, in practice they frequently gut it, so that reforms adopted by the legislature may be eviscerated and weightless by the time they reach the level where they are supposed to be acted upon.

The 1993 constitution does not give parliament an explicit right to oversee *(kontrolirovat´)* the executive branch, a power considered essential to the checks and balances between the American legislative and executive branches. However, as parliament has gained experience in using the powers it does have—particularly the budget process, investigations, hearings, and the Auditing Chamber[35]—it has gradually acquired greater de facto power to oversee the bureaucracy's compliance with legislative requirements.

The bureaucracy's ability to derail the implementation of policy decisions made at the center not only contradicts the primacy of law, but also hampers the ability of a reform-minded central leader to ensure the implementation of his wishes. Because of the power of the bureaucracy to issue regulations on how laws are to be implemented, it can distort and water down a leader's reform policies. After the Law on State Enterprise was passed in 1987—which attempted to expand the freedom of enterprises to plan their own production and trade with other producers—a commission was formed to review all relevant government instructions and to annul those that were found to contradict the law. Over 1,000 legal acts had been fully or partially rescinded by the beginning of 1989, and another 3,500 were being scheduled for action.[36] Nonetheless, the abject failure of the Law on State Enterprise— conceived as a centerpiece of Gorbachev's early economic reforms—to alter significantly the relations between enterprises and ministries, suggested the continuing ability of the state bureaucracy to subvert intended reforms that would strip it of its power. Much the same pattern has continued into the post-Soviet period; laws passed by parliament still often take the form of highly general "wish lists" of objectives, leaving it to the state bureaucracy to translate these into specific binding rules.

PRESIDENTIAL DECREE POWER

A third threat to the primacy of law is the willingness of the president to ignore constitutional or statutory limitations in the pursuit of political ends. The clearest example, of course, is President Yeltsin's set of decrees in September and October 1993 that dissolved parliament. They were unconstitutional, even though they called for

---

[34]Ibid., pp. 424–425.

[35]The Auditing Chamber (*Schetnaia palata*) is an independent auditing agency created by the parliament, comparable to the General Accounting Office in the United States. Like the GAO, it serves the legislative branch by conducting audits of the books of executive agencies and presenting reports of its findings.

[36]Ibid., p. 429.

a national referendum to determine the constitutional principles that Russia was to adopt for the future. Yeltsin further authorized the army to use crushing military power to suppress the resistance to these decrees, and for many citizens, the artillery shelling of the parliament building in October 1993 was more than the outcome of a national tragedy—it was the final sign that President Yeltsin was willing to use dictatorial means to defend his power. Yet his actions had the result of resolving a constitutional crisis and allowing a new set of constitutional institutions to begin operating, their legal legitimacy buttressed by the outcomes of popular elections. But his defiance of the law set a dangerous precedent for a future president.

Apart from the high-stakes but hopefully unique case of September–October 1993, there is another and less spectacular threat to the primacy of law in the president's power. As we have seen, the constitution grants the president the right to issue decrees (edicts, or *ukazy*) which have the force of law unless and until the parliament passes legislation that supersedes them. The constitution stipulates, however, that presidential decrees may not violate existing law. In April 1996 the Constitutional Court ruled that the president may issue an edict to "fill gaps" in existing legislation. That is, where the constitution calls for a federal law but parliament has not yet acted, a presidential decree may establish legal standards until a law is adopted that supersedes it.[37]

President Yeltsin has used his decree power extensively in matters such as privatization, banking reform, and criminal procedure, although he has invited the Federal Assembly to adopt substitute legislation in these areas. Opponents have accused Yeltsin of exceeding decree-making power and have claimed that he has in fact violated current law. As we have seen, the president's decree power enables him to modify the status quo without action by the parliament and then to use his veto power under the constitution to block opposing parliamentary action. The combination of decree and veto power makes the president very powerful in influencing legislation, since he can threaten to veto legislation he dislikes and to govern by decree (except for those areas where the constitution requires that policy be set by a federal law). Moreover, his right to initiate legislation, his ability to threaten to dissolve the Duma (e.g., by putting up patently unacceptable candidates for prime minister and forcing the Duma either to confirm one or be dissolved), and his ability to block a bill in the Council of the Federation by using carrots and sticks, mean that he has leverage over the legislative process at a number of pressure points.

---

[37]This was the view of a majority of the court in a decision on a set of challenges to a presidential decree regulating elections of chief executives in the territorial subjects. The court struck down, however, a key part of the ukaz which demanded that the territories obtain the president's permission before they held gubernatorial elections. They were entitled to do so without higher level approval, the court held, so long as they had enacted their own appropriate legislation.

That the scope of presidential decree power is still contested was evident in the blistering dissent of one member of the court. He heatedly disagreed with the majority's claim that the president possessed the right to "fill gaps" in existing legislation. If the constitution requires a law that does not currently exist, he declared, the president can introduce a bill to parliament and urge parliament to pass it, but the president may not usurp the rightful constitutional authority of parliament to make law.

The distance between the majority and minority opinions on this major issue indicates that the subject of the president's decree authority will remain disputatious for some time.

See *Sobranie zakonodatel´stva Rossiiskoi Federatsii*, no. 19, 6 May 1996, item 2320, pp. 4950–4960.

A vivid example of the president's use of his decree power to override existing constitutional and legal principles was his June 1994 decree aimed at fighting organized crime. This granted the police extraordinary powers to search homes and businesses and seize records and documents whenever they possessed evidence of involvement in organized crime. Moreover, the authorities could arrest and detain suspects for up to 30 days without charging them. Notwithstanding the code of criminal procedure and constitution, not even a judge's warrant was required for these actions; the procuracy's own authority was sufficient. The president's decree undoubtedly reflected the public pressure to combat organized crime, and he did invite parliament to pass a law superseding the decree. The law, however, remained mired in controversy within the Duma, partly because of the reluctance of both reformers and communists to authorize extraordinary powers for the police.

The June 1994 decree was patently unconstitutional, and lower court judges even held it to be so, but Yeltsin waited until June 1997 before rescinding it. Still, he did finally rescind it, at the urging of his own legal administration and the Human Rights Commissioner, as well as at the assurances of the procuracy that the decree was entirely useless in fighting crime.[38] Moreover, a great many presidential decrees annull one or more previous decrees, usually as a result of the adoption of a federal law superseding the decrees' provisions. Thus there is reason to believe that as the volume of legislation increases to meet the needs of the postcommunist system, the president's decree authority will become narrower and more technical.[39]

Some indication of the scale of the president's use of his decree power may be seen in the fact that over the 1994 and 1995 period, parliament passed 461 laws, 282 of them being signed by the president. Around 100 of the latter were major regulatory or distributive policy acts in areas such as budget appropriations, social welfare, and reform of state political institutions, law enforcement, and the judicial system.[40] Over the same period, the president issued approximately 4,000 decrees, most of them of minor significance, such as appointing individuals to state positions or awarding honors for merit. A few, however, were highly important because they shaped major national policy. These included the terms of the privatization of shares of the state television and radio company, the delineation of powers of regional government, and the determination of which enterprises were subject to privatization for cash. Often the parliamentary opposition vehemently objected to the president's use of his decree power to bypass the regular lawmaking process, but had no legal means to counter it.[41]

---

[38] *Segodnia,* June 18, 1997.

[39] This is the position, for instance, of a rising young member of the Our Home Is Russia faction in the Duma, Vladimir Ryzhkov. See his article, "Mify i skazki sovremennoi politiki," *Nezavisimaia gazeta,* 30 May 1995.

[40] *Segodnia,* December 23, 1995.

[41] In spring 1996, after President Yeltsin issued an edict reaffirming earlier edicts on the right of members of collective and state farms to acquire parcels of land from the farm as private property, the communist–agrarian coalition in the Duma hurried through the legislature a law "clarifying" the procedures under which farmers could exercise these rights. The "clarification" had the effect of annulling farmers' right to own land as property.

The greatest threat that presidential power poses to the primacy of law is not the *strength* of the president's decree-making power, however, but the *weakness* of his ability to control the bureaucracy. By invoking presidential authority, officials of the executive branch sometimes act with impunity. A clear instance is the savage brutality of the federal army's military operations in Chechnia. Until hostilities ceased in the fall of 1996, the massive bombardments of Grozny and other cities, against villages and refugees fleeing the fighting, and against other civilian targets, aroused outrage in Russia and throughout the world. At times the president appeared powerless to control these operations. Some of the president's commands to the army to stop bombing were simply ignored, with the army denying that there was any combat going on at all—merely "mopping up operations" against "a few bandit units." Following a brief visit to Chechnia in August 1996, President Yeltsin's newly appointed national security advisor, General Alexander Lebed´, bitterly accused the federal authorities of utter incompetence in prosecuting the war. The combination of unrestrained violence together with severe military ineptitude indicates that for all his nominal power, the president has little actual ability to control the conduct of the armed forces. It is this breakdown in political and legal accountability for the exercise of power by state authorities that is the gravest consequence of the overcentralization of power.

CRIME AND CORRUPTION

Both criminality and official corruption have been stimulated by a substantial rise in the power of organized crime. But although organized crime has been discussed extensively in the Western and Russian press, reliable indicators of its scale are elusive.[42] By all accounts, however, organized crime is deeply entrenched and broad in scope. A recent article in the newspaper *Izvestiia* observed:

> 'Godfathers' of the mafia exist in many countries, but there for the most part they control illegal business, such as narcotics, gambling, thieves' hang-outs. Here they have established total control over ordinary commerce. As a result we pay for our daily bread, for our basket of consumer goods, around 20–30 percent more. In the farmers' markets exotic fruits cost less than tomatoes and cucumbers—because of the tribute to the mafia that is paid. Thus the population is supporting two states with its money—the legitimate government and the criminal one—that exist in parallel. Or rather, the legal state more and more depends on the power of the criminal one.[43]

Public outrage over the scale of organized crime prompted President Yeltsin to issue the June 1994 decree mentioned earlier granting the procuracy and police extraordinary powers of search and seizure until it was rescinded by another decree in June 1997. Apart from its flagrant violation of the constitution, it was only one

---

[42]A useful but somewhat lurid account of the subject is the book by Stephen Handelman, *Comrade Criminal: Russia's New Mafiya* (New Haven, CT: Yale University Press, 1995).

[43]"Neizvestnaia voina . . . s korruptsiiei," *Izvestiia*, October 22, 1994.

more in a series of anticrime campaigns which were aimed at fighting organized crime, but which were ineffective in making significant headway against it.

A disturbing report on the severity of organized crime was given by Interior Minister Anatolii Kulikov at a press conference in June 1997. Kulikov declared that there were some 9,000 criminal groups in Russia with around 100,000 members. He asserted that the number of registered crimes by organized groups had increased by almost 95 percent during the previous 5 years. He claimed that law enforcement bodies were making headway in solving crimes but acknowledged that some 3,700 murders committed in the first half of 1997 alone remained unsolved.[44]

Government Corruption One reason government laws and decrees have done relatively little to reduce organized crime is that the law enforcement organs themselves are deeply corrupted. In one widely cited incident, in the summer of 1995, the then newly appointed Interior Minister, Anatolii Kulikov, sent out a truck carrying a cargo of vodka on a 700-kilometer trip across southern Russia. Out of the 24 times that police stopped the truck, they had demanded bribes 22 times. As a result of his investigations, General Kulikov fired a number of senior police officials, including four generals. One official fired was the deputy chief of police of Moscow.[45]

The chairman of the Duma Committee on Security, Viktor Iliukhin, declared in April 1994 that in 1993, some 1,500 officials were investigated or arrested in connection with corruption charges. About 50 percent of them were high-ranking employees of the executive branch, and 27 percent were officers in law enforcement agencies. Corruption pervades government more generally. Stephen Handelman observes that "In 1993, more than forty-six thousand officials from all levels of government in Russia were brought to trial on charges relating to corruption and abuse of office, according to Acting Procurator Aleksei Ilyushenko."[46] A sad comment on the severity of corruption was the fact that Procurator Ilyushenko himself was arrested in February 1996 and charged with taking bribes.[47]

As the investigations of official corruption continued, the Interior Ministry's own internal security unit announced in June 1996 that over 1,200 police officers had been convicted of crimes during 1995, 533 for abuse of official position.[48] The First Deputy Procurator General disclosed at a conference in July 1996 that 14,000 corruption cases had been initiated over the preceding two years, and one in three cases involved state officials.[49]

Public perception that the new post-Soviet elite is more corrupt than the old communist elite is reinforced by the enormous growth of opportunities to use public office for private gain and the weakness of enforcement of existing rules. Public

---

[44]RFE/RL Newsline, Vol. 1, No. 53, Part I, 16 June 1997.

[45]OMRI Daily Report, August 23, 1995.

[46]Handelman, p. 285.

[47]OMRI Daily Digest, February 26, 1996.

[48]OMRI Daily Digest, June 19, 1996.

[49]OMRI Daily Digest, July 9, 1996.

scrutiny of official behavior is weakly developed and many scandals unearthed by the press peter out with no action taken. Many gray areas exist where the standards of legal conduct are unclear or unwritten, allowing practices to flourish that would be illegal on conflict-of-interest grounds in other societies. Public officials commonly hold gainful positions as shareholders, board members, consultants, or employees of private firms with which they have close working ties. Members of parliament write laws affecting organizations in which they have a personal financial stake. Members of the government maintain close relations with executives in state industries. Senior government officials demand large "fees" for meetings with Western businesspeople. In the atmosphere of unregulated and cozy ties between business and government, suspicion is rampant, and many officials are reluctant to play a sucker's game by not taking advantage of opportunities for self-enrichment which, they assume, everyone else is enjoying.

Lax Budgetary Practices   Budget practices unfortunately encourage the exercise of unaccountable influence over the allocation of resources. Particularly vulnerable to abuse is the practice of creating special-purpose off-budget funds in order to shelter state revenues from legislative scrutiny. These can serve, in effect, as huge slush funds for public officials. This device has become particularly popular as the development of private property has created huge opportunities for quick profits through favorable government licensing, privatization, taxing, and other policies. Now and then an indication of the scale of the problem is revealed. At the federal level the two major categories of protected funds are those for social support and those under ministry control. Local governments also sometimes create their own off-budget funds.

Vast streams of revenue are removed from outside scrutiny this way. A sum equal to almost two-thirds of the state budget goes into social funds such as the pension fund, the employment fund, and the medical insurance fund. They are channeled not through the state treasury but are often held in commercial banks, often at well-below-market rates of interest. This, plus the fact that they are not subject to regular audits by parliament or the government's own controllers, renders them susceptible to misallocation. A bill which would require all off-budget funds to be approved by the Duma, ensure that they were kept in the state treasury rather than commercial banks, and subject them to regular audits, was proposed in parliament, but could not muster enough votes to survive a first reading. The president, in his message to parliament in 1997, again urged that these off-budget funds be placed under budgetary control.

Conclusion

The reformers' ideal of a "law-governed state" has not been realized in practice. The precedence of law over political and administrative power in the state would reduce the ability of officials in the bureaucracy, the security police, and the president to exercise power arbitrarily. Respect for the law on the part of officials and citizens would help establish habits of civic initiative and responsibility, which are essential to democracy. These are among the reasons that legal reformers have actively propagated the ideal of the "law-governed state" and have taken several steps that begin to put the ideal into practice. As with many other institutional reforms, however, success in the realm of law will ultimately require large-scale changes in political culture and behavior.

The radical implications of a shift to a law-governed state have generated opposition from a number of entrenched interests both inside and outside the state. In some cases the opposition is due to bureaucratic unwillingness to relinquish administrative power, in other cases it stems from the lucrative opportunities that lax and corrupt fiscal practices create for self-enrichment by officials. The continuing hold among many who wield power and among many in the population of the traditionally skeptical attitude toward the law—the view of the law as no more than an instrument of the policy goals of those in power—may also impede movement in this direction. However, there is ample evidence that a substantial base of support exists for the concept of law as a set of impartial rules to which both state officials and ordinary citizens would be subordinate. Despite serious limitations and setbacks, a slow and long-term movement in the direction of the rule of institutions rather than individuals can be discerned since the fall of the Soviet order.[50] As we have seen in this chapter, both reformers and their opponents can agree on a core set of legal principles that are essential to the primacy of law. They have enacted a number of reforms which have strengthened law and legal institutions. The constitution now corresponds much more closely to the actual political system than it did in the Soviet era, and some of the changes in legal institutions and codes strengthen civil rights. But Russia remains far from being a "law-governed state." The weakness of law enforcement and old habits of treating the law instrumentally continue to impede progress toward the primacy of law.

---

[50]Robert Sharlet, "Reinventing the Russian State: Problems of Constitutional Implementation," *The John Marshall Law Review* 28:4 (Summer 1995), p. 786.

Chapter 8

Whither Russia?

Interpreting Russian History

Observers who offer interpretations of the direction of Russia's political development generally belong to one of two schools of thought. One emphasizes Russia's uniqueness, shaped by the long history of Russian autocracy and the country's vast physical expanse. Russia's future is seen as largely determined by its past. As Russia was, so shall it be. Those adhering to this way of thinking remind us that generation after generation, Russia's political culture has reinforced habits and values which perpetuate authoritarian rule: submissiveness to authority, unwillingness to assume risk and responsibility by the community, suspicion and mistrust in personal relations, passive acceptance of the centralized state. This system of values is relieved by occasional outbursts of fierce rebelliousness which, though, are not necessarily democratic. Russia's political history, according to this outlook, does not lead in a straight line toward a widening of the sphere of personal liberty and respect for law. Rather, over time, Russia oscillates between long periods of autocratic stasis and decay and moments of radical egalitarianism directed against the existing order. The cultural syndromes of patrimonial rule, clannish court politics, and mutual alienation between rulers and people, meanwhile, form recurrent features of Russian politics.[1]

The alternative view holds that history in Russia, as elsewhere, must obey universal laws of social development. With social modernization come certain irrevocable changes in people's outlooks and demands, and different demands on social organization, those who belong to this school of thought would argue. Like other authoritarian regimes, the USSR was affected by the greatly accelerated international mobility of capital, values, information and ideas, which affects the political legitimacy and economic viability of every state.[2] An authoritarian regime cannot forever hold back

---

[1]A fascinating and influential essay demonstrating the recurrence of certain cultural themes in Russia's history is Edward L. Keenan, "Muscovite Political Folkways," *Russian Review* 45:2 (April 1986), pp. 115–181. An important interpretation of Russian history arguing for the continuity of the drive for patrimonial, imperial, and autocratic rule, is Richard Pipes, *Russia under the Old Regime* (New York: Charles Scribner's Sons, 1974).

[2]Lucian Pye, "Political Science and the Crisis of Authoritarianism," *American Political Science Review* 84:1 (1990), pp. 3–20.

the tides of history. From this perspective, an observer would predict that given the right conditions—peace abroad, and stability and appropriate institutions at home—Russia will experience a progressive, if uneven, evolution toward wider individual rights and responsibility through liberal democracy and the market economy.

Moreover, some historians also suggest that Russia's traditions include much more than simply the one-way unfolding of the autocratic principle. They point out that Russia's history also includes institutions of community self-government in city-states such as Novgorod; that in the nineteenth century Russia experienced rapid economic growth and a wave of liberalizing political and legal reforms; and that in the twentieth century, regardless of the political intentions of the Soviet rulers, a large base of support developed for such bourgeois institutions as private property and representative government.

We choose our point of reference depending on which interpretation we prefer: we decide how to compare Russia with other countries, and which aspects of Russian history to emphasize. Economists generally insist that economic laws are universal, and therefore the same formulas for macroeconomic stabilization that work in Latin America and Southern Europe must work in Russia.[3] For their part, many political scientists see Russia as a case of a partial transition to democracy from a communist form of authoritarian rule. In this light, some aspects of Russia's recent past can be compared with the abrupt political turnabouts experienced by Brazil, Argentina, Peru, and other major Latin American states over the last 20 years.[4] As is the case with other states that have replaced authoritarian regimes with new democratic institutions, Russia's newly formed political system must withstand the political pain of wrenching economic restructuring.[5]

Those who stress the uniqueness of Russia's political development say that Russia cannot be understood by comparison with other countries.[6] They would argue that "transition" in Russia has occurred only at the most superficial level and that in

---

[3]For instance, see the World Bank's World Development Report (1996), which focuses on economic transitions from communist to market systems.

International Bank for Reconstruction and Development [The World Bank], *World Development Report 1996: From Plan to Market* (New York: Oxford University Press, 1996).

[4]Samuel P. Huntington, *The Third Wave: Democratization in the Late Twentieth Century* (Norman, OK: University of Oklahoma Press, 1991).

[5]Adam Przeworski, *Democracy and the Market: Political and Economic Reforms in Eastern Europe and Latin America* (Cambridge: Cambridge University Press, 1991), p. 191; see also idem, "The Games of Transition," in Scott Mainwaring, Guillermo O'Donnell, and J. Samuel Valenzuela, eds., *Issues in Democratic Consolidation: The New South American Democracies in Comparative Perspective* (Notre Dame, IN: University of Notre Dame Press, 1992), pp. 106–134.

[6]The 19th century Russian poet Fedor Tiutchev wrote an often-quoted verse expressing this idea:

Umom Rossiiu ne poniat´,
Arshinom obshchim ne izmerit´;
U nei osobennaia stat´:
V Rossiiu mozhno tol´ko verit´.
(One cannot grasp Russia with one's mind,
One cannot measure it with an ordinary yardstick;
It has a special character:
One can only believe in Russia.)

fact the changes of the last decade have undermined political order but have not shaken the bureaucratic class's monopoly on power. Hidden power centers preserve many of the technological and organizational resources of the old regime, they claim. The close personal ties among the ruling elite enable those who exercised power in the past to retain it today, even if they have converted their political posts into lucrative opportunities for private profiteering in the new quasi-commercial business environment. These observers point to the strong influence of the security forces in the presidential administration, the power of the old regional elite in many of the subjects of the federation, particularly the national republics, and the insulation of decision-making on matters of national security from any democratic control through bodies such as the Security Council. For them, the post-Soviet order has created a façade of democratic processes behind which much of the same oligarchy that ruled in the past has held on to power.

Some historians would interpret the problem of creating a new political order in post-Soviet Russia as one more phase in the long history of Russian statehood. Over the centuries, Russia has experienced periods when state power expanded, and other periods dominated by political disorder and conflict. Robert Tucker argues that Russian history moves in cycles in which long periods of autocratic rise and decay are punctuated by shorter spells of modernizing reform followed by phases of breakdown and disorder.[7] Eugene Huskey points out that the present-day Russian presidency not only replicates certain organizational features of the Soviet period, with the presidential administration paralleling and overseeing the government in much the same way that the CPSU penetrated and controlled the government, but that it also resembles the organization of executive power under the autocracy: Like many observers, he concludes that a national culture such as Russia's is able to replicate basic patterns of political organization in different guises over history.[8] Indeed, in Russia many thinkers today reject the search for developmental models not drawn organically from Russia's own heritage. Paradoxically enough, many who reject Marxism–Leninism as well as Western individualism prefer to ally themselves with communists, as defenders of the principle of an autocratic state, against liberals and pluralists.

Where one locates Russia in its own and world history, then, affects whether or not one sees Russia's current transition as substantial and unidirectional. We are observing Russia at a single point in time and one in which the establishment of a new political order is incomplete. We also have only incomplete information about how the present Russian regime works. Although the Soviet regime went to great lengths to conceal its political processes from prying eyes, the accumulation of scholarly research and the regime's long stability enabled outsiders to gain a good deal of knowledge about how the system worked.[9] Curiously, although far more

---

[7]Robert C. Tucker, "Sovietology and Russian History," *Post-Soviet Affairs* 8:3 (1992), pp. 175–196; idem, "What Time Is It in Russia's History?" in Catherine Merridale and Chris Ward, eds., *Perestroika: The Historical Perspective* (London: Edward Arnold, 1991), pp. 34–45.

[8]Eugene Huskey, "Yel´tsin as State Builder," *The Soviet and Post-Soviet Review* 21:1 (1994).

[9]Thomas F. Remington, "Common Knowledge: Soviet Political Studies and the Problem of System Stability," in Daniel Orlovsky, ed., *Beyond Soviet Studies* (Washington, D.C.: Woodrow Wilson Center Press, 1995), pp. 159–192.

information on many topics is available today, our *understanding* of Russian politics is more fragmentary and unsettled than in the past because of the greater variation in patterns of behavior across regions, the dispersion of state power into multiple new structures, and the rapid pace of organizational change. Still, let us sum up our survey of the Russian political system, and see whether some overall trends are coming into focus.

Democratic Transition

POSTCOMMUNIST REGIMES AND GLOBAL CHALLENGES

Throughout Eastern Europe and the former Soviet Union, new democratic institutions have inherited the responsibility for managing, reforming, or dismantling the inefficient bureaucratic machinery of the ancien régime. These societies exhibit wide variation in their ability to subject the government of the state to the control of representative institutions. The unfavorable economic and political legacy of communist rule is widely recognized, but certain features of contemporary international society also impede democratic consolidation, notwithstanding the strong impact of the accelerated global diffusion of trade, finance, ideas, values, desires, and aspirations. Across the world today, the representative forms which emerged from the spread of universal political rights and the establishment of the sovereign national state as a universal form of political community themselves appear unable to satisfy the demands of publics in many developed societies for effective political voice.

In much of the developed democratic world, this is a period of widespread if inchoate antagonism toward central governments, elected representatives, and political parties as such. Electronic communications media are displacing sites of direct, face-to-face association. The simulacrum of participation created through television seems to leave a sense of unfulfilled desires for involvement and influence even if the information functions performed by older forms of political representation are replaced effectively by the ability of politicians to reach citizens via television and citizens' ability to speak to politicians via polls. The crisis of confidence in parties, parliaments, and other aggregative structures in Western democracies posed by new technologies of "hyper-democracy" has a counterpart in the difficulty of representative institutions in gaining effectiveness as means of governance in Russia and other postcommunist societies. Because the communist regimes gave high priority to modern communications for mass mobilization and control, the new representative institutions are being established in a society which is already saturated by television. Unlike Central Europe, however, Russia lacks recent working models of democratic representative institutions which can be adapted to the postcommunist environment. Its parties, electoral systems, and legislative bodies thus face the even greater challenge of building their capacity for governance in the face of widespread public skepticism, severe policy dilemmas, and the considerable head start television has in structuring political communication.

In some important ways, the postcommunist transition in Russia and other former Soviet states has differed from the paths taken by Central Europe. In Russia the dismantling of the communist system occurred in the absence of a negotiated agreement among outgoing and challenger elites over new rules of the game. Recent theories of democratic transition emphasize the importance of pacts containing mutually agreed rights and guarantees protecting each side against the possibility of sweeping defeat as the political arena is widened and new democratic decision-making procedures are established.[10] The successive constitutional schemes devised by Gorbachev and Yeltsin between 1988 and 1993 were instruments designed to enable them to achieve their policy goals by giving constitutional status to an existing power base. Not surprisingly, these arrangements were not accepted by their opponents and proved unstable. In their rivalry, Gorbachev and Yeltsin followed somewhat parallel strategies, employing electoral democracy to mobilize mass support in the soviets as a counterweight to the communist party apparatus, then transferring their base of operations to an executive presidency. In this game Yeltsin held the advantage. In the first place, he sought and won office in three direct elections in three successive years, culminating in his landmark election to the Russian presidency in 1991. Second, Russia was a political community with a national identity and national culture whereas the Soviet Union was not. Therefore the democratic opening weakened and ultimately destroyed the Soviet Union as a state but made Russia's post-Soviet statehood possible.

Rather than following a roundtable agreement between regime and opposition on the rules governing new parliamentary elections in Central Europe, Russia's elections of 1989, 1990, 1991, and 1993 were held at the initiative of the leader of the day seeking a popular electoral base for his power. Although these elections had profound consequences for the mobilization of new political forces, other groups whose power was vested in the old state and party bureaucracy had no stake in the success of these arrangements and finally rejected their authority in coup attempts of 1991 and 1993. Neither the reform leaders nor the communist opposition made a "credible commitment" to abide by the decisions reached under the new democratic order.[11] Like the Provisional Government of 1917, the provisional USSR and RSFSR constitutional regimes of 1989–93 had few defenders when they were dismantled. These precedents offer little encouragement to those appraising the prospects for consolidation of the current, post-1993 constitutional system.

However we assess the influence of contextual factors such as geography, political culture, international politics, and economic and cultural globalization on the course that Russia's long-term political evolution will follow, most observers would agree that the choices that Russia's leaders have made in the decade of the 1990s

---

[10]For instance, see Giuseppe DiPalma, *To Craft Democracies* (Berkeley: University of California Press, 1990).

[11]The concept of "credible commitment" to a set of institutional arrangements that determine how a group will reach political decisions has been the subject of much recent research. The argument of much of this literature is that the economic and political development of societies will depend on the nature of their institutions, and that to the extent that elites are willing to bind themselves to fixed procedures for exercising power, they facilitate socially beneficial cooperation.

Douglass C. North, "Institutions and Credible Commitment," *Journal of Institutional and Theoretical Economics* 149/1 (1993), pp. 11–23; Barry R. Weingast, "Constitutions as Governance Structures: The Political Foundations of Secure Markets," *Journal of Institutional and Theoretical Economics* 149/1 (1993), pp. 286–311; Elinor Ostrom, *Governing the Commons: The Evolution of Institutions for Collective Action* (Cambridge: Cambridge University Press, 1990).

will be tremendously important for the future. The economic and political rules of the game they lay down now, and the precedents they set through their own behavior, will guide successive generations of politicians and ordinary citizens. They can set in motion cycles of expansionism and conflict in relations with the country's neighbors, or new relationships based on common security interests. They can leave behind an economy organized around self-sustaining economic growth, or economic collapse. Their choices will affect future patterns of political development, including the likelihood that civil liberties will be respected, or will instead be sacrificed to the imperative of a new authoritarian order.

NATIONAL IDENTITY AND POLITICAL CHOICE

Zbigniew Brzezinski, a long-time student of Russian and communist political affairs who served as the U.S. national security advisor under President Jimmy Carter, observed that Russia must make a fundamental choice between two models of development: it "can be either an empire or a democracy, but it cannot be both."[12] A democratic Russia would not threaten its neighbors or regiment its own society for the sake of imperial rule, he argued, but if Russia in the post-Soviet era attempts to reestablish a political and military hegemony in the territory of the former union, that would spell the end of democratic reform. Brzezinski expressed the fear that imperialistic tendencies in Russia appear to be gaining ground. The surprisingly large vote for Vladimir Zhirinovsky in the December 1993 parliamentary elections can be seen in this light. Russia delayed the withdrawal of its military forces from Estonia and Latvia in order to pressure the leaders of those countries to grant political rights to the Russian minorities living there. It continues to maintain troops in Moldova, Georgia, Armenia, and several other former republics of the Soviet Union. It has actively promoted the reintegration of the former republics into a more closely knit Commonwealth of Independent States.[13] Similarly, addressing the United Nations in September 1994, President Yeltsin declared that Russia had special rights and responsibilities in the territories on its borders that used to make up the former Soviet Union, to help bring about the settlement of armed conflicts and to defend the interests of the 25 million Russians living outside the Russian Republic.[14] Many saw these statements as indications that the imperial tendency in Russian policy was gaining ground at the expense of democracy.

Brzezinski is surely right that Russia cannot be both an empire and a democracy: only a democracy would be willing to develop relations with other countries on the basis of equality and mutuality of interests rather than the domination of the weaker by the stronger. It is also undoubtedly the case that within Russia, antidemocratic forces are vying with democratic forces for supremacy. The triumph of an

---

[12]Zbigniew Brzezinski, "The Premature Partnership," *Foreign Affairs* 73:2 (March/April 1994), p. 72.

[13]The head of the Russian Foreign Intelligence Service warned Western governments not to oppose the reintegration process or to attempt to deny Russia its rightful status as a great power. At the same time he maintained that in seeking the reintegration of the CIS, Russia was not asserting any imperialist interests. See Fred Hiatt, "Russia's Spy Chief Warns West: Don't Oppose Soviet Reintegration," *Washington Post*, September 22, 1994.

[14]John M. Goshko, "Yeltsin Claims Russian Sphere of Influence," *Washington Post*, September 27, 1994.

authoritarian ultranationalist would reverse the movement toward democracy and return to an imperialist foreign policy. But the efforts by Russia's leaders to define a new national identity which includes the interests of Russians living in the "near abroad" and to assert an outward-looking foreign policy are not in themselves signs of an imperialist resurgence. They do, of course, demonstrate the strong desire among Russia's political leadership to assert Russia's power and status in the post-communist world.

The transition to a democratic political system in Russia, in short, is bound up with the reconstruction of Russia as a national state. Throughout Eastern Europe, an ethnic criterion has historically applied to the construction of nationhood—that is, the state was the political expression of an ethnic nation, whereas in the classic Western European pattern, the state as a territorial political unit arose before the nation formed.[15] Russia, however, has not employed an ethnic conception of nation-hood historically but instead tied its national existence with the political mission of building and maintaining a multinational state. This was true even in the Soviet period, particularly under Stalin, when the regime imposed a strongly Russian national identity on Soviet society, disguised as "Soviet nationality." As the former chairman of the Foreign Relations Committee of the Federation Council of the Russian parliament, Vladimir Podoprigora, put it in a recent article, for Russians in the past "the phrases 'the great Russian people' and 'the great Soviet people' were readily interchangeable."[16] Now the post-Soviet and postimperial Russian state is seeking to define the boundaries of its national interests. It is hardly surprising that the fate of the 25 million Russians in the "near abroad" (meaning the other former republics of the Soviet Union) should be central to the national and state interests of post-Soviet Russia. By the same token, however, as Russian democratic leaders take pains to point out, Russia must construct its relations with the newly indepen-dent states of the former union on a basis of equality and mutual respect for sover-eignty. Indeed, as Podoprigora puts it:

> A large people and a large territory have always generated a sense of boundlessness and might, encouraged the illusion of the inexhaustibility of spiritual and physical forces, and a sense of national greatness. To maintain this perception, neither the Russian nor Soviet government spared the people. And the people themselves offered themselves up in sacrifice to this idea. But it did not justify itself. It exhausted the people's powers without bringing spiritual satisfaction. The aspiration to achieve recognition of national greatness, to win greater roles in solving world conflict situations, than we can allow our-selves, is not only fraught with new difficulties for the people, but also sometimes places us in a false and ridiculous position. Would it not be better to concentrate for a certain historical period on solving our own problems? Perhaps in this position there is not national greatness, but there is national honor. And that is the main thing.[17]

---

[15]Anthony D. Smith, *The Ethnic Origins of Nations* (Oxford: Basil Blackwell, 1986), pp. 134–137.

[16]Vladimir N. Podoprigora and Tatiana I. Krasnopevtseva, "Russkii vopros kak faktor vnutrennei i vnesh-nei politiki Rossii" [The Russian Question as a Factor in Domestic and Foreign Policy of Russia], *Segod-nia,* October 18, 1994.

[17]Ibid.

The reconstruction of national identity thus complicates Russia's progress toward democracy since the transition is not occurring within historically settled national borders. But there is another factor as well impeding the establishment of democratic institutions in Russia. Throughout Russian and Soviet history, the state has played the dominant part in initiating phases of intense social change, and personal leadership has been crucial in moving the state. Gorbachev and Yeltsin illustrate this pattern in their attempts to use power in an authoritarian way to achieve democratic goals such as *glasnost´*, democratization, legal reform, a market economy, and a new foreign policy. One problem with the use of autocratic power to impose democracy, of course, is that it undermines the very institutions it endeavors to create. For that reason, the revolutionary changes which have occurred in Russia over the last decade have been more effective in breaking down the fabric of the old system than in constructing a new institutional framework to replace it. Like Gorbachev before him, and like other great Russian reformist rulers, Yeltsin has found himself in the dilemma of relying on highly centralized, personal power to enact reform instead of entrusting power to institutions he cannot control.

Does Democracy Matter?

For these reasons, Russia's transition to democracy is partial and incomplete, in contrast to the more rapid consolidation of democratic institutions in Poland, Hungary, the Czech Republic, and Slovenia. Among the countries of the Commonwealth of Independent States, however, Russia may be the most democratic. But what do we mean when we say that one political system is more democratic than another? And is it even desirable for Russia to become more democratic? After all, as we saw, many people inside Russia and outside believe that to break the resistance of communist and bureaucratic forces to market competition, it is necessary to follow the so-called "Asian model" of authoritarian rule and rapid capitalist development. Jerry Hough, for instance, criticizes American policymakers and Russian advocates of "shock therapy" for neglecting the relevance for Russia of China's economic development path, as well as the experience of other, less repressive, Asian countries such as Singapore, Taiwan, South Korea, and Thailand.[18] As we saw, around one quarter of the population of Russia, in a 1994 public opinion survey, agreed with the proposition that what Russia needs now is a leader such as Chile's Augusto Pinochet—a figure associated in Russians' minds with savage political repression and a brutal but effective market-oriented reform policy. Is it in fact the case that the Chinese and Pinochet strategies are superior to one in which market-oriented reform is pursued simultaneously with political liberalization?

Surveying the evidence from a wide range of cases, Samuel Huntington examines the consequences of democracy in three areas, economic, military, and political.[19] He points out that while there are notable exceptions, political democracy

---

[18]Jerry F. Hough, "Schlock Therapy," *Washington Post,* January 30, 1994.

[19]Huntington, "The Modest Meaning of Democracy," p. 18.

tends to be associated with higher levels of social wealth than are nondemocratic systems. It has long been believed that this correlation came about because wealth tended to produce democracy; that is, citizens in wealthier countries demand political rights, particularly as property-owning middle classes emerge which seek to protect their interests. To be sure, nondemocratic regimes in the modern world represent a very diverse lot, economically speaking. Few democracies have succeeded in maintaining successive average annual economic growth rates of 8 or 10 percent for a decade or more, as has China. But neither have many "produced the total economic catastrophes that nondemocratic governments have often generated."[20]

A second area in which to compare democracies' economic performance with that of nondemocracies is their record in yielding equality in the distribution of wealth and income. Huntington concludes that democracies are associated with moderate levels of inequality both in assets and in incomes: democracies, in some cases, seem to require some degree of inequality as a stimulus to growth. But maintenance of high levels of inequality, as well as high levels of equality, appears to require large doses of political repression and are thus incompatible with democracy.[21]

With respect to their level of military effort and the aggressiveness of their foreign policy, the difference between democratic and nondemocratic regimes is clearer: democratic regimes tend on average to be far less militarized; and communist regimes were the most militarized of all. In communist regimes, the ratio of military manpower to the total population was about twice that for other authoritarian regimes in the early 1980s, and the latter were about twice as high on this measure as democratic regimes.[22] A growing body of research also suggests that among democracies, a kind of "zone of peace" exists: democracies do not fight wars less often than nondemocracies, but they do not go to war against other democracies.[23]

In the political domain the consequences of democratic institutions are most apparent. Democracies have higher levels of public order and stability than do nondemocracies; this is because democracies enable citizens to turn out leaders and change policy direction, albeit usually only incrementally. Democracies by definition guarantee political rights to citizens, among them the rights to participate in the political process through speech, association, and voting. These rights, in turn, are important conditions of other significant benefits for society, including stability, order, and prosperity.[24]

If, then, democracy matters, how close does Russia come to being a democracy?

DEFINING DEMOCRACY

Many distinguished scholars have proposed definitions of democracy. One of the most widely cited is that of Robert Dahl, who distinguished two basic dimensions along which a given polity might change over time or which vary across a range of

---

[20]Ibid., p. 19.

[21]Ibid., p. 20.

[22]Ibid., p. 22.

[23]Ibid., p. 23.

[24]Ibid., pp. 24–25.

political systems: *participation,* or the right of all adult citizens to freely exercise political rights, such as the right to vote in popular elections and to be elected to political office, the right to express themselves, to acquire information, and to organize free associations, including parties and interest groups; and *contestation,* or the degree to which political leaders must compete for power by gaining the freely expressed consent of citizens.[25] Certainly one can suggest additional criteria for judging whether a political system is democratic or not. Philippe Schmitter and Terry Lynn Karl propose two other defining features of democracy: elected officials must be able to exercise their legal powers free of the threat that their actions will be overruled by unelected powers, such as army commanders; and the state must be able to govern itself without being dominated by outside powers.[26] Let us briefly review the record of evidence that has been presented in this chapter to ascertain how far Russia may have advanced in meeting these tests. Let us take them up in reverse order.

POLITICAL AUTONOMY

By the standard of Russia's freedom of influence by outside powers, the only source of external control that might potentially be significant is that of international financial organizations such as the International Monetary Fund and consortia of major private Western banks; these public and private financial institutions have certainly pressured Russia to adopt certain strict guidelines for fiscal and monetary policy as a condition for extending loans and other forms of credit. Some Russian politicians have claimed that Yeltsin's government has effectively turned control of Russia over to these bodies and allowed the West to colonize Russia. But these accusations seriously distort the nature of Russia's relationship with world financial organizations. Yeltsin and the radical government officials who launched the economic reform program in 1992 believed that the only way to make Russia's break with communist rule irreversible was to carry out rapid and decisive measures to stabilize its economy and establish private property rights. In this they had the strong political support of Western governments and financial institutions. But Western influence has been limited and it appears that the pressure of the IMF and other external powers has been used much in the same way that it is used elsewhere: when governments must take unpopular measures such as raising taxes, cutting spending, and devaluing currency in order to restore fiscal health, they find it convenient to use the IMF as a whipping boy, blaming the pain of the stabilization program on the IMF so as to escape public condemnation.

Quis Custodiet Ipsos Custodes? Who will guard the guardians, an old question asks. As to whether Russian leaders are able to govern without fear that the military or another unelected power center will intervene, we should note that the countries that have moved away from communist rule in the former Soviet Union and

---

[25]Robert A. Dahl, *Polyarchy: Participation and Opposition* (New Haven, CT: Yale University Press, 1971).

[26]Philippe C. Schmitter and Terry Lynn Karl, "What Democracy Is . . . And Is Not," *Journal of Democracy* 2:3 (Summer 1991), pp. 81–82.

Eastern Europe have generally been free of military coups. It is the Southern European and Latin American cases where democratic transitions have sometimes been reversed by military takeovers. On the other hand, we have observed that the KGB's successor organs, freely citing national security concerns and relying on the president's vast powers, have been able to claim a large sphere of power which is partly free of legal or political accountability. The military occasionally ignored President Yeltsin's demands for cessation of hostilities in Chechnia, and have resisted any serious attempt at structural reform. The danger posed by the security police and the military arises from their ability to operate autonomously, outside effective democratic control, in their own spheres of power rather than from the threat that they will intervene directly in politics.

Electoral Competition The third criterion is that of contestation, the degree to which public authorities must compete for their power by gaining the freely expressed consent of the citizens in open elections. In this respect we can examine the degree of electoral contestation both at the federal and regional levels of government. At the federal level, we have seen that parliamentary elections were held just as the law required in December 1995; turnout was very nearly 70 percent and all sides accepted the results without seeking to have them overturned. The vast majority of sitting Duma members ran for reelection, although fewer than half succeeded in winning seats, and while the splintering of democratic forces across a large number of parties, combined with the 5 percent threshold to receiving party list seats, kept all but a handful of their candidates from winning, the overall proportions of the vote for pro-communist, centrist, and pro-reform parties were similar in 1995 to those in 1993. Even more significant, from the standpoint of the regularization of electoral institutions, was that the second presidential election was held on schedule on June 16, 1996. For the most part, it was conducted freely and fairly, and the losers accepted their defeat.[27] As has been emphasized here, the elections stimulated a process of party-building, which is a crucial element of stable modern democracy.

At the regional level electoral contestation is much less free and fair. In many regions, powerful executives can manipulate the rules of competition, ensuring that they are reelected to office and that their corresponding regional legislative bodies are packed with their supporters. The heads of executive organs dominate the regions: there is little separation or checking and balancing between executive and representative branches in the regions. Instead, the representative branch has largely become a compliant source of support for powerful regional executives. Although most were placed in their positions by President Yeltsin, the degree of power most enjoy now is such that they are not effectively controlled either by the president or by local electoral or representative institutions. The round of gubernatorial elections in the fall of 1996 did not overcome this. Overall, we would judge that the criterion of contestation in the political system appears to be largely met so far as politics at the federal level is concerned, but not always in the case of politics in the regions.

---

[27]The integrity of the election was certainly marred by the egregious exploitation of the mass media by the president's campaign managers; the communist candidate received very little coverage, and most of that was negative.

Citizen Participation Finally, how open is the Russian political system to citizen participation? In one respect, the communist regime met this test of democracy, since no category of the population was excluded from citizenship rights by virtue of sex or race or property, and the regime made extensive efforts to make citizens share in the obligations of citizenship—among them the obligation to vote, to serve in the army, and to express support for the regime. Indeed, in terms of the formal rights of citizenship, the inclusiveness of the Soviet regime of the past stands in contrast to the exclusion of certain ethnic groups from the rights of citizenship today in some of the successor states. Nearly a quarter of the adult population of Estonia, for instance, was denied the right to vote in parliamentary elections in September 1992, on the grounds that as members of alien ethnic minorities, they did not qualify for citizenship.[28] Formally, Russia has continued the inclusive citizenship policy of the Soviet regime, and it has not erected any barriers to civic rights on ethnic or other grounds.

Substantive rights to participate are a different matter, however, since the Soviet regime suppressed most of the political rights that make civic participation democratic: the right to form associations freely, the right to express political opinions openly and acquire information, and the right to run for office. In this respect Russia is significantly freer than was the Soviet regime. Again, however, there is a gap between the performance of the political system at the federal level and that of the regions in this respect. In some regions, political freedoms have been curtailed by authoritarian governors. Press liberty is not secure, even at the federal level. On October 17, 1994, a bomb planted in the briefcase of a young journalist working for a Moscow newspaper exploded, killing him and destroying many of the documents he had gathered. Since he had been collecting evidence about high-level corruption in the armed forces, many believed that his murder was the work of those who wanted to put an end to his investigations. His death was one of several cases of murder and persecution that year of journalists who offended powerful political interests.

Yet the great majority of Russians consider themselves to have more political freedom than they did under the old regime. Two-thirds and more of Russians surveyed in 1993 report themselves to be freer to say what they think than they were in the past, freer to join any organization they wish, and freer to practice any religion.[29] And high proportions of the public continue to express support for the general principles of democracy. To be sure, as Raymond Duch points out, people tend to express much higher levels of support for abstract political principles, such as free elections and the desirability of party competition, than they do on more concrete issues such as the willingness to tolerate freedom for those whose views are considered threatening to social order.[30] But the abstract support for democratic principles is matched by the gradual emergence of autonomous public associations. The end of the communist regime has stimulated groups to organize for the protection of their interests. New institutions for articulating and aggregating these interests

---

[28]On the evolution of the political systems of the Baltic states before and since independence, see Anatol Lieven, *The Baltic Revolution* (New Haven, CT: Yale University Press, 1993). Discussion of the citizenship law in Estonia and the 1992 elections may be found on pp. 274–289.

[29]Richard Rose, "After Communism: What?" *Daedalus* 123:3 (Summer 1994), p. 52.

[30]Raymond M. Duch, "Tolerating Economic Reform: Popular Support for Transition to a Free Market in the Former Soviet Union," *American Political Science Review* 87:3 (September 1994), p. 599.

remain fragile. But, as we saw in reviewing the emergence of new political associations and parties, the spread of political and property rights has resulted in the emergence of a more competitive and pluralistic environment.

Perhaps the most powerful factor affecting the likelihood of a democratic outcome in Russia's transition is the nature of the public's expectations of the future. Where time horizons are short because people do not expect a stable future, they tend to seek short-term rewards. They avoid investing much material or political capital if their rewards are uncertain or subject to a high probability of being taken away from them. It is quite possible for a social setting in which people believe that one must take advantage of others before one is taken advantage of to go on this way indefinitely: society need not necessarily advance to a state in which there are higher levels of social trust and cooperation, and hence social progress, including economic growth and democratic self-rule. But where people begin to reinforce one another's expectations that they are able to cooperate in common endeavors without relying upon a harsh, dictatorial, central authority, a "virtuous cycle" results in which more complex and effective organizational forms evolve.[31]

The vast size of Russia and the historical pattern of its development, through which the greatest share of social resources were subject to state ownership and control, make it unlikely that such a process of democratic consolidation in the postcommunist era will be anything but slow and uneven. At the same time, we have reviewed some of the historically new factors that make democracy a possible outcome of Russia's transition: the absence of a bitter global struggle between capital and labor over control over the means of production, the dense network of international communications linking societies across state boundaries, the high educational attainments of Russia's society, and its unwillingness to return to dictatorship. Although sometimes it appears that Kremlin politics boils down to the incestuous interplay of a few powerful cliques, political leaders of a variety of ideological camps are increasingly acting as though they believed that they are all better off accepting a common framework of democratic institutions in which to articulate their demands and resolve their differences.

---

[31]This is a simplified restatement of the argument made by Robert D. Putnam with Robert Leonardi and Raffaella Y. Nanetti, *Making Democracy Work: Civic Traditions in Modern Italy* (Princeton: Princeton University Press, 1993).

Index